Philosophy and Salvation

Philosophy and Salvation

An Essay on Wisdom, Beauty, and Love
as the Goal of Life

CARLOS BLANCO

◆PICKWICK *Publications* • Eugene, Oregon

PHILOSOPHY AND SALVATION
An Essay on Wisdom, Beauty, and Love as the Goal of Life

Copyright © 2012 Carlos Blanco. All rights reserved. Except for brief quotations in critical publications or reviews, no part of this book may be reproduced in any manner without prior written permission from the publisher. Write: Permissions, Wipf and Stock Publishers, 199 W. 8th Ave., Suite 3, Eugene, OR 97401.

Pickwick Publications
An Imprint of Wipf and Stock Publishers
199 W. 8th Ave., Suite 3
Eugene, OR 97401

www.wipfandstock.com

ISBN 13: 978-1-61097-380-9

Cataloging-in-Publication data:

Blanco, Carlos.

    Philosophy and salvation : an essay on wisdom, beauty, and love as the goal of life / Carlos Blanco.

    viii + 286p. 23 cm.—Includes bibliographical references and indexes.

    ISBN 13: 978-1-61097-380-9

    1. Philosophy—Religious aspects. 2. Religion—Philosophy—History. 3. Virtue—History. 4. Salvation—Philosophy. I. Title.

BJ1518 B53 2012

Manufactured in the USA

Contents

Acknowledgments | vii

Introduction: The Salvific Dimension of Thought | 1

Part 1: In Search of *Fundamentum*
1. Philosophy beyond Science | 7
2. The Senses of Being | 18
3. The Dynamism of Being | 39

   Excursus: On the Dimensions of Being and the Limitations of the Principle of Non-contradiction | 49

Part 2: *Fundamentum* in History
4. Consciousness beyond the World: Freedom | 59
5. Freedom beyond Itself: Solidarity | 94
6. Solidarity beyond Itself: Creation | 122

   Excursus: A Salvific History for All | 143
   Excursus: From the "Thrownness" into the World to the Kingdom of Ends | 155
   Excursus: The Concept of Religion and the Scope of Theology | 161
   Excursus: The Names of Humanity and the Utopia of a Redeemed Past | 172

Part 3: Questioning as Salvation
7. Death as Challenge | 181
8. Wisdom, Love, and Beauty | 192

Epilogue: Only a God Can Still Save Us | 209

Appendices

APPENDIX A: Hegel: History, Theodicy, Art, and Redemption | 215

APPENDIX B: Dilthey and the Legitimacy of the "Sciences of the Spirit" | 225

APPENDIX C: Religion as Illusion in Sigmund Freud | 230

APPENDIX D: The Conception of God as *Das Ganz-Andere* in Rudolf Otto | 241

APPENDIX E: God, the Future, and the *Fundamentum* of History in Wolfhart Pannenberg | 256

APPENDIX F: The Rose and Its Reason | 270

Bibliography | 275

Acknowledgments

I am immensely grateful to Evan Martino and Elliot Billingsley for their assistance in editing this text.

Introduction
The Salvific Dimension of Thought

When we ascend to high peaks, we become inevitably seized by the impression that it is not possible to climb to still more prominent heights, and even less to discover a new peak with passion and tenacity, so that it is vain to aspire to crown a superior vertex. Everything has been already conquered; everything has been unveiled; there is nothing to elucidate. What is left is to indulge ourselves in our conquest, to contemplate the vast landscape that others have opened for us. We thus feel tempted to avoid any responsibility to move forward, to promote life and imagination, to fight, to engage in a new search which may extend the horizons of life and thought: what is left is to delight ourselves in our own complacency.

An exhausted age must learn to fascinate itself and to become imbued in the surprise of the unusual, the verve of the gift of life. It is true that we do not know the ultimate root that binds us to this space and this time, but we treasure a force that enables us to continue to promote the power of being, to push history forward: that is, to create. An emaciated era is left to concentrate all the strength of its intellect and will, all the inspiring nutrient irradiated by science, technology, the humanities, art, institutions, and, moreover, the inscrutability of each individual, in order to enjoy the sense of wonder, and to succumb to enthusiasm. This may give us unto a quest that perhaps lacks a definite term, but nonetheless reveals our deep purpose: to place us on the cusp of the creative energies of life; this entails the responsibility to expand its scope, to find a "further," an "*ulterior*," a "*plus*" to that which is already given. However, we shall not conceive of this goal as a final truth that will resist the passage of time and the trial of the future, but as a pure intuition, as an inexhaustible calling, as a perpetual source of inspiration.

Introduction: The Salvific Dimension of Thought

There is something in thought that is salvific, as if the epiphany of the redemption longed-for by humanity appears in the realm of philosophy.

The vocation of philosophy is not the theoretical contemplation of ideas, or the attempt at reaching ecstasy before the empyreal beauty of concepts, or the mere proposal of a critical analysis of the world that surrounds us. These indeed are moments of philosophical thinking, which epitomizes thinking itself, since it approaches knowledge from an integrating, ultimate perspective that is not susceptible to being satisfied by means of a partial insight. Instead, it intends to reach, even though asymptotically, a *fundamentum*, a "foundation." Philosophical thinking, moreover, has a higher ambition: that is, it is destined to save humanity.

To "save" means to set a different scenario, in which negativity, which has become inexorable, posing a burden which is impossible to carry any more, may be overcome by a statement, by a word, by a *positivitas*, by a thought in which the previous negativity does not triumph but is removed and annihilated. Only thought can create such a new *positivitas*; thought alone envisions the revocation of this negativity, so ineluctably powerful that it claims for itself the whole sphere of reality.

When negativity is so intense that it is confused with reality, and when human aspirations are humiliated by violent reality that dashes every dream and confines thought to a subsidiary task (the methodical dimension without the ethical scope),[1] the necessity of salvation emerges as urgently as ever.

We all seek salvation. We all become prisoners of negativity. Humanity wants to be saved: to be saved by the arts, by science, by technology, by politics. We want to overcome the untenable power of negativity that so often enslaves us. But, where is the saviour to be found, and where is the source of salvation?

Salvation may only come from the infinite springs of the word. The word saves us: the word of science, the word manifested in art, the word of a society which promises something for itself . . . Humanity understands itself through language: human beings use words in order to know each other and to cooperate in the edification of something that may transcend them. The word invites us, and in fact leads us to transcendence. This is salvation: to inaugurate a new world in which the former negativity may be overcome. Those religions that offer salvation

---

1. T. S. Eliot wrote, prophetically, in *Choruses from the Rock* (1934): "Where is the wisdom we have lost in knowledge? Where is the knowledge we have lost in information?"

Introduction: The Salvific Dimension of Thought

do so through the word: whoever listens to their doctrine drinks the water of life, because the word is life.

And the word becomes philosophy when it thinks about the world, history, and the human being. It becomes philosophy when it no longer remains in the realm of the analysis of reality, but it dares to seek to understand, in search of a meaning which may help us gain knowledge of ourselves, freedom, and possibilities of action and thought.

Philosophy is called to save humanity, inasmuch as it cannot escape the responsibility that belongs to its deepest essence: to reach the core of things. It is not for philosophy to stay on the surface, but to be immersed into the complexity of the world, to let reality speak to us, discovering the word that remains unknown and hidden in the midst of an apparent lack of meaning. Philosophy is therefore humanization, and humanization is the salvation of humanity.

The philosophical experience provides a permanent consolation through the power of thought to create and transform. Humanity can be relieved from its languid sadness by means of reading the great works of philosophy and feeling itself part of such an intellectual adventure. The withered melancholy provoked by the impending fate of a lethal nothingness ascends to the vivid and passionate enthusiasm for knowledge and for the salvific energy of thought, in which the world is not tyrant's fixed dominion, but humanity's home to improve.

The salvation that flows from philosophy perpetually faces the insurmountable barrier of death. Philosophy can teach us to stand before death with dignity, to be aware of the fact that the scope of humanity is broader than that of the individual, for humanity survives in its members, and that only from death does life renew itself. In truth, philosophy offers no comforting answer to the persistent problem of our meaning as individuals: why, with the capability of posing such compelling questions about the sense of our existence, we have to return to the dust we come from, in which consciousness will vanish into the unconscious? Why must we die?

For this grave matter, religions shall outlive philosophy. Philosophy does not save us from death, but it saves us from life. It helps us guide our life. We philosophize because we hope to obtain answers, not merely to ponder, but rather to know. We philosophize to understand and moreover, to redeem a humanity torn by its lack of meaning: we philosophize in order to find a meaning, and, if we fail, we philosophize to build a meaning. Once we open the gates of philosophy, and we penetrate its world of concepts, categories, streams of thoughts and theories, we unfold the veil

Introduction: The Salvific Dimension of Thought

of salvation. By participating in this fascinating struggle for understanding, we redeem ourselves, and redemption is the salvation that cleanses the wounds of humanity. By collaborating in the effort to comprehend made by our fellow human beings throughout the centuries, we discover ourselves. We achieve salvation because we learn to understand ourselves as beings in search of meaning.

We have inherited a longing for understanding present, in its highest expression, in philosophy. Through philosophizing, humanity has saved itself. It has not been captured by the obvious, and it has been able to overcome the frontiers of its *hic et nunc*, ascending into the kingdom of ends. Through philosophizing, humanity has vehemently shown that it cannot be satisfied by the world alone, but it needs to create a world beyond all others, integrated by the arts and the sciences, but which aspires to an ultimate foundation, to a *fundamentum*, to the deepest possible understanding.

By philosophizing, we have saved ourselves, and we are still doing so. Humanity will only die once it ceases to philosophize, once what is transient prevails, and once it becomes enslaved by that which does not seek to understand but limits itself to provide a mere description of the surrounding reality.

I think that there is an intellectual, philosophical salvation for humanity: we just need to follow the luminous path of centuries of ideas, doubts, questions, and challenges of philosophical thinking. This shows, as in an unrestricted divine epiphany, that humanity needs to understand if it wants to set the conditions to liberate itself from the oppressive power of negativity, from a lack of hope that has surpassed the bleak threshold beyond which we can no longer resist.

PART 1

In Search of *Fundamentum*

1

Philosophy beyond Science

IN OUR ATTEMPT TO understand ourselves as beings that constitutively challenge, by thinking, that which is given, and whose ultimate horizon is always that of creation, that of searching a *novum* that may reach a radical emancipation from the sameness of the world, we must first analyze the course taken in our days by "thinking" as such, which is epitomized in the current state of philosophy.

For many, the heyday of the scientific view of the world and its incontestable epistemological success has led to a gradual "cornering" of philosophy, the "love of wisdom" which can only be "freedom to think." This apparent "victory" of the natural sciences manifests, in our view, an extremely limited paradigm on the most genuine role of philosophy. Philosophy is guilty, in any case, of the emergence of this restrictive perspective, because it has normally conceived of itself either as the "explanatory force" of the world or as the "interpretative instance" of reality.

In the beginning, philosophy did not compete with science to provide an explanation of the structure and the functioning of the world, because the latter (which is principally defined on the basis of its methodology) had not been yet born. Science is the "beloved daughter" of philosophy, and when it downed, it subsumed a vast part of philosophy in its booming domains, behaving like a child who "devoured" his own parent. The philosophical disquisitions on the universe, nature, and the human mind gradually appeared as empty speculations that were to be superseded by a genuinely scientific vision of the world, by the "Comtian" stage that might purify archaic conceptions of its unverifiable metaphysical elements through a strict working methodology (as the one assumed by the natural sciences). However, philosophy found its precious "refuge," its comfortable winter quarters, its perpetual "immunity" in the task of "interpreting" the world. Philosophy thus believed that it was the sole possessor of the sphere of "sense," and in its monopoly of this arcane area it excluded the natural sciences from any search of "understanding" (Dilthey's *Verstehen*), of seeking a meaning of that which the natural sciences themselves discover.

However, our time radically mistrusts the possibility of deciphering a meaning that always escapes us, because it is indebted to the present interpretation of the world and it is ultimately captive of a certain scientific conception about how the world works. The influence on the question of the meaning of human existence of Copernicus sun-centered thesis, of Darwin's theory of evolution (with the discovery of the absence of a "special" biological character of the human species within the dynamism of life), and of Einstein's ideas on the physical world has far surpassed the impact of the deep and subtle disquisitions of philosophers. In any case, the reflection on the "ontological position" of humanity within nature (cultivated by authors like Thomas Huxley, Max Scheler, and Helmut Plessner) should not be disdained. The fact that we are a late link in the evolutionary chain of life should not induce us to forget the extraordinary importance that the birth of culture with *Homo sapiens* possesses, even in pure evolutionary terms.

The idea of "meaning" is always dependent upon the current state of our knowledge of the world and of ourselves. Philosophy should attempt neither to explain the world nor to understand that which science reveals about nature but to formulate a hypothetical meaning: philosophy must aspire to become the creative force of world and meaning. Philosophy has to create its own world.

The disenchantment of thinking is its worst tragedy. Instead of mistrusting the world and history, the past and the present, thinking surrenders to the incorrigible tendency towards sameness.[1] It renounces the critical questioning of that which is given, on the basis of a future that cannot be anticipated.

---

1. In this work, we will constantly use the word *sameness* as a philosophical concept. Its equivalent terms in other European languages are *identitas* (in Latin), *mismidad* (in Spanish), *Selbstheit* (in German).

After the death of thinking, only two options remain. The first one consists of a selfless capitulation to the natural sciences. Philosophy will serve the natural sciences. It will systematize its claims in order to strengthen the scientific view of the world, and it will try to extrapolate its methodology the field of both the social sciences and the humanities; a task that, somehow, has been carried out by analytical philosophy in the Anglo-Saxon world.

The second one is the interpretation of human realm on the basis of its past, through the (permanently unfinished) exegesis of the different visions of humanity which have been proposed over the centuries. Philosophy inexorably becomes history of philosophy, and the human sciences constrain themselves to "revisiting" the different possible approaches to the products of human activity in space and time. However, this option is extremely weak. Its fragility stems from the latent danger of becoming absorbed by the natural sciences.

Interpretations, inextricably connected with the exercise of subjectivity, raise suspicions in those disciplines which feel closer to the scientific view of the world, whose goal is no other than that of overcoming the intellectual vulnerability of the humanities. Increasingly relegated to a subsidiary role and incapable of articulating a project for humanity, philosophy cedes its own realm to the natural sciences and the analytic discourse. Philosophy renounces the enunciation of claims, the elucidation of the future, the creation of a *novum*, and it thus succumbs to the overwhelming pressure of the natural and the social sciences. The quantitative dimension and, within the social sciences, the thorough study of historical phenomena and the access to the sources from the past through the cultivation of philology (on whose methodological centrality to the sciences of the spirit Dilthey deeply meditated at the end of the nineteenth century) become the common aspiration of all branches of knowledge.

This oppressive dichotomy faced by philosophy can only be solved by vindicating the legitimacy of thinking turned towards the future. Since the future is intractable for the natural sciences (and for the kind of philosophy which, just as analytic philosophy, surrenders to the scientific methodology and does not aspire to create), it offers a scenario of inexhaustible freedom that rescues us of any potential methodological rigidity. Thinking can then demand a legitimate place within the universe of science, for it is referred to a horizon that, by its own concept, always remains alien to the scientific understanding of the world. Thinking can now revisit the past and the present without raising suspicion, because it does not pretend to offer a scientific explanation of them but to challenge them. However, and in order to accomplish this goal, it has to understand the past and the present in the most accurate way. It therefore needs to use the instruments provided by both the natural and the social sciences in their multifaceted forms. In any case, philosophy does not seek to "exhaust" any possible understanding. Its goal consists of thinking, *id est*, of opposing any possible "conclusion," any potential "sameness." Therefore, it never becomes petrified in the analysis of that which is given in past and present: it incessantly moves towards a future that is always new.

Philosophy is creation; philosophy is offering; philosophy is proposal. It constitutes, thus, an attempt to open thought to the future, to that which is not given yet in the *hic et nunc* of history. Upon thinking, human beings expand the energies of life, and they become the vanguard of being. Philosophy does not intend to replace the natural sciences in its laborious longing to clear the structure and operation of the universe. Philosophy does not pretend to substitute the scientific view of the world, by claiming a "deeper comprehension" of that which the natural sciences, by virtue of a transferable and communicable methodology (whose "objectivity" stems from its presuppositions, so that once an agreement has been convened on them, they do not only explain the present state of things in the world but also predict future situations) have achieved in the last centuries.

Philosophy does not seek to identify a sense where the natural sciences only discover causes, effects, and an inextricable combination of chance and necessity. Philosophy aims to *create*, that is, to *innovate*, to glimpse the possibility of a *novum*, a new meaning of insight, a different approach to the human realm and the world itself. Philosophy shines as the expression of the longing for growth that fills the human spirit, which experiences a constant desire for freedom, for self-affirmation against "that which is given." Thinking, as an insubordinate goal, constitutes an eminent manifestation of this will to liberty.

Nevertheless, philosophy cannot remain alien to the dynamism of the natural sciences. It should not look for a perennial refuge against the scrutiny of science and technique. Rather, it should become imbued with the spirit of the natural sciences in order to expand the horizon of its understanding and to reach higher pinnacles of depth and freedom. The provisional character of scientific statements means that it is not possible to exhaust the knowledge of the world. Nevertheless, there is no legitimacy in using this indeterminacy as a fragile excuse to ignore the results of the natural sciences. Rather, the provisional nature of scientific statements should be regarded as the fruit of a common phenomenon that also affects philosophy: the incessant capacity for acquiring a deeper understanding of reality. If science is to a certain extent provisional, the human intellect is susceptible to growth, so that a given understanding of the world will not indefinitely constrain its scope. In this way, the provisional character of philosophical statements recalls not only the perspective of an "unclosed" history (which Dilthey examined in his writings)[2] but also the human capacity for growth, for challenge, for emancipating itself from any given "sameness." The provisional nature of philosophical statements is a source of freedom and encouragement to show confidence in the future and the human power to create.

However, the provisional nature of its statements is much more severe in philosophy than it is in science. The scientific understanding of the world is aware of its provisional scope, and it rarely succumbs to a nostalgic remembrance of old theories. The object that unifies the scientific task remains "inalterable" (Parmenides) in its perpetual movement (Heraclitus): the universe. Any hypothesis is but the expression of a common attempt at elucidating the structure and functioning of the universe that "is there" as inescapable frame of reference. Nevertheless, for philosophy, the transitory nature of its statements becomes the most painful uncertainty. The fact that we are historical beings implies that our understanding of the human world cannot entirely detach itself from the historical moment under whose light those ideas have emerged. Human nature does not cease to experience the intense affections of history. Our historical life provides us a higher power of penetration, a deeper capacity for "descending" into the meaning of human existence, but it is also a sour source of confusion and distress before the huge piling of events, ideas, proposals, and feelings that inundate the course of times. We can fall captives to melancholy for ancient archetypes imagined *in illo tempore*, but we shall always realize that the light coming from the past, as brilliant and fascinating as it may be, will be insufficient for the orientation of thinking in our days.

The "pending rest" between past and present (history) raises an insurmountable barrier. Undoubtedly we can find inspiration in the thoughts of our ancestors, in the words of the greatest masters of philosophy, science, and art, but we shall never discover, even in their most powerful rays of wisdom, a valid torch for today. We must think; we need to look at history with hope and courage: we have to create our own world

---

2. Cf. Dilthey, *Der Aufbau der geschichtlichen Welt in den Geisteswissenschaften*, 237.

and we have to take possession of the inheritance that we have received. Tradition, the sentiment of belonging to a common creative desire which binds us to our forefathers, can offer support against any threat of despair. As unintelligible as the present history may seem, and as darkened as our creative capacity may appear, we shall always dispose of the legacy of wisdom, beauty, and love which we have inherited from the immense efforts made in the past. In it shall we find a fountain of inspiration, from whose waters we can drink without ever exhausting it. *Gratitude*, veneration for the grandeur of the past and the intellectual and artistic depth that it has bestowed upon us, leads to the firm desire to move thought forward. The love of wisdom is the will to think and to participate in the same longing for understanding and creation that invaded the spirits of times past. The love of wisdom demands the inauguration of the future.

Science discovers the fountain of the excess of energy that we possess. However, it does not reveal its aim, its ultimate possibilities. It does not unfold the goal to which we must commit the gift of life, complexity, intelligence, and sentiment. Philosophy must offer a free "elucidation" of the destiny of our capacity for enlarging the frontiers of being and to expand the horizons of life. Philosophy, as offering, as longing for "newness" and interpretation, is not subject to a goal alien to the act of creating. Philosophy recalls love of wisdom, love of life, love of novelty: love of the deepest possibility that the human being possesses. Philosophy must shine as love, detachment, commitment, courage, and confidence, as the *novum* that emancipates us from the inexorable concatenation of causes and effects, of instrumental reasons that cannot foresee an end goal. It must therefore overcome necessity. It must express our longing for authenticity and immediacy, for an *a priori* that may be a real *alter* to the world. Philosophy constitutes the vivid proof of our unwillingness to constrain ourselves to the contemplation of the world in its sameness: we want to create and to inaugurate room for freedom; we wish to *think* in a genuine sense; we seek to edify our own world.

The epistemological "prerogative" of the natural sciences, which emanates from their explanatory success of the structure and functioning of the world, is the result of a certain methodology, of the existence of a way to "contrast" its statements. However, science does not elucidate how we should face the future. Science examines the sameness of the world, its "self-identity," but it does not teach us how we should create our own world, how we should live in community, how we should imagine the future. Science does not emancipate our mind from the tyranny of instrumental goals. It does not offer a pure, unconditioned end. Its gnoseological triumph (the sonorous criticism of the "despotism" of science and its destructive power, leveled in the past decades, is only a timid complaint, which does not address the "core" of the insufficiency of science: its submission to mediated reality, to the concatenation of causes and effects that fills the natural universe, to the sameness of the world) cannot conceal the existence of severe challenges, which show the limit reached by our scientific understanding of the world.

However, the so-called sciences of the spirit (Dilthey's *Geisteswissenschaften*), "personified" by philosophy, should not pretend to monopolize the realm of understanding. Their task does not reside in turning any attempt at "interpreting the world" into their sole patrimony. Rather, they must promote the continuous *hermeneutic growth* of humanity, so that interpretations may become deeper and more edifying, in order to acquire a greater awareness of everything at stake in each concept, idea, and proposal. The search for a certain "totality," that is to say, the quest for a way of binding the parts into their whole, does not constitute the sole goal of the sciences of the spirit. The natural sciences seek to discover how the parts intertwine in the world as "totality," as their whole.

Science does not need a "spokesman," be it of philosophical or sociological nature, to act on its behalf. Science itself, on the basis of its method, establishes its own and more reliable understanding. The fact that science (both on account of its degree of development and of the frontiers erected by its own method) is incapable of covering all the realms of human life is a different matter. There is no science of art, politics, ethics, and religion, if by "science" we understand the application of the hypothetical-deductive method, in which empirical contrast plays an essential role. In an analogous way, there is no "science of science," that is to say, no hypothetical-experimental study of scientific activity itself. An "excess" of understanding always remains, even in the scientific accomplishments concerning the unfolding of the structure and functioning of the world, because the question about the meaning of scientific discoveries "for us" cannot be silenced. This "mystery" does not correspond to a quest for objectivity: it is a display of subjective creativity.

Philosophy should not seek to replace science, whose method has been proven as the most efficient strategy to find explanations in terms of causes and effects (even if through "probabilistic models," "patterns of inference," "justified generalizations") of the vast majority of phenomena in the world (by virtue of the "happy conjunction" of experimental observation and hypothetical-deductive reasoning, supported, in the fundamental disciplines, by mathematical language). Philosophy must pose questions. It needs to delve into the meaning of scientific discoveries for mankind. However, it should not impose, *a priori*, a certain conception on science. Philosophy must come into a critical dialogue with science, in order to remark its limits and challenges, its *ignoramus*, even if this task seems to repress the premature enthusiasm of many scientists. Philosophy can offer a broader, "more holistic," perspective, which may be useful for science itself, as it manifests the whole scope of that which remains to be explored. In addition to this, philosophy can show certain directions that science might take in its attempt at answering the numerous questions still at stake. In different occasions, philosophy has not constrained its activity to offering a synthetic perspective. Rather, and by virtue of fine and detailed analyses of the human life, philosophy has granted a series of enlightening considerations for science itself. An example of this "philosophical service to science" is the study of human emotions by the different phenomenological schools.

The vigor of the great philosophical questions has promoted the scientific enterprise. Philosophy succumbed to itself, and it perished to the intensity of its own fire. The quest for explanations of cosmic phenomena, without the need to point to supernatural, mythological, and superstitious entities, planted the beautiful seed of modern science.

Both science and philosophy share a common goal, sometimes explicitly stated, yet normally assumed in an implicit way: to alleviate human suffering. Behold their convergent (yet not exclusive) responsibility. By satiating our longing for knowledge, science mitigates our suffering, our grief before the orphanhood of answers and the vastness of our questions. Philosophy and the humanities expand the horizon of our thought, and they offer us a critical mediation on history and the possible forms of social organization, so that we may edify a world in which the capacities of all individuals can be fully displayed.

Philosophy is called to foster a fruitful exchange with the natural sciences by broadening their scope. Philosophy must listen to science with humility, because it does not enjoy any kind of epistemological privilege. The task of philosophy resides in propitiating a deep reflection about the foundations, scope, and challenges of science, especially with regard to its role in society and our understanding of ourselves.

The relationship of science to philosophy must be governed by a principle of "hermeneutic solidarity": philosophy should not remain alien to scientific discoveries in its interpretation of world, history, and mankind, but it should also perceive the necessity of contributing to the acquisition of a deeper conscience of the limits of science and the provisional nature of many of its statements. Science will provide a "material basis" on which to establish philosophical reflection, whereas philosophy will offer a "hermeneutic perspective," whose goal consists of interpreting scientific findings with regard to a possible understanding of the human life. On the one hand, philosophy should not act as a "science in parallel" to the elucidation of the material structure of nature. Rather, it should pay attention to the achievements of the various scientific disciplines. In any case, philosophy should always be aware of the provisional character of most scientific enunciations and their insurmountable limitations. Science, on the other hand, will not be able to supplant philosophy in the human search for "creative interpretations," bound to different cultures and historical moments, whose reference is the meaning of scientific advancement for mankind, both individually and collectively.

Science provides the hermeneutic clue for unfolding the material order of the universe. However, the fact that science is capable of unfolding the mechanisms that allow human beings to stand as a "challenge against the world" does not confute the reality of our challenge to the world. Science offers the possibility of explaining the origin of this capacity for defying the world. The so eagerly expected scientific explanation of the genesis of human subjectivity may account for the origin of our mental powers, and it will surely expand our current conception of matter (just as quantum mechanics has forced us to broaden our present ideas on the nature of matter). However, the explanation of the origin of something does not exhaust the understanding of the full range of its possibilities. There is a *semper plus* to any scientific explanation: science can unveil the mechanisms behind the emergence of subjectivity, not the very nature of *my* subjectivity, especially in those aspects that concern how I can make use of my subjectivity. The task of philosophy is condemned to a perpetual lack of resolution. The principal questions posed by Kant (What can I know? What ought I to do? What can I hope?), summarized in this mystery, "What is man?," are ultimately unsolvable. The enigma posed by very individual subjectivity, by every individual consciousness, by every human being, will always remain.

Neither the natural nor the social sciences (which are incapable of explaining my subjectivity, unless it is done on the basis of subsuming it into patterns that will always generate some "explanatory darkness"), not even the attempt at returning to the transcendental subjectivity of a Hegelian universal spirit displayed in history, of whose inexorable development I constitute a mere moment (because this spirit cannot be "myself," while at the same time being "someone else": our subjectivities would vanish in a lethal net of objectivities), might crown such a peak. This irretrievable incapacity nonetheless opens a potentially infinite space of reflection for philosophy, and it is deeply connected with the essence of artistic creativity, because there are infinite possible subjective experiences, whose most eminent "incarnation" takes place in aesthetic works. Science can unfold the objective dimension of subjectivity (as a process of the central nervous system), but this accomplishment shall not conceal the need for creative interpretations of that which scientific understanding cannot exhaust.

Philosophy seeks to understand the human world in every historical stage. It also aims to "anticipate" the future, which always remains open. Philosophy can helpfully pose the question of how we should edify the time to come, so that it may correspond to the demands that every age poses. Philosophy, as offering and commitment to the possibility of creating, addresses the necessity to think of our place in the world, and to discuss the way in which we should use the excess of energy that we possess. It therefore highlights the depth of the mystery of how we should live, and of how we should unveil that meaning for which many eagerly long as creation, as *novum*, as challenge to the sameness of the world.

Philosophy interprets the world. Moreover, it seeks to create its own world. Philosophy should neither intend to compete with the natural sciences in the elucidation of the structure and functioning of the world, nor constrain its task to interpreting that which is already given. Philosophy must open itself to the future, to a *novum*, to creating that which shall be subject to interpretation. Inspired by the legacy of both the scientific view of the world and its own tradition, it must fuel the flame of novelty. Philosophy converges with aesthetic creativity: it offers the possibility of creating something new.

Philosophy is committed to challenging that which is given. However, it must, first of all, understand the nature of "that which is given" and its relationship to consciousness. Thinking about the world seems therefore equivalent to displaying its full possibilities in our minds, by contemplating in it a fountain of incommensurable inspiration for imagining newness and for crossing the gates of a universe of purity: the realm of the unconditioned, the kingdom of freedom. Philosophy shines as criticism of the world and fascination for the creative power of life. Thus, it becomes passion, *enthusiasm*, love of wisdom and longing for creation.

The vocation of philosophy is none other than thinking about human life. The paradoxical "presence" of the future gives us the possibility of creating a way of understanding that may propitiate our growth, the broadening of our interpretation of world and history. Behold the opportunity to gain new freedom.

2

The Senses of Being

THE EXPRESSION "SENSES OF being" refers neither to the classical question of the manifold meanings of "being" in Aristotle, through his "discovery" of analogy (a topic which was brilliantly examined by Franz Brentano[1]), nor to the analysis of the categories of classical metaphysics and logic. It does not concern the elucidation of the idea of being in Heidegger, which, by its own concept, cannot be clarified at all (Heidegger blames the Western metaphysical tradition of darkening "being," but he does not offer any alternative to this "veiling" of being; his analysis of *Dasein* as the entity that wonders about being incurs in a flagrant vicious circle, because the meaning of *Dasein* becomes the hermeneutic clue for understanding being, while being becomes "that about which *Dasein* wonders"; being is not captured in its purity, in its *creating* power, but only in the concrete existential problem of the "being-there").[2]

---

1. Cf. Brentano, *Von der mannigfachen Bedeutung des Seienden nach Aristoteles*.
2. As Nicolai Hartmann writes, in clear reference to Heidegger: "Sinn' ist unter allen Umständen (in allen seinen Bedeutungen) etwas, was ‚für uns' besteht—genauer für uns oder für etwas, was unseresgleichen ist, und sei es auch nur ein postuliertes logisches Subjekt. Ein Sinn an sich wäre ein Widersinn. Es ist also noch zu wenig, wenn man sagt: an sich selbst braucht das Seiende als Seiendes keinen Sinn zu haben. Vielmehr muss man sagen: an sich selbst kann es gar nicht Sinn haben. Es kann nur „für jemand" Sinn haben. Sein Sinnhaben für jemand aber—wenn es ein solches gibt—ist jedenfalls nicht sein ‚Sein'. Das Sein des Seienden steht indifferent zu allem, was das Seiende ‚für jemand' sein könnte. Hier liegt der Grund, warum Heideggers ‚Welt' eine auf den Einzelmenschen relative (je meinige') ist. Das Abgleiten der Seinsfrage in die

Phenomenology, as conceived by Husserl, has shown very modest philosophical results on our understanding of "being." The best application of phenomenology was accomplished by Heidegger in *Sein und Zeit*: if we intend to reach "things themselves" ("*Zu den Sachen selbst!*," to follow Husserl), we inevitably face the mere "being-there," the entity that has been thrown into the world. Conceptually speaking, phenomenology "dies" after *Sein und Zeit*.[3] The "thing itself" is *Dasein* and its condition of a "fallen" entity whose destiny is death (Heidegger's *Sein zum Todde*).

By "senses of being" we understand the way in which *being*, the pure and unconditioned intuition (although not constrained to its "unconditionality"), the *power* that fills everything, relates to itself in its *perpetual growth* as being. These modes of being become manifestations for consciousness: they are the meanings acquired by being in its reference to consciousness, to that entity which "appears without appearing"[4] and stays

Sinnfrage läßt es anders nicht zu" (*Zur Grundlegung der Ontologie*, 42).

3 Classical philosophy, since the pre-Socratic thinkers, tried to identify a principle without principle, the untimely force from which everything emerges, lying in the origin of all reality. Modern thought, since Descartes, wonders about the subject that formulates every possible question about the entity. Both aims converge in the very act of a subject's questioning the *fundamentum* of every entity: in the question about being, which transcends all questioning about the entity. For Heidegger, the essence of philosophy resides in the perception of the ontological difference between being and entity. (The necessity of differentiating being and entity is extensively examined in *Identität und Differenz* [1957], particularly in the section "Die onto-theologische Verfassung der Metaphysik," which deals with the historical oblivion of the ontological difference between being and entity and the subsequent polarization of the metaphysical discourse around the entity and God.) Metaphysics cannot limit itself to merely standing as the logic of the entity, Heidegger proclaims. Philosophers after Parmenides were all victims, according to him, of confusing being and entity. For Heidegger, only poetic compositions, like the perdurable verses of Parmenides and Hölderlin, have been capable of delving into being. But the more we approach being, the more we perceive of its distance: being escapes us, and it is "the last smoke of evaporating reality" (Nietzsche, *Twilight of the Idols*, VIII, 78). To reach being is to reach nothingness, and to understand nothingness is to understand being, because being and nothingness are the same and unique *fundamentum* of totality, which is and is not. The brilliance of the work of Heidegger is patent in its capacity for joining the purely theoretical discourse about being as radical *fundamentum* (*Grund*), as a *fundamentum* that becomes emptiness, a fathomless abyss that evades all possible understanding (*Ab-Grund*), with the reflection about history, mankind, and society, because the idea of being is inexorably connected with the history of the West. The decay of being is followed, according to Heidegger, by the decay of the West. It means the suppression of Western culture, its dissolution into technique. The recovery of being is the revival of the flame of the West. Nevertheless, being cannot be the sole patrimony of Western thought: being has to become the "spiritual fate" of humanity, the overcoming of any dialectic.

4. The phrase "to appear without appearing" is intended as a translation of the

in search of the deepest meaning of its own being. In the different senses adopted by being it is possible to contemplate its capacity, its orientation towards itself, it's "being itself." Being *exercises its own being*, and this necessarily involves exercising its own "*being-able-to.*"

In its different modes, being shows, first of all, its "being": the absoluteness of its "being"; its "being centered upon itself." Second, in its "being-able-to," being manifests its openness to itself, its *freedom* for itself, its *potentiality*. Being "can be." It "can exercise itself for itself." It relates to itself not only as being but also as "power." Consciousness apprehends this intrinsic potentiality radiated by being for itself as *manifestations of being*.

BEING-"BEING-ABLE-TO"

Through its "being-able-to," being relates to itself as ultimately "unfounded," as *free*, as capable of indefinitely founding itself and unlimitedly relating to itself. Being "possesses itself." Being is, first of all, "being-able-to," because "it can be itself." The most fathomless and cryptic purity of being is not "the immediate undetermined," just as for Hegel, but that which "can continuously determine itself": the susceptibility to "being itself." Being "can be itself." Therefore, its "being-able-to" shines along with its own being: being is "being-able-to," and logic is a manifestation of this fundamental power of being.

BEING-NULLITY

Being-nullity consists of being as it is unfounded on its own being: being as *lacking a 'fundamentum' which may stem from its own being*. Because the *fundamentum* is susceptible to being questioned (no frontier emerges for consciousness in its capacity for interrogating that which is given: consciousness is opened to non-being), being is orphan of a firm ontological basis: it stands on its own being. Being finds itself "suspended" on its own ontological space. This radical indeterminacy inexorably links it to "non-being," to nullity, to absolute emptiness. Being, in its most basic relation to itself, appears as "not-being-able-to": being is not (*esse non est*, inasmuch as it is not founded upon itself). It is hanging on the most fragile thread. However, this fusion of being and nullity, this "being-not-being-able-to," is not the result of the manifestation of being to consciousness,

---

Spanish expression "*comparecer no-compareciendo.*"

which "denies it" and "nullifies it." Rather, it points to its deepest nature, to being in its primeval mode. This relationship of being to itself as nullity is the fruit of its own potentiality: it is not the product of the activity of consciousness. Since being relates to itself as "being-able-to," as *power*, it is not founded upon itself alone: it is also founded upon that which is not "itself" in its mere "being." It therefore opens itself to nothingness, but to a kind of nothingness inextricably bound to being: nothingness as slave to being (nothingness is not constrained to its own nullity). Nothingness "manifests" being's "being-able-to" with respect to itself, its susceptibility to a *fundamentum* that is always ulterior to itself. Then, nothingness recalls the *ulteriority of being*, its "absence of foundation," which shines as the rubric of its most egregious freedom, of its "being-able-to-be-itself" and therefore "being-able-to-be" that which "is-not-able-to-be." Nothingness is indebted to the deepest power of being.

BEING-APPEARANCE

Being-appearance is the world, its spatio-temporal condition, its dimensional "being-able-to," which is constrained to a "frontier," even if it can be overcome. Being inasmuch as it is limited by itself is "that which appears there": being in its *hic et nunc*, which is "the appearance to consciousness of the spatio-temporality of the world." Being-appearance, the world, is a limited continuum, in which any trace of infiniteness (as infinitely large or infinitely small) is absent, and only consciousness will recover it. Through consciousness, the world not only appears but it also "does not appear," because consciousness is part of the world (it "appears"), but it is a challenge to the world, too, a negation of its "merely being there," of its "appearance." Consciousness defies finiteness, but the world only appears as "finiteness." Consciousness challenges the mere appearance of the world: in the realm of consciousness, the world "appears and does not appear." As being-appearance, being relates to itself as limit, as "frontier," as finiteness. "That which appears" corresponds to our general understanding of reality in a positive sense, as *positivitas*, as "that which is given" and limits itself to "merely being-there." Consciousness inasmuch as *act* constitutes a challenge to the world: it "does not appear," for it questions the mere appearance of the world, its "limitation" to a given spatio-temporal frontier. However, any product of the activity of consciousness becomes an object of the world. Any result of the activity of consciousness is inherently limited, finite, as it is constrained to the spatio-temporality of the world. Being "in a limited way" is being-appearance: it is being as spatio-temporality that defines itself on the basis of its own spatio-temporality. It is retracted to itself in order to become "sameness." It is founded on its "mere appearance."

BEING-BECOMING

Becoming constitutes the spatio-temporal manifestation of "being-able-to" which is intrinsic to being. Becoming represents a transition from a given "appearance" into a new one. However, the result of this movement inexorably leads to "sameness," a return to being inasmuch as it "possesses itself" in a limited, finite way. The being that *moves*, the being that exercises its "being-able-to" in a spatio-temporal form, shows its intrinsic power in its *limit*, in its "being finite." Finiteness is a possibility of being (just as infiniteness, which is "simply being": an infinite proposition, unreservedly large and infinitesimally small). Therefore, the finiteness of being obeys the freedom of being. The "being-becoming" of the world is the evolving capacity of the universe, its suitability for the acquisition of new states, of new forms of appearance.

Becoming manifests the "multiplicity" of the world. Through finiteness, being deprives itself of its indeterminate unity in order to consecrate itself to diversity. Through finiteness, being challenges itself in its "movement," in its "being-able-not-to-be" that which "appears-there" (in a given spatio-temporal location). However, this challenge posed by the world to itself is immediately annulled through sameness. The act of becoming seems illusory for consciousness. Zeno's paradoxes have not lost their intellectual depth. Movement, becoming, "cannot be," if by "being" we exclusively understand "being-appearance" and "being-sameness." Becoming cannot be captured by the power of understanding, for any apparent "becoming" always recalls a given "sameness," a given "state" of the world in its *hic et nunc*. The world has never remained in some sort of "vacuum," emancipated from any given state, from any given sameness, from any given "appearance." If change is analyzed from a more accurate perspective, it is possible to realize that it can only consist of a continuum of states, of a continuous "appearance," of a continuous "sameness." Being-appearance and being-sameness are never abandoned. It is true that becoming, if we should interpret it as the negation of any state, cannot be grasped. We do not see "movement." We do not feel "transformations": we perceive of divergent states, not "movement itself." Movement silently evaporates at any attempt at capturing it. However, we need to notice that the irreducibility of *hic et nunc* represents an imposition of consciousness, a sign of its tyranny, which aims to grasp the finite and volatile reality of the world in accordance with its aspirations towards infiniteness. No trace of infiniteness emerges within the world. We only contemplate finite states. The irreducibility of *hic et nunc* is not a property of the world but a feature of consciousness, which tries to discover something "infinitesimal" and "infinite," something "irreducible" in the world. The world, inasmuch as it appears before consciousness, recalls an irreducible *hic et nunc*. Nevertheless, the world as world, the world as "that which simply appears there," the world as sameness, is simply its spatio-temporality, which is inherently finite (instead of infinite or infinitesimal). Any shadow of infiniteness is the product of the activity of consciousness. No light of infiniteness shines in the world. It is consciousness that recalls infiniteness in its ambition to understand the world, *id est*, in its will to challenge the world in its sameness in order to enlarge the frontiers of all that is given. Being-becoming is different from being-appearance and being-sameness. It cannot be grasped through their canons.

Being-becoming is the possibility that being has to relate to itself *qua* different, *qua* distinctive with respect to itself through finiteness. Being-becoming is constrained to limits, but it exercises its power in its variation within those limits. Being-becoming manifests the irrevocable power of being, which not even in its finiteness can be deprived of its "being-able-to." Becoming recalls the freedom of being with respect to itself. There is becoming because being can "possess itself" *qua* mutable, *qua* indigent and vulnerable. That which is finite is susceptible to being "divided" into parts. Consciousness will never grasp being-becoming, because in order to challenge the world, its mere appearance, it needs to project infinite categories on something that is finite: it has to subsume the reality of the world into a concept (and a concept is potentially opened to infiniteness).

Becoming "is never given." It links that which is given, the parts to which being-appearance is susceptible on account of its finiteness. Becoming is the power of finiteness, its freedom, the capacity of the parts for relating to each other. Nevertheless, consciousness perceives of infiniteness. For consciousness, the mere appearance of the world seems potentially infinite and inexhaustible. One can always challenge it in its sameness, in its simplicity, in its "positivity." Matter is manifested to consciousness as potentially infinite and infinitesimal, but science teaches us, and both ordinary experience and logical reasoning teach us, that it only consists of finiteness, of its spatio-temporality, of parts in dynamic interaction. However, this finiteness cannot be grasped by consciousness, which is avid for infiniteness (*qua* infinite or infinitesimal). Consciousness contemplates variability, but it is unable to explain (in its deepest ontological meaning, in the core of intelligibility of reality) the origin of that profusion: how this variability has emerged, if states, "sameness," "appearances-there," have always existed. Consciousness "sees" states, but it does not observe the transition from one state into another, for it apprehends any possible transition as an objectified reality in its *hic et nunc*, as a potentially infinitesimal structure. Consciousness is incapable of conceiving of discontinuity. Consciousness is convinced that "*natura non facit saltum.*"[5] Consciousness subordinates everything to continuity, which is equivalent to "infinitesimalness," to indifference, to submerging any part into a primeval and infinite unity, in whose vastness any trace of finiteness evaporates.

For consciousness, "atoms" do not exist *stricto sensu*. The fact that physics teaches us that matter is composed of elementary particles does not confute this evidence: we cannot "imagine" the atom or the ultimate subatomic particle (if science ever discovers it beyond the *pléiade* of elementary particles admitted by the standard model) because we can always "think beyond its finiteness." We can always conceive of an even smaller particle. Consciousness cannot cease to challenge such a hypothetical "ultimate component" in its finiteness. Consciousness cannot conceive of a frontier, of a barrier, of a "limit." Consciousness cannot imagine a limit for spatio-temporality. It cannot think of a day without yesterday and a day without tomorrow. Consciousness constantly seeks a *plus*, for it challenges the world through its "infiniteness," through its unlimited power to "go beyond that which is given." Consciousness does not understand the world in its sameness, in its finiteness, for it always tries to defy it, to negate it in its sameness, to question its finiteness, its limitation. Consciousness cannot renounce the contemplation of the world as an inexhaustible reality, which is potentially infinite and infinitesimal. It does not capture finiteness, limitation, frontier, the spatio-temporality of the world: its being-becoming, its being-appearance, vivid witnesses of the freedom that being has to relate to itself through finiteness.

---

5. This famous gradualist principle was assumed by Charles Darwin in his theory on the mechanisms of evolution. Cf. Stauffer, ed., *Charles Darwin's Natural Selection. Being the Second Part of His Big Species Book Written from 1856 to 1858*, chapter 8, "Difficulties in transitions," 25: "Do quite new organisms appear? "Natura non facit saltum." Kinds of transitions."

Being-becoming is therefore the rubric of the finiteness of the world. Infiniteness does not become: it "lives" in its own infiniteness. Any change is illusory, because it is diluted in its own infiniteness. That which is infinite "suffocates" any flame of finiteness, of partiality, of limitation. By swimming in infinite waters, reality deprives itself of any trace of multiplicity. It is indifferent. It loses any power to relate to itself through differentiation. Infiniteness absorbs any breath of partiality. That which is infinite is immutable.[6]

All that is susceptible to becoming is finite, for it can change, it can acquire a different state, but this transition is not dissipated into an ocean of infiniteness which dissolves any "drop" of finiteness. The world, *qua* "appearance" enfolded over itself, can change: it can "become." Consciousness seeks to challenge the sameness of the world in a radical way. Consciousness intends to subsume finiteness into infiniteness, partiality into the undifferentiated totality, into *being*, into the fathomless purity. Only when it discovers being as *ulteriority*, being as infiniteness and purity which nonetheless continuously transcends itself even in its own infiniteness (so that it is also able to limit itself), consciousness opens itself to *novum*, to a newness that "overwhelms" infiniteness (in whose realm everything "is already given" and there is no possibility of newness): the purity of being is *creative*, for it overwhelms itself in a continuous and infinite way, so that its infiniteness does not consist of "being already there" (diluting any trace of finiteness) but of its unlimited capacity for transcending itself: of its power to *create*.

BEING-SAMENESS

Being relates to itself as "sameness" as soon as it constrains itself to a certain state. The "sameness" of being is the self-exhaustion of being in a given state. Sameness is intrinsic to the world: being-sameness is the result of being-appearance whose becoming leads to a new form of being-appearance. Being-sameness is therefore the rubric of the potentiality of

---

6. It is true that set theory, and especially the mathematical study of infinite series, forces us (at least since Cantor) to qualify many of the traditional philosophical statements regarding the idea of infiniteness. However, the considerations which we have just exposed on the relationship of finiteness to infiniteness are meant to recall an "existential understanding" of infiniteness, which is closer to the traditional philosophical conception of infiniteness as "absence of finiteness," "overflowing of finiteness," "overcoming of finiteness," which can be complementary to the mathematical notion derived from set theory.

being *qua* being-appearance and being-becoming. Sameness is the mere appearance of being, its simple "being-there," that which is given and founded upon itself. The *limit* acquired by being in order to "possess itself" in a finite way shines as being-sameness. Being-appearance, being-becoming, and being-sameness, although understood by consciousness as different senses of being, actually constitute three projections of a common phenomenon: that of "being as world," that of being as endowed by itself with spatio-temporality.

Being-sameness is therefore being-appearance inasmuch as it is limited to "appearing": the mere appearance of being can be understood as being-sameness. A sense of being does not represent a new ontological "level," as if being had the necessity to conquering new stages in an inexorable way. If being obeyed some sort of ineluctability, it "would not be" *stricto sensu*, because being is freedom, it consists of the exercise of its own "being-able-to": it is the possession of being by itself, so that nothing can anticipate the path which being will take. Being cannot be forced to follow a certain series of stages. There is no final goal for being: being is freedom, it is the perpetual possibility of being, its ulteriority, its capacity for crossing any barrier and open any horizon. There is no ultimate ontological frontier. Being "is for itself" freely, and it finds no goal beyond the exercise of its own freedom. The senses grasped by consciousness are the manifestations of how being can project its "being-able-to," but they neither exhaust the possible modes of being nor address the deeper truth of being (which recalls, after all, the freedom of being: its "being itself"; but this remains undefinable, for it challenges any concept and intuition). Consciousness understands that being is its "being-able-to": being is *power*; it is a relation to itself. Behold the vivifying light of creativity.

BEING-CONSCIOUSNESS[7]

Being-consciousness is the world in its challenge to itself. Being-consciousness is therefore "appearing without appearing," the radical questioning of

---

7. Several authors have criticized the idea of "consciousness," regarded as too narrowly linked to Western culture. According to Clifford Geertz, "the Western conception of the person as a bound, unique, more or less integrated motivational and cognitive universe, a dynamic centre of awareness, emotion, judgment, and action organized into a distinctive whole and set contrastively both against other such wholes and against its social and natural background, is, however incorrigible it may seem to us, a rather peculiar idea within the context of the world's cultures" (*Local Knowledge*, 59). However, even in other cultural traditions it is still *possible* to conceive of the idea

the world in its sameness: it is the unlimited longing for more, for *novum*, for freedom and creation. Through consciousness, being exercises its power inasmuch as *questioning*, as freedom to defy all that is given within the realm of the world. Being seeks to understand itself, to contemplate itself, and to love itself because it challenges itself in a radical way, in such a profound form that it opens itself to creation. Being-consciousness is the rubric of the lack of satisfaction of being, of its perpetual desire for "more," of its disposition to cross any frontier without succumbing to any given limit. Being-consciousness manifests the deep rupture within being itself. Thus, it shows its most eminent freedom: that of "being for itself," that of non-conformism with whatever may stand in the world. Through being-consciousness, being looks for itself as infiniteness, as unity, as *fundamentum* (but as a free *fundamentum*, which is not founded upon itself but "hangs" on its "being-able-to," on its openness to its *alter*, to "not-being-able-to": being as opened to non-being), and it becomes capable of questioning "questioning itself" in the highest possible interrogation (why questioning?; why the "why"?).[8]

---

of consciousness in a "Western" sense. As strange as it may seem in the context of the historical and cultural variety of mankind, it cannot be denied that the Western idea of consciousness ("return to oneself," "reflexivity," "for-itself") represents a *possibility* for human thought. Similar considerations can be posed concerning psychoanalysis. As important as the unconscious dimension may be for our lives, *it is possible to think of consciousness; it is possible to think of oneself as a conscious being*. Factual evidence can probably disclaim the pretension that we principally determine ourselves as conscious beings; perhaps it will show that consciousness is filled with unconscious elements. However, it will not prevent us from the possibility of conceiving of consciousness. Even if it were true that our general understanding of consciousness were delusory (a thesis that has not been proven), we could still conceive of consciousness as a *possibility: we could think of consciousness as "consciousness in a strict sense."* Of course, the idea that consciousness is an illusion constitutes an easy and regressive strategy, which discourages science from developing new tools to unfold the nature of conscious phenomena and their place in the physical world. To deny the reality of the vast range of phenomena which has not been explained by science is a subtle tactic to conceal the gravity of their challenge. If everything is delusory (consciousness, freedom. . .), science, reason, art, and all that we contemplate is also delusory. Everything succumbs to the most dramatic state of darkness.

8. The infiniteness of consciousness can only be discovered through our interaction with other individuals who stand before the same horizon of mystery. Emmanuel Levinas has seen in "the other" not the negation of the *ego* but the epiphanic moment of the infinite being, *"l'absolument autre,"* in which the divine is not captured by the structures of this world; rather, it conveys a constant challenge to the world, an absolute "other" that is actually a face, *"un visage"* that enables us to realize that we are not unique in our uniqueness: we must transcend ourselves in order to assume the condition of ex-tatic beings. (Following Rudolf Otto, we can argue that using "the divine

BEING-FREEDOM

Freedom expresses the exercise of its "own being" by being itself. Freedom is the possession of being by itself. Being relates to itself as freedom inasmuch as *power*, as potentiality that allows it to "live for itself." The free being falls outside itself, so that it radically opens itself and abandons any "sameness." However, the free being can "freely" acquire a certain state of "sameness": it can limit itself; it can "merely appear" and find delight in such a constraint. Being is opened to itself inasmuch as it is free: it is "free" for being and it is free for exercising its own being-able-to.

Being unitarily lives its own freedom, and it therefore becomes *ethics*, relationship to itself in order to display its highest power, its courage. The *ethics* of being evokes its subjective "being-able-to," its capacity for committing itself to a norm that may preserve it in its freedom: the ethics of being inasmuch as being-freedom is the condition of possibility of its

---

[*das göttliche*]" instead of "the deity [*die Gottheit*]" does not necessarily impoverish the idea of a personal God, for neuter terms frequently "indicate the mysterious overplus of the non-rational and numinous, that cannot enter our "concepts" because it is too great and too alien to them" [*The Idea of the Holy*, 203].) If, according to Horkheimer, we all long, in the deepest dwelling of our soul, for the totally-other [*Sehnsucht nach dem ganz-Anderen*], it seems that this melancholic sentiment must be addressed, first of all, to "others" surrounding us: nostalgia for humanity. (On the importance of this notion in the thought of Horkheimer, cf. Sánchez, *Anhelo de Justicia. Teoría Crítica y Religión.*) The dream of Horkheimer—that justice may prevail over the "curse" of history—is echoed by Rahner in *Schriften zur Theologie*, 6:85). In this way, the tension between all that is ours and all that is not becomes solved in the service to universality, to humanity, so that whatever is singular may be integrated into a totality capable of illuminating the obscurity that torments our spirit, sharing our doubts and anxieties with others. Humanity is always there, and every one of us can take comfort in humanity. The presence of mystery and the constant opening of the horizon of possibilities demand something that may be an end in itself, something that can actually assume disinterested, universal goals: something thrown into mystery, which can become a sign of hope. Society is the task of everyone, a calling for commitment, for the action of the subject, for the *ego* that reaches its full subjectivity in delivering itself to a *tu*, to the community of persons. Levinas's idea of the epiphany that takes place in the contemplation of others is powerful, indeed, and it is shared by many religious, cultural, and philosophical traditions: to see God in the face of our brothers and sisters, because the "others" constitute a challenge, a question, an exhortation for commitment; the divine is an invitation to an ontological opening, to transcending ourselves, to seeing something unconditioned in those who surround us. As Levinas has written in *Totalité et Infini*, "l'expériénce absolue n'est pas dévoilement mais révélation. Le visage parle." Levinas's philosophy offers no excuse for refusing to become involved in the improvement of a contradictory reality: "Dieu invisible, cela ne signifie pas seulement un Dieu inimaginable, mais un Dieu accesible dans la justice," and "la métaphysique se joue dans les rapports éthiques."

"possessing itself" as free. In order to reach its free possession, being needs to subordinate its inexhaustible impetus, its infinite force, to a limit, to the modesty of a frontier that enables it to persevere in its own "possession" of itself, so that its freedom does not turn into an arbitrary and even destructive force but becomes a *creative power*.

Being-freedom, as ethical being, recalls the commitment of being to its own freedom, to its determination to be free, which stems from its deepest "being-able-to." However, and in order to be free, in order to exercise its exuberant and vital power, being must grant itself ethics (as Kant foresaw: it is by virtue of his freedom that the subject autonomously links himself to the moral law: the subject universalizes the exercise of his own freedom in order to overcome the constraints of an anarchic experience of liberty): it must consecrate itself to its own power inasmuch as "norm." The ethics of being points to the exercise of freedom: being is ethical in order to conquer its freedom and "be worthy of itself." Ethics is consubstantial to freedom, because it refers to a "free freedom."

BEING-SOLIDARITY

Solidarity constitutes the overcoming of freedom: it is "free freedom," freedom committed to love, freedom committed to the unification of multiplicity and the elucidation of a common goal: it is the universalization of freedom. Being-solidarity approaches the category of universality, of fraternity, of openness to others in order to *create*. Being-freedom is manifested as a subjective power: I can be free; I want to grow; I wish to create. In freedom, being is consecrated to itself. In solidarity, being integrates world and consciousness through its longing for harmony, coherence, order. Its deepest will does not consist of challenging the world, not even challenging itself, but living-together to expand the energies of life. In solidarity, being becomes universality and it "lives itself"[9] as plurality.

Being, in its susceptibility to be fragmented, becomes reconciled with itself through solidarity. Being is now society, political organization. Ethics turns into politics, into the concord of freedoms for the construction of a community, of a space in which freedom may be exercised "freely" and universally. Being-solidarity seeks universality. It intends to escape its own freedom. Therefore, it opens itself to plurality, to multiplicity, to the harmonization of all that is different on the common ground of a *political 'ethos:'* ethics in its aspiration to set the conditions of possibility for a

9. "Se vive," "se posee," "se ejerce" . . .

plural exercise of freedom. Ethics *qua* politics, *qua* common experience of the power of being, is the responsibility of being inasmuch as plurality with respect to itself. The *political 'ethos'* is the responsibility of humanity with respect to itself: humanity must be collectively free, so that all of its members can exercise their freedom. Being-solidarity is the free consecration of being to universality, to the unification of that which is diverse into a convergent life: into its "living for others," into commitment to plurality (vivified by the possession of a political space, of a common *telos*), into freedom experienced as community.

BEING-COMMITMENT

Being relates to itself as commitment when it offers its freedom to an "*alter.*" It entirely renounces its own sameness and freedom in order to reach the highest degree of solidarity with others. Its goal is fathomless purity, the detachment from itself. Through commitment, being becomes free to "deprive itself of its own freedom." However, its aspirations transcend the enjoyment and satisfaction of communal life and social recognition: its energies are ineffably oriented towards *novum*, creation. Being-commitment represents the radical predisposition for creation.

BEING-PURITY:

Being relates to itself as purity through its shining as that which is inexhaustible, fathomless, and perennially evocative: as the overwhelming suggestion that never succumbs to any constraint. Being-purity is the ineffability of being.[10] Any discourse on the ineffability of being trembles before the limpid perception of its beauty, its simplicity, its abnegation. Only admiration is suitable. Being-purity evades any attempt at grasping its freedom, its power, its majesty . . . However, its trace is left as intuition, immediacy. In being-purity, being relates to itself as the unconditioned, as that which does not obey anything else: as that which is by itself and for itself, but universally radiates its resuscitating light. It is youth detached from itself and opened to compassion.

Being-purity inspires fascination and enthusiasm for so much limpidness, so much simplicity, before such a profound and overwhelming

---

10. Gabriel Marcel poetically referred to the "rooting of being in the sphere of mystery" (cf. Marcel, *The Mystery of Being*).

virginity. The heart which does not look for itself can be conquered by the contemplation of purity: it has been captured by a silent fervor, by peace, by commitment and dedication to creation, to universal life, to displaying its freedom as growth, as the edification of *novum*.[11] Through wondering at purity we feel exhorted to consecrating ourselves to the latent beauty that surrounds us, to the great and captivating architectonics that covers us, to abnegated beauty, to silent wisdom, to the free and generous love of which we perceive when we are possessed by the noble light of purity. Then, the universe emerges before our eyes as the greatest work of art, because it is capable of exhaling the breath of purity and abnegation, the wind of fathomlessness. We know that nothing in the world is pure, for everything is conditioned by the fierce necessity of matter, by the voracious inexorability of life, by the self-sufficiency of cosmos in its sameness, but being goes beyond the world: being is its *power*, its openness; being is creation, *novum*. Consciousness grasps, even in the midst of this vertiginous world, that golden blow, that delightful air which recalls purity and inexhaustibility, the deepest and most penetrating intuition.

BEING-CREATION

Through being-creation, being relates to itself as power for *novum*, as the radical and fathomless openness to that which "is not." Being-creation is consecration to the "wholly-other." It is therefore being committed to non-being, to "not-being-able-to." It is being absolutely detached from itself; it is being escaping its own freedom and its own solidarity in order to exercise its power through creation, through the edification of that which "does not appear" and has not been imagined by consciousness.

---

11. Humanity can create history, and thought can reach novelty. The past was present, and it was also novelty. Let us grant the possibility that the present is novelty, too. Can't there be a place for originality, for creativity, for the "author" as such? Can we indefinitely return to the past in the quest for something truly original? Isn't there room for something completely new, as a utopian limit, which may be capable of revealing something truly original? The space of originality is that of ulteriority: what is unique can be understood from the infiniteness of being, from the possibility of a perennial broadening of the horizon of understanding. Thinking as such, the act of posing questions as the capacity for tending towards the *fundamentum* and transcending any dialectic, constitutes the most eminent manifestation of ulteriority. Beyond any possible phenomenological reduction a core always persists, and it will be examined by every age with a renovated spirit, because every time must have the right to go back to the *fundamentum*.

Being-creation opens itself to "not-being-able-to." It recalls being-nullity and being-power: it points to the most irreducible magnificence of being, to its deepest truth. Being-creation manifests the latent vigor of being, its evasion from any *fundamentum* which is not its "being-able-to," its serene but grandiose courage, which allows it to long for the impossible, for non-being, so that it may commit itself to a perpetual disposition for growth and dedication, for radiating its sublime purity in order to shine as wisdom, beauty, and love.

BEING WISDOM-BEAUTY-LOVE

Through wisdom, being possesses itself as understanding, truth, and growth. Wisdom radiates depth, the contemplation of *fundamentum* as possibility: constant openness, perennial disposition to enrichment, transformation, and learning. Through wisdom, being exercises its own power in order to grow, in order to relativize itself and create glimpses of novelty. Through beauty, being enjoys its own power by contemplating the unconditioned purity acquired once it freely commits itself to creation, to *novum*. Beauty recalls service, dedication, generosity: the capacity for committing oneself to contemplation, to renouncing one's own selfness in order to "fall" before a reality whose evocative nature conquers our spirit. Through love, being "stands for itself" as abnegation, as radical commitment to that which lies "outside" its ontological space. To love means to consecrate oneself to others, and this *alteritas* resides in "that which is not," in its "not-being-able-to." Being loves when it commits itself to non-being and prepares itself for creation. Wisdom, beauty, and love take root in the same and fertile ground: that of commitment, limpidness, creative openness that perceives of the incommensurability of an unconditioned meaning. Wisdom, beauty, and love represent the rubric of being in its inexhaustibility.

The most genuine compassion stems from love, because love involves feeling its dramatic absence in this world and this humanity. In the realm of love, we perceive of the most terrible of all punishments: the impossibility of incarnating its ideal in the fragility of nature and the vulnerability of humanity. Love lightens the torch of clemency, but this mercifulness does not recreate itself on its own condescendence: it is creative compassion, it is a wise and beautiful love, it is a love that understands the urgency for the edification of a *novum* in which tears and sadness may vanish. It is aware of the impossibility of a full accomplishment of purity: being as freedom, being as limpid power, being as creative impetus never appears in the sameness of the world, in the *hic et nunc* of nature and history. However, this void constitutes an invitation for seeking wisdom, beauty, and love with even greater enthusiasm. It offers a vivid exhortation for creation, for dreaming of the impossible in order to witness the highest potentiality of being (its commitment, its abnegation).

Being wisdom-beauty-love cannot shine without commitment: it is being in its purity, being detached from itself and alien to any temptation of vanity. It is being opened to creation, to transcending itself and radiating its light in an uninterested and limpid way: it is being as *service*. This is the reason why being as wisdom, beauty, and love "contemplates" that which is ultimately impossible, for it longs for committing itself to something, for donating its power to "others": it wants to grow and learn. This is the strongest root of the tree of its deepest happiness.

BEING-ULTERIORITY

Through ulteriority, being shines as the "incessant power to be," as the radical openness to a *plus* (each instantiation of ulteriority recalls one of the countable elements of Cantor's series). As ulteriority, being relates to itself through its latent possibility of novelty. Ulteriority is the *power of being*,[12] its "suspension" on "the unfounded," on the abyss which does not radiate darkness but light: the light of possibility, of creative power, of openness. Being susceptible to a perpetual questioning by itself (not only by consciousness), by virtue of its "being-able-to" (that leaves it unfounded on itself), is being-ulteriority: a *semper plus* that manifests the deepest truth

---

12. Understanding is, in this way, a "fusion of horizons" (Gadamer), a broadening of the subject by the object and of the object by the subject. Being is susceptible to *any possible hermeneutics*: it is the condition of possibility of every hermeneutic projection. Every division (and moreover, the differentiation of sciences, as developed in the Western tradition) is essentially mutable, dependent upon that which every age may be ready to admit. We all perceive, in every age, of the necessity of transcending our own categories in order to *let ourselves* be dominated by being. In the dialectic of dominating and being dominated, of action and passion, the truth of being is actualized. This is the only possible way for metaphysics to avoid nihilism, which was prophetically envisioned by Nietzsche: if, instead of disclosing the entity, we unfold the power of being (to use Paul Tillich's famous expression), which through its act of creating constitutes a constant overcoming of the horizon of emptiness and nothingness that threatens thought and history. The sole metaphysical refuge against nihilism and the risk of totalitarianism and dogmatism (the "black holes" of thinking, in which the intellect closes itself), is *ulterioritas*, the conviction that there is always a "beyond" (*semper plus ultra*).

of being. Ulteriority shows the humility of being, its permanent disposition to overcoming itself and extending its latent energies in order to enlarge its own frontiers. In the realm of ulteriority, being is bound to itself through its "turning" to "more," to a *plus*, to a perennial *novum* which can never be exhausted, to an unreachable peak that unlimitedly opens the paths of being.

It is tempting to regard the senses of being as moments in a process of *ascension*. However, there is no *scala entis*, no "ladder," no concatenation of levels, each of which "overcomes" the preceding one. There is no limit, no peak for being. The different levels only manifest the way in which being possesses itself: the exercise of the power of being. Being grows, because it relates to itself as "that which can be." Nevertheless, it does not climb any mountain: there is no pre-established path that being must inexorably follow. Being "is for itself."[13] Behold its freedom . . . But the liberty of being is so intense and powerful that it does not constrain itself to returning to its original purity. Being does not seek its sole understanding, its selfish revisiting. The freedom of being consists of its capacity for *creating*, for *committing* itself to the "unlimited," to the "impossible," to an endless process which allows it to "live itself" unreservedly. Being shines in its most elevated form through its *ulteriority*, through its incessant possibility to transcend itself, through its condition of "*semper plus*," through its inexhaustibility, through its limpid abnegation to being, to living, to opening itself.

The senses of being constitute the *constant possibilities of being*. They should not be contemplated as moments within an evolutionary process. *Ulteriority is the constant of being*, which emanates from its "being-able-to." Being "evolves" because "it is for itself," and it relates to itself as *power*. This is the reason why it corresponds to that which is pure, fathomless, and inscrutable: to *creation*. Therefore, the senses of being ought not to be interpreted as spatio-temporal successions in the *life of being* but as *permanent possibilities of its "being-for-itself."* We speak in terms of "senses" because our power of understanding requires some sort of classification, some analytic insight into the modes of being. However, being simply is, and through its "being itself" being shows its power, its "being-able-to." Being and "being-able-to" are so closely connected, so inseparably bound that the act of being is already "being-able-to," and any attempt at grasping the *fundamentum* of being violates its fathomless purity. However, there is no point in recalling a primeval unity of being in which all oppositions

13. "El ser se es."

fade, as certain trends of mysticism and metaphysics suggest, because "unity" is already a concept, and it already constrains the freedom of being, its mere "being for itself," its commitment, its creation, its *novum*. It is not only language that trembles but also intellect itself and our devout wish for understanding.

Every sense of being is its *truth*, its authentic mode to relate to itself and exercise its own "being-able-to." Truth is the possession of being by itself, *id est*, its freedom. The truth of being is its being-nullity, its being-appearance, its being-becoming, etc. Truth, concerning consciousness, is the perception of the depth of being, of its inexhaustibility, of its *potentiality*. Thus, truth is not the mere verification of the appearance of being inasmuch as world: it is not simply *adaequatio rei et intellectus*. A profounder idea of truth highlights not only the "objective" awareness of being as world but also the possibilities of being, its inexhaustible susceptibility to a *plus*: its ulteriority. The *reality* of being is the way in which it relates to itself, its truth and therefore its freedom, its "being-able-to," its inexhaustibility.

A superficial understanding of truth and reality identifies both notions with the mere appearing of being. Therefore, that which is real and true consists of the simple "being-there" of the world, of its sameness. Consciousness cannot desist from demanding an ulterior justification that challenges the world in its sameness. Through this enterprise, consciousness discovers the freedom of being, its power, its truth, which is also its deepest reality. "Objective" truth represents but a minuscule part of the colorful truth of being: being is true inasmuch as it is, as it "possesses itself," as it grows and looks for *novum*, as it *creates*. Every age of humanity will acquire a certain understanding of being. Science will elucidate the prolix mechanisms, the structure, the functioning of the world, of the being-appearance defined by its sameness and closed on itself. However, consciousness will ask for more, for it seeks to delve into the *truth* of being, into its freedom, its possibility, its creativity. Consciousness is perennially avid for "more" (as a beautiful rubric of the ulteriority of being): it will intend to conquer new levels of understanding within the infinite depth of being. On behalf of this intense longing, consciousness will aspire to creation, since the edification of *novum* "extends" the truth of being and allows for the growth of being in its truth, for its transcendence over itself.

The truth of being is manifested to consciousness as *painful uncertainty*, as lack of definition. However, this is a sign of its freedom. "The real" is the truth of being in its exercise of its own "being-able-to." Every sense of being is real inasmuch as it shows a latent possibility of being, its truth as possibility. But the truth of being *grows*, because being "expands itself," transcends itself and "ulteriorizes" itself. Being exercises its own being. Science will conquer new pinnacles in its attempt at a global understanding of the structure and functioning of the world, and it will project its intellectual impetus to the arcane domain of consciousness, but it will ultimately realize that its horizon is inexhaustible. An infinite and green forest emerges before the eyes of science. It is always possible to pose more and vaster questions and seek a deeper understanding of reality. The truth of being-appearance (the world) is its reality, which science laboriously elucidates through a methodology that takes the world in its objectivity. Science reduces the elenchus of questions that can be addressed to nature to those which *are meaningful*, that is to say, to those which are focused on the world *qua* world, in order to overcome a constant temptation that threatens the activity of the human intellect: that of questioning the world on those realms in which it can offer no answer. The epistemological success of the natural sciences is subsidiary to its method (and yes, there is a method, against Feyerabend, for there is a way to contrast any meaningful scientific statement; otherwise, the energies consecrated by some of the most outstanding intellects of mankind to the elucidation of the structure and functioning of the world would have been in vain; of course, this does not mean that there is no room for creativity, intuition, originality, and construction of new concepts in science: all it says is that any new statement must be contrasted, it must be "set" in a way that may be consistent with theory and experience), to its capacity for adequately recognizing the being-appearance of the world, its sameness, its "limit." Science imposes "humility" on concepts and statements: their submission to a certain way of contrast. Science humbly renounces the grandiose constellation of questions posed by classical metaphysics. The restriction of its frame of interrogation has allowed science, since Galileo, to discover the optimal way of dealing with the world in its truth, *id est*, in its reality of mere "being there," justified in its own sameness.

Science "decrees" a series of requirements or "postulates" (such as the intelligibility of the universe) that might be regarded as traces of consciousness. They could even delegitimize its pretension of objectivity. However, we should not forget that these axiomatic principles are constrained to the smallest, indispensable number, and they immediately yield to the "manifestation of the world by itself" through an empirical method that subordinates the judgment of the intellect to the reality of the world in its "being there." It is true that the scientific enterprise *confirms* the intelligibility of the world, the existence of a series of laws that allow us to understand the way in which the universe functions, the reason behind the phenomena that our senses contemplate and our reason evaluates. Nevertheless, the demand of intelligibility is prior to the beginning of the scientific adventure. This priority should not be taken chronologically but "conceptually." The presupposition of intelligibility of nature points to the necessity of the human reason for discovering the "logic," the meaning, the order that binds together the multiplicity of the world in accordance with an underlying unity. The mystery resides in understanding the "happy coincidence" that has enabled the convergence of both one of the deepest longings of the human intellect (intelligibility, sense, rationality) and the evidence emanating from the world itself: the synthesis of mathematics and physics. However, and even if the universe lacked intelligibility, consciousness would never desist from looking for it or to "construct" it.

Science surrenders to the world. The questions that it poses and the concepts that it produces answer the demands imposed by the world. The nature of science consists of the discovery of the world in its truth, in its "worldliness." The realization of the limits of the scientific intellection, the awareness that there is a "meta-discursive level," is a result of the perennial dissatisfaction of consciousness, of its capacity for formulating an incessant chain of questions: it is the fruit of its *longing for freedom*, expressed as a challenge to the sameness of the world. This is the reason why consciousness cannot cease to radiate the light of philosophy: not on account of its wish to compete with the scientific view of the world but of its longing for understanding and creating, for grasping a deeper truth, for a *meaning*, for "experiencing" the freedom of being, the *power* from which everything comes and to which everything leads. Consciousness is eager to perceive of that which may be pure and fathomless, of that which may not be conditioned by the inveterate concatenation of causes and effects that fills the universe: love, beauty, and wisdom; that which transcends any given truth, for it manifests being in its limpidness, freedom, and creative force. Consciousness cannot abdicate its capacity for self-transcendence, its "questioning itself" even to tremble in its most solid foundations. Unsatisfied with the elucidation of the mere "appearance" of the world analyzed by science, consciousness asks for a meaning: it impetrates freedom. Consciousness cannot capitulate to the world, not even to the wonders of its structure and functioning, which embellish the scientific enterprise:

it is avid for *creation*. Consciousness wants to edify its own world and its own *truth*.

3

The Dynamism of Being

THE SCOPE OF CONSCIOUSNESS

CONSCIOUSNESS CONTRADICTS THE SAMENESS of the world. It is the most radical challenge to the world. Consciousness does not merely contemplate "all that is given," the phenomenology of the world. Rather, it questions the world in its sameness in order to expand the horizons of the world itself. The world does no longer become exhausted by its own sameness but it is now regarded as something provisional and partial in nature. Consciousness rejuvenates the world. The world no longer subsumes everything into itself, for consciousness stands as a perpetual challenge to the world. Totality has been broken, and it is not enough to reconcile world and consciousness through an absolute consciousness that may unify objectivity and subjectivity. Nothing can be considered as "the highest possible reality." There is no absolute totality. There is no "end." Consciousness is left to its own creative impetus. The true peak does not consist of the unification of all that is given but of creation, surprise, wonder, and freedom: of pure, niveous, irreducible intuition.

However, how should we define "that which appears without appearing"? It is a new form of appearing in the *hic et nunc* of the world. Its "non-appearance" is a new way of appearing, for it is evident that it still appears before us, as something that "stands out there." Sameness must therefore be complemented with "otherness." Sameness is no longer the only form of reality that prevails. This simultaneity of appearance and its negation constitutes the basis of thought.

Heidegger's exhortation to denouncing and overcoming the "forgetting of being" in Western philosophy can be interpreted, from the perspective which we have just exposed, as the rebellion against a subtle tyranny in our metaphysical tradition: the tyranny of sameness. May Parmenides prevail (the harmony and immutability of being, seated on its eternal throne and alien to any form of dynamism and negation) or may Heraclitus triumph, in both cases thought surrenders to sameness. If we agree with Heraclitus's *panta rhea*, we will accept that individual entities cannot be regarded as forms of "sameness," for everything is constantly flowing and nothing is ever "equal to itself." However, the totality of the world remains "the same." It is now the objectification of sameness. Thought is not seen as a challenge to the ultimate sameness of the universe. There is no "broadening of being." For Heraclitus, there is a *logos* which governs the world in its becoming, a *logos* that is immanent both to cosmos and human beings. There is an eternal recurrence of everything to everything: everything flows, and "everything" is the eternal sameness of the universe.

Thought challenges any form of sameness: that of a static universe and that of a dynamic cosmos, the product of harmony and the result of dialectic. Thought establishes a new ontological space. It expands the horizons of being. Inasmuch as questioning, thought incorporates both being and nothingness, affirmation and negation. It subsists as "appearing without appearing." This sort of "interrogative phase of being," which emerges with the birth of thought, should not be examined from the narrow perspective of sameness. There is no "identity" in thought, a "selfness" with which it must commensurate. No higher unity remains to solve the contradiction between world and consciousness in a new form of sameness. There is no final pinnacle to conquer, and this is the reason why there is room for history, for that which cannot be expected, for a real opening to the future. Heidegger's elusive being can be regarded as the absence of a final frontier for thought, as the expansion without an apparent limit, as the inexhaustible possibility. There is something instead of nothing because in the realm of apparent infiniteness, which is prior to both being and non-being, it is possible that there be something, just as it is possible that everything disappears and nothing persists.

The human questioning about being constitutes the most fascinating adventure of thought, the true beginning of the "human" as such, and its positioning in the proper space of being: it is the starting point of the philosophical salvation of humanity. Such a question breaks through our entire existence. It is, in fact, the question about the question itself.

In human life, only wisdom, beauty, and love radiate pure freedom, unconditional commitment: the liberation from any shadow of "sameness," of reiteration, of constraint. The path of beauty, love, and wisdom opens the room for limpid abnegation, diaphanous commitment, and radical freedom, which cannot be apprehended by concepts or historical structures. Wisdom, love, and beauty invite us to contemplation, to *Gelassenheit*. However, this contemplative attitude does not suspend the endeavors of humanity. Rather, it becomes aware of the impossibility of "capturing" love, wisdom, and beauty. Their inexhaustibility represents a vivid sign of perennial freedom. There will always be something that humanity shall not possess, but of which it shall passionately dream. It is true, as Angelus Silesius, wrote, that the "rose is without 'why': she blooms, because she blooms,"[1] but humanity needs to pose the question about the "why": it is our spiritual task, and we cannot reject it, because in our wondering about the rose that blooms we are giving a voice to the universe. We cannot remain in *Gelassenheit*: we have to think, so that the universe may speak through our lips.

The intensity of the opposition of nature and freedom, necessity and subjectivity, reason and will, which affects the entire Western philosophical tradition, can only be solved through the perception of the *ego that grows in space and time*: the *ego that edifies history*. Reason and will, necessity and freedom, nature and spirit . . . they all converge with the *ego*. The *ego* integrates, through its growth, reason and will, for it is capable of expanding all that is given. The *ego that grows* does not cease to appear as an object of the world, immersed within the inexorable concatenation of material causes. However, it beautifully rejuvenates reason and it freely broadens necessity. By edifying history, the *ego that grows* in the paths of human time overcomes the mere appearance of nature without depriving itself of its ineluctable connection with nature. The *ego that grows* assumes contradiction, the innermost essence of consciousness as "appearance without appearing," as a part of nature that nonetheless overwhelms the vast realm of nature. All the creations of human subjectivity are objects of nature. They can never be detached from their condition of natural

---

1. "Die Rose ist ohne warum; sie blühet, weil sie blühet . . ." (*Cherubinischer Wandersmann*, Buch 1, 289). This verse was influential in Heidegger: cf. his *Der Satz von Grund*, 70ff.; cf. Caputo, *The Mystical Element in Heidegger's Thought*, 60–66.

entities. There is no "third world" composed of the products of human activity (as Sir Karl Popper suggested).[2] The fruits of the human endeavor for transforming the world and conquering understanding inevitably become fragments of the natural world. The free broadening of necessity to which we refer is nothing else than the capacity of consciousness to challenge "that which is given": its interrogative power. The world is no longer regarded as an absolute reality which accounts for its own justification. Rather, the world is subject to a radical questioning, to a courageous act of challenge. Consciousness expands the horizon of reality through will, spirit, rebellion against necessity. However, the result of this enterprise irrevocably becomes a new form of necessity, a new part of nature: a new element of the world.

Science teaches us that the universe has evolved over time. But any new discovery inaugurates a new challenge, and any scientific answer generates a new question, for from where does everything come? From where does being come? Why the universe? From where do the laws of science stem? Why the "why"? These and other questions pre-eminently express the "piety of thought" (Heidegger) and moreover, the mysticism of reality, since, as Wittgenstein writes in his *Tractatus*: "it is not how the world is that is mystical, but that it is."[3]

Consciousness tends to be considered the greatest challenge faced by the scientific view of the world. According to Thomas Nagel, "consciousness is what makes the mind-body problem really intractable."[4] However, the greatest mystery is not the existence of consciousness itself, even in the "strongest" sense in which it can be evoked, but the possibility that the human mind has of formulating such a radical concept. As both David Hume in *A Treatise of Human Nature* (1739) and Daniel Dennett in *Consciousness Explained* (1991) have shown, that to which we normally refer when speaking about consciousness does not have an empirical basis, because any attempt at reaching consciousness ("myself") in an introspective manner always leads to a particular perception, never to something like a "self." The "self" is never grasped, and there is therefore solid ground for the suspicion that consciousness (as the manifestation of the self to the subject) represents an abstraction which does not exist in reality.

---

2. Cf. Popper, *Objective Knowledge*.

3. "*Nicht wie die Welt ist, ist das Mystische, sondern dass sie ist,*" (Wittgenstein, *Wittgenstein's Tractatus* 6.44).

4. Nagel, "What Is It Like to Be a Bat?," 435.

The idea of a continuous, unitary, simple "self" is most probably illusory. This very plausible option helps us preserve the unity of the scientific view of the world: instead of postulating a frontier in evolution between the objective processes of nature and an autonomous kind of reality that substantially differs from matter (as Alfred Russell Wallace suggested[5]), and which would have emerged by means of unknowable causes at a given time, the gradual unfolding of the structure and function of those mechanisms which we generally associate to consciousness seems to show that there is no such a gap but a progressive increase in the complexity of the nervous system that capacitates for higher-order faculties. Nevertheless, even if such a naturalistic explanation were achieved, a problem would still remain: the fact that we can formulate the idea of consciousness as a reality which cannot be reduced to material processes. In an analogous way, the mystery to be solved does not concern "how we create the idea of infinity," since it is clear that we never imagine infinity as such (we always link it to specific representations that try to recall the absence of finiteness): the *explanandum* is how it is possible, from a material, naturalistic point of view, to formulate the idea of infinity, a concept that deliberately detaches itself from any association to "finite" representations (even if in practice this is never achieved at all). No genetic explanation is satisfactory. To justify how we reach the concept of infinity does not explain how it is possible for us to mean what we actually mean by infinity, if we are finite beings. The fact that we can explain how we reach the concept of consciousness does not unveil how it is possible for us to mean what we actually mean by consciousness.

Even if there is room for the legitimate suspicion about "what we actually mean by consciousness," arguing that it does not hold to empirical evidence, it is still a fact that we can mean such a concept, at least as a logical possibility. Therefore, an unsolved question remains: how to account, scientifically, for the possibility of understanding concepts such as consciousness, infinity, and nothingness, which deliberately "detach" themselves from any empirical ground.

The challenging problem concerning the relationship between matter and mind (whose implications reverberate practically in every great philosophical question: nature vs. freedom, causality vs. intentionality, facts vs. values, quantity vs. quality, matter vs. spirit, syntax vs. semantics, body vs. soul, objectivity vs. subjectivity, exteriority vs. interiority. . . all of them corollaries of the almost insurmountable difficulty of reconciling

---

5. Cf. Wallace, *Natural Selection and Tropical Nature*, 209.

the physical and the mental dimensions) is an extension of the traditional mystery, highlighted by the pre-Socratic thinkers, of the connection between particularity and universality. It would be misleading to regard it as an isolated philosophical problem.

The evolution of being interlaces the whole of reality and thought: necessity and freedom, nature and spirit, appearance and its negation. Matter, life, and consciousness belong to a common evolutionary projection of being (immediacy, purity, that which is absolutely undetermined; the fathomless and ungraspable, that which overwhelms any concept and transcends any given category). The evolution of being consists of the broadening of its domain. It points to its growth. The emergence of the spirit turns this growth into a free expansion, whose goal resides in creating territories of newness, even if such a work will necessarily conform to the inexorable laws of nature. Under the empire of consciousness, the creation of new forms no longer obeys the blind impulse of physical and biological necessity. Natural selection, whose centrality in the transformation of living entities was so clearly understood by Darwin,[6] no longer prevails. The impetus that moves the evolution of being is no longer guided by the exclusive will to preserve life: there is longing for newness.

The question about the destination of this process cannot be answered, because the goal is no other than growth itself, creativity, newness, the display of the potential infiniteness of being. The train of creativity has no definite destination. The reward of the trip is the noble contemplation of its evoking landscape. Freedom is the goal of being.

Idealism never succeeded in providing an adequate explanation of why something had to emanate from the absolute principle. The rupture

---

6. The centrality of natural selection for the evolution of life does not exclude the possibility that the science of the future may discover new mechanisms which also play an important role in evolutionary dynamics. The work of Lynn Margulis on symbiotic cooperation in the genesis of eukaryotes, and more recently, the concept of "facilitated variation," coined by Kirschner and Gerhart, point to the possibility of refining the traditional binomial consecrated by the neo-Darwinian synthesis (random genetic mutations—the source of variability—and natural selection as the "filter" of those variations). See Kirschner and Gerhart, *The Plausibility of Life*. We cannot know if the science of the future will find other principles, in addition to the existing ones, which shall enable us to carefully explain the fascinating complexity that stems from the evolution of life. Any scientific dogma is always under the challenge of refutation. Nobody can question (at least nowadays) the centrality of natural selection and genetic mutations in evolution, but this explanation may seem too vague when confronted with specific details that demand a more accurate scientific approach. We cannot exclude the possibility of further theoretical improvements and even substantial modifications.

inside the absolute, which is assumed by the great masters of German idealism (Fichte, Schelling, and Hegel), is a postulate. The absolute might have remained in its perennial silence. There is no sufficient reason to claim that the absolute had an internal necessity to escape itself and create its own *alteritas*. No reason can be offered for violating the eternal, indifferent, and unitary purity of being. Reason cannot account for the emergence of multiplicity if multiplicity is not regarded as an internal moment of unity itself. The absolute must be its own and absolute self-transcendence.

There must be "more" to all that is given, to any form of sameness, because we can always think of such a *plus*. The absolute cannot consist of the original, immediate, and eternal indifference. Rather, it has to stand as the capacity for "more," for *ulteriority*; as the inexhaustible possibility to transcend all that is given. Being is its self-transcendence, its "more," its ulteriority. We are tiny aliquots in the incommensurable cascade of the self-transcending of being. However, every drop, as small as it may be, is absolute, inasmuch as it constitutes an inexorable force, without which being could not reach its self-transcendence. Human beings, endowed with consciousness, represent the avant-garde[7] of an infinite torrent whose destiny is its perennial self-transcendence. Through us, being imagines itself. We are, as Wittgenstein noticed, a "limit of the world."[8] However, being is constantly transcending itself, so that any limit is illusory or at least provisional. The limit rubricates an arbitrary abstraction of a temporal moment and a spatial location, but the frontiers of being exceed any constraint and they become infinitely diluted. We are the instantiation of the

---

7. The so-called anthropic principle, both in its strong and weak versions, can be interpreted as the condition of possibility, for the knowing subject, of understanding the fact of the universe as a meaningful reality. It is therefore a "subjectivization" of cosmic objectivity, a humanization of the scientific understanding of cosmos, which offers a frame that allows us to grant an existential meaning to the universe. It represents the hermeneutic moment of confluence (Gadamer's *Horizontverschmelzung*) of *Naturwissenschaften* and *Geisteswissenschaften*: the hermeneutic moment in which the objective converges with the subjective in the human questioning about being and the absolute. It is not a discursive content of science or philosophy but a frame, a contour, a methodological or even a programmatic principle which actively involves the human being who knows the universe. However, "finalism," the perception of Teilhard de Chardin's "Ariadna's thread" in the evolving display of the material being, cannot be regarded as a scientific cause *stricto sensu*. Science can neither confirm nor refute finalism, which cannot be derived from the procedures of the natural sciences. Copernicus left us in a state of bitter solitude, lost in a vast cosmos. The anthropic principle seems to emerge as a desperate, yet consoling attempt at restoring the centrality of mankind inside a huge universe.

8. Wittgenstein, *Wittgenstein's Tractatus*, 5.632.

creative energy of being, of the power underlying its constant capacity for transcending itself (which through us is manifested as self-consciousness, as the questioning of all that is given). We personify the pinnacle of the creative power of being, matter, and life. We can only hope for more variety and greater creativity, for a deeper challenge to that which is given. The original purity of being will not cease to shine in those realities which reveal an inexhaustible intuition "incarnated" in the finiteness of space and time: love, beauty, and wisdom.

THE SOLITUDE OF CONSCIOUSNESS

If its sole and most absorbing goal consists of the struggle against the world, consciousness becomes a new form of sameness. Its rebellion against the sameness of the universe, against the fact that everything in the world obeys inexorable laws which reiterate the inflexible dynamics of material reality, succumbs to a new and equally darkening slavery. Secluded inside its narrow borders, consciousness suffers the most severe form of solitude. The solitude of consciousness is the most punishing state of isolation, because it is possible to take awareness at it and it is eventually avoidable. The solitude of consciousness can adopt four fundamental manifestations:

Self-Sufficient Consciousness

Consciousness has so deeply understood its difference from the sameness of the world that it ends up believing in its own absolute power. Moved by unredeemed *hubris*, consciousness thinks that the scope of its present possessions suffices. It has already crowned the pinnacle of life. There is no further need to know more, to question more, to broaden even more the horizons of its interpretations in order to capture that which is pure and unconditioned, that which nothing can "possess," for it shines through its own beauty, wisdom, and love. Self-sufficient consciousness is dominated by overconfidence in its own power. Self-sufficient consciousness is enslaved by itself. It has not descended into its innermost nature with the intention of gaining freedom but for the sake of its own self-affirmation. In its "abasement" towards itself, it has nonetheless forgotten that it is not enough to deny the world: a new world must be edified.

Apathetic Consciousness

Indifference darkens the strength of apathetic consciousness, which tries to stand in "neutrality" before life. It does not wish to challenge the world. It does not aim to challenge itself. The fountain of its satisfaction flows from the achievements of other people: their thought, their action. There is no room for commitment, because everything is in vain; everything falters and withers. Apathetic consciousness prefers the obscurest anonymity. Its aspirations are not focused on thought and creation but "survival." Its highest goal does not transcend the brief illusion of life. All is grey and empty. Life is indifferent. Life consists of a chain of reactions: I am not the agent of any project but the summation of the accidents that constitute the path of my existence. To live means to resist as long as the impulse of life palpitates in our hearts. There is no vital horizon. No novelty can be discovered in nature and history. No enriching evocation stems from life. Ambiguity and lack of definition are the rubrics of existence. Our stoic duty resides in living without any apparent reason, for neither life nor death is worthy of our deepest effort. There is no passion; there is no enthusiasm; the flower of hope does not blossom. Apathetic consciousness incarnates death in life, the renunciation to creation. It refuses to look for a sea of originality and a land of fascination.

Distressed Consciousness

The waters of despair have inoculated their lethal poison into the soul of distressed consciousness. It feels assaulted by the most intense and inscrutable fear. Life cannot be understood. Life is threatening. The act of living is enslaved by the constant shadow of the absence of meaning. It is impossible to catch the slightest glimpse of purity and real freedom. Life is the source of apprehension. It is no longer contemplated as a fountain of possibilities. Only negativity, pain, and evil emanate from it. However, distressed consciousness does not seek death. It is not attached to life, but it is not possessed by courage. Death inspires a greater fear than life. Distressed consciousness is condemned to live under the tyrannical government of a continuous and pungent anxiety. Unrest, angst, trouble, torment, disquietude—there are not enough terms to describe the emptiness of its existence. According to a distressed consciousness, there is nothing worthy of honest commitment. We must live, because death is even more unpleasant than existence, but life constitutes a severe and incurable torture. Distressed consciousness lives in a state of bitterness. Its discouragement leads to suspicion about other people's intentions. Its apprehension affects not only self-sufficient and apathetic consciousness but also the constellation of those who venture to think and work. Distressed consciousness is dominated by the will to destroy. It wants to prevent the irruption of novelty and the display of the longing for creativity.

Suicidal Consciousness

For suicidal consciousness, fear of life is not accompanied by an equivalent apprehensiveness towards death. The pain of life is so intense, and its negativity so clamorous and merciless, that suicidal consciousness, endowed with courage and power, deprives itself of the gift of life. Life is a burden too onerous to be carried any longer. Death is regarded as a source of freedom, as a heroic action which defeats the natural attachment to existence and the preservation of vital autonomy. If according to Spinoza, everything tries to persevere in its own being, suicidal consciousness feels the deepest and most transcendental freedom: that of detaching itself from the universal laws of the world.

The four forms of consciousness we have just described share a common condition: solitude. Consciousness is not opened to a new reality. Its horizon of possibilities is severely diminished. Consciousness, taken now as "sameness," as a new manifestation of the world, is enslaved by its own finiteness. Even if it believes in its self-sufficiency, and it thinks that in its potentially infinite power the source of its redemption lies, it finds no reference beyond itself. Everything is mediated by the demanding filter of an insatiable consciousness. There is no gift, no commitment, no purity, no freedom, no creation. Consciousness becomes an extension of the world. Individuality vanishes, because it has not been consecrated to anything but itself. It has become a mere element of the dynamism of the world. It does not seek to create through love, beauty, and wisdom. It does not offer the immensity and colorfulness of its energies to a *novum*.

Humanity must not feel imprisoned by its past. It should not believe that it is subject to an inexorable destiny which defeats even the highest endeavors of will and thought. Humanity needs to listen to the calling for freedom, newness, and creativity. Humanity has to become disciple of mercy, contemplation, and understanding, but it must not constrain the pinnacles of love, beauty, and wisdom to any foreseeable future. Rather, it should conceive of them as the expression of the unlimited.

EXCURSUS: ON THE DIMENSIONS OF BEING AND THE LIMITATIONS OF THE PRINCIPLE OF NON-CONTRADICTION

The unquestionable merit of Aristotle in the history of Western philosophy resides in his attempt to found any and all rational content upon a first principle: "the most certain principle of all is that regarding which it is impossible to be mistaken; for such a principle must be both the best known (for all men may be mistaken about things which they do not know), and non-hypothetical. For a principle which every one must have who understands anything that is, is not a hypothesis; and that which every one must know who knows anything, he must already have when he comes to a special study. Evidently then such a principle is the most certain of all; which principle this is, let us proceed to say. It is, that the same attribute cannot at the same time belong and not belong to the same subject and in the same respect."[9]

The principle of non-contradiction, first principle of all reasoning, according to Aristotle, constitutes a universal, necessary, and evident *fundamentum*, which precedes any discursive reasoning. It is grasped by the intellect as a necessary object. Being a necessary object, every thought about contingent reality must bear, implicitly, the principle of non-contradiction as the true condition of possibility of the contingent *qua* contingent.

In the philosophy of Aristotle (which represents a formidable attempt to offer a rational solution for the problem of movement, of becoming, of the inherent alternation between being and non-being in the same subject), the principle of non-contradiction is not susceptible to negation (since it is the very source of all possible negation; it is a necessary object). However, the principle of non-contradiction is not the only necessary object. In fact, any attempt to prove that the principle of non-contradiction is a necessary object involves setting a hypothesis, and therefore using the method of *reductio ad absurdum*, which already presupposes the principle of non-contradiction and the impossibility of two opposite attributes to analytically subsist in the same subject (*tertium non datur*).[10]

---

9. Aristotle, *Metaphysics* IV: 3, 1005a 19–b 18.

10. According to Kant, the principle of non-contradiction is the supreme principle of analytic judgements. However, if we include in its enunciation the spatial and temporal variables, we can argue that the principle of non-contradiction is also the supreme principle of synthetic judgements. In Aristotle's formulation, the "temporal

Part 1: In Search of *Fundamentum*

The principle of non-contradiction is a formal expression of the mode of being of that which is contingent, of whatever can be and cannot be. The principle of non-contradiction does not rule over itself, because as a principle which cannot be denied, it falls out of the domain of negation, and hence it is not an object of itself but belongs to the realm of necessity (which is not covered by the structure of the principle of non-contradiction). It seems legitimate to pose the question of whether a single principle, in this case a necessary object, suffices to provide the *fundamentum* of the reality and the thought of the contingent *qua* contingent, and moreover, if it can be seen as the supreme principle of every possible judgment, regardless of its dealing with the contingent or the necessary.

The concept of "structure" of the principle of non-contradiction is problematic, because (rigorously speaking) a necessary object is not structured, since all structures are possible modes of organizing diversity in accordance with a unifying principle. However, in a necessary object there can be no diversity, only uniqueness. The notion of "structure" must be substituted with or, better still, preceded by that of "constitution" of the principle in the realm of necessity. A necessary object appears in the realm of necessity: it dwells (*habitatio principiorum*), in its own way, in the sphere of necessity.

The structure of a necessary object is only valid *quoad contingentiam*, in respect to the mode of being of all that is contingent and to its proper characteristics, but it cannot be attributed to a necessary object as such. We will call the mode of being of everything necessary, that is to say, the sphere in which necessary objects constitute themselves, the *superformal realm*. The superformal realm founds the sphere of contingency, which in physical reality shows dimensionality and dynamism, the capacity for adopting different states and different deployments of every specific object in connection with the totality of reality. The superformal realm gives sense to contingency, and it constitutes the true rational foundation for the existence of all that is contingent, of all that

---

synthesis" is present, and this was subject to Kant's criticism (*Critique of Pure Reason* B192). We think, nonetheless, that there is no valid objection against the introduction of the temporal variable, because universality in the synthetic realm involves regarding temporality as a constitutive element of that which is "synthetic." A different problem (of no lesser importance) is the possibility of determining two simultaneous events, and whether the very concept of simultaneity is actually applicable to a synthetic judgement, or if, on the contrary, there is no temporal instant at all, since every instant is potentially infinitesimal. This issue implies dealing with the themes of reference and absoluteness in judgements.

shows alternatives and opposite modes of being. It therefore transcends any possible formalization, and the "constitutiveness" of every necessary object ruling over that which is contingent resides in it.

We can identify three "projections," or modes of being, which are compatible, yet discernible, with all that is necessary: necessity as *fundamentum* of the lack of alternatives; necessity as *fundamentum* of the infinite continuity which gathers all possibilities of the contingent; and necessity as *fundamentum* of the "integrability," or systematic totality (susceptible to mutual relations), which is present in that which is contingent.

Let us name the first mode of being *intensive*, the second, *extensive*, and the third, *abtensive*. All necessary objects, and therefore everything that founds that which is contingent, can be therefore reduced to these three modes of being of whatever is necessary. There are, as a consequence, three fundamental principles, or three fundamental necessary objects, of reality: the *principle of non-contradiction*, which is the intensive *fundamentum* of contingency, as it rules over, and constrains, any possible alternative, the *principle of transcendentability*, which is the extensive *fundamentum* that gives sense to the existence of different degrees of reality which are mutually transcendible, and the *principle of harmonizability*, which is the abtensive *fundamentum* of the cohesion between the constitutive elements of reality.

Just as the principle of non-contradiction makes negation and the existence of alternatives meaningful, the principle of transcendentability conveys the significance of the transition from one degree of the real being into another, and the principle of harmonizability founds the cohesion of the whole system of reality. None of these three principles rules over itself. In effect, if we were to transcend the principle of transcendentability, nothing would give sense to sense itself. If we negate the possibility of indefinitely transcending every form of the real being, we are still defending the idea that it is possible to assert and to deny, and therefore to establish a difference in entitative degrees between what is asserted and what is denied, the very thing over which this principle rules. If we negate the principle of harmonizability, we should therefore accept that it is not always possible to integrate every concrete entity in relation to other entities which constitute reality, but if this were the case, we would not be able to negate in any form, because negating involves establishing a link between different objects, that is to say, a mode of unifying them in accordance with a principle that rules over them.

The realm of potentiality is founded upon the constitution of all that is necessary, too, and the unification between potentiality and reality, between *potentia* and *actus*, comes from the very subsistence of superformality as the sphere of the first principles. In this way, there is a reason mediating between possibility (in its two dimensions: as non-contradictory and as indefinite openness to opposite modes of being) and reality, which is the subsistence itself of the superformal.[11]

The superformal realm cannot be the sphere of the absolute, because it includes different necessary objects with different applications. The uniqueness of the absolute, which "principiates" all necessary objects, is the *ultraformal* realm. We approach the "logical absolute" in itself from the mode of being of necessary objects, which found any rational inquiry. The absolute appears as being (by virtue of the intensive principle), as supremacy (by virtue of the extensive principle), and as totality (by virtue of the abtensive principle).

The ultraform is Hegel's *reine sein*, the transfinitization of any form of becoming. The ultraform is being, which is seen as absolute. Pure being is not opposed to pure nothingness, but nothingness, in its non-absoluteness, identifies itself with being in its absoluteness, with the pure being: thus, the Hegelian equality between *reine Nichts* and *reine sein*.[12] Nothingness is not and being is: *categorumen* is the synthesis of the ontological space of being and the nullitive non-space of non-being, of that which is and that which is not.

---

11. From a pluralistic perspective of the necessary, the classical principle of the hierarchy of the sciences becomes problematic because it is not possible to speak in terms of a single principle ruling the whole of knowledge. Such a hierarchy can be interpreted, however, from the point of view of *reciprocality* between the premises and the conclusions of the different sciences.

12. The fundamental equality between pure being and pure nothingness is stated by Hegel in *The Science of Logic*: "Nichts ist somit dieselbe Bestimmung oder velmehr Bestimmungslosigkeit und damit überhaupt dasselbe, was das reine Sein ist" (1:67). In the preface to *Phenomenology of Spirit*, Hegel formulates the idea that the principal problem of philosophical systems resides in their incapacity for leaving disjunctions behind (that is to say, to situate themselves in the superformal realm, in the contemplation of the principles of the contingent in order to envision the overcoming of any possible dialectic) and move into the *development*, into the very act of *becoming*, into the process itself, into the *entasis*, which is the primordial tension that constitutes the "act of existing" of being. On the structure of *Phenomenology of Spirit*, cf. Hyppolite, *Genèse et Structure de la Phénoménologie de l'Esprit de Hegel*.

Any determination involves a certain type of negation (as Spinoza famously expressed in his *omnis determinatio est negatio*),[13] but the transcendence of all determinations is the absolute itself, regarded as absolutization of every being and every non-being: the absolute unifies and does not unify, it integrates and it does not integrate being and non-being; it infinitely transcends every possible contradiction, and it is therefore unreachable by human thought, which cannot dispense with the alternative modes signified by the three fundamental, necessary principles.

Nothingness lacks a non-mode of non-being, and since we are compelled to negate every verb, every attribute, and every predicate when referring to nothingness, it is therefore elusive for language. Nothingness is not opposed to being as such, because nothingness is defined in terms of non-opposition, and, strictly speaking, of "non-definition": nothingness is not. What is cannot be opposed to what is not, because any opposition is applied in the realm of being. The absolute, as the "selfness" of being, integrates the non-absolute, too, for the non-absolute non-absolutely determines the whole of reality: that which is empty, what is nullitive, is sub-nullentity of any entity.[14]

Human intelligence can understand that any manifestation of being hides the lack of non-being, and since void is the proper mode of non-being, in every being, void is absent, and the absence of void is the proper mode of being, in such a way that in the true absolute, in the transfiniteness of any potential infinity, both the non-absolute and the absolute converge, in the sense that they can be necessarily and non-necessarily derived from one another. If non-being is not, being is. The absolute, absolutely considered (in contrast with the absolute contemplated as the supreme principle of the relative), excludes nothingness, non-absolutely not considered, in such a way that the absolute, absolutely regarded, assimilates being in its absoluteness and excludes non-being in its non-absoluteness. From this perspective, we arrive at the formal equality between the absolute and the non-absolute in *categorumen*, in that which is and that which is not, interpreted from the mutual conditioning of being and non-being. The fact that being is implies that non-being is not: this is perhaps the simplest deduction of the fundamental equality of being and non-being.[15]

13. Cf. Spinoza, "Epistle 59," in *Complete Works*.
14. In set theory, the empty set is necessarily a sub-set of all sets.
15. Jean-Paul Sartre's distinction between *être en soi* and *être pour soi*, which

Part 1: In Search of *Fundamentum*

What stands beyond any possible doubt is not the principle of non-contradiction but the fundamental integration of being and non-being, the overcoming of all differences: openness as transcendence. Within the infinite space of being, whose only limit is openness itself, there will always be a solution to any dialectic and a response to any conflict. Our hope is anchored in the infinite space of being, and it is only there that we can find the redeeming power which we are avidly seeking. Language does not allow us to grasp the very moment which links all oppositions and which points to the fundamental equality of being and non-being. The overcoming of duality, of mankind by mankind, and the discovery of the transfiniteness of being encourage us to discover freedom and openness as the true essence of being, in which we must truly contemplate the salvation for which we are eagerly longing.

The principle of non-contradiction does not capture the original purity, the primeval, unconditioned, and limpid intuition: that which is radically *a priori*. Rather, it is based upon the distinction between being and non-being. Contradiction does not certify impossibility: as conscious beings, we are those who "appear without appearing," the rubric of the most powerful paradox. The principle of non-contradiction strengthens the sameness of the world, but we seek to challenge the

---

corresponds to his phenomenological ontology, represents an eloquent sign of the difficulties involved in any attempt to overcome duality. Sartre rejected many of the Western philosophical dualisms (potency/act, essence/appearance), seeking to overcome them in the new dualism of "in-itself/for-itself": "in-itself" corresponds to the unmoveable core, to the ontic "selfness," which is infinite and insurmountable; "for-itself" is the pure relation, the lack of concretion, which stems from the annihilation of the real by consciousness, that reduces it to mere relativity (some sort of "nothingness," of nullity, inasmuch as negation of the real). From this new dualism, Sartre deduces the impossibility of the absolute (and therefore of the divine): it would be contradictory (an "in-itself/for-itself"), a pretension of integrating being and nothingness. However, Sartre's commitment to overcome dualism made him fall into another form of duality (not only in the dualistic terminology, which may be inevitable, but also in the argumentative process itself). The true overcoming of any duality demands the awareness of the fundamental equality of being and non-being and the perception of the possibility of integration offered by the openness of being regarded as *entasis*, as creative tension. The absolute is being itself: it is the transfiniteness of everything, the "selfness" of the unfolding, the pure transcendence. The absolute is being and is not non-being: the absolute absolutizes, it completes and gives fullness and meaning to the ontic becoming and the non-ontic non-becoming; it is the very force of being and non-being, the very power of openness, the "selfness" of duality. It is therefore the "selfness" of the duality of act and potency. The ontology of Sartre is primarily exposed in *Being and Nothingness* (1943).

world in its sameness. The principle of non-contradiction rules over sameness *qua* sameness, but it does not govern the contradiction to sameness itself: the questioning of "that which is given." Before the verve of questioning the power of the *tertius exclusus* succumbs.

That which is original is *power* inasmuch as *possibility of novum*. However, *novum* in its authenticity cannot constrain itself to displaying that which has been already initiated in the precedent moments. Hegel's *Geist* evolves over time and space, but it simply develops that which already exists in the "idea *an sich*" before its self-alienation. Hegel does not conceive of the possibility of a true *novum*. The real *novum* needs to be able to break the continuity established by reason between the past, the present, and the future, although it must be inserted within the concatenation of "that which is given," within the chain of "sameness." The true *novum* cannot be imagined as another possibility within the absolute mind which, just as in Leibniz's philosophy, incorporates all possibilities and chooses the best of them: *novum* must emanate from a possibility which has not been anticipated at an earlier stage and which does not preexist in some sort of divine *kosmos noetikos*. *Novum*, understood as rupture, as will, as freedom, as "impossibility," has to be possible: *creation*, youth, the truly golden spring, must be possible.

PART 2

Fundamentum in History

4

Consciousness beyond the World: Freedom

CONSCIOUSNESS BEYOND POWER: FREEDOM

IF THERE IS A word capable of condensing, better than any other one, the set of aspirations that define our societies, the deepest wishes of our civilization, and the most universal dynamic of both the individual and collective actions, no doubt that such a term is "power."

Power—and moreover, Nietzsche's "will of power"—shines everywhere. Our world seems to live in a never-ending quest for power. We want to know because knowledge gives us power over nature, humanity, and ourselves; we want to achieve economic success because this will enable us to acquire goods in order to obtain power over the products of our endeavor; we want to gain recognition because social celebrity means power, too: the power that our ideas can exert upon our fellow human beings.

Any form of power is a will to influence others; any form of power is therefore power over something that is alien to us. Money, pleasure, domination, technique—they are all projected on external objects. Mastery over oneself can be regarded as a form of "self-power," of power aimed at controlling our own personality, but this is not the most common sense of "power." When we say that someone is powerful we mean that he or she has the capacity for influencing others: individuals, groups, the academic and scientific communities. Different kinds of power can modify the world surrounding us: they can act over the "other" and over "others." They can in fact conquer the other's "self-power." Someone becomes powerful over another person when he or she can invade his space of autonomy: when he or she can gain part of another's self-power.

Power is, in this way, ecstatic: it arises from a certain person, and it needs to be applied to something that is external to that person. Humanity exhibits its power over nature by mastering it, by subjugating it, and by using it in order to satisfy its increasing needs. Humanity conquers the spaces of freedom of nature, gaining its self-power. Nature ceases to be nature in order to become an expression of the power of humanity over the world. Humanity itself yields to the endogenous powers that it generates: some individuals have power over others individuals, some countries over other countries, some social groups over other social groups, some authorities (political, intellectual) over other authorities. Self-powers, the spaces of freedom and capacity of action on the individual level, are gradually emptied to be conquered by strange self-powers, which, themselves, lose their condition of "self-power" in order to become inserted into other self-powers.

What a great paradox! On the one hand, we are powerful if we have self-power, if we are capable of mastering ourselves and decide about our universe of possible actions, if we become owners of ourselves, but on the other hand, we are powerful if we externalize our power, if we apply our self-power to the world, which is alien to us. We have to empty ourselves, to lose our self-power, in order to conquer someone else's self-power, in order to absorb the autonomy of the others. The interior power becomes an exterior, ecstatic power, which needs to go out of its possessor in order to affirm itself as power, even if in doing so, the others lose their self-power. This loss is reciprocal: others lose their self-power because whoever is powerful, thanks to his self-power, deprives them of their space of autonomy. But the powerful person is also losing his self-power: in order to show himself as powerful, he needs to externalize his power, losing autonomy. He becomes dependent upon the external world, upon nature and humanity. He becomes powerful by ceasing to be powerful for himself. The powerful one has a need of those who are deprived from power,[1] or who have less power than him, in order to express his power. He needs to empty himself, to give away his self-power, which is now turned to the

---

1. As Nietzsche wrote at the beginning of *Also Sprach Zarathustra*: "Du grosses Gestirn! Was wäre dein Glück, wenn du nicht hättest, welchen du leuchtest!"

Consciousness beyond the World: Freedom

world, to obtaining someone else's self-power, but at the expense of not projecting his power over himself. He wins strange power, but he loses his own power.

The powerful one becomes a slave of the world. He needs a world to exhibit his strength. Every king needs a kingdom: the powerful need to apply their power on anything or anyone. The powerful have to be expelled from themselves into a world which is strange for them, because the dynamism of that world, even if eventually falls subject to their power, will always remain alien to them, since it works according to its own mechanisms, and its principle of action will always belong to another being. Those who are powerful can conquer that principle of action, but they will never be able to substitute it. They need to assimilate it by means of their self-power, losing their sphere of interiority, their world, in order to possess strange worlds.

The tragedy of power consists of its looking for domination and, in so doing, becoming controlled by the external circumstances. The powerful one longs for infiniteness outside his subjectivity, but he only finds finiteness. His only alternative is to increase his power even more, to seek more and more power, but since he cannot find the infiniteness he desires inside himself, he needs an infinite world outside him that does not actually exist. It can never be reached. Even the most powerful individual of all times would have still wanted more power, because he would have longed for a truly infinite scenario in order to project his self-power, an ambition that exiled him from the sphere of his individual subjectivity. We externalize our action because we are incapable of living with our internal power, with our self-power, with the world that we can create for ourselves from our own principle of action, without the need to conquer strange principles of action.

Power is void. We need power because we lack something in ourselves. Due to this void that exists in "our world," we have to conquer external worlds, and we have to become prisoners of "ecstaticity," of the irresistible potency that expels us from ourselves, projecting us on strange existences, in order to gain dominion over them, so that we may obtain the existence we have lost. We need to multiply ourselves in principles of action which are alien to us because we have been incapable of gaining the unitary principle of action which is in us.

Power expresses indigence, lack of peace with nature, with the human being, and with oneself. The goal of a peaceful society is to let all its members "introject" their will of power upon themselves, focusing their insatiable will of power over the vast world of their interiority, over their principle of action, over the potentially infinite universe which does not need to conquer the self-powers of others to gain its own world, but which builds a world from itself: self-power is the truly creating power, the power of whoever constructs the world from himself, instead of having to gain strange powers in order to edify that world.

It has been said, and here there is much credit to be given to Michel Foucault, that there is a relationship between truth and power. Truth reflects power: the truth of those who hold social power, of those who have the capacity for running the means of production of truth. The powerful impose their truth in an unceasing struggle for power, and it is almost impossible to conceive of an absolute truth which may be independent from the antagonistic wills of power.

Without pretending to refute the validity of many of these considerations, we should not forget that power is associated with void. If power is indigence, so is truth. We are incapable of conceiving of a transcendental truth, of an unconditioned truth which conditions all other truths that emerge from the dynamics of power, of a *fundamentum*, because we are still under the domain of void: we lack self-power. In the hypothetical scenario of a world in which power were principally self-power, the power over oneself that does not need to conquer strange self-powers, a truly free power which is not indigent to the circumstances, to the external world, but whose connection with other powers is voluntary instead of imposed by the will of domination, void would become possession. We would be independent from that which is external to us and we would be enslaved to our internal world alone, which is ours, for it arises from our own principle of action and cannot subjugate us.

Such a world is imaginary. The history of humanity is the chronicle of the externalization of power, and it has rarely been the epics of self-power. It is true that the externalization of power is a sign of human non-conformity, which is the cause of the conquest of new worlds, but the cost paid has been too high. Everyone loses with the externalization of power: the powerful, forced to seek strange self-powers, without realizing that true power lies in the edification of their own world, and those who fall under the domination of others, because they cede their self-power to an external agent.

The goal of a peaceful society is the humanization of power, the discovery of power as an internal, not external force; the possibility that all members of the political community may recognize themselves as the carriers of a unique power, instead of seeing themselves as subjugated by a strange power. The final goal has to be that no one may lose himself. We need pure goals on which to focus our self-powers.

Knowledge is the kind of good which best resembles infinite power. We can always know more without running the risk of conquering the self-power of others, without endangering their freedom. In knowing, we open our world and we open ourselves to the world, but we do not need to enslave anyone. It is clear that there are risks linked to the use of knowledge, for those who know more can benefit from the self-power that they have gained in order to dominate others. However, the diffusion of knowledge makes it possible for everyone to project his own self-power: if everyone knows, the danger of subjugation by external agents diminishes, since we all become less susceptible to an eventual conquest by someone else.

COMMUNICATION, KNOWLEDGE, PEACE, AND FREEDOM

The history of humanity shows that there is no direct relationship between knowledge and peace: not always those who have known more, and those whose minds have been capable of ascending above what is immediate in order to open new worlds to the human intellect, have been those who have contributed the most to the edification of a culture of peace.

Many faculty members of the University of Vienna became affiliated to the Nazi party, as so did the distinguished German physicists Philipp Lenard and Johannes Stark (who supported the so-called *Deutsche Physik*). The great Italian inventor Guglielmo Marconi belonged to the fascist party and he was a member of the fascist grand council. Hitler was enthusiastically welcome after the *Anschluss* in 1938 by hundreds of thousands of Viennese people, residents of one of the principal European centers of music, literature, and thought. A city that used to perform Mozart's operas and mystically delight in Beethoven's sonatas fell under the spell of Adolf Hitler, and it developed indiscriminate hatred against so many people, so many fellow citizens and human beings. How could this happen? We must never abandon the collective memory of humanity, which is one of our most valuable treasures: *corruptio optimi pessima*, "the corruption of the best is the worst one," as the classics said, and our recent history manifests that the greatest spirits of a time have seldom failed. This is the fundamental contradiction of the human being: with the power of reason we build the sciences and the universe of ethics, but with the power of our selfishness we destroy our brothers and sisters.

Nevertheless, humanity seems to maintain the hope that a moment shall come in which such a direct relationship between knowledge and peace will be possible. We normally say that a certain people has been or is more violent because its members lack education, or because they are ruled by fanatic leaders who eclipse their faculty of understanding, submitting every human action to the judgment of power and not to the discernment of the intellect. We also realize that as the educational indexes of our countries have increased, and more and more people have gradually had the opportunity to access higher education, information, the cultivation of reading and thought, the free exchange of ideas and opinions, the conscience of solidarity, of mutual respect, of sensibility towards the problems of others, of concern about the future of the planet, of attention to those groups which have traditionally suffered discrimination, of the importance of dialogue, etc., have notably advanced. In fact, Hegel believed that the history of humanity was the vivid narration of our conscience of freedom, along a path full of traumatic dramas which belong to the dialectic of a process whose meaning generally escapes us, but whose long-term outcome is a higher conscience of freedom, of autonomy, and insertion of every individual into the human community and its fate.

The question is not therefore referring to the existence *de facto* of a direct relationship between knowledge and peace, since it has been absent in most episodes of human history, but to the possibility of establishing, both theoretically and practically, a connection between knowledge and peace. In order to do so, we must first reach a certain degree of consensus regarding the definitions of the terms involved.

What is knowledge? It is not my pretension to summarize here thousands of years of history of philosophy both in the East and the West, with conceptions of knowledge that are normally divergent among themselves. The goal is to find a way of categorization which can help us understand the basic elements which appear in what we intuitively regard as knowledge. Some of the greatest minds of humanity, such as Aristotle, Ramón Llull in his *Ars Magna*, Athanasius Kircher, and Leibniz (who had a lifelong obsession with the idea of *characteristica universalis*, which would include the fundamental concepts of human thought in order to build, from them, more complex judgements, in resemblance of a mathematical composition), have made important efforts in the enterprise of categorizing reality.

Consciousness beyond the World: Freedom

The twentieth century, with the so-called linguistic turn in philosophy both in the Anglo-Saxon world (through analytic philosophy) and continental thought (by means of the emphasis that hermeneutics has given to language), seems to encourage us to regard knowledge as a linguistic scenario of narrative nature, as an epic in which different agents—or to use the terminology developed by the Franco-Lithuanian semiotician Algirdas Julien Greimas (1917–1992), "actants"—intervene. Greimas identified six principal actants in all narrative discourse: subject, object; sender, receiver; supporter, oppositionist.[2] This actantial model in semiotics, in spite of its structuralist background, can still provide some light on our aim to define knowledge and peace.

Which are the actants in the plot of knowledge?

Subject: every human being capable of knowing, and especially those who generate knowledge: the scientists and the thinkers.

Object: the real and the possible.

Sender: the history of the human search of knowledge. Since the dawn of our rationality, we have looked at the sky, contemplating the stars and wondering, just as Bertrand Russell, why they iridescently shine, until Einstein and Bethe gave us the answer.

Receiver: the whole of humanity. Knowledge is not only addressed to the wise; it is meant to reach every man and woman who needs, by nature, to know in order to live.

Supporter: the historical, social, cultural, institutional, and personal conditions which favor the active participation in the epic of knowledge. For example, we can think of the deep impact that the foundation of the Library of Alexandria by Ptolemy I had for Hellenism. The library became the centre of ancient wisdom, and it contributed to the definition of the Hellenistic *paideia*, an ideal of culture and classical education for all the peoples living under the influence of Hellenism, which included the fundamental works of poetry, philosophy, and science. This library also had consequences for the non-Hellenistic cultures which were in direct contact with Hellenism, such as Judaism. The *Letter of Aristeas*, full of legendary data, is meant to legitimize the Greek translation of the Hebrew Bible, known as the Septuagint, a translation that was necessary not only for the Greek speaking Jews of the Diaspora, but also for Judaism itself and for its participation in the ideal of culture, so that their most precious book could be added to the list of the most relevant writings that humanity

---

2. Cf. Greimas, *Structural Semantics*. Cf. also Greimas *On Meaning.*.

had produced up to that moment, in such a way that the collection of the sacred texts of Judaism might find a place in the Library of Alexandria.³

Oppositionist: what is the antagonist, *par excellence*, of knowledge? *Prima facie*, it is ignorance, but knowledge as a task is opposed by fanaticism, dogmatism, prejudices, and intolerance. The oppositionist to knowledge is the lack of an open mind, the absence of humility in those who venture into knowledge, the lack of social recognition of the enterprise of knowledge and, more than everything, the deliberate refusal to learn from everyone and everything, motivated by pride, ideology, culture, or religion. Whoever does not prepare himself for a constant quest and for a continuous act of posing questions (which are, according to Heidegger, the "piety of thought"⁴), is vehemently opposing knowledge.

What about peace? Let us return to Greimas's schema:

Subject: individuals and societies.

Object: the individual and the collective, the peace of everyone with oneself and the peace of all societies among themselves.

Sender: the history of the human quest for peace and the history of tragic absence of peace; after all, the history of humanity as such.

Receiver: humanity in its entirety.

Supporter: those conditions which promote peace, especially the spirit of toleration and dialogue, the mutual knowledge of all human beings and cultures, education, the memory of the peoples, and the hope to build a more fraternal future.

Oppositionist: selfishness, hatred, and ignorance. According to Kant's ethical philosophy, selfishness is the radical evil, and hatred and ignorance normally respond to a selfish sentiment: selfishness in treating others, the refusal to regard them as peers, as brothers and sisters instead of enemies. In addition to this, voluntary ignorance is generally due to selfishness, in the sense of refusing to open oneself to other perspectives, to "otherness" as such.

Knowledge and peace share the subject, the sender, the receiver and, to some extent, the supporter and the oppositionist. Even if the object

---

3. On the impact of Hellenism for the identity of Second Temple Judaism, cf. Collins and Sterling, *Hellenism in the Land of Israel*; Collins, *Jewish Wisdom in the Hellenistic Age*. Martin Hengel's work *Judentum und Hellenismus* (ET: *Judaism and Hellenism*), is still a classic. On the influence of Hellenism on the formation of the Hebrew canon, cf. Carr, *The Formation of the Hebrew Bible*; Evans and Tov, *Exploring the Origins of the Bible*.

4. Cf. Heidegger, "Die Frage nach der Technik," in *Vorträge und Aufsätze*.

seems to be different, there are reasonable grounds to think that there is a deep convergence between that which is sought by knowledge and that to which peace aspires.

I dare to say that one of the most beautiful dreams that humanity has had is that of indefinite progress. The Enlightenment wondered at the achievements of human reason, of science, of technique, and critique in such a way that it ended up believing that the liberation fostered by the increasing degree of knowledge might emancipate us from all kind of dogmatic oppression and from sterile confrontations motivated by the absence of reason. Happiness would be given by a state of continuous, unending progress, based upon knowledge and reason, which allow us to understand and to transform reality. Instead of fearing anything or anyone, the human being should trust reason as a source of freedom. Sadly, the history that follows *Les Lumiéres* has proven that the dream of the Enlightenment has not been fulfilled. Even if it is still an "unfinished project" (Habermas), the truth shows that its promises have not been brought into effect. Knowledge, science, and technique hide an immense destructive power, which does not always promote the humanization of world and history.

Humanization: that is the question. In a first approach, the world appears to us as a hostile, strange, unknown reality. It generates fear, but by means of knowledge and its application through technique we are capable of humanizing the world, or at least we believe to be doing so, heroically overcoming the many evidences that contradict this presumption. We protect ourselves from the vagaries of the world and from its blind nature, which does not express itself in terms of justice but of mere survival, although we finally become the dominating species and end up soullessly subjugating the world. Regarding the human world itself, we try to design norms, institutions, manners, and social structures which should help us humanize the relations among human beings. However, this endeavor demands a great effort, and as Sigmund Freud brilliantly proposed, it has the result of painfully repressing our inner passions, relegated now into the unconscious, and which may eventually come up again, generating much suffering.

There is a double face in the process of humanization: many times it dehumanizes, and many times it is not universal. Not every person has profited from the human longing for humanization of world and history. There are many victims of the human desire to progress, whose testimony rarely becomes public, because such a will for improvement has seldom covered a parallel will for power and dominance.

In any case, we are also aware of our inability to conceive of a goal for humanity and history other than an increasing humanization of all the conditions of the individual and social worlds. We cannot renounce the utopia of transforming knowledge, of turning the capacity of the human mind for linking one fact to another by means of causal explanations and interpreting reality, into peace, into a more humane world. As human beings, we interpret the world and history. What was strange for us in the beginning becomes assimilated to our conceptual and vital categories through thought and action: we adapt the world to our world, and history to our history.

Science submits the multiplicity of world phenomena to a set of laws and, above all, to a series of methodological procedures which allow us to understand what is apparently different as a manifestation of a common, underlying reality. Thus, physics has been able to discover the four fundamental forces of nature, showing that the variety of natural events may be reduced, after all, to the concourse of four basic interactions. More recently, physics is attempting to offer a "theory of everything," which may integrate those four forces (although a true "theory of everything" is ultimately impossible, as Gödel's theorem manifests).

With the unfolding of the DNA structure, James Watson and Sir Francis Crick amazed the world with the discovery of the key of life. Genes are fragments of DNA and they express heritage of millions of years of evolution. Darwin had ennobled, almost a century earlier, the human quest for knowledge when he proposed a synthesis which unified the natural history of life on earth, making the more complex species stem from the simplest ones.[5] The beauty of the theory of evolution resides in its capacity for establishing a link among all forms of life. The fascinating variety of beings on Earth ultimately stems from a primitive manifestation of life. The discovery of the evolution of life, and of how its fabric, sewed throughout millions of years, has propitiated the emergence of the peak of complexity represented by the human mind, constitutes one of the greatest achievements of science: the finding of the "common ground,"

---

5. For an introduction to the philosophical implications of the theory of evolution, cf. Rosenberg and Arp, *Philosophy of Biology: An Anthology*, with contributions by E. Mayr, S. J. Gould, C. Lewontin, and E. O. Wilson, among others. Cf. also Ayala and Dobzhansky, *Studies in Philosophy of Biology: Reduction and Related Problems*. On the contributions of Darwin to biology, cf. Mayr, *The Growth of Biological Thought*, 394–534.

the substrate that bounds all forms of life. The theory of evolution provides a synthesis which strengthens the scientific vision of the world. It offers a fertile field of meditation for all realms of knowledge. Diversity becomes actually integrated into a global picture, into the architectonics of knowledge.

The seventeenth century facilitated an almost unmatched advancement in the scientific understanding of the world when Sir Isaac Newton, in his *Mathematical Principles of Natural Philosophy* (1687), perhaps the most important scientific work in human history, broke the rigid separation that the Greeks, and especially Aristotle, had established between the physics of earthly phenomena and the physics of astronomical phenomena. In Aristotle's view, the stars were ruled by special laws, as they constituted some sort of semi-divine world, different from the Earth, but the penetrating genius of Newton arrived, showing that the same laws which can be applied to the earth are also suitable to explain the physics of celestial bodies. Another victory of the human intellect and its progressive, to use a notion broadly cultivated by the German theologian Rudolf Bultmann, "demythologization" of world and history[6] (which is analogous, to a certain extent, to Max Weber's idea of "disenchantment of the world [*Entzauberung der Welt*]"[7]).

Knowledge is not always cumulative; even less often is it immutable. It may be legitimate to speak in terms of "accumulation" in the realm of the natural sciences because, being true that although Einstein corrected Newton's mechanics and his theory of gravitation, Newton's physics can be still applied as a limit case of Einstein's. This does not happen in the human sciences. There is little in common, with certain exceptions, between ancient, medieval, and early modern anthropology. They will inevitably converge in particular aspects, in specific information which may be valid today despite having been relativized or qualified in its scope, but they will rarely coincide in the methodological underpinnings. On the other hand, the scientific method is still valid, as it was in the times of Galileo, and it represents one of the greatest achievements in human history. It is the same method that has made it possible to correct Galileo's ideas

---

6. Cf. Bultmann, *The New Testament and Mythology and Other Basic Writings*.

7. As Max Weber wrote, "Jener grosse religionsgeschichtliche Prozess der Entzauberung der Welt, welcher mit der altjüdischen Prophetie einsetzte und, im Verein mit dem hellenischen wissenschaftlichen Denken, alle magische Mittel der Heilssuche als Aberglaube und Frevel verwarf, fand hier [in Calvinist asceticism] seinen Abschluss" (*Gesammelte Aufsätze zur Religionssoziologie*, 1:94). On the disenchantment of the world in Max Weber, cf. Schluchter, *Die Entzauberung der Welt*.

without a significant alteration of its foundations. It is therefore a method which possesses an immense conceptual and explanatory power, an immense humanizing power, since it allows the human mind to advance in its understanding of the world. Its success has encouraged its application, although with not few problems, to the realm of the social and human sciences, becoming the "ideal" of rationality, rigor, and knowledge *stricto sensu*.

This is the reason why any "sociological theory" of science, such as Thomas Kuhn's,[8] fails to account for the true development of our scientific understanding of the world: there may be different paradigms changing over time in a given scientific discipline, but the fundamental paradigm of science, as condensed in its scientific method (a conjugation of theory—hypotheses- and experiments in different possible combinations) has not been significantly altered. There is only one scientific paradigm, with different manifestations and "subsets" of rules in accordance to the various scientific disciplines. The concatenation of paradigms creates modifications within each branch of science, not "revolutions" in the way in which science works in a global sense (the basic assumptions of the scientific method do not become "revolutionized" but expanded to account for more and more complex phenomena).

Science is knowledge *par excellence*, but science is not peace *par excellence*. The science that unveils the mysteries of the universe and shows us the fascinating world of elementary particles, the science that even arrives at chaos theory and acquires conscience of the illusory character of its predictive potential, is also capable of producing the most sophisticated weapons, and it allows us, for the first time in history, to destroy the planet and to annihilate ourselves. Science also inspires fear of the possibility that human relations may become less and less humane, that technique may invade every sphere of existence, without leaving any space for creativity, fantasy, and life, so that the artificial may supersede the natural, and some individuals may use the power of science and technique to dominate others. We come back to our initial consideration: experience has made contemporary minds pessimistic about the ability of science and knowledge in its most general sense to bring peace to the world and to our personal cosmos. The opposite idea seems to be an outdated utopia of the Enlightenment, discredited by recent historical events.

---

8. On Kuhn's concept of paradigm, cf. his work *The Structure of Scientific Revolutions*, 43–51.

Consciousness beyond the World: Freedom

As human beings, we have always wished to live better, and we have always longed for a fuller, more humane life. Even many of those who have committed horrendous crimes have justified their perverse actions on the basis of their necessity in order to achieve a better future for their people. Humanity has constantly looked forward. We have not been captives of our past. We have looked to our past, and in some periods of history the present has been hostage to the past, to withered conceptions and deciduous powers but, since the Enlightenment, humanity only has future. The present becomes relativized on the basis of the future, and we can no longer think that the past possesses a legitimacy which may prevail over the value of the present in its path to the future.

Our imagination is captivated by the power of the future. We believe that science will find a vaccine against aids and cancer, that current conflicts will be solved, that the present powers will pave the way for those of the future, that the contents of our ignorance will not be a mystery in years, decades, or centuries, and that those ideas which we now take for granted and as universally valid will be subject to criticism over time. Let us examine our consciousness on this point, and it may be true that we actually think that everything will change, perhaps for better, in the future, but, in any case, in the end everything will become different. We no longer believe in a return to the past. We are convinced of the irreversibility of time, of the arrow set by the second law of thermodynamics, and we conceive of the world and history on the basis of this concept: history continues its course over time and there is no alternative other than going forward.

Humanity places its hope in the future, in a future genius who may explain what today remains enigmatic, in a future technology that may make our lives more comfortable, in a future peace agreement that may help those peoples that are in conflict to understand and love each other, in a future time in which we will conquer worlds which are almost unreachable for us today. Centuries ago, humanity looked to the past, to the initial golden age, to Ovid's *aetas aurea*.[9] Plato looked to Atlantis, the everlasting

---

9. Since Mircea Eliade's *The Myth of the Eternal Return*, it is commonplace to attribute to ancient civilizations a cyclical conception of time and life. Without trying to delegitimize this thesis, which undoubtedly offers many interesting insights into some essential aspects of the categorization of reality of the different ancient cultures, we agree with Jan Assmann, who remarked that in Egypt the situation is more complicated (cf., among the many works of this German Egyptologist, *Das kulturelle Gedächtnis: Schrift, Erinnerung und politische Identität in frühen Hochkulturen*). The explicit denial of history as the necessary expression of the human becoming in time and space is difficult to find in the Egyptian civilization. Together with a model of sacred time we find

myth of a higher civilization which was later destroyed, but which remains unsurpassed. After it, everything has been a sign of decadence. The Bible tells us about the Garden of Eden, as the initial state of perfect and inaugural harmony between the human being, God, and nature. However, sin brought our fall, and man and woman had to abandon that idyllic place in order to enter the crudeness of history.

After Greece and Rome, after their superb art, their mathematics, their culture, the loss of classical wisdom came, and humanity went back into darkness. Europe did not experience a conceptual revolution capable of surpassing Greek mathematics until the seventeenth century, with the discovery of the concept of function and the invention of infinitesimal calculus by Newton and Leibniz. Zoroastrianism, prophetic and apocalyptic Judaism, and Christianity incorporated the idea of a linear history oriented towards its consummation. They did not look only to the past: their eschatological doctrines made the past and its understanding depend on the future. This was certainly an important step, but we had to wait until the philosophical and scientific developments of the seventeenth and eighteenth centuries so that the Western conscience might open itself to the perspective of the future in a definitive way, to a large extent by virtue of the secularization of central notions of the Judeo-Christian tradition. Hans Blumenberg, in *The Legitimacy of the Modern Age* (1966), defends the view that modernity has no "mortgage" contracted with the Judeo-Christianity, although it is hard to deny, as Karl Löwith showed in *Meaning in History* (1949), that the modern discourse on humanity and history has been powerfully shaped by a series of patterns which cannot be understood without the influence of theology.[10] A different question (and

---

a "profane" form of the temporal: besides *neheh*, the cyclical eternity that constantly returns to itself, the beginning of the *exitus* and the summit of *reditus* of the cosmic totality, which integrates both the human and the divine, we also discover *djet*, the permanence. The Egyptian mind, even within the domain of the sacred reality, was capable of envisioning a double sense of time: a universal and circular way, of ascent and descent, of departure and return, and a unidimensional way which expresses the harmony and stability of all the internal movements. The "sacred" time runs parallel to the "profane" time. Any apparent newness becomes subordinated to a superior order, which, up to a certain point, "transcends" history: the theological order, which guides and defines history.

10. Modernity, as Heidegger remarks, has "conquered the world as image" (Cf. Heidegger, "Die Zeit des Weltbildes," in *Holzwege*, 81–85; See also Taylor, *Hegel*, 7). The human being, as *subiectum*, posits himself before the entity [*Seiende*] as object of his thinking, becoming the true being [*Sein*] of the entity: through analyzing, transforming, and creating the entity, humanity makes it meaningful. The human being is therefore, as Protagoras famously remarked, "the measure of all things: of things

here Blumenberg's thesis is greatly illuminating) is whether this fact has to "enslave" the modern imagination, binding it to Judeo-Christian ideas. Otherwise, we would have received a poisoned legacy.

The future has become a synonym for hope. Ernst Bloch dedicated his *opus magnum*, *The Principle of Hope*, to the study of the human hope in a better future, and this idea has been greatly influential on the so-called "theologies of hope" (just as the theology of Jürgen Moltmann), which highlight the orientation of Christian thought towards the dynamics of the future, of an open future which may be capable of revealing a more humane horizon. However, we should not become hypnotized by some sort of ventriloquist future which acquires its own personality, evanescently escaping our control, as Daniel Bensaïd lucidly realized in several of his writings,[11] but we must actively edify what is to come.[12]

---

which are, that they are, and of things which are not, that they are not" (Freeman, *Ancilla to the Pre-Socratic Philosophers: A Complete Translation of the Fragments in Diels Fragmente der Vorsokratiker*, 80B1), the microcosm that assumes the aspirations of being.

11. Cf. Bensaïd, "L'Humanité au-delà du Capital," 139–46.

12. The philosophical discussion about the nature of history has been generally polarized by binomial linearity/circularity. The cyclical conception of time was adopted by Nietzsche in his theory of eternal return [*ewige Wiederkehr*] as an attempt at overcoming nihilism, in contraposition to the Zoroastrian and Judeo-Christian idea of linearity. For Nietzsche, to a large extent inspired by Schopenhauer's *The World as Will and Representation* (1818), being is will to power, which persistently returns to itself and constitutes its sole horizon. Judeo-Christianity envisions an intrinsic newness in each instant of history, and it sees the origin of time in divine creation. Judeo-Christianity chooses unidimensionality over bidimensionality, linearity over circularity, while at the same time it preserves a cyclical element in the liturgical organization of the calendar and in the representation of history as if it gravitated toward a single *kairos* or central moment. Against this apparently insurmountable dichotomy, it seems necessary to project our thoughts on an ulterior dimension that may be capable of overcoming duality. Time connects two realities, two realms: one is subjective, and one is objective. Time relates the conscience of the subject with the external universe, of which the subject is a part. Time provides us the idea of becoming, of the dynamic progression of being, of the difference between self and alterity. In time, we acquire conscience of our own development, of our own personality. Time is not a substantial reality, something *in se*, but an ontic *link* between two worlds, a bridge that joins subjectivity and the objectivity of cosmos, a fascinating and inscrutable dimension of human reality, that defines it in its immanence and its transcendence, in which its determinations take place. In the subject and the object, both tendencies live together: linearity and circularity. Humanity, on the one hand, thinks of new things and envisions progress, but, on the other, it is always returning to the same basic questions and is perennially captured by the same fundamental anxieties. Nature is ruled by evolutionary laws that have fostered transformation, but we also realize that it remains under the domain of cycles, of regenerations, of life and death, and the conservation

Part 2: *Fundamentum* in History

In any case, the future has also become a synonym for uncertainty and even fear. We do not know what the future will bring to us, for in times past it has shown horrendous things, whose memory brings bitter sadness. Theodor Adorno said that to write a poem after Auschwitz is barbaric,[13] and this is partially true: after such a concentration of inhumanity it is very difficult to compose poetry, yet not impossible. Humanity has continued to cultivate the arts and the sciences. Humanity has continued to live and to make an effort to live in a humane way. There are some beautiful words by Pablo Neruda that express this idea:

> It is today exactly one hundred years since an unhappy and brilliant poet, the most awesome of all despairing souls, wrote down this prophecy: "A l'aurore, armés d'une ardente patience, nous entrerons aux splendides Villes." "In the dawn, armed with a burning patience, we shall enter the splendid Cities." I believe in this prophecy of Rimbaud, the Visionary. I come from a dark region, from a land separated from all others by the steep contours of its geography. I was the most forlorn of poets and my poetry was provincial, oppressed and rainy. But always I had put my trust in man. I never lost hope. It is perhaps because of this that I have reached as far as I now have with my poetry and also with my banner. Last, I wish to say to the people of good will, to the workers, to the poets, that the whole future has been expressed in this line by Rimbaud: only with a *burning patience* can we conquer the splendid City which will give light, justice

---

laws become relevant not only in the theoretical sphere but also in the "pragmatics" of nature, in which an equilibrium prevails, a preservation that coexists with change and variability. Energy is conserved, but, in this context of preservation, many transformations take place. Within the human conscience, is it not true that we are always trying to move forward while, at the same time, we are posing the same questions again and again, the same unceasing voices of the spirit? The cyclical and the linear dimensions coexist in the subjective and objective spheres, in the intrinsic and the extrinsic realms, and time is the link connecting both tendencies, which converge in the human act of becoming in the universe. This act of becoming is shaped by the determinations that mankind bestows upon itself and those which are alien to it, being a form of becoming in which human freedom always projects infinite horizons even in the midst of the finiteness of the world, and both the subjective and the objective actions, that seem to diverge, actually converge in the consecution of the very act of constantly becoming something new, which assimilates the past and assumes the future, predicting it and bringing it back, while respecting the uniqueness of the present.

13. "Kulturkritik findet sich der letzten Stufe der Dialektik von Kultur und Barbarei gegenüber: nach Auschwitz ein Gedicht zu schreiben, ist barbarisch, und das frißt auch die Erkenntnis an, die ausspricht, warum es unmöglich ward, heute Gedichte zu schreibe" (*Prismen: Kulturkritik und Gesellschaft*, in *Gesammelte Schriften* 10:30).

and dignity to all mankind. In this way the song will not have been sung in vain.[14]

Why should we lose hope? Our worst mistakes stand in contradiction to our great achievements. Misery and destruction contradict the resonant sublimity of music and the magical beauty of science, but why should we think that mistakes are inevitable? Why should we think there is no possibility of a better future? Why should we become captives of the past? Why shouldn't we boast of our power to overcome what is now given, inspired in the conviction that the future, as the scenario of the unpredictable and unknown, is therefore a space of novelty and hope?

Death is a terrible reality which has frightened us since the dawn of our rationality, but it is also a transforming force that allows for the renewal of history. The worst criminals of the past no longer exist, and they have fallen into bitter oblivion, while the great creators, the sages, the humanists, and the saints of the different religions exist in the memory and pride of humanity. Our children study their lives and examples in school because we want them to do so, because we wish that they may find inspiration in these outstanding figures, and we also pretend that they know the bad testimonies as a way of prevention, even though we also realize that the knowledge of history has rarely stopped it from being repeated.

The uncertainty of history is also the diaphanous certainty of the horizon of novelty offered by the future. The uncertainty of history can therefore plant the solid seed of the tree of hope. In this way, our initial question on the possibility of achieving a direct connection between knowledge and peace turns into the following problem: is it possible to have hope in knowledge leading to peace?

One could think of the relationship between knowledge and peace as if they were two opposite poles: knowledge, the synonym of theory, on the one hand, and peace, the effect of action, on the other hand; theory and praxis, contemplation and action. Knowledge would then consist of what is abstracted from reality, the pure theory which avoids mixing itself with action, not to become "polluted" by its partiality, contingency, and relativity. Also, action may be suspicious of theory, because the latter is often incapable of opening itself to the reality of the world. The natural sciences have managed to establish a happy and concordant harmony between theory and praxis, between knowledge and its applications. Technology has given prestige to science, even more than the capacity of science for

---

14. These words are taken from Pablo Neruda's Nobel lecture in 1971.

explaining how natural phenomena work, but in the social and human sciences, such a narrow connection remains unattained.

We should not forget, however, that our democratic systems would be unimaginable without the theoretical and humanistic enterprise of so many great thinkers over the last centuries (and already in Greece), who illuminated, with the power of their ideas, the social reality and the way to organize it in freedom and justice. This is the reason why every remark on the apparent uselessness of the humanities against the proverbial utility of the natural sciences must be regarded as superficial and unfair. A culture which does not value the humanities, reducing everything to what seems to be "practical," will inevitably become simple and insubstantial, and it will easily fall to the tyranny of fanaticism and intolerance. The cultivation of those disciplines which are hypothetically useless constitutes a precious sign of freedom, indeterminacy, and human greatness. The tragedy of our time is that the dedication to these disciplines is only possible in those countries whose main concern is not mere subsistence.

We must leave behind the idea that knowledge essentially corresponds to pure theory, to the realm of disinterested aims, as opposed to action, guided by practical interests. The human being interprets his world and the world. Any form knowledge, even that which might seem to represent the quintessence of objectivity, is subjective inasmuch as it projects a human prejudice over the world. Science is not simply objective: it is objective from the point of view of human subjectivity. We categorize the world in accordance with our concepts and prejudices. For example, we accept that it is possible to understand nature and to unfold its laws, but it could be otherwise. It might be a happy coincidence, as the Hungarian physicist and Nobel laureate Eugene Wigner remarked in an essay on the application of mathematics for the natural sciences.[15] There is no *a priori* argument that may tell us that the universe of mathematical forms of which we conceive in our mind can actually describe with accuracy the cosmos of physical objects.[16]

---

15. Cf. Wigner, "The Unreasonable Effectiveness of Mathematics in the Natural Sciences," 1.

16. In any case, and since science primarily studies interactions between material bodies, it seems reasonable to suppose that these interactions, which involve different "unities," ultimately correspond to a quantitative treatment, as the one incorporated by mathematics, for this approach operates with "unities," by establishing relationships among them. In Cartesian terms, if science examines *res extensae*, it is by virtue of their extension, of their quantitative dimension in space and time, that they are susceptible to an intellection in mathematical terms. Instead of a happy coincidence, we would be contemplating a necessity imposed by nature itself and the quantitative

The scientific image of the world is ruled by the prejudice that reality is intelligible. As Gadamer showed, understanding always bears a pre-understanding, and this is the basic pre-understanding of the natural sciences: that we live in an intelligible world that is subject to universal laws, which equally rule in any point of the universe, provided that a set of analogous conditions is fulfilled. Our enunciations do not simply refer to the state of things but rather they depend upon a system of conceptual reference given by our own mind. In the last decades, the results obtained in the fields of physics and mathematics, and especially in branches such as quantum mechanics and chaos theory, have genuinely contested our devoted and passionate faith in the intelligibility of the world and the power of reason to understand and predict the full range of its phenomena. Many things escape us, but the scientific enterprise is still alive and untamed, although science is more aware of its limitations.

There is no solid pretext to associate knowledge with pure, disinterested theory, voluntarily unlinked from action. Any form of knowledge is already an act of humanization, just as any action over the world provides us with knowledge about the world. In knowing, in opening ourselves to that which is strange, we also learn to know ourselves, and we achieve some kind of liberation from our preconceived ideas, from our environment, and from our own history. Few experiences are as gratifying as that of learning, of envisioning something new, which takes us away from the *hic et nunc*, from the here and now, which is often oppressive. Even the apparently exotic reflections of the first philosophers on cosmos and the *arkhe* of nature were indispensable for the human mind to emancipate itself from the chains of a magical conception of world, initiating the path of the rationalization of the world.

Knowledge, and the use of reason which leads to it, is available to everyone, not only to the wise and powerful. The evidence of reason is the most liberating certainty. Knowledge defeats any authority, and it establishes itself as the authority. We are normally captives of prejudices, and knowledge itself is not alien to this reality, but the most extraordinary feature history resides in our capacity for gaining awareness of these biases.

Jürgen Habermas has expressed with remarkable insightfulness the link that exists between knowledge and interest. The empirical-analytical sciences have a technical interest, aimed at dominating nature in a Baconian sense. This does not mean, however, that everything done by these disciplines is intended for a practical application but rather that even those

---

relations established by the objects that integrate it.

enunciations that apparently remain in the theoretical sphere are subject to a series of validation (or, following Popper, falsation) procedures that actually reinforce the scientific method. We induce the conditions of the experiments in order to legitimize the theoretical assertions on the basis of our ideal of a hypothetical-deductive science.

The historical-hermeneutical sciences seek to interpret the world and history in such a way that the subject may actually understand himself. Understanding does not operate for its own sake: we understand in order to understand ourselves. This is the intrinsic interest from which it is useless to try to escape, for any development in the realm of the human sciences allows us to know ourselves in our present situation, something that might eventually bring light on how we must act.[17]

Habermas recognizes a third class, the critical science, guided by the emancipatory interest of reason: that reason may make itself become free, promoting a dialogue free of domination between all rational agents. Genuine communication could only exist in an emancipated society. We might add that objectivity is actually the asymptotic, infinite limit of intersubjective communication.

The critical science converges with what Western thought has generally called "philosophy." And the "love of wisdom" which has inspired the philosophical endeavor throughout the centuries is not alien to the world of action. Philosophy has rarely been empty speculation, deliberately disconnected from real events. Philosophers have been influenced by the space and time in which they lived, and with their ideas they have influenced their world, too. In this sense, philosophy has always been political (having to do with *polis*, with the human community). Philosophy has manifested a luminous vocation of understanding and humanization, and is there anything as eminently political as the will to understand and to humanize? Moreover, philosophy has constantly fostered, by its own nature, dialogue. Philosophy has generated questions which demanded dialogue, a shared reflection between men and women. Philosophy has enhanced human communication, and this is perhaps the greatest achievement of philosophical thinking: to have established the intellectual and social conditions so that humanity did not cease to pose questions, being able to transcend itself and to ascend beyond that which is given.

Communication can reify reality and generate suffocating structures, but it helps individuals and communities to achieve a broader space of understanding, to overcome partialities, and to allow for new spaces of

---

17. Cf. Habermas, *Technik und Wissenschaft als "Ideologie."*

action and reflection. In this sense, it is possible to speak in terms of a *pluralistic humanism* which does not conceive of individuals on the sole basis of their insertion in pre-established structures and cultures (as isolated entities which archetypically repeat structural invariants) but according to their constant capacity for reshaping those structural relations. By means of communication, human beings gradually break the coercion of natural and social structures, acquiring a higher conscience of their freedom. There is no way back from the conscience of freedom. The same humanity that discovers its subjection to structures is actually capable of imagining how to overcome those sclerotic patterns. Humanity regards itself as captive to what has been pre-established, but it also dares to initiate the epic adventure of knowledge, which is the source of new spaces of life and thought.

Communication allows human beings to escape themselves, in an act of fugitive flight from their "selfness," and it helps cultures open themselves to a reciprocally fruitful interaction. Communication is therefore the foundation of historical progress, which can only consist of the acquisition of a larger space of realization and liberation. The achievements in the realms of knowledge and human relations gives a testimony to the power of communication, which offers the instrument to overcome any form of ignorance and relationship constituted in terms of domination.

Progress can be understood as the openness that each subject offers and that humanity has been able to perform throughout the centuries. It affects all the dimensions of existence. Despite the numerous and almost ineluctable facts that contradict the idea of progress (hunger, poverty, underdevelopment, the loss of the horizon of service and cooperation), the fact of knowing more and living in a time which is always different (equally capable of assimilating that which comes before it) is a manifestation of progress. Progress is the truth of being. Progress is openness, intensity, experience, knowledge, longing, art. Progress synthesizes the totality of being and mankind, and it is the constant elevation of being by being itself; it is an expression of immanence and transcendence, the rubric of the tension which creates and originates old and new worlds; it is the concretion of the absolute in history: progress therefore becomes the biography of being, the display of its potentiality, the overcoming of any possible duality in an infinite "looking forward."[18]

18. The progress of society is mediated by the establishment of an "entatic" (tense, *entasis*) relationship between the quest for *fundamentum*, on the one hand, and the constant necessity of opening ourselves beyond any absolute foundation, on the other. Today, the inevitable dialectic between the search for a non-dubious basis of morality

Science, art, thought, technique—they are all the embodiments of progress. However, they also point to its indeterminacy, in which its mystery and attraction reside. We do not know in which direction progress is leading us, but we do understand that it is carrying us along the ontic space, which is being itself, inviting us to follow it into totality, into a *categorumen* that integrates both being and non-being. In the very act of "being carried by being" we become aware of our fate: to create.

Let us read the classics again and again, let us immerse ourselves into the beauty of the great verses that humanity has produced, and let us enjoy the achievements of science and its exploration of the intimate structure of the universe. Knowledge increases our longing for the absolute, because we would like to have infinite, unconditioned wisdom, and although we understand that this is impossible, we still seek it. Behold the seed of salvation: the infinite wish, which makes us equally infinite.

Only from the conscience of the supremacy of the subject which opens itself to being and totality can we transform any *id*, any sub-conscience, any under-determination which pressures the autonomous core of personality, into a bridge between the subject and the object.[19] Faith

---

and human rights and, at the same time, the wish not to "close," with transcendental and metaphysical reasons, any possible discussion about these topics, seems to be a vivid proof of the "entatic" element that travels through history and thought. As humans, we are almost unrestrictedly defining ontic spaces. We long for absoluteness while we also shy away from it. If we were to equate absoluteness to truth, we would inexorably admit that we ardently seek the knowledge of truth, but we also fear it with no lesser fervor, because it can exhaust and paralyze the continuous movement of being. Against such a compelling dialectic, conscience, as infiniteness that opens itself to absoluteness, must emerge as the unbreakable *fundamentum*. To take an active part in being, to involve ourselves in being, to acquire conscience of our condition of entities in being, is a truth that is always new: truth as novelty and moreover, truth as openness, as the freedom of the subject to set its path in the horizon of being. This creativity exhorts us to make of the *ego* an *alter*, and of the *alter* an *ego*.

19. Psychoanalysis poses at least four challenges to modernity and its conception of humankind, as Michel de Certeau has written: "La psychoanalyse en détèriore les postulats: l'apriori de l'unité individuelle (sur lequelle reposent une économie libérale et une société democrate), le privilége de la conscience (principe de la société 'éclairée'), le myth du progrès (une conception du temps) et son corollaire, le mythe de l'éducation (qui fait de la transformation d'une société et des ses membres l'éthique d'une élite)" (*La Fable Mystique* 1:17). In spite of the legitimate criticism of many of Freud's theories, no one can doubt that his ideas constitute an inexorable source of inspiration for any philosophical consideration of autonomy and freedom. Freud did not conceive of psychoanalysis as a mere medical theory aimed at treating neurosis but as a theory of culture (which, according to him, has been developed at the expense of the satisfaction of our instincts, sacrificing them in favor of the community and the edification of the collective human reality: this is exposed in his *Introductory Lectures*

in the possibility of a humane shaping of the pre-established structures is robust confidence in humanity, which is firmly rooted in the nature of communication. The communicative action sets a symbolic means for individuals and communities to contact each other. Communication always establishes a space that transcends the partiality of the individual and the community. Communication is therefore the space of universality. This is the reason why any project of humanization must pursue what Habermas has called a "communication free from domination," in which subjects and groups may express all their vitalities.

Pluralistic humanism, the kind of humanism that does not ignore the results of structural analysis on the way in which history, society, economy, and science condition our understanding of ourselves, and which does not intend to impose a certain *a priori* conception of the human being, assumes the hope in a more humane future. Thus, pluralistic humanism is the humanism of communication.

The natural and the human sciences can equally contribute to promoting a higher conscience of freedom, as both of them help suppress the chains of ignorance. The goal of history can only reside in the actualization of the infinite human capacity for communication. The inherent dehumanizing power of science, technique, and thought cannot hide an important certainty: communication lets us become aware of any dehumanizing potential.

The great sapiential, cultural, and religious traditions of humanity seem to converge in the formulation of the ethics of humanization, which fosters the human potential for knowledge and freedom; the ethics which, without falling into the naïve (and seldom ideological) pretension of making the individual subject solely responsible for his actions, in order to exonerate the system (social, economic, cultural. . .) and its structures from any possible blame, manages to highlight that only free communication can promote the flourishing of the genuine possibilities of the human being. This humanity, humanized through communication, will also come into dialogue with the physical world, and instead of treating the surrounding cosmos as the object that we can merely possess, we will learn to regard it, as Haber as has written, as a "fraternal nature." We will therefore recognize its "subjectivity."

If knowledge is the pre-eminent path to peace, then it also points towards salvation, which appears as the capacity for overcoming the negativity that forces us to direct our energies outside, to the external world.

---

on Psychoanalysis, delivered in 1915–1916 and in 1916–1917).

Peace is the recognition of oneself, of humanity, of the world, of the "I" in the "other"; it is the capacity for accommodating the totality of the world and humanity into our own interiority and to project our interiority onto the world and humanity. Peace is therefore the absolute exchange, the pure communication, the shared fullness, in which the interior worlds open themselves to each other freely, which is not motivated by void and dispossession, by the negativity that lies as the basis of power. Peace is the self-power which does not need to empty itself in order to dominate other worlds.

The salvation that thought brings to us constitutes a permanent challenge to any form of power. Power does not save but rather condemns. Power divides humanity, and it abruptly breaks the human being within himself. Salvation, on the contrary, is vocation of union, of participation in a common fate, in the creation of a new scenario which we may all share. Knowledge is an infinite, inexhaustible enterprise, which will continue giving a meaning to the human life in future generations. Knowledge is in itself salvation, because it opens us to a world which goes beyond our singularity, integrating us into the dynamism of the cosmos and history. Knowledge is the eminent expression of the opening of mankind to being.[20]

The intellectual has to be a prophet, and to address his thought and his action to those who have been forgotten, because they decide the destiny of humanity, since they show our true and genuine possibilities. There can be no collective success as long as we tolerate the failure of so many who cannot enjoy a life worth being lived. Michel Foucault proclaimed the death of man, and we can renew this statement by saying that a model of humanity in which some people while others have been deprived of their humanity cannot subsist. Through the prophetic critique of power, alienation, and injustice let us look to the future and to the past, let us live,

20. We can argue that in openness itself and in guaranteeing the conditions that make openness possible the tendency towards absoluteness and truth resides, and the goal of our existence has to be the perception of the radical nature of this calling for self-transcendence in the infinite space of being, which is also a vocation to dialogue and tolerance, as the ways for the fulfilment of our fate: to be ourselves. We are here in order not to know why we are here, and this is the great paradox that we face. However, this indeterminacy constitutes an invitation to openness and quest, to look for ulteriority and self-transcendence, for culture, wisdom, and goodness. . .: it is an exhortation to grow in our humanity and to give a meaning to the universe. The ineffability of the universe demands to be conveyed through our own voices and, to use Rilke's words—"happy are those who know that behind any language there is the ineffable" (Rainer Maria Rilke: "Glücklich, die wissen, dass hinter allen Sprachen das Unsägliche steht" (*Sämtliche Werke* 2:259ff.).

let us change, let us imagine, and let us think; let us join ourselves and let us obliterate the differences in the infinite space of truth. The intellectual will find no home in power; his only abode will be all cultures and the vast ocean of knowledge.

The challenge of humanity is the universalization of all that has been achieved, seeking peace and concord as the horizons of fullness. The centuries preceding us have made fundamental contributions to the understanding of the human being (freedom, equality, fraternity/sorority) and nature (science, technology), but the challenge of the future is the universalization of these conquests, led by the conviction that we all participate in a common fate, a shared vocation, legitimately diversified in the different peoples and cultures, but capable of edifying a pluralistic humanism.

The new civilization which all the peoples of the Earth must build together cannot conceive of knowledge as a possession but as an attitude of openness to the richness of life, as a sincere exhortation to challenge the past, the present, and the future in order to broaden the horizons of humanity. Instead of a culture of "having," we will follow the path of "being," and our shared masters will be those voices, full of depth and authenticity, which have proclaimed throughout history the need to grow as persons, not as mere owners of dehumanized objects: Amos, Isaiah, Buddha, Socrates, Jesus, Saint Francis of Assisi, Eckhart, Spinoza, Marx, Schweitzer. Humanity will then overcome itself and the *übermensch* foreseen by Nietzsche will be born, whose goal will not be to dominate but to understand, to imagine, and to love, solid means for the inauguration of fruitful and dignifying scenarios in history.

As Albert Schweitzer announced with outstanding lucidity, we have become "übermenschen," "mais le surhomme souffre d'une imperfection funeste de son esprit. Il ne s'est pas élevé au niveau de la raison surhumaine qui devrait correspondre à la possession d'une force surhumaine."[21] This *raison surhumaine* needs to be defined by the convergence of rationality and sentiment, of dispassionate logic and vivid compassion, so that the true "*übermensch*" will be someone capable of giving himself to others. The trace of the most genuine love, which is the preeminent sign of peace, will luminously shine in his spirit.

---

21. Taken from his Nobel lecture, "The Problem of Peace."

THE ESSENCE OF FREEDOM

Freedom, if regarded as a power against the world, becomes reduced to autonomy. It does not stand as "free freedom," as a kind of freedom that is not subject to any sort of "sameness," may it be that of the world or that of subjectivity itself in its unredeemed longing for independence from the surrounding cosmos. Autonomy expresses the closing of freedom over itself, its "seclusion" within its own limits, its darkness. Its sole wish resides in challenging the world, but this act of courage against the universe does not lead to the will of creating something new. Ruptured by its own being, captivated by its capacity of decision, by its ability to gain a high degree of emancipation from the oppressing necessity imposed by the world, a consciousness whose sole scope lies in its autonomy cannot show commitment to creation. The spirit of detachment does not blossom in its spirit. The soul of abnegation, the beauty of delivering oneself, with depth and courage, to expanding the energies of life and broadening the horizons of the possible, to building a new world which may not be constrained to the sameness of the tangible universe, does not flourish.

The solitude of consciousness is the product of its most intimate self-referential inclinations. The defeat of this state of solitude demands commitment to a *novum*, to broadening the limits of the possible, to creation. Consciousness becomes donation, detachment, sacrifice, and freedom, for it feels the vocation to serve a goal which may transcend its narrow nature. Thus, consciousness turns into a creative spirit, whose power of fascination is now possessed by the desire to plant the seed of novelty and to cultivate love, beauty, and wisdom. This consciousness is no longer the mere expression of "for-itself" [*für-sich*], whose definition involves its radical opposition to the world (the "in-itself," *an-sich*), but the incarnation of abnegation, goodness, commitment, passionate quest.

The conviction that the world is entirely insufficient to satisfy the deepest longings of consciousness leads to the assumption of a task: that of venturing through unknown paths. To challenge the world implies to flee from the comfortable situation of "merely appearing" as another object inside the nets that sow the vast clothing of the universe. The perception of the state of indigence into which consciousness is inexorably condemned to fall can be eclipsed by a profound fear towards this condition. A tormented consciousness will seek to return to the world, although this wish may be hidden behind the subtle curtains of the attempt at a "*fuga mundi*." Nostalgia for immutability, melancholy for the victory over the oppressive domains of space and time, conceals a refusal to committing oneself to the deepest vocation of which we can think: to create.

The individual cannot flee from its vocation to challenge the world. We are not "beings-in-the-world": we are "beings-against-the-world." The nature of consciousness points towards the inescapable necessity of questioning everything that is given. No *factum* can stand before consciousness without the concomitant feeling that it is susceptible to some kind of critical interrogation. The human being can hardly avoid the contradiction which he or she represents with respect to the world. As Max Scheler claimed, man is the "ascetic of life," the eternal protestant against reality, the perennial Faust, a beast "cupidissima rerum novarum."[22] The human being is capable of breaking any limit. The extension of its most inextricable power allows for the negation of the will of life, as Schopenhauer remarked through his idea of *Verneinung des Willens zum Leben*. To challenge the world does not mean to try to destroy the world. Rather, its ultimate meaning is associated with the attempt at making the world "less worldly." This "demundanization of the world" can be understood as the will to question the world in order to eventually transform it. We know that the world suffers a process of continuous modification. Heraclitus's intuition, "everything flows" (*panta rhei*), has been prolixly confirmed by the natural sciences. There is no time to rest in the vastness of the universe. The cosmos experiences a constant mutation. However, this set of variations does not constitute a series of real "changes." It merely vindicates the world in its sameness. Movement exists, but it serves a higher goal: stability. The world, as a whole, stays in identity with itself. Nothing is created either destroyed: it is only transformed. Any hypothetical mutation obeys inexorable laws. Its ultimate direction is the consolidation of the cosmos. Therefore, any alteration becomes subordinated to the impossibility that the world may "come out of itself."

The world is condemned to be itself and to perpetuate itself as such. Only with the advent of human consciousness the possibility of "non-appearance" emerges. Only then it is viable to "escape the world" into a "non-world" (which nonetheless does not cease to appear as part of the world). To propitiate that the world may lose its "worldliness" involves questioning the world with passion and commitment. From this act, the possibility of a *novum*, of a future which does not repeat the patterns of the past, the horizon of a true history, arises. To turn the world into a "less worldly" reality can be interpreted as an invitation to live as historical beings and

---

22. Cf. Scheler, *Die Stellung des Menschen im Kosmos*,

to delve into this condition. We cannot be deprived of our mundane character. We are parts of the world, but our deepest tragedy stems from the contradiction that defines our existence: we are also "outside the world" in the inexhaustible realm of consciousness. Because we appear in the world and we stand as objects of the material universe, we have the chance to pose a challenge to the cosmos and to question everything that is given before our eyes. We are not ethereal beings, pure spirits; we are not equal to the angels of Scholasticism (pure forms, limpid intelligibility entirely detached from any connection with matter). The human being can never become a pure form of "non-appearance." Contradiction must be intrinsic to that kind of being whose deepest nature resides in its (at least theoretically) unrestrained power to challenge the world. We must have the right to possess a history, but history is inevitably mundane, as it is subject to change (the basis of growth, worsening, and improvement). To make the world less worldly implies to vindicate the autonomy of history as a "non-world" which is nonetheless part of the world. In such a "non-world," in such a new world, novelty is possible and there is true future, which cannot be predicted from the inexorable concatenation of the preceding elements.

We must not look after being. We must not look after the world. We must challenge both of them. Our care of the world can only be understood in terms of our necessity to have a world which we can challenge in order to grow as humanity. It seems trivial to state that there would be no humanity without the world, but if we analyze this truth in a deeper sense, we can realize that our worldliness ultimately offers the possibility for our growth as humanity, since we have the capacity for challenging all we judge as irrevocable and therefore unfair. Our duty is not to look after a world whose sole goal lies in the reiteration of its ineluctable patterns: we must challenge it in order to show its latent possibilities.

THE QUEST FOR THE PUREST INTUITION OF LOVE, BEAUTY, AND WISDOM

Humanity constitutes the pinnacle of the creative powers of life. We represent the fruit of an arduous process, of an almost indefatigable struggle to expand the energies of life and autonomy against all those potencies which challenge them, against the impulse towards inertia, death, and absence of self-regulated activity. Our duty lies in broadening, even more, the horizons of life. We must display, with greater intensity, the possibilities of being: we must achieve the kingdom of the spirit. Among the different orientations that evolution could take, one of them has led to increasing degrees of complexity, and it has eventually enlightened the flame of consciousness. We do not know the goal of this movement. We do not know its ultimate destination. We do not know its deepest underlying reason. However, we do know that we can maximize the possibilities that nature, turned into conscious life, has granted us. Even if we are the product of chance, this fortuitous condition should not be interpreted as a rubric of tragedy but as a sign of gift, surprise, and wonder. We incarnate the fascinating evidence that there is room for the highest level of creativity in the order of nature.

The human being has to contradict the sameness of the world until he finds a truly free world, his "own world." The sameness of the world does not constitute a pure form of unity. It can be captured by concepts. Our mind seeks a deeper unity, a unity which no idea or image could ever grasp. Only the unity that carried the fountain of its "non-appearance" might be regarded as pure and free. A non-objective unity which is nonetheless present in the world only flourishes as love, beauty, and wisdom. We can always love more, know more, and long for more beauty. Any power, any concept, any desire recall these ultimate realities.

Nevertheless, love, beauty, and wisdom are not the beginning but the end of a mental itinerary which involves both intellect and will. Consciousness challenges the world and "destroys" it in its unity. The world, instead of appearing as a merely unitary phenomenon, conceals a vast multiplicity. The loss of its primeval unity, of its simple "sameness," after the advent of consciousness opens room for the quest of a true unity: that which defies conceptualization, because it points to the primordial intuition, to being in its purity. However, this true unity stands at the end of the dynamism of world and history. World and history should not evolve from unity into a combination of unity and plurality but from unity as sameness into pure unity (through the activity of consciousness, that eagerly looks for that pure unity which cannot be experienced in the world). Love, beauty, and wisdom represent pure intuitions which contain the seed of their infinite overcoming.

In order to accomplish the goal of achieving the purest possible idea of love, wisdom, and beauty, we must challenge the multiplicity experienced by our senses. The apparent dependence of these realities upon world and history needs to be questioned. We have to reach that which is unconditioned but is also susceptible to appear in the territories of world and history, even if only as intuition.

Both the individual and humanity have to contradict the world and themselves with the intention of crowning a pure intuition, their "world," their freedom, *stricto sensu*. This can only be obtained if the determinations imposed by the world are defeated by the power of understanding. We must act as subjects beyond the pressures of the "sameness" of the world, of objectivity. However, it consists of a strenuous process which encourages us, both individually and collectively, to reach emancipation from the tyranny of the sameness of the world, as the way to access a world of freedom, a world rescued from itself: a world in which the world does not have to succumb to the rigid canons of necessity but is able to commit itself to contemplation, to "quiescent activity," to that which transcends space and time, in spite of never ceasing to appear within the borders of space and time. We seek the deepest level of our contradiction to the world (the fact that we are physical beings although we challenge the "mere appearance" of the world) as the gate to the purest intuition, to the truest freedom: to love, beauty, and wisdom.

In our rebellion against the oppressive shadows of "sameness," we feel exhorted to using all the energy that life has bestowed upon us. We are incapable of unfolding the ultimate reasons that bind us to this world, but we perceive of our power to challenge the world through intellect and will. We aspire to the ultimate and most radical wisdom about the universe, history, and humanity. Only through creativity we can fulfill our highest ambition. Behold the *salvation* of humanity: to challenge the world in order to create, in order to become servants of freedom, purity, and the limpid commitment to an end in itself. We must not be ransomed from any dark condemnation: we must achieve salvation in an unfinished history whose horizon is finiteness. However, this history offers the possibility of committing ourselves to something pure, to that which would be radically aprioristic, to that which nothing could exhaust and no one could possess. Finiteness allows us to create a world. That which is radically *a priori* is ineffable; it is the transcendence of any given transcendence; it is the free and unconditioned unity, which fuses both intellect and will. We create the world and the world creates us. To create is to commit oneself to something beyond ourselves. It is purity; it is novelty; it is gift. Through creation, we cease to be a mere extension of the world. We are no longer a form of sameness. We breathe the fervor of life, contemplation, and fascination for the opportunity that we enjoy to stand before the world and against the world. We therefore feel ourselves as the avant-garde of being, as the rubric of surprise, as the possibility of continuously challenging reality. Thus, we can conceive of the human being as *capax sapientiae, capax pulchritudinis, capax amoris*.

That which is absolutely immediate, the pure *a priori*, the unconditionally "other" with respect to everything that is given; Rudolf Otto's "totally-other," the ultimate reality which cannot be projected onto another realm; the limpid; the "holy"; that which is not susceptible to any conceptualization; that which cannot be felt, exhales the breeze of freedom. We can never capture it, but we are able to appreciate it in specific works, in concrete instantiations in time and space. However, it never becomes exhausted by any operation of will and understanding. It is being, the eternal spring, *novum*, that which nothing and no one possesses: it is commitment, creation, the longing for more; the *ulterior* nonetheless rooted in world and history, whose feet walk upon the fragile hills and the feeble pastures of the Earth and fly through the volatile skies that cover the space of the real and the imaginable.

Because love, beauty, and wisdom are never constrained to any entity but become "evaporated" at any attempt at grasping them, they presage the ineffable, radical, and unconditional limpidness. They are expressions of being, which challenges any form of "having." The triad of love, beauty, and wisdom recalls division, irreducible fragmentation of the ultimate reality. We know that love, beauty, and wisdom actually converge into an unknown form of being, but our reason is not prepared to regard them as pure unity.

The trinity of love, beauty, and wisdom is reminiscent of the Scholastic triumvirate of *bonum-pulchrum-verum*, but endowed with freedom. Love is not only the good which we seek in fulfillment of moral law but the free and generous commitment to something that may transcend our own beings. Beauty transcends the medieval *pulchrum*, in whose magnificence the splendor of the Creator shines: it is that which cannot be grasped, the rubric of the subsistence of an inscrutable foundation, whose power of evocation cannot be exhausted. Wisdom is no longer understood only as *verum*, as the possession of a truth that stands as *adaequatio rei et intellectus* and forces the intellect to surrender to that which is given. Rather, it is regarded as the internalization of truth, as the service to a purity that overwhelms us, as the conversion of any sign of truth into a rubric of freedom, in order to foster life and broaden the frontiers of being. The truth of the world is the fierce necessity of life, the inexorable laws that govern the vastness of the universe, the smallness of the individual and the impossibility of founding reason upon itself. Wisdom, on the contrary, is the perception of our legitimacy to challenge the world and to expand the limits of truth. Wisdom appears as the disposal of our own lives with regard to a future that defies "that which is given."

The convergence of love, beauty, and wisdom cannot be explained: it is subject to intuition. It has to be contemplated. It needs to be shown. In the world, it is hardly possible to combine the amorous with the wise, and the wise with the beautiful, but we are called to feel and discover that these three ungraspable ideals obey a primeval *power*, a synthesis of activity and contemplation. We can love whatever is beautiful, and it can grant us the sublime light of wisdom, but beauty frequently differs from love.

Beauty must be contemplated. Through love, we have to commit ourselves. In wisdom, we can understand ourselves. Beauty and love recall the power of sentiment, whereas wisdom represents the elevation of rationality, science, and thought. The highest goal, the noblest and most splendorous challenge to the world, consists of turning contemplation into devout commitment and pious understanding. The integrity of love, beauty, and wisdom can only be achieved through the fusion of the three of them. However, this ideal cannot be accomplished. Beauty, love, and wisdom, the highest expressions of our challenge to the sameness of the world, can never condescend to the objectivity of the world.

Beauty will be sought first through nature. We will seek to imitate the fervent beauty of the natural world. This longing for *mimesis*, motivated by the feeling of overwhelmingness before the beauty of the forests, the mountains, the oceans, and the most various landscapes of the earth; the admiration for the beauty of the immensity of the skies: they will all become a source of inspiration for our quest of beauty. Nature will be regarded as our true home. The human genius will tremble before the creativity of nature, which has enlightened, by virtue of apodictic laws and causes that are perhaps unknowable, wonders that weaken any sentiment of complacency for the achievements of mankind.

Nevertheless, the beauty of nature will be regarded as an empty reality. The glorious cascade of harmony, strength, and polychromy that flows through its egregious channels will be an object of admiration, but we shall realize that this current of creativity is blind. Beauty is not the goal of nature. The evoking density of its beauty is the result of a process whose sole objective resides in supporting and reaffirming the sameness of the world. The expansion of the creative energies of matter does not seek the pure and unconditioned dimension.[23] We long for that which does not

---

23. Some theological trends have advocated for a "naturalistic" representation of

obey a concatenation of means. We want that which does not serve the mere perpetuation of life, the simple appearance of the world. The beauty of nature has to be examined through the demanding filter of the human *ego*. Consciousness must become the judge of beauty, for we seek a new universe, a universe of such depth, intensity, purity, and transcendence that it inevitably overwhelms the scope of the beauty of nature. Therefore, we shall look for a *wise beauty*, for a beauty that may shine as wisdom. The beauty of nature is silent, but we need a wise beauty, a beauty that may lead our life, a beauty that can teach us to stand as owners of the energy that palpitates in our hearts, in order to use it for the goal of an integral creation, whose destiny may be that of improving the existence of humanity and revealing the inexhaustible truth of world and life.

The wise beauty is the will to create an aesthetic realm that may fulfill our longing for growth. This beauty must help us overcome the present frontiers of humanity. It must be a source of youth. A wise beauty understands that nature is governed by the primacy of strength over love, by a cryptic conjunction of chance and necessity. The fittest survive, the weakest perish. Wise beauty dreams of a world in which beauty may be sought as a free goal that serves nothing else. The cosmos, as seductive as it may seem for the longings of our senses, is slave to necessity. There is no true freedom, no pure creation, and no abnegated commitment to an end in itself. The spirit as radical *a priori*, as "wholly-other" with respect

---

God. An example of this attitude can be found in the writings of Gordon Kaufman (1925–2011), especially in his book *In Face of Mystery*. God should be regarded, according to him, as the "creativity of nature." The power of nature to create forms of admirable beauty and sophistication is undoubtedly overwhelming. It inspires deep mysticism. However, if the theological discourse wants to be meaningful for our time, it cannot avoid the "historical dimension." History (humanity) is part of nature, but it demands a different kind of understanding. The extraordinary creativity of nature, such an outstanding display of energy and beauty which charms our imagination and fascinates our reason, has no goal other than "strengthening" the world in its sameness. The laws of matter are inexorable. The light of real *novum* cannot be perceived. Cosmos and nature only seek to "persevere in their being" (to recall Spinoza's famous philosophical statement). No free *telos* can be contemplated. The dynamism of nature reaffirms the world: it does not deny the world. No love stems from nature. Human consciousness therefore rebels against the sameness of the world, against its universal reiteration, against its cycle of causes and effects. Human consciousness longs for freedom, newness, and true creation capable of breaking with the past. This is probably the reason why no theology and philosophy can ever feel satisfied with the mystifying contemplation of nature. The search for words, the longing for understanding and newness, the quest of free love, beauty, and wisdom (not as the collateral processes of the irrevocable laws of matter): this will is too onerous a burden to subsume it into the silence of nature.

to the sameness of the world, does not shine. Wise beauty must open itself to love. It needs to experience the deepest metamorphosis into a wise and amorous beauty, into a beautiful and tender wisdom, into a wise and beautiful love. Thus, beauty would be contemplated as a reality that transcends its aesthetic dimension: beauty as a form of wisdom, and love as the goal of the enrichment of consciousness through the powers of understanding and sentiment. This creative beauty is no longer a projection of an *ego* in search of fulfilling its indomitable desires through the contemplation of natural beauty. Rather, it precedes any form of aesthetics and any concept: it is fathomless purity; it is *being*; it is that which never becomes exhausted within any "structure," for it never appears. However, it is also part of the world: it is the rubric of the beauty of contradiction. It is ineffable. It shines as pure freedom. It consists of an unlimited power of evocation. It is being as possibility. It is the free power committed to creation.

The spirit, that which is pure, that which cannot be exhausted, cannot appear in the world: it must be *conquered* through creation. The spirit permanently challenges any form of appearance: it is freshness, life free from the rigid canons of necessity. In art, we seek this purity as beauty. In science and thought, we try to create it as wisdom. In history, we look for it under the manifestation of love. But love ineluctably vanishes from history. Pure beauty abandons any work of art. Wisdom, the most intense depth of the spirit, has never been expressed in the vulnerability of words. Love, beauty, and wisdom must be regarded as the ultimate goal, as the ungraspable treasure of our human odyssey. We know that we can never achieve their profoundest nature. We can never contemplate pure beauty, love, and wisdom. However, this conscience of impossibility is the rubric of our deepest possibility: that of standing as a perpetual challenge to everything that is given; that of incarnating a spirit that can be subject to constant rejuvenation, improvement, and learning. The growth of mankind, its most radical possibility, would not be feasible if history obeyed a prefixed paradigm. History needs to be regarded as the scenario in which we can advance not only in the realm of the material forces that transform the world but also in the sphere of thought, in the intensity with which we may perceive of beauty, love, and wisdom. If this growth followed a linear pattern, if any vestige of rupture had disappeared, if history were free from the shadows of contradiction, humanity would become deprived of its liberty. Humanity must be capable of creating its own world at any given moment. It must be able to turn back to the past in order to interpret it. The meaning of history has to dwell in each age and ultimately in each individual, in each opportunity of contemplating the past and of turning it into a meaningful reality for our present time; in each possibility of acting in the *hic et nunc* and in every occasion of envisioning a future that has not been given to us.

5

Freedom beyond Itself: Solidarity

SOLIDARITY AS SYNTHESIS OF ETHICS AND POLITICS

THERE IS A COMMON enterprise in which every consciousness must participate: that of challenging the world in order to create our own world. The evasion from this commitment to contradicting the world, which emanates from an inner vocation, would turn us into mere parts of the world, into simple extensions of that which is given. We would stand as gears inside the vast machinery of the world, and we would lose our historical condition. No true future could be contemplated.

The horizon of this common task is the basis of human *solidarity*. We are all twinned by the insurmountable contradiction that we represent. In order to accomplish our goal of challenging the world, we need to question the world together. The challenge posed by mankind will always be greater than that of an isolated individual. If the edification of history as an alternative space to the deaf sameness of the world constitutes the primordial sign of our defying the world, and if history is never the work of a single individual, the human task must be the endeavor of the whole of mankind. There is an inescapable duty for humanity: to propitiate that every individual may become a true challenge to the world. The task of critically questioning the world cannot be the privilege of a few: behold the seminal principle of any form of social justice. The power of certain individuals over others needs to be minimized in order to foster the power of humanity over itself.

Humanity cannot suffocate the energy of the individual. Neither can it eclipse the latent powers of the world. Rather, it must extend all of them, and it must seek to engage them in the edification of a scenario in which an unceasingly open and free future may turn possible. The individual must be capable of challenging humanity, for this challenge will rubricate freedom and creativity. But the individual must feel encouraged to challenging the world with others. Thus, the resulting challenge will exceed by far the power of the individual to question the world. The challenge that we pose on account of the deepest contradiction which we incarnate is not unilaterally focused on the world: it affects any form of "sameness," be it that of the world or that of humanity. We need to challenge everything that "merely stands," everything that seems unsuitable for critical questioning, everything whose sole goal is itself. There can be no peace in the world. True peace could only blossom if it were possible to challenge, in a free and radical way, any eventual sameness. Our peace consists of our irrepressible rebellion against any absolute (world, humanity) that blinds our eyes before the beauty of novelty.

Consciousness, by creating its own world, becomes free. Freedom represents an ethical experience, for its goal is the growth of the subject. This is the reason why freedom can "freely" submit to a limit, as it preserves its "autonomy," instead of succumbing to the temptation of turning itself into an absolute, unquestionable reality. The ethical experience of freedom can be understood as solidarity. Freedom as ethics recalls responsibility, the need to maintain liberty and to make it coextensive with the liberty of others. This free submission of freedom to an ethical order stems from its dignity, power, and scope. This submission would be the product of coercion if it simply obeyed the demands of the community as the prerequisite for a social experience of freedom. Ethics primarily refers to the free subordination of liberty to the order established by consciousness: freedom, eager for creation, in its longing for exercising its deepest power, feels the commitment to edifying a new world. This commitment can be regarded as self-alienation, but unlike the Hegelian *Entfremdung* it is free activity that is not governed by the inexorable laws ruling over the display of the idea: consciousness freely commits itself to fostering the horizons of life and thought.

Freedom runs the risk to become a new form of sameness if it does not abandon itself. It needs to be opened to solidarity, so that the ethical experience may become *political existence*. This way of reasoning is not intended to suggest that the individual is constituted first as an ethical being and later transformed into a "political animal," into a social being. There is no "after" that should be interpreted chronologically, as if the subject living in the state of nature of classical political theory actually existed. The individual does not appear *in statu naturae* before signing a social contract. This discourse can only be taken symbolically, as a sharp philosophical metaphor that accounts for the implications of social life for every individual. "Historically" speaking (if we refer to history in a broad sense, including those stages of prehistory in which consciousness, in its strongest meaning as self-consciousness, had already appeared), the available evidence points to the fact that every individual has been born inside a certain political community, as primitive as it may appear to the eyes of the modern idea of state (and even to the concept of "civilization" which follows the Neolithic revolution). The political dimension is the social experience of freedom. It is true that probably no single individual has been capable of freely submitting himself or herself to a political community. Necessity, inertia, the imperative of survival, or the impositions of violence (conquest, migrations...) have almost universally determined the membership of an individual in a certain society. However, by "free commitment" of the individual we mean the way in which the free subject, that is to say, consciousness capable of disposing of its own power, must face the edification of a world that may transcend its own freedom.

Solidarity can be contemplated as the synthesis of ethics and politics: ethics becomes politics because freedom can be socially lived; politics is internalized as ethics because the individual acquires consciousness of his vocation to broadening the horizons of humanity. The freedom of the individual is no longer secluded in its own and suffocating sameness. Rather, it becomes opened to the collective experience of solidarity: it turns into solidary freedom.

When this longing for participating in the spirit of solidarity takes place freely, instead of stemming from blind obedience to an external imposition, to coaction, whose sole weapon is fear, not persuasion, freedom has dignified its own power, for it has committed itself, possessed by abnegation and detachment, to the edification of something that may transcend itself. Freedom does not seek a reward in its commitment to solidarity. Its sacrifice is generous, and its goal is creation. Such a commitment is discovered as an end in itself, as a presage of the unconditioned, of that whose worth is founded upon nothing but itself. The individual needs to drink from the fountains of humanity in order to find the inspiration for which we are all eagerly looking. Opening ourselves to the uniqueness of each face; admiring the revelation of creativity encouraged by the vast and beautiful diversity of cultures, philosophies, and religions that have enriched human history with their deepest ideas and works; understanding the teachings (even if provisional) of science about the structure and functioning of the universe. . ..: by all these means, the possibility of *novum* does not die. No potential source of inspiration should be rejected. Rather, what we must do is to cultivate any flower that offers even the slightest signs of love, beauty, and wisdom in the garden of those who wish to create.

The historical task of Europe resides in offering the world a paradigm capable of summarizing its troubled history into a series of ideals suitable for enhancing the fraternity of peoples and cultures. Europe is in debt to the world, after centuries of exploitation and soulless invasions, and its way of reconciliation and redeeming itself from its past mistakes resides in the extension of its social model, of a solidarity lived in freedom which can aspire to become a solidarity of the spirit, whose goal is not only to change the economic and social conditions, but to expand a human ideal: the primacy of art, science, and love in interpersonal relations, leaving room for individual freedom, in such a way that anyone can manifest his own ideals, even if they are contrary to the utopia of solidarity, by virtue of the perennial validity of the principle of toleration towards disagreeing opinions. The Europe of ethics is the Europe of solidarity, in which the perspective of the ends prevails over that of the means, and morality precedes efficiency.

Europe is in urgent need of a solidarity of the spirit, which positively affirms that our deepest and purest goals, our "salvation," our dreams of love, beauty, and wisdom, are not to be found outside the world, in those infinite skies whose sole contemplation threatens our mind because of our smallness before such a huge universe, nor in the ephemeral delectation with our non-satiable wish for material accumulation, but in humanity itself: in sincere dialogue, in art, in science, and in whatever can constitute an end in itself, instead of a means for an unknown goal. The end is humanity, and all that contributes to its growth, that is, all that broadens our being, is already "spirit," it is already humanity, it is the transcendence of the individual through his commitment to a profounder aim, so that singularity may be ennobled, exalted to a more sublime summit. The discovery that individual freedom grows if it is transcended as solidarity is a core teaching of contemporary European history. The achievements of our social model, the conquests of our welfare state, the beauty of European solidarity (which overcomes any apprehension motivated by the current economic crisis)...: they all point to the primacy of a solidary freedom, of a freedom committed to creating a project that may embrace the freedom of others. This is the philosophical destiny of Europe.

SOLIDARITY AND THE PASSION FOR HISTORY

The creative genius of mankind shone with unique intensity when Denis Diderot coined (in the peak of the Enlightenment, when the true possibilities of reason, both profitable and destructive, came to light) this neologism, *solidarité*, inspired by the Latin term *solidus*, "solid," not in the sense of an inert object, in which life is absent and all is death, but of a compact union of diversity, in such a way that everything may contribute to everything, and the individual may become exalted by its integration into the collective, finding a degree of stability and strength higher than if it were left to indigent solitude.

Jean Beaufret asked Heidegger: "comment redonner un sens au mot 'humanisme,'" "how to find a meaning again for the term 'humanism,'" immediately after the end of the Second World War. Heidegger replied in his celebrated *Letter on Humanism* (1947). Today, we must pose a similar question regarding the concept of solidarity (which was coined in the closing stages of the Enlightenment, when the true possibilities of reason, both profitable and destructive, came to light) and its philosophical and political translation.

Solidarity precedes Marx and goes beyond him, but it cannot ignore the thought of this great German thinker, and moreover, it cannot forget his ideal of a convergence between possibility and necessity ("from each one according to his possibilities and to each one according to his needs," as it is expressed in the *Critique of the Gotha Program*), for which it is essential to propose, in an intrepid way, the principle of solidarity between all human beings as the ruling norm of social organization.

The greatness of Marx resides, negatively, in having granted a privileged role to the historicity of human relations in philosophical reflection, and, positively, in having conceived of an ideal of reconciliation, after highlighting that although a heart-breaking void remains in history, we do not have to tolerate it as an insuperable fact, for even though it is true that an "estrangement," an "alienation" subsists, it is also certain that we imperiously look for our appropriation of the historical happening

Freedom beyond Itself: Solidarity

itself. However, it is important to realize that this estrangement cannot be solved: a full human appropriation of the different events will never take place, since it would suspend history. We must learn, just as Pushkin, to suffer, perhaps in an unlimited way: "But, O my friends, I do not wish to die, I want to live—to think and suffer."[1]

Thanks to Marx, Western philosophy has become aware of the imperative of uniting theoretical reflection with *praxis*, encouraged by the painful shadow of negativity that invades history, which is far away from having shown its full potential regarding the improvement of human life: we must own history, so that it may illuminate our thought. This is the meaning of the eleventh thesis on Feuerbach: "philosophers have hitherto only interpreted the world in various ways; the point is to change it [Die Philosophen haben die Welt nur verschieden interpretiert; es kommt aber darauf an, sie zu verändern]."[2] Thought cannot be deprived of the power to transform the world, to assume the weight of history. We must implement the perspective of an open future, against the thesis of an "end of history" (Kojève, Fukuyama), which reproduce the patterns of the eschatological imagination. The quest for solidarity has to legitimize the attitude of a permanent critique, even though accompanied by the commitment to an effective realization of the ideal of solidarity. This is the only way to preserve the power of dialectics to overcoming the difficulties that will inevitably burst into history.

There is no absolute spirit, beyond the opening itself of history, which consists of the broadening of being, that is neither negative nor positive, neither detrimental nor fruitful for humanity, but it is neutral and blind. Our task resides in taking ownership of history, in building a meaningful history for all the members of the one human family through solidarity. We must find in the indefatigable display of the energies of life signs of permanence and purity, rubrics of love, beauty, and wisdom.

Courage towards history: this is solidarity, whose end transcends the purely social and economic sphere, because the "solidarity of the spirit" seeks to foster the emancipation of reason and the longing for love, beauty, and wisdom, so that we can think for its own sake and we can look for pure goals, as the pre-eminent sign of freedom, and solidarity aspires to freedom for all . . . Life: this is the aim of solidarity. Thinking is our "destiny," but a fate that is an open, free, and insatiable *telos*: that which the future grants us. We have come to this world and to this history in order

---

1. Pushkin, *Elegy* of 1830.
2. Cf. Tucker, ed., *The Marx-Engels Reader*.

to think, and thinking is the solution to the enigma of our presence in this vast world and the mystery of the incisive course of this inscrutable history. Thinking is the epiphanic goal of solidarity.

Solidarity is a form of compassion, as it manifests the will to suffer with those who suffer and to rejoice with those who rejoice, by participating in the sentiments of others and generating emotions whose reference is not only the intimacy of the individual subject but also our feelings as humanity. Compassion would cease to be authentic if it became the veiled expression of the conscience of superiority, of the hypocritical benevolence that, behind the pretension of clemency, is actually humiliating for those who stand below. Instead of suppressing the individual dreams, the project of solidarity is capable of offering a new frame and a greater space in which to propagate all our latent energy that needs to be liberated. Hope is the intangibility of the ideal of solidarity, its openness to an inexhaustible future, which is always there, and cannot be reduced to any specific time and any specific project. Solidarity combines, in a beautiful mixture, the tangible and the intangible, reality and utopia, the finite and the infinite, by creating a new language.

Diogenes the Cynic anxiously looked for a man, while running along the streets of Athens with a candle lighted at day, and we are told that he did not find what he was seeking; but we should not be surprised at this, for we do not know the deepest nature of human beings. Probably, we shall never achieve a satisfactory answer to this question. However, this evidence must not inspire sadness: the human being is a perennial mystery, because our most intimate truth cannot be elucidated outside history, and while there is history (and we have powerful reasons to believe that history will never reach any culmination), the human being will still be an unanswered question. Dilthey was prophetically insightful when he claimed that only from the end of history could we project our imagination back to the past, in order to understand the meaning of each particular event and history as a whole. Only a consummated future would shed light on the meaning of the present. Let us convince ourselves that the end of history perhaps will never come, so that we will never be capable of looking back to the past to obtain a global perspective on the course of history, by knowing the dénouement, the "closing" of its arcane process. Let us admire the sublime prodigy that every stage of history unveils something new about humanity, so that the words that we are now pronouncing will not be the final verbs, but our children, and their children as well, will have something to say, and no one will have exhausted any possible discourse. Let us venerate the treasure of an unclosed history.

Solidarity cannot exist without respecting the intrinsic value of history. On account of this, solidarity cannot become a non-temporal truth that avoids its confrontation with the changing reality of times. Solidarity is shaped within history, and we think of solidarity by paying attention to the needs and dreams of humanity in history. Solidarity also dies in history, when it forgets that it cannot "finitize" history, extinguishing the flame of the course of chronology by creating a non-historical arcadia in which the passing of times is interrupted, as in a sudden twilight. The passage of times is ineluctable, and it is the incontrovertible truth against which it is useless to rebel: there can be no perfect society, if by "perfect" we understand a project that should take place regardless of all historical conditions. Solidarity seeks to offer an ideal, but of historical nature, which is susceptible to a temporal realization because it becomes the principle of intelligibility of history itself: by creating a more just and mutually binding world we manage to understand history. On the contrary, inaction against injustice darkens the centuries, our longing for the future withers, and the content of both our individual and collective life becomes emptied. For solidarity, the ethical maxim that the human being should always be considered as an end, never as a means, must determine history, instead of the blindness of the historical events eclipsing the ethical ideal.

It is difficult to grasp the essence of justice. Amartya Sen has remarked[3] that rather than reaching a theoretical consensus on the transcendental nature of justice, we must offer an interpretation of this concept that may generate comparative judgments on "degrees of justice." There is much truth in this insight, and the search for a final characterization of justice probably needs to be abandoned. However, any assessment of that kind bears an implicit idea of justice. It is impossible for us to bury the shadow of definition, even if it is tacit. Our challenge lies in leaving room for different theories of justice, while at the same time committing ourselves to the *growth* of our conscience of justice. This goal will be easier if we assume the perspective of a perennially open history, whose essence points, precisely, to its indeclinable state of incompleteness.

Justice cannot be separated from the realities that every age may be ready to accept as just. It is convenient, in any case, to postulate a hope: that no single period will go back in the understanding of "the just" (although historical evidence continuously refutes this noble expectation),

---

3. Cf. Sen, *The Idea of Justice*.

but that true growth in our conscience of justice will occur so that our idea of justice will satisfy the inherent potentialities of the human beings, which will inexorably increase over the course of times. Our idea of justice is much more demanding than it was for the classical world of Greece and Rome. We cannot accept slavery, because we have developed a notion of the human being that recognizes a series of capacities in all the members of our species, and it attributes inalienable rights to individuals. And this process will go on *in crescendo* as we acquire a more developed idea of humanity and nature in general. Many things that are nowadays contemplated as just will undoubtedly scandalize the future generations. Let us trust that no single step backwards concerning the rights that we have arduously conquered will be made, and that the social discernment on justice and injustice will be always attached to the lucid realization of the potential of humanity in any given moment. Only if the human possibilities had been exhausted we would have reached a final understanding of justice, and we have strong reasons to think that this will never happen.

Solidarity, although the result of a material reflection on history, seeks to discover something intangible, something "spiritual" in history; not a sphere that is completely alien to the course of times but the beauty of history itself as it is susceptible to satisfying the demands of the human mind, uniting any apparent divergence in a common horizon. The spirit is the link that communicates the different parts, and the solidarity of the spirit pretends to humanize history, not only in its material dimension but also in its "spiritual" aspect, which cannot be reduced to the tyrannical domain of quantity, because it penetrates the deepest realm of our intellect and our sensibility. It does not aim to realize the ideal of solidarity only in the effectiveness of social and economic structures: it wants this ideal to become our window into history, our way of being, our greatest wealth, a source of hope before the ill-fated silence of time and space.

Solidarity is not built objectively alone: it has to be, above all, internalized by each individual as a robust conviction, as enlightening ethics. The transformation of history is not enough: thought has to be "redeemed" from the vacuous vice of selfishness, and if this cannot be achieved, that is to say, if by means of art, science, philosophy, and love, by means of reason and sentiment, solidarity does not stand as the deepest fountain for inspiring our thought, we will hardly build up the ideal of collective solidarity. The simple acceptance of the current state of thought, the submission to the hypothesis that the human being is in need of no "liberation" at all, of no rescue, of no earthly apperception of that which

Freedom beyond Itself: Solidarity

religions call "salvation," would mercilessly condemn history to the acrimonious sorrow of the murkiest apathy, surrendering to the past and to the present and darkening any possible future, by substituting it with gloomy determinism. Solidarity must believe in an unredeemed history, and it must display the possibilities of humanity in the openness of history by conceiving of an undefined, infinite "salvation" for humanity that is never completely actualized.

Solidarity thinks of a world whose goal may be humanity: a humanized history that is not left to the arbitrariness of blind forces, and about which reason has something to say, although not through a final verb but by declaiming a word which may inaugurate a new discourse. Solidarity must not fear history, as it constitutes an attempt to historicize humanity and to humanize history: to historicize humanity means to show that there is nothing absolute, nothing alien to the power of change that stems from the human will to edify something better, for there is always "more" in history; to humanize history involves the creation of a new language in which all human beings, not only some of them, may foster the flourishing of their fullest potential, by finding in communication, art, science, and love goals which serve no further goal.

What should we choose: freedom or equality? Solidarity nowadays cannot ignore any of the terms, and it must try to overcome them in the ideal of fraternity/sorority, asking humanity for commitment, responsibility, and sacrifice to renounce some freedom if by doing so we gain equality, and to renounce some equality if by doing so we grow in freedom. The question will concern the limit, that is to say, how much freedom and how much equality we are to collectivize so that the individual, in his singularity, can reach true freedom and authentic equality at the same time. Maybe by bestowing upon the category of "end in itself" the priority that it deserves we will find a solution to this problematic integration. Let us lose some freedom if we acquire more equality, but let us take refuge in art, knowledge, and love, in which we will be infinitely free; let us tolerate some inequality, if it may be redeemed by the contribution to the collective good according to the possibilities of every person, and let us enter the dwelling of beauty, wisdom, and love, for something that can possess us all will equate us all, as it transcends us, not because of introducing us into non-existent worlds but because it eludes the unilateral control of the individual, defeating the rigidities of any human power.

Solidarity is the humanization of power, the dream a power that can expand the vital energies of all individuals, a power that can lead us to ends and not to infinitely concatenated means that lead to no goal at all. Solidarity longs for a power that unites and does not separate, for a power that comforts and does not embitter.

The solidarity of the spirit is also the quest for a freedom that dares to transcend itself, to liberate itself from its own "narrowness," as it is open to "create," to inaugurate the *novum* in history, to enlarge the horizons of thought and life. It is a solidarity in which the intangible prevails, and in which the analysis of society is not limited to the examination of class dynamics, but it also attempts to understand the irreducible sphere of individuality, the mystery of the singular face, the enigma that personal wishes do not necessarily converge with a general will.

Perhaps there is no general will at all, but there is a common aim for establishing the conditions of possibility so that everyone can have a legitimate interest which does not harm the inclinations of others. Solidarity is therefore the attempt to assimilate that which is alien to that which is owned; it is the radiant concourse of otherness, which expands the horizon of the individual by "increasing" the scope of his subjectivity, and at the same time, by opening him to others by means of understanding (intangible, spiritual aspect) and of the sharing of goods (tangible, material aspect).

The "group in fusion" of Sartre's *Critique of Dialectical Reason* must be integrated by truly free men and women, and "truly" is not an arbitrary imposition that violates freedom itself. Rather, it means "susceptible to harmony," to being inserted into a greater horizon, into a broader context of intellection, in which the individual is not regarded as an atomized reality but as a being that is eager for communication and in need of others. Solidarity is the conscience of our fragility, of our state of orphanhood. It also consists of the awareness of our strength once we become united as humanity, which is, after all, a path towards liberty. As Rousseau remarked in *The Social Contract*, the individual, "in *giving* himself to *all*, gives himself to nobody."

Solidarity has a redeeming aspiration: it wants to save humanity; not by means of a supra-historical liberation but through a historical emancipation. Solidarity is faith in history, faith in life. Solidarity is love of history, and it is therefore the aim to save history, turning it into a scenario which is perennially open to new horizons, to new possibilities, to a "more" that does not encapsulate the "human" in peremptory structures but rather exhorts us to feel the exuberance of time and life, the impenetrable wonder of the instant, the pious beauty of change and the unbeatable movement of the centuries.

Solidarity is hope in future, because there will always be a future, at least while the time of humanity lasts, this is, the finite limit that a mysterious power has granted us to live in this vast and esoteric universe. We must "live deliberately," as Henry David Thoreau proclaimed,[4] being fully humane, and extending the radius of action of our spirit to its highest pinnacle: our capacity for communication, for science, for art. Solidarity is eminently mystic, if by "mystic" we refer to something that may find a deeper meaning even in the midst of evidence. Mysticism revives the light of the ineffable, and the ineffable is the future, for we do not know why we have come to this world and why there is a future. This is mysticism: it is a beautiful and learned lack of understanding, *ducat ignorantia*, which liberates us from the gelid chains of oppressive intellection. Solidarity does not pretend to exhaust the mystery of history but to humanize it.

Solidarity of the spirit understands that the problems of humanity transcend the abolition of social injustices: humanity is an endemic problem in itself, because it constitutes the patent expression of dissatisfaction, of irresolution, of the paradoxical orientation towards that which is insatiable, to a future that is always open, whose energies necessarily remain indomitable. Injustice transcends the specifically material dimension: there is no perfect society because there is no perfect humanity, fully reconciled, in whose kingdom the pure and ultimate may settle down. On the contrary, humanity is history, temporality, finiteness, and this is its great treasure, our perennial source of optimism and hope. In this way, solidarity of the spirit does not pretend to become an irrefutable truth but an instrument to set the conditions of possibility for all members of the human family to freely display their vital energies, to cultivate art and knowledge, love and passion, but within a frame of indefectible finiteness, which is the pious humility that time stoically imposes upon us.

---

4. "I went to the woods because I wished to live deliberately, to front only the essential facts of life, and see if I could not learn what it had to teach, and not, when I came to die, discover that I had not lived. I did not wish to live what was not life, living is so dear; nor did I wish to practise resignation, unless it was quite necessary. I wanted to live deep and suck out all the marrow of life, to live so sturdily and Spartan-like as to put to rout all that was not life, to cut a broad swath and shave close, to drive life into a corner, and reduce it to its lowest terms, and, if it proved to be mean, why then to get the whole and genuine meanness of it, and publish its meanness to the world; or if it were sublime, to know it by experience, and be able to give a true account of it in my next excursion" (*Walden*, chapter 2).

Part 2: *Fundamentum* in History

The deepest injustice that troubles the human being resides inside every of our souls, in the intangible sphere of our singularity, in looking for something that is unknown without ever reaching it, in our incapacity for knowing how to reach happiness and how to discover purity in the midst of necessity, chance, and power. This is the deepest human problem: our ignorance of why we have come to this colossal universal and what we can expect from our existence on this fertile earth. Let us edify a world in which everyone can freely meditate upon these questions, once the agonic chains of material need have been broken, and let us expand the energies of life through the objectification of a project of solidarity which will enable us all to consecrate our lives to the most sublime goods of the spirit: knowledge, beauty, love, communication, the creation of new worlds, passion, and unlimited fruition.

Solidarity of the spirit does not propose a final ideal of a good life. Rather, it tries to establish the conditions so that every human being may become the agent of his ideal of "good life," by offering wisdom, beauty, and love as the potentially inexhaustible horizons that lie before us. They grant humanity the possibility of finding a meaning for its finite existence, while at the same time they do not generate useless frictions between men and women, for the fact that I know does not deny the freedom of the others, just as my delectation with beauty does not prevent the enjoyment of others.[5]

Solidarity is always idealistic, because it proposes an ideal. History without an ideal becomes enslaved by the physical universe, and it turns into a mere prolongation of biological evolution, of the events which must inflexibly occur in this recondite region of cosmos, over which we possess no control at all. History is only worthy of such a name if it can express a human reality, and reason is human, thought is human, and human is the indestructible will of power over history, the will for humanization, for the subjection of time and space to an ideal which can humanize these arcane concepts. In this sense, solidarity continuously evokes a degree of dissatisfaction with the present and a decorous hope for the future: because solidarity does not believe that history inexorably follows a pre-established path, but it trusts the possibility of improvement, of "more," it does not

---

5. The fact that someone knows more than others may become dangerous only if we conceive of knowledge as a means, not as an end. If knowledge is an end in itself, it is power, but a constructive power, a self-power that participates in a ubiquitous, infinite good: that of wisdom, of which anyone can participate without ever exhausting it. My delectation with beauty does not make the fruition of others impossible and my burning passion does not forbid their wishes.

Freedom beyond Itself: Solidarity

renounce its ideals, in spite of the contradictions of the ages and solidarity itself. Solidarity is possible as long as it retains a "holy utopia" worthy of our fighting, which is the utopia of solidarity.

Solidarity has to proclaim the legitimacy of the Humanities and any kind of hypothetically "useless" knowledge, as a proof of the prevalence of the category of "end in itself" (opposed to the eclipse of reason provoked by the focus being put on its unilaterally instrumental dimension). Science thinks of itself as "aseptic," alien to any valuation that is external to the mechanisms set by its own method. The Humanities, on the contrary, provide us a voice that vividly appeals to us, as they deal with our deepest worries. The Humanities exist for their own sake, because their goal is no other than giving expression to the imperishable longings that have accompanied us for centuries, and to the new ones that will emerge in the future. The Humanities are called to stand as a refuge, even in the fragile consolation of literature and philosophy, for this family to which we belong.

The enigma of history is the act itself of posing the question: we have come into this cosmos to formulate the supreme question, but in order to do so we must reach a genuine independence from the natural conditions, becoming ends and not means, and leaving away the shadow of exploitation of some human beings by others, by turning power into an instrument of collective progress, instead of a tool of traumatic oppression.

Solidarity cannot pretend to exclude randomness from history, for the shadow of unpredictability also hides mysticism, a seed of surprise that encloses the magic of time, the portentous fascination induced by the overwhelmingness of that which we cannot foresee. Solidarity wants this inexorable arbitrariness to become a positive power, a humanizing energy, a firm platform that may allow us to broaden the frontiers of being and the limits of humanity, expanding our "*élan vital*" as much as possible by eliminating any restrictive barrier and leaving all gates unceasingly open.

Michel Foucault spoke, with his characteristic clairvoyance, about the importance of resisting *le chantage* of Enlightenment: the apparent necessity to take a stand in favor or against this eighteenth-century movement (even while acknowledging that it is not possible to examine modern Western philosophy without understanding the meaning of *Les Lumières*). Against this attitude, Foucault proposes[6] a philosophical *ethos* that consists of interpreting the Enlightenment as a permanent disposition for a critique of our historical being. Therefore, Foucault suggests a "negative"

---

6. Cf. Foucault, "Qu'est-ce que c'est les Lumières," in *Philosophie. Anthologie*.

intellection of the Enlightenment, by focusing on its *pars destruens*, and leaving in suspense, at least for the moment, any constructivist pretension. However, it seems legitimate to pose the question regarding the viability of this approach, that is to say, of whether human thought can remain in a state of continuous criticism that does not become a project for the future. Foucault may be right when he says that we should prefer a discourse that obtains real transformations to the bombastic promises of a "new man," but nothing can conceal the human wish for totality, because humanity is still there, and it goes beyond the mere sum of individuals, as problematic as the concept of "humanity" may be. Solidarity can be considered as a "limiting attitude," as the expression of courage, because it is committed to the perspective of totality, not only to the respect for the autonomy of the parts (even though totality is finite). This is the reason why solidarity cannot escape the horizon of finiteness.

The principal difficulty of any historical ontology, as that of Foucault, lies in its attempt at examining, diachronically, how we become subjects of knowledge, ethics, and power (to recall Kant's three famous questions: how we become human beings, after all): they tend to forget that the human mind is unable to elucidate the meaning of the past, nor the effective way in which we have become what we are now. The past will always be subject to controversy (which is a healthy sign of intellectual vitality). We cannot clarify the past: we can unveil the meaning of the present and prepare the meaning of the future. To look for the deepest roots of a certain discourse is a vain, endless, and distressing task. Precious energies are wasted in it. Various and unsolvable disagreements will imprison our mind, but we need to think, to innovate, and to create: we must think of the new. Thus, the relevance of transcendental constructivism still persists. We must orientate our thought towards the future, not to a fathomless and everlastingly confusing past, which will always refuse any attempt of interpretation capable of providing an idea of what we must do right now. Let us look back to the past with respect and interest, but let us not retain our thought in the endless debate about the past. Let us rather open ourselves, just as science, to the future. Let the archetypes of the past not enslave our imagination: let them grant us light and inspiration instead of answers to our present responsibility and our future expectations. History is never repeated at all.

Can humanity renounce the elaboration of a theory that not only looks back into the didactic past, showing its limitations and engaging itself into an inexcusable deconstructionist endeavor, but which also seeks to edify the future, assuming the many risks that this task offers? Aside from genealogy as a goal and archaeology as a method, brilliantly used by authors like Nietzsche and Foucault, why should we not long for a reactivation of constructivist transcendentalism, in spite of the danger involved by partiality? Is it not worth doing, as soon as we keep an open future, which may prevent all of us from the temptation of "closing" history? We can conceive of reality as the asymptotic limit of intersubjectivity, as the ideal situation in which truth would have been elucidated if we had achieved a consensus that "exhausted" all possible interpretations of that which appears before us as real (this is impossible, for every new human being that comes into this world is already novelty, an extension of being, the right for a new hermeneutic). Moreover, isn't nonconformity congenital to our mind, which can never feel satisfied after having "clarified" the past, but always orientates its thought towards the future, in such a way that, because the future does not exist yet, the human mind will be encouraged to build it up? The historical perspective offers the possibility of taking distance from the present, and it helps to relativize the *hic et nunc* of history in light of past experience. This is the reason why the liberating potential of our historicity needs to be used in order to edify a more humane future.

By remaining comfortably installed in an attitude of criticism we might be capitulating to the unfair *status quo*. We need to propose a pluralistic humanism, running the risk of partiality and opening ourselves to the exuberance of evocations that history and cultures emanate, but we have to do something: we have to act, we have to commit ourselves to the improvement of our human condition, because humanity rejects inaction and moreover, injustice. Solidarity of the spirit, which incorporates, as a theoretical basis, a pluralistic, non-dogmatic humanism, participates in all those "micro-political" movements which, inspired by the ideal of solidarity, struggle for the edification of a history in which no one will be a foreigner in the one human home.

SOLIDARITY AND THE CONSCIENCE OF FINITENESS

Solidarity must assimilate the idea of "finiteness" as one of its central categories. We are finite, and so is our history. No single theory can therefore seek to bring the nostalgic infiniteness of mathematical forms to the revealing finiteness of space and time. The greatness of history lies in its finiteness, the root of its subversion, for its subjection to the domain of chronology offers the possibility of appreciating the treasure of time itself, so that, instead of postponing dreams indefinitely, it longs for materializing them in the *hic et nunc* of the ages.

Solidarity is a finite theory about a finite humanity in a finite history, and it will never be able to express a superlative, yet vaporous and ungraspable, infiniteness, which rejects any critical judgment from a finite rationality. We have not been made for the infinite, and the pinnacles to which we aspire need to be found in the realm of finiteness, in which both our immanent transcendence and our transcendent immanence reside: contradiction in its purity, which is reality in itself, that does not claim for a final reconciliation beyond the subsistence of contradiction itself, this is, beyond respect for the legitimacy of a perennially opened history.

Solidarity does not represent a hermeneutical clue capable of expelling the shadow of mystery, as the definitive solution to its untamed enigma, but the enunciation of history itself as a humane and open entity, which must always possess a future. Solidarity is the expression of the vivid longing for an ever-promising future. Solidarity is temporality, but a temporality healed by the power of dreams. Solidarity is the convergence between the temporal and the eternal in the ideal of a fraternal humanity, which leads history in such a way that it can offer a universal future, available for all. Solidarity is deep faith in the reality of humanity, in the truth that humanity does not simply consist of an additive compilation of different persons in different centuries. Rather, it is a spirit, a link, a form of communication which is indeed constituted by individual subjects, but an entity of its own which expands the vital energies of the individuals by offering them a greater ocean to sail and a vaster landscape to contemplate.

Humanity is the act of broadening the horizon of the singular subject in order to bestow upon him a worthier scenario of his elusive individuality (the exceptional mystery represented by the uniqueness of each person, by the fact of being oneself instead of another). Humanity is the affirmation of the individual, and solidarity cannot pretend to underestimate individuality: it must open it to a larger sphere, for we imperiously need, as individuals, a great challenge, something that may captivate us with enthusiasm, taking us beyond ourselves. We cannot talk alone: we want more voices and more glances, more hands to touch and more bodies to hug. We want more, and this will of "more," this "ulteriority" of our spirit, can only be realized in the context of humanity: not in the space of an evasive nature which shares no word with us but in the face of others; and humanity is all faces, it is the astonishing sea that lies before us. Humanity is finite, but it is the most unlimited reality that we have in the realm of

Freedom beyond Itself: Solidarity

finiteness. Solidarity, as the expression of a project for humanity, formulates a courageous will for the individual to grow in his subjectivity, so that he can know himself better and become more aware of his own possibilities. But in order to achieve this goal it is necessary for the individual to look at himself in the mirror of humanity.

We need nowadays a kind of solidarity which is aware of its own finiteness, and which does not seek to be interpreted as an absolute, irrefutable truth, but lucidly understands that its *raison d'être* is that of giving testimony of a very real dream, of a possibility which is not a mere illusion and which can take place in history, in any history and period of history. In this sense, solidarity cannot be subject to a rigorous definition, which would enclose it in very narrow and inelastic margins, disabling it to become shaped and reformed by history itself (which is the origin and the goal of solidarity, since it is the attempt to humanize history). Any definition is a form of limitation, but we look for a type of solidarity that may surpass all the limits of those presumptuous categorizations that seek to stand as infallible and omniscient dogmas.

Solidarity is neither in favor of nor against religion, which belongs to the intimacy of the individual person, whose deepest meaning cannot be explained by any social system, as it is related with the perception of our impotence, of our finiteness, of our fragility, which can generate attitudes as divergent, but after all as similar, as fear and enthusiasm before that which remains unknown. Wittgenstein noticed that religious language is, by its own nature, incommensurable with the language of reason.[7] Religions tend to offer a hope in the afterlife, and let it be welcome for whoever wants to believe in it. The concern of solidarity has to be history, not a hypothetical meta-history; solidarity must be focused on finiteness, not on infiniteness, which would paralyze any passionate, even though peaceful, struggle for a better world. Solidarity therefore needs to tolerate religions and to exalt, above all, science, love, and art, and if religions foster human creativity they will have to be respected, but if they eclipse and hinder the human longing for emancipation from ignorance and for liberation from the atavisms of cultural prejudices they will have to be fought, not in themselves, but in their different expressions.

Solidarity shares with religion the keeping of a burning hope. Nevertheless, its flame is drastically reduced to the horizon of history, the only space about which our rationality can acquire any sort of knowledge. However, and since human life is not only reason, but also radiating

---

7. Cf. Wittgenstein, "Lectures on Religious Beliefs."

sentiment, solidarity must not pretend to imprudently suppress the emotional dimension associated with any form of religiosity and art but to help it flourish superabundantly, as soon as it does not oppose the human dream for a more just world. We want to broaden the horizons of being: we want to think more, to know more, to ask more, to enjoy more, to love more...: inasmuch as religions contribute to this purpose, they will befriend solidarity, but inasmuch as they aggressively darken the human energy, stealing our vitality, they will have to be confronted, not by means of blind force, which bears the seed of vaster violence, but with the indestructible power of love, knowledge, and art.

The question about the nature of the human being is necessarily linked to the elucidation of the role of the future in history. To ask, just as Kant, "what is man," is also to wonder about the meaning of the future for men and women, because the primary evidence that we possess is the constant "presence" of a future, at least during the era of humanity. It is always possible to postpone the posing of the question and its eventual answer to a day after today, to a "tomorrow" which is always there, in such a way that the definition of the human being necessarily becomes relativized by the horizon offered by the future.

Because there is a future, the human being is *homo absconditus* (Ernst Bloch);[8] because no past and no present have the last word about the future, we are mysterious and hidden beings, which have not yet unfolded all we can do, for good or for bad. History offers a critical mediation which allows us to contextualize the horizon of humanity: we know the range of our capabilities, the science and the love we can generate, and also the pain we have been given to suffer, but this awareness is always limited: it is constrained by the power of the future. We cannot reject the possibility that tomorrow the human being will be capable of more, of better or worse things. If the human being continues to exist in this huge universe whose silence so much frightened Pascal, is a mystery to come, "pointing" towards a hypothetical future in which the meaning of "humanity" might be disclosed. While there is a future, every hermeneutic of humanity will be provisional, an anticipation of the meaning for which we are longing and which can never be fully achieved in the present. History will continue to offer the intercession needed to relativize any pretension of universality

---

8. On *homo absconditus*, cf. the third part of Bloch's *The Principle of Hope*. On the idea of *homo absconditus* in the philosophy of Ernst Bloch, cf. Green, "Ernst Bloch's Revision of Atheism."

concerning human nature. While there is a future, the human being will be *homo absconditus*.

There is no humanity without a future. A humanity which had become a pure present, the Boethian perfect possession of an interminable and immutable life, would no longer be human, for it would have been deprived of the beautiful possibility of change, of envisioning all that may come tomorrow, of creating and dreaming. Humanity without negativity, humanity assuming now the condition of absolute spirit, humanity lacking the dialectical mediation of void that encourages the edification of a new, broader space, would no longer be human.

We seek to know the deepest core of our nature, but we must realize that the future turns humanity into *abscondita realitas*. Humanity is "hidden," it is wholly-other with respect to itself, so that it can relativize every historically acquired (or even naturally received) determination. There is an asymptotic, infinite, unreachable limit, since it is always possible to think beyond the human reality given in the present, because we can constantly conceive of a future which, in opposition to eschatology, is not consummated but actualized in its radical, insurmountable openness, and whose anticipation can only be accomplished by paying the highest attention to the forms that the human phenomenon has adopted in both the past and the present. Our sole consolation as humanity, the only antidote against the shadow of finiteness and ignorance, is to take refuge in the paradise of our creations: cultures, art, science, the infinite ocean of knowledge, the plurality of civilizations and the variety of interpretations of the world. Critical questioning is granted by the omnipresence of the future: because there is future, we can relativize any form of knowledge and any civilization, and we can also find in the richness of the human realm, and actually in every single facet, a challenge for our subjectivity, an exhortation to relativize ourselves and to fight for a history in which every member of the human family may be capable of shaping his own future and of enjoying the extant polychromy of human works throughout the centuries.

We do not know the deepest essence of the human being and the true scope of our capacities. As humanity, we have not said our last word. Our truth is still hidden, factually produced in history, with a sole transcendental and invariable *fundamentum*: the presence of a future. *Homo absconditus quia homo futurus*: this is our highest treasure, the gift of time, the possibility of perpetually going beyond ourselves.

Part 2: *Fundamentum* in History

The human being appears as the expression of a quest, as the personification of a constantly new question posed to being, and history emerges as the ontic space which reveals the true horizon of humanity: history as a window to being. Humanity is the challenge of being.

SOLIDARITY AS ETHICS

Solidarity is the primacy of ethics over efficiency, of spirit over matter, if we understand "spirit" as the intangible ideal that allows us to be ends instead of means. Solidarity of the spirit keeps the correspondence between the realms of potentiality and necessity, guided by the conviction that the human reality can only be grasped once both poles of the binomial are integrated: what we can do and what we need to do, the openness offered by nature and the limitations that nature itself burdensomely imposes upon us. The reality of our individual and social condition only emerges in light of these two certainties: that, on the one hand, we can and we need, but, on the other hand, we must not arbitrarily separate our capacity from our necessity.

Solidarity of the spirit thinks that even within a society in which the principle of convergence between capabilities[9] and needs prevailed, the end of history would have not been reached, because there is no final pinnacle for history but an unredeemed ascension to the future. Solidarity of the spirit believes, however, that humanity can find nothing more fruitful than love, beauty, and wisdom. Knowing, loving, and enjoying beauty—we give a sense to life. Cosmic silence stands in radical contrast with the word that humanity discovers in goals like wisdom, beauty, and love. The contradictory nature of reality prevents us from unveiling pure wisdom, virginal beauty, and immaculate love, but we are always approaching them, even if asymptotically, and the dignity of the human being lies in his power to open his mind to new horizons. It is therefore necessary to universalize this tendency, so that all (not only few) can know, love, and achieve the highest delectation. Solidarity is a clear longing for universality.

Solidarity of the spirit preserves utopia, the "non-place" which finds a "space" inside the human mind as an ideal towards which we can be indefinitely inclined, although we are aware that perfection is alien to any

---

9. Although the use of the concept of "capability" does not necessarily imply the adoption of the so-called capability approach (Sen, Nussbaum, and the like), there is certainly a close connection with it. For a succinct exposition of the idea of "capability" in relation to the utilitarian, the "welfarist," and the Rawlsian ideas of equality; cf. Sen, "Equality of What?"

Freedom beyond Itself: Solidarity

human enterprise. However, solidarity of the spirit respects the independence of history, for it does not pretend to exhaust it. The contradictions of the centuries cannot be modified by exclusively transforming the material conditions of production: a new scenario has to be prepared, so that human beings can freely think, love, and enjoy. The ultimate goal of solidarity of the spirit is, indeed, pristine freedom. The passion for human dignity that drives solidarity towards the future allows us to conceive of a society in which the intangible, that which joins us without endangering our individuality, that which integrates us without mutilating the sharp mystery of our uniqueness, can finally emerge in this history.

The spirit, the union of diversity, is the destiny of solidarity: the internalization of the ethics of ends, of the ethics of solidarity, freely objectified in the edification of a more just world. Thus, solidarity is a song of hope in the possibilities of the human being.

Solidarity is a ruling principle, rather similar to the regulatory ideas of pure reason for Kant, and it is materially expressed in the establishment of a series of objective conditions that facilitate that everyone may display his abilities at most and satisfy his needs without constriction, as soon as the requirement of universality is fulfilled. Possibilities vary, as do needs. Solidarity does not seek to "petrify" a given state of the human nature at a given time, but it proposes the ideal of solidarity for every stage of humanity, which is always algid. As soon as rationality emerges, humanity is capable of solidarity. If solidarity is, first of all, ethics and spirit, then the path towards solidarity cannot consist of the completion of a series of historical and socioeconomic requirements. On the contrary, solidarity has always been there, and it is the constant vocation of humanity. We can contemplate, both in our minds and our hearts, the inextinguishable flame of solidarity.

Solidarity is an ethical ideal, defined by the pretension of using the given state of technique and science to obtain the highest degree of display of the vital energies of the human being. Justice is the expansion of this latent energy. Solidarity dreams that the broadening of the individual being will not be restricted to a few but it will be universalized, because solidarity is continuously affected by the phantasmagorical shadow of partiality.

Solidarity has never been as possible as it is now, because humanity has never before reached such a developed state of technological progress, global awareness, appreciation for different cultures, perception of the ecological challenges, admiration (mixed with criticism) for science, etc., as it has done today. Humanity has never been as ready as it is now for solidarity.

Part 2: *Fundamentum* in History

There is nothing as complex as solidarity, and only that which demands passionate engagement deserves honest dedication ("nothing was done in history without passion"—Hegel). Solidarity wants to preserve the heterogeneity of the human phenomenon by enabling every one, and not only a few, to become aware of complexity. This beautiful concept must be no longer the entertainment of scholars and academicians. No one should possess this noble idea as his sole property, making us believe that he is the only one capable of understanding the path that humanity has taken, if there is any path at all, so that those who do not enjoy his privilege cannot create any collective project. This anti-democratic attitude clashes with the spirit of solidarity, which is the philosophy of the many against the labyrinth of subtleties of the few. Simplification consists of believing that solidarity is not suitable for humanity. True awareness of complexity resides in realizing that history remains unfinished, and that there is no absolute truth which can absorb the finiteness of time, but it also consists of the commitment to the universal participation in the task of complexity, by enabling all human beings to unreservedly develop their potentialities.

The absolute is history itself, the process, the finiteness that is, for us, infiniteness, the "true infinite" of Hegel,[10] which reveals a spirit, something that remains, while at the same time changes; a contradiction that cannot be reduced to the oppressive domain of the concept, but which rather liberates us from understanding, opening ourselves to the power of sentiment, art, and love. Complexity is not the sole possession of learned scholars but rather the truth of human existence. Solidarity wants to exalt complexity, to authenticate it by preventing it from standing as the exclusive property of a few, so that it can become the wealth of the many, whose lives, instead of being complex, are defined by the simplicity of the search of mere survival, even though humanity has never been as capable as it is nowadays of producing in great abundance. The complex life cannot be the sign of distinction of a certain social class but a truth that may be internalized by all human beings. In order to do so, it is necessary to give everyone the chance to have a complex life, emancipated from the urgency of the immediate needs of life and opened to the noble polychromy of

---

10. "True infinite," for Hegel, does not consist of the mere opposition of finiteness and infiniteness, but it is a synthesis of both finiteness and infiniteness. True infinite cannot be the antithesis of finiteness, because an infiniteness conceived in terms of opposition to finiteness is still finite. The true infinite is both finite and infinite: it is the overcoming of both infiniteness and finiteness. It is therefore pure indeterminacy and pure freedom. According to Wolfhart Pannenberg, the idea of "true infinite" is one of the central concepts of the philosophy of Hegel. Cf. Pannenberg, *Gottesgedanke und menschliche Freiheit*, 81; Pannenberg, *Metaphysik und Gottesgedanke*, 94.

history, art, and science. Let complexity not be simplified by a few: let us all vindicate our right for complexity, and in order to be equally susceptible to the complex it is necessary to be equally susceptible to broadening the horizons of being, history, and knowledge.

This is the dream of solidarity: that all human beings may work in order to improve their lives, to create, to know, to love, to exchange, and to bequeath beauty. The incentive of labor is humanity itself, the end and not the means (material possession), and this is the reason why solidarity seeks to radically reduce social inequalities, for the asymmetries in the valuation of labor hide the tragedy of the subordination of some men and women to others, and the unequal consideration of human dignity from one individual to another. An ethical conversion is needed in order to captivate the effervescent power of imagination in ends and not in means, so that human beings may not be blinded by money as the universal tool for an unknown goal but by the goal itself, by human welfare, by the overflowing cultivation of art and science, by the possibility that everyone may love and come into dialogue without the restrictions imposed by prejudices and social differences. The mitigation of the unjustifiable inequalities in income that exist nowadays, aside from the urgency for a civilization of austerity and solidarity, alien to the ostentation of wealth, power, and luxury, is a challenge of our time. The struggle against social injustice verifies the sincerity of our commitment to the ideal of solidarity, of our conviction that the end, and not the means, sets the value, and that ethics must prevail over efficiency, for the purpose is not to produce but to live and to expand the energies of all singular lives.

As long as we tolerate the persistence of a society which allows some individuals to accumulate so much wealth as it now happens humanity will have failed. Philanthropy poses no solution at all, for it can be regarded as the cosmetic make-up of the capitalistic machinery that perpetuates injustice and inequality. The fact that, by means of social and economic development, everyone may become individually richer is in vain if the differences are so large that they implicitly express an unfair comparative valuation of the work of some people in comparison to the work of others. Solidarity protests against the scandalous concentration of prosperity and power, and it proposes a way to overcome the contradictions that such a phenomenon generates: solidarity. The excessive wealth of a few may be bearable if, at least in theory, everyone else can satisfy his basic needs. However, it is still contrary to the project of treating every human being as an end, and never as a means, for solidarity wants to recognize the unique greatness of each individual life and the intrinsic dignity of his work.

A difference of ten times in income, this is, in the estimation of the value of the work of a certain individual in comparison to other, might be tolerated, but the problem is rather different: it has to do with the idea of "limit." Our world knows no potential limit to the accumulation of income. Some individuals earn thousands of times as much as others. Can any discourse inspired by solidarity ignore this fact, and become blind before it, by taking refuge in the ideal of equality of opportunities, of *equalitas ex ante*, which is different from *equalitas ex post*? Does not solidarity have anything to say concerning *equalitas ex post* and its implications regarding *equalitas ex ante*? If there is such a great disparity in the result it is because there is too much inequality in the beginning, and by correcting the latter it is possible to emendate the first, but an even more drastic effort is required, because it is also necessary to fight against an excessive inequality *ex post*, and the precise understanding of "excessive" has to be judged collectively and democratically, guided by both reason and sentiment, by all we can tolerate and all we judge as impossible to admit, for it goes against human dignity.

Extreme suspicion concerning wealth and power must be complemented, however, by unlimited admiration for those who cultivate the inexhaustible goods of humanity: art, knowledge, love, communication, and fantasy. Solidarity must encourage the highest appreciation for the work of scientists, humanists, and all those who voluntarily give themselves in service of others. To substitute the republic of efficiency and economic injustice with the paradise of arts and sciences: this is the dream of solidarity, to promote all that does not discriminate, all that does not raise walls between human beings and does not foster the asymmetric distribution of power, all that encourages those realities which cannot be depleted, whose use does not prevent the benefit of others: the infinite wells from which everyone can drink without ever becoming exhausted.

Liberalism feels comfortable in defending equality before the law, without any further specification. At least since Locke, this movement has privileged individual rights—principally, of course, the right to private property—over collective rights, and it has hardly promoted a critical examination of the prevailing social order, which makes certain laws exist instead of others. While uncovering, under the illusion of respect for the procedures, its lack of an approach capable of critically analyzing the asymmetry of power that subsists within a certain society, liberalism prefers to support negative freedom, the indifferent ability to do something, instead of positive freedom, which is the effective possibility to perform something.

However, and since law is a social convention, historically mutable, which responds to the state of a society at a given time (not the innocent consecration of an eternal principle, but the ratification of a will which does not always benefit the whole social body), it is legitimate to wonder whether it is enough to support a vague equality before the law which does not simultaneously endorse the imperative of achieving real equality through the law. The first option bears little commitment, while the second one belongs to the very essence of solidarity. It justifies a reasonable suspicion about any kind of juridical formalism, for this attitude normally hides an indolent reluctance to envision any possible modification, even subversive, of the established order on behalf of a more just world, in which equality may not be a chimera, a mirage impressed in the bombastic letters of legal codices, but a political, social, and economic objectivity.

Equality before the law: why only this? Why does liberalism stop its reflection here, instead of taking a step further by critically assessing the underpinnings of a certain law, its social substrate, which does not always recall a truly just order? Why can't we have an effective, material equality that guarantees, in a more convincing way, the formal equality before the law, easier to reach if society is integrated by men and women who have been equated in their respective powers, so that no one has any sort of relative advantage that might eventually grant him privileges over others? The same logic that impels liberalism to adopt the principle of universal equality before the law—the will for justice—inspires the aim of solidarity to achieve equality through law. However, solidarity dares to go further, and it does not suspend its quest for justice in obtaining formal equality. It is aware that formalism is the tip of the iceberg that conceals a vast body of inequalities that, if not corrected, will seriously hinder any aspiration for true equality before the law.

What belongs actually to each individual? Are we solely responsible for our achievements? Have we obtained what we possess in a completely pioneer, innocent, inalienable way? Can anyone deny that he has benefited from a given social order, from the available knowledge, from the technique that we all have inherited, from the ruling laws, from the work of many others, both past and present? Individual freedom . . . But are not the circumstances influential in the effective exercise of freedom? Is it not legitimate to transform the circumstances in order to conquer freedom?

Part 2: *Fundamentum* in History

Freedom is not given: it is socially conquered. The freedom of some individuals generates victims among the others. Thus, solidarity fights in favor of a freedom which may be real for all: a freedom without losers, which is a humanized freedom.

We all owe so much to history and humanity that it is even shameful to proclaim our self-sufficiency without paying attention to this incontestable evidence. The dark prison of the ego is, after all, extremely disturbing. Language, science, arts, social relations: let us admire the achievements of each person, but let us not forget that if someone contributes to the general welfare, he does so because he has previously received many things from society, most of which remain unnoticed. We are children of mystery, and solidarity wants to express this sentiment of gratitude. Humanity can be the fountain of many evils, too, but it is also the source of the solution for the deficiencies that now exist and for the imperfections that will emerge in the future, in an endless process, because misfortune will constantly appear in the human world, but so will the energy to overcome it.

Solidarity gives voice to the scandal of social injustice, armed with the conviction that there is more to unite humanity than to separate it, and personal preferences never justify the ostentatious differences in power, knowledge, and happiness that we suffer. The principal cause of the barriers that we have built up is our own historical responsibility, and it does not result from a hypothetical natural order that reveals little or nothing about social organization. Solidarity promotes an encouraging hope in the future by enabling that the vast range of determinations which emerge from the blind combination of chance and necessity that vivifies nature may become humanized, transformed, and sweetened according to the ideals that we, as humanity, propose, so that words can finally triumph over cosmic silence. Social equality replaces natural injustice and social dream supplants natural evidence. But solidarity is also aware of the evidence that no single ideal will ever exhaust the richness of history and the complexity of the human phenomenon. This is the reason why charity cannot be completely excluded, even though it has to be constrained to the realm of the personal and intimate deliberation, to the space of mystery and non-rationality, which is often the source of rationality and commitment.[11]

11. On rationality and commitment, cf. Sen, "Rational Fools," 317–44. It is interesting to notice that one of the core ideas of Max Weber's *The Protestant Ethic and the Spirit of Capitalism* is that non-rational assumptions may be the source of rational principles. In this sense, the non-rational belief in predestination in Calvinism, which stems from faith, not from reason, offers the foundation for a process of

Freedom beyond Itself: Solidarity

We can dream of solidarity, and it can become the content of the indescribable emotions that one feels while listening to the most sublime music. Capitalism is too focused on the immediate reality, on the absence of a collective project, on the satisfaction of limited and short-term interests. Solidarity transcends the here and the now of history because it thinks of the future, assuming it in a radical way, as the perennial possibility to change history.

Mystic means capable of infusing hope in everyone and struggling against fatality. Mystic involves regarding history as a potentially infinite path of possibilities for humanity. Mystic means deeply human, but in such a way that "human" becomes "humanity": not the addition of fragmented individuals but the commitment to an august enterprise to which everyone can contribute. Solidarity is therefore lack of conformism and rejection of the present: it is a providential confidence in the future. We possess an invincible power, which resides in our reason and our sentiments: our ability to set the conditions that will make history become less random and more merciful than it is now, so that the word of humanity, instead of being silenced by the deafness of this huge and blind universe, will be listened to, even if we are the only ones to hear it.

Solidarity implies confidence that beyond this vast and speechless cosmos we have ourselves as humanity. Solidarity is peace and virtuous concord, in which humanity no longer fears history, but uses the chances offered by time to create, to know, to love, to enjoy, and to communicate, living instead of dying.

---

strict rationalization that defines the emergence of capitalism. However, the question is whether humanity has to accept that unexpected outcomes alien to our rational control will ineluctably appear and shape history, establishing new "rationalities"; or whether it is rationally possible to conquer the power of the non-rational source of creativity that humanity possesses. What should we expect from ourselves, both from our rational and non-rational dimensions? This is the challenge to be met.

6

Solidarity beyond Itself: Creation

THE LONGING FOR SOLIDARITY is too fragile. It easily becomes will of power. Closed over itself, absorbed by its own and powerful energies, it turns the quest for a deeper integration of humanity into its sole commitment. It does not contemplate the possibility of growth, *novum*, creativity: the overcoming of both subjectivity and humanity. Twilight emerges upon history, for no horizon beyond the conquest of solidarity can be foreseen. If the danger of freedom resides in the tyranny of individuality, in solidarity mankind enjoys such a high degree of centrality for thought that it is no longer possible to transcend humanity. Purity, limpidness, the irreducible intuition that transcends any concept and any desire (without succumbing to the forces of reason and the arcane and unconscious impetus that live in the human mind), now seems too distant. Humanity suffices, and the possession of itself is regarded as the highest pinnacle to which one can aspire. Any love, any sign of beauty, any timid rubric of wisdom is condensed in humanity. Any wish points to mankind. No continuous challenge is perceived, no intrinsic call to transcend all that is given.

Any philosophy based upon mistrust darkens the future and usurps the creative enthusiasm of humanity. Any philosophy founded upon universal suspicion sets the scenario for its own destruction, because an analogous apprehension as that which compels it to mistrust the intentions of others reverts on its own motivations. Thus, such a philosophy will be regarded as the fruit of envy, resentment, and rancor; as the product of the lowest passions and the absence of creative impetus. The constraint of thought to the paradigm of suspicion condemns us to an inescapable net of mutual apprehension that suffocates any creative energy. We can all mistrust each other. However, our longing for love does not need suspicion but creativity, discovery, future, and experience; criticism must be a tool, not an end.

Consciousness committed to creation is capable of overcoming, through its detachment, the shadow of resentment. To create means to defeat rancor in order to discover purity, limpidness, inexhaustibility: that which unites without ever annulling individual identity. Freedom absorbed by itself is blind to universality. Solidarity exclusively focused on itself becomes deaf to creation, to the expansion of individual energies: to the demands that move our spirit towards the perennial opening of everything, including the conquests of solidarity. Solidarity must propitiate the full disposition of freedom, as to lead consciousness towards creation, commitment, search of the unconditioned. Any past suspicion disappears if we are possessed by the enthusiasm for creation. The past therefore becomes a noble source of inspiration, an enlightening experience that manifests our common humanity and our membership in a shared history. The past exhorts us to understand the legacy, which we have received, in order to "possess ourselves." But creation is the triumph of the future, the longing for a tomorrow, the fascination for that which has not yet emerged. Creation exhorts us to rescue the past from its self-absorption as to revitalize it and resuscitate the withered energies. We need to revive our heritage. The sentiment that has to prevail in our soul is the honest ambition that history may move forward and the future may show its full potency. We must obliterate any trace of rancor, in order to lead consciousness toward its deepest longing: love, beauty, and wisdom.

PROPAEDEUTIC MOMENTS OF CREATIVE CONSCIOUSNESS

Solidarity must open itself to creation. It needs to be vivified by *novum*, by the future in its truth (as a horizon which enables the emergences of newness, the incessant youth of the spirit). Creative impetus stems from three moments that antecede creation itself. In these moments, the individual *prepares himself* for creation, for the glimpse of purity, novelty, irreducibility.

Part 2: *Fundamentum* in History

Life

To create means to live in the most intense degree. Life, the disposition of its own possibilities towards a goal, a "teleonomy" (to take Jacques Monod's expression[1]), a horizon that is susceptible to different orientations (this intrinsic indeterminacy in its ontological space makes life a challenge to the world in its sameness; this challenge will become radical with the advent of consciousness), is the antechamber of creation. If through its evolution, the material world only reaffirms itself in its own sameness, in its constant return to itself (so that any appearance of newness, any form of becoming, is but an internal display of that which was given in the initial conditions of the universe), with the emergence of life an innovation of extraordinary consequences has taken place. Life is part of the world. It is subject to the irrevocable laws, which run the totality of the world. However, life does not constrain the scope of its action to contributing to the preservation of the world in its sameness through a pre-established path. Rather, life sets its own orientation, the precise direction that the world shall take in its return to its own sameness.

Through life, the world begins to challenge itself. Behold a primitive, yet fascinating manifestation of freedom as indeterminacy. The totality of the world subsumes any apparent innovation in its inexorable mechanisms. No newness rises in the world. When we refer to physical reality, we can indeed declaim, in a bereaved elegy: *Nihil novum sub sole*. Everything was already given in the initial concentration of energy from which it all arose. The birth of life, that deep mystery which still captures the attention of scientists, constitutes the origin of a challenge to that absence of newness within the physical world. The biotic world has room for "novelty": no new energy is created, but within the realm of potential transformations of matter-energy that happen in the living forms the direction which the world shall take cannot be predicted. Life "reacts" to the world in different ways. The plasticity of living systems, their capacity for adaptation and evolution, indicates that the final outcome of living processes cannot be predicted in precise, "mathematical" ways. Life enjoys some sort of "freedom" to dispose of its own world, of its own *Umwelt* (to recall Jakob von Uexküll's famous concept).[2]

Consciousness challenges the world in its sameness, because consciousness "appears without appearing": it is part of the world, yet it is

---

1. Cf. Monod, *Chance and Necessity*.
2. Cf. Von Uexküll, *Umwelt und Innenwelt der Tiere*.

the strongest negation of the world. Consciousness is not satisfied with the mere appearance of the world: it seeks to defy it and to create its own world. However, consciousness is primarily life: consciousness flourishes because life exists.

Understanding

Because it is fully consecrated to living, and it has become aware of its deepest capacity as a pinnacle in the evolution of the world, consciousness *understands* the world. The second moment for creative consciousness corresponds to understanding. Consciousness unfolds the truth about the possibilities of the world: they are constrained to the world itself. Newness cannot stem from them. Consciousness seeks to challenge that impossibility. Consciousness understands the fragility of the immensity of the world and it commits itself to challenging its power.

Consciousness understands "the impossible." Therefore, it contemplates "the impossible" as a possibility that emanates from the vastness of being, from its "ulteriority." Although the analogy may seem risky, it is inevitable to perceive of "signs" of the emergence of *novum* (newness which, from a purely mechanistic point of view that postulates an inexorable concatenation of causes and effects, according to which everything is "contained" *in nuce* in the preceding elements, is simply impossible) in the fundamental levels of logic and science. Gödel's theorem states that "in any consistent system which is strong enough to produce simple arithmetic there are formulae which cannot be proved-in-the-system, but which we can see to be true. Essentially, we consider the formula that says, in effect, "This formula is unprovable-in-the-system." If this formula were provable-in-the-system, then it would not be unprovable-in-the-system," so that "This formula is unprovable-in-the-system" would be false: equally, if it were provable-in-the-system, then it would not be false, but would be true, since in any consistent system nothing false can be proved-in-the-system, but only truths. So the formula "This formula is unprovable-in-the-system" is not provable-in-the-system, but unprovable-in-the-system. Further, if the formula "This formula is unprovable-in-the-system" is unprovable-in-the-system, then it is true that that formula is unprovable-in-the-system; that is, "This formula is unprovable-in-the-system" is true."[3] In some sense, these formulae "emerge out of nothing." They are true, but they cannot be proven in the system. They cannot be inferred from the

---

3. Lucas, "Minds, Machines and Gödel," 112–27.

initial axioms (otherwise, they could be susceptible to proof). "The impossible" appears as possible; *ex nihilo* (if this ambitious metaphor should be tolerated) formulae which were not "possibly contained" in the initial axioms emerge. They cannot be deduced *more geometrico*. A "hiatus" subsists within elementary logical systems. It forbids an "axiomatized" understanding of totality, for consistent formulae which would disprove the completeness of the axiomatic system would always arise. Here we find a valuable seed of "openness" and "growth."

Consciousness can understand that totality transcends the rigid limits established by the material world. Totality will be understood as the incessant capacity for crossing any given frontier. The understanding of world, life, and consciousness as forms of a fundamental "being-able-to" anticipates the commitment of consciousness to creation. In its understanding of the surrounding reality and of itself, consciousness becomes prepared for turning into "creative consciousness." First, it was necessary for it *to live*, to feel the power of its living force, as distinct from the mere appearance of the world. Second, consciousness needed the fine tools of its analytic power: the criticism of the world and the perception of the singularity of the human mind.

Consciousness does not fear death. It does not regard death as an inexorable force which limits its creative impetus. Rather, it realizes that the exercise of the full range of its possibilities demands the overcoming of the threatening presence of death through its commitment to creation, to "the impossible," to *novum*. This way of living, this conscious and undaunted consecration to life, which does not surrender to world and death, enables consciousness to understand the *contingency* of the world. The world "is merely given." It is defined by its own "sameness." However, consciousness can challenge the world through thought. The act of questioning the world, of interrogating it in its deepest essence, rubricates a vivid triumph of consciousness. Consciousness can presage that which is necessary not in the mere appearance of the world but in the possibility of "the impossible": in the marvel of creativity.

Creation points to the ineffability of purity. Not everything deprived of the possibility to become an object of the world is impossible. Love, beauty, and wisdom, those limpid, unconditioned, "inexhaustible" intuitions, never succumb to any form of objectivity. They are never "constructed" in the world. No one can grasp wisdom, beauty, and love. They are not tools that one might eventually possess. They never belong to a certain "*hic et nunc*" of the world: they are freedom, purity, and abnegated commitment.

Longing

Consciousness lives in the world and it lives for itself. Consciousness understands the world and it understands itself. It is therefore ready to become creative consciousness. However, it must look for it anxiously: it needs to seek to reach the stage of creative consciousness. The third propaedeutic moment is that of *longing*.

Prior to conquering itself as creative consciousness, it must become *creative will*. In its quest for life and its search of understanding, consciousness interprets itself as the pinnacle of the possibilities of the world. By recognizing the contingency of the sameness of the world and the inextricable connection of being with "being-able-to" (the suspension of being in its own possibility), consciousness has become aware of its innermost power: to challenge the given reality in order to create. The longing for creation internalizes the will of life and the desire of understanding. In this longing, in this will which freely possesses itself and whose desire finds no constraint, life and understanding shine in their full majesty. He who assumes such a powerful longing for creation loves life and understanding, for volition radiates the glare of life and the light of understanding. Through its intense longing for creation, the will is in full possession of itself. It can therefore commit itself to *novum*. Defying the world through the mere act of living does not represent a true challenge. Life is still captive of the ontological space of the world. Life is still subject to the inexorable laws of nature. It is susceptible to various possibilities which expand the horizons of physical matter, but unlike understanding, it does not radically challenge the world. Understanding transcends the simple resignation to choosing one among the elenchus of available options. Understanding questions the limit posed by the world. Understanding is opened to "the impossible" and the discovery of the truth of the world. Through the power of understanding, consciousness rescues the world from itself and returns it to its original purity, to its truth. The longing for creation, the will focused on "that which cannot be," means that the exercise of the potentiality which is inherent to consciousness seeks something beyond merely challenging the world: it wants to extend the frontiers of the world.

Part 2: *Fundamentum* in History

The longing for creation demands an equal longing for conceiving of oneself as creator. In spite of the disturbing awareness of the material impossibility of raising a true *novum*; in spite of the evidence that everything that appears in the world is subject to the irrevocable laws of nature, to the inevitable concatenation of causes and events, mind has already "contemplated" that which is impossible: freedom, creation. The longing for creation, as the fruit of life and understanding, leads to the ambition to "generate," in the *hic et nunc* of history, that which cannot be. However, this powerful longing is aware of the saddening reality that any actual realization of "the impossible" would become a new form of sameness, an objectification of an intuition too pure and beautiful as to descend to the vulnerability of life. It would therefore suffocate the radiant light of *novum* in the distressing silence of the mere "appearance" of the world.

However, and in spite of experiencing the power of contradiction, the creative will commits itself with passion to love, beauty, and wisdom, those unrealizable intuitions, those rubrics of "impossibility," of "nonbeing," which are nonetheless felt as life, understanding, and longing. The ulteriority of being shines in them: we could always delve with greater courage into love, beauty, and wisdom, because they are inexhaustible, and they never constrain themselves to any limit. They never become objects, "actualizations" of a possibility. They are "impossible," so that they reflect the purity of being, its primeval character: gift, surprise, and mystery. They emanate *creative freedom*, a faithful novelty which, although it does not detach itself from history (for it does not betray that which is given in the world, those hopes and longings which have been cultivated throughout the centuries, the intense appetite of love, beauty, and wisdom which so many have fostered in the past and still fuel in the present), it does dare to transcend any possible longing and to enlighten the perpetual flame of desire: there is always room for more love, more beauty, and more wisdom; it is always possible to become enthusiastic at such a golden triumvirate, because it has never been "actualized." In fact, any realization of this noble triad would turn it into an object. It would become exhausted and it would lose its freedom. It would succumb to necessity, to that which is not creative, to that which is conditioned and is therefore incapable of releasing the halite of purity, authenticity, truth, *creation*.

COMMITMENT

Creative consciousness stems from the commitment to *novum*, to an elusive purity which is therefore inexhaustible: love, beauty, and wisdom inasmuch as *freedom*. The three of them will never become realized in the *hic et nunc* of world and history; however, the human spirit will never cease to seek them passionately. They cannot be reduced to any specific manifestation in a certain time and a certain space, for they recall such a deep and limpid purity, such a profound and ultimate truth, that any determination of these fundamental intuitions would betray their authenticity (again, behold the relevance of Spinoza's claim: *omnis determinatio est negation*). We can always aspire to a deeper acquaintance with love, beauty, and wisdom. All great cultures have venerated this trinity as the most elevated good on which the unredeemed longings of the human spirit could be focused, but no single individual and no single civilization have been capable of discovering the ultimate "objectification" of love, beauty, and wisdom. This triad cannot be subsumed into the narrow margins of our intellect, our will, and our sentiment. Its purity is too intense and innocent for us.

The search for love, beauty, and wisdom, in spite of the passion with which it must be embraced, has also irradiated the light of peace: the contemplation of their weakest signs bestows upon us the gift of "quietude," as we realize that we can seek nothing higher than love, beauty, and wisdom. They also inspire fascination, because they are "fearful," "*mysteria tremenda*" on account of their depth, power, and purity. We feel encouraged to praise them and to commit ourselves to their quest. Such a commitment can adopt three principal dispositions: ascetic commitment, heroic commitment, and creative commitment.

Ascetic Commitment

The ascetic, so deeply admired by Schopenhauer, renounces his own "selfness" and radically distances himself from the sameness of the world. For the ascetic, the world is as vain as his own *ego*. He must flee from the world and his own subjectivity. He must overcome the frontiers of objectivity and consciousness in order to penetrate into the ultimate home: silence. The deepest truth of being lies in the absence of activity and passion (the Spanish mystic Miguel de Molinos popularized this idea in the seventeenth century through his appeal to *quietism*, although it is clear that this thesis finds much earlier roots in the most important mystical and ascetic movements of great world religions). Commitment is free because the ascetic deliberately renounces the goods and pleasures of the world and his own consciousness (art, science, and love) in order to consecrate his soul to the pure-transcendent, the absolute-indeterminate, vacuum, nullity, the fundamental equality of being and non-being: *nothingness*. For the ascetic, totality has been broken in its sameness. Its emptiness has been finally shown: behind the apparent magnificence of world and consciousness, behind the polychromy of phenomena, behind the incandescent magic of intelligence and will, there is nothing. The ascetic has discovered the deepest truth, in whose silent ground being is rooted. The ascetic commits himself to this truth not with passion, but with abnegation: enthusiasm is a vestige of the sameness of world and consciousness.

Nevertheless, the ascetic commitment is not free. Rather, it is the inexorable product of having discovered the emptiness of world and *ego*. The ascetic understands the whole of reality, and he believes that he has conquered true wisdom, true love (the renunciation of love), and true beauty (the absence of contemplation: the mere act of "being there," which points to nothingness). Beyond silence, there is nothing else for which to look. The ascetic is a servant of himself. His commitment is not utterly pure, because he has turned his commitment into his reason of being. We must look for a free commitment.

Heroic Commitment

The hero is entirely committed to humanity. Detached from himself, he does not succumb to silence. Rather, he feels a deep love for his brethren. This love encourages him to challenge any given "sameness" which constrains the human longing for freedom. His wisdom consists of his renunciation to himself in order to consecrate his energies to humanity. He becomes blind for anything that is alien to the deepest desires of mankind. The beauty which he passionately venerates resides in humanity. The hero loves humanity, he rejoices in humanity, and he "knows" humanity. Humanity is the truth of his existence and the truth of the world: the world has been born for humanity, and humanity is now leading the world.

The hero is not committed to creation but to liberation. He does not conceive of freedom as the pure sunrise, as the enthusiastic edification of *novum*, but as the courageous triumph over the present state of slavery. The future is subsidiary to the past. The hero is not committed to thinking of that which may be new. The *telos* of history is determined by the longings of mankind and its vocation to liberty. However, to create is to show so great courage as to break with the past and the present, even if this demands the imagination of new goals for humanity. To create is to commit oneself to unlimited purity, to the radical intuition, to the limpid and self-contained *a priori*, which is therefore free to the highest degree, for it is never exhausted in a specific desire, not even in the most vehement ambitions of freedom. To create is to love, to know, to contemplate, to praise the ephemeral condition of the infinite, the incommensurable joy, the sign of the eternal, of the being which does not remain in its inveterate silence but speaks to itself in the constant expansion of its horizons.

Creative Commitment

Commitment to creation goes beyond humanity. Its scope transcends the rigid frontiers of mankind: there is a *semper plus*, an *ulterior* to any given form of sameness. Creative commitment is opened to the future: it is longing for *novum*. The *novum* is that which challenges the concatenation of causes and effects that rules over the dynamism of the world. It also challenges the selfishness of mankind, whose sole goal consists of achieving its own humanization. Creative commitment relativizes the human realm: it opens itself to nature, to the greenness of life. However, it does not fall into the temptation of staying in nature; neither does it pretend to integrate world and humanity, nature and subjectivity, necessity and freedom, into an absolute consciousness which overcomes any determination.

For creative commitment, that which is "given" must be transcended into that which "is not given," into creation, into the sunrise which does not limit itself to planting the seed of a twilight. Creative consciousness perceives of "the surprising," "the inexhaustible," "the pure." Creative commitment consecrates its strength, its spirit, its passion, its enthusiasm, to creation as end in itself. Its aspiration is no other than creation as inexhaustible and free goal.

Creative commitment values all potential sources of inspiration. It is therefore opened to other cultures, to the extraordinary religious, philosophical, and artistic variety of humanity. Leibniz's "je ne emprise presque rien," such an intense longing for new ideas, such a deep attempt at broadening the limits of our rationality, expresses the fundamental sentiment that inspires creative commitment. This unredeemed desire does not lead to dissipation and eclecticism. Instead of merely accumulating opinions and theses, creative commitment eagerly looks for its own criterion.

Creative commitment consists of opening the mind first in order to later "concentrate" its energies in the discovery of that which is permanent: love, beauty, and wisdom.

Creative commitment does not turn its challenge to world and humanity into a goal. It does not succumb to indifference. It does not take refuge in ascetic silence and holy inaction. It desperately looks for newness, and it perceives of the ruthless opposition of a universe in which novelty seems impossible, because every seed has been already planted: every effect emanates from a given cause, and every idea is inferred from previous logical possibilities. Creative commitment knows that its struggle for newness may be in vain, but it finds in this "gigantomachy" the reason of its existence: its commitment to something which can be considered as an end in itself. Love is the goal of its love; contemplation is the goal of its contemplation; wisdom is the goal of its wisdom. Creative commitment finds the deep unity that connects love, beauty, and wisdom: commitment to *creating*, to venerating the wonder of *being*, the creating power from which everything stems and to which everything leads.

Creative commitment feels the greatest pleasure in loving love, embellishing beauty, and understanding wisdom. However, this pleasure is not constrained to the narrowness of its spirit: creative commitment lives in detachment from itself. Its pleasure is "ecstasy," a creative pleasure, a pleasure which encourages it to go beyond itself and to look for the future, instead of recreating itself in the fruition of the *hic et nunc*.

The philosophy of Hegel forced the idea to descend from its celestial heights, in whose glory Plato had placed the archetypes, the "real," the ultimate *nooumenon* beyond the obscure appearance of this earthly world. In Hegel, nature and history are the life of the idea: they consist of the *kenosis* of the idea, which abandons the fathomless purity of logic (the idea in itself), the *kosmos noetikos*, in order to "incarnate" itself in space and time. This *sincatabasis* obeys its will to acquire a deeper knowledge of itself. The idea looks for nothing but itself. It wants the highest form of freedom. The idea lives in world and history, which are no longer deceiving shadows which eclipse the beatific vision of truth. However, the idea is capable of taking flight because it already possesses wings, endowed with such an intense power that the immutability of heavens becomes distressing. The idea must cross heaven and Earth, for it is orphan of space and time: it must grant itself its own space and its own time, its own life. The idea cannot remain in the heaven of intelligibility which Plato had regarded as its most eminent home. It must leave that warm shelter to discover itself as absolute. Nevertheless, there is nothing new, no creation, nothing to be conquered. The Hegelian idea loves itself and conquers itself, but this arduous struggle is empty, because the idea only gains that which it already carried with itself: it crowns itself, it ascends to itself, and it challenges itself.

We should not conceive of the idea as Plato's celestial archetype, as *Ipsum Esse Subsistens*. The idea cannot be the eternal, if by "eternal" we exclude the possibility of participating in temporality. There would be no novelty, no change, and no growth at all: it would be an "imperfect" idea, incapable of assuming dynamism. But the idea cannot limit its activity to looking for the synthesis of eternity and temporality in its self-alienation as nature and history, for it will have gained nothing. Its achievement will be illusory: the idea will not have abandoned its own realm. It will have sinned and it will have broken the divine commandments. It will have been expelled from the original paradise. But its goal will have been utterly selfish: the understanding of itself and the acquisition of a higher conscience of its own freedom.

The idea must descend onto the Earth. It must become finiteness in order to integrate infiniteness and finiteness, but it must be opened to *creation*. The idea must seek to ascend, and it must become convinced that the highest peaks in which it initially dwelled are not the most sublime pinnacles: there is room for "more," which can never be exhausted. The idea must live in a perennial flight from any form of "sameness." To create means to conceive of a vocation for the idea. The idea must be creative, it must negate itself and suffer the infinite pain, but the goal of this tragedy can be no other than commitment to novelty, to true freedom, instead of returning to itself. The spirit must be conquered. It does not appear *in nuce* in the display of the idea. The spirit is an unattainable peak, but such a dedicated quest already reflects the depth of the spirit: it is love, it is beauty, it is wisdom; it is intuition. The idea must be ready to discover novelty, the *mysterium tremendum et fascinans*, *being* in its purity, which unceasingly challenges all that is given, even the power of the idea in its sameness.

Creative Commitment against the World: Culture

Creative consciousness will be in need of looking for its *world outside the world*. It will edify a world in which freedom from the inexorable concatenation of causes and effects that rules over the natural cosmos may prevail.

In such a new world, the flower of youth, spontaneity, and freshness will grow. The trees of love, beauty, and wisdom will be contemplated with passion and delight. In its rebellion against the world in order to build its own world, creative consciousness will freely commit itself to that which transcends its own subjectivity: the discovery of the purest intuition, the unconditioned, that which could be a perennial source of evocation, whose reply to our eager questioning would not be silence but the tenderness of words: love, beauty, and wisdom. This discovery will be of creative nature, instead of a mere "unfolding" of the reality which remains hidden behind the dark curtain of the sameness of the world. Creative consciousness "will open the window of being," and it will let "being flow in its most intimate power," in order to contemplate how being transcends itself, how it grows.

Through culture, consciousness committed to creation lives in freedom. "It lives for itself" in solidarity, because culture always overcomes the sphere of individuality. Culture always achieves a certain degree of universality: it is that which stands before any consciousness. Culture obtains emancipation from the individual creative consciousness and it becomes the patrimony of the human community from which it has emerged. If its latent universality is intense enough, culture will turn into the possession of the whole of mankind: it will be universal culture, whose tradition, whose gallery of creativity and evocation, binds us to a fundamental longing: the wish for a free world, for a humane world, for a world in which novelty may be possible and we can express the excess of energy that lives inside us; a world in which we can reflect the perennial lack of satisfaction that dwells in our spirit, a world in whose extension humanity may come into dialogue with itself.

Culture finds inspiration in the world in its sameness. The works of culture are always of a worldly nature. Culture dwells inside the world, but it shows a passionate struggle against the world. Culture, just as consciousness ("that which appears without appearing," the world that denies itself in its worldliness), reflects the human longing for *novum*, for a world which does not justify itself in its sameness. In its commitment to culture, consciousness discovers its potential freedom. It overcomes the inscrutable antinomy that opposes freedom and necessity: culture is part of the world, for it takes roots in the punished grounds of Earth (it is therefore sameness, silence), but through culture we achieve an intuition of that which is inexhaustible, pure, limpid, sincere: a fathomless truth which recalls creativity, the infinite power to raise *novum*, to broaden the scopes of being. Through culture, the opposition of consciousness and world reaches its climax: culture is part of the world, but in its worldliness it radically challenges the world. It is therefore "non-world," a heaven on Earth, a voice in the middle of the desert. Any attempt at capturing this moment of emancipation of culture from the world is in vain: we know that culture constitutes an extension of the world, a fictitious cosmos if we pretend to detach it from the material world. We are unable to apprehend the deepest essence of culture, its *truth*, for it points to creative freedom, to the pure intuition which is not subject to categorization, to infiniteness.

Through culture, consciousness seeks to find the beauty which the world does not offer. The art of nature is silent; it is blind; it is not made of flesh and bones. It simply displays that which is inexorable. Beauty does not shine in the world for its own sake. It is a happy manifestation of necessity, but it is not the goal of the evolution of matter and life. There is no *free beauty* in nature, a beauty which may stem from love, from the wish for commitment to a truth that may transcend us: a commitment to that which would never become a form of "sameness" but it would carry the incandescent flame of perennial evocation, of infinite suggestion, of true *novum*. It is not a wise beauty, for it is not aimed at propitiating *growth*, learning, an experience that may submerge us into a deeper truth of being (commitment, service, love): the beauty of the world is closed over itself. It is the fortuitous corollary of the dynamism of the world. The genuine light of beauty does not shine in nature. Consciousness will find a source of inspiration in the beauty of the world, for we shall always remain in an eager quest of evocation and ideas about how to "materialize" our unrestrained longing for novelty and creation. However, consciousness will notice the insufficiency of the world. Culture will offer consolation to consciousness, a "fortress" against the sameness of the world. Nevertheless, consciousness will inevitably lose its battle if it does not come into the realization that creation, the *novum* which it passionately seeks, can never "appear" in the world. Rather, it must be perceived in the power of love, beauty, and wisdom; in their pointing to purity and freedom: to peace.

Creative Commitment with the World: Science

Through science, consciousness reconciles its creative impetus with the sameness of the world. Culture projects its longings on a new world. Culture emanates from an intense rebellion against the tangible world. Science approaches the world with a different spirit. It does not seek to challenge the world but to *understand* the dynamism of nature.

Science is creative because it corresponds to the refusal of consciousness to simply contemplate the world in its dynamism. Consciousness does not silently observe the vast movement of the universe. Rather, it sharply penetrates into its structure and functioning, in order to create its own world of understanding, in which the silence of the mere appearance of the world may be substituted with the music of intelligence. Rationality shows the concatenation of causes and effects that governs the world, the deepest "reasons" underlying the visible manifestation of cosmos. It is true that science explains the world in its sameness, so that it does not challenge the world, but we should not forget that the scientific enterprise (probably initiated before the Greeks, although it remains a subject of historical evidence that the greatest contribution of Greek civilization to the history of the human spirit consisted of giving birth to a reflection on nature founded upon *logos*: the quest of an explanation of the phenomena of the world through looking for its ultimate reasons), which reached a state of consolidation after the discovery of the appropriate *method* to achieve its goal in the 16th century (whose clear precursors were the spirit of the Renaissance, some late-medieval developments, the Islamic science, etc.), constitutes a form of questioning the world.

Consciousness committed to creation through science seeks to reach the *truth* of the world, its deepest structure, the "intelligibility" that must permeate the whole universe (behold a postulate of consciousness: the intelligibility of the world). In spite of its provisional nature, the scientific enterprise does not cease to look for that which may be "permanent": necessity, the rationality of the world as reflected in its inexorable and universal laws. Creative consciousness cannot regard the world as governed by contingency. It needs to believe that everything in the world is the result of an inexorable process ruled by irrevocable laws (even if these laws are sometimes local and not always universal, and even if these laws correspond to probabilistic patterns). Over the centuries, science will achieve a deeper understanding of the structure and functioning of the world, but its fundamental mission will remain: to understand the world in its sameness. This understanding seems to us too "fragile," because consciousness looks for a kind of understanding that does not limit itself to simply highlighting the concatenation of causes and effects that governs the dynamism of the world. Consciousness is not satisfied with an explanation of the world: it longs for giving it a meaning. But at this point the power of science diminishes. Its understanding of the world leads to an explanation, not to a meaning. Consciousness must therefore "*create*" its

Solidarity beyond Itself: Creation

own world, it has to edify the dwelling of culture, in which such a meaning may be freely sculpted, painted, written with beautiful words, and felt through suggesting melodies.

Through scientific intellection, consciousness has *created* a world. It is insufficient for its high aspirations, but at least it represents a space of understanding and intelligibility, in which the world is radically questioned by consciousness. The world is no longer "that which merely appears there," because science has discovered the deep roots of its structure and functioning, the ultimate necessity which it obeys. Through science, consciousness calls itself: it reflects its own lack of satisfaction, its longing for understanding, its *commitment*. The advancement of science is the fruit of the consecration of so many great minds to cultivating the flower of scientific knowledge. The abundance of material interests, the will to dominate nature (on which Sir Francis Bacon insisted at the beginning of the modern age), the translation of science into technique, should not darken the evidence that many men and women have committed their lives, their intelligence, their perseverance, their fantasy, their creativity, to the task of unveiling the structure and functioning of the world. This goal has often prevailed over the search for economic profit and social recognition. The will of understanding, "curiosity," the wish for "something more," our lack of satisfaction with that which is given, overflows the narrow space of technical interest.

Consciousness has sought understanding since its earliest stages. Even the mythological discourse reflects a deep longing for understanding. The myths were looking for something "beyond" the visible phenomena. Science is perhaps the most eminent rubric of how consciousness is incapable of merely contemplating the world: consciousness is in constant need of seeking something deeper. Through science, consciousness challenges the world.

Consciousness longs to commit itself to the pure, to that which we could contemplate endlessly. However, consciousness does not find it inside the world. Its creative commitment to the world is its challenge to the world: science. But consciousness will realize the fragility of the scientific enterprise. Its intrinsic vulnerability is due to its limited offering: it does not show that which is fathomless, that which is free: that which is new. Science only reflects the greatness of the world, the splendor of its sameness. Consciousness may become fascinated by the sumptuousness of the world, the greenness of nature, the brightness of the sky and the limpidness of crystalline waters. Possibly, it will be raptured by the honest sentiment of feeling itself part of that vast and majestic reality, which is capable of displaying such a richness of prodigies and evocations. Nevertheless, as soon as consciousness delves into the truth of the world, into the structure and functioning of that gallery of sublime images which conquer its sensibility, it will prophetically notice that it all obeys necessity instead of freedom: nature is not the result of abnegated purity, of authentic creation.

Creative Commitment beyond the World: Philosophy

Through the consecration of its energies to philosophy, consciousness creates a world which is no longer defined by its opposition to the cosmos that appears before our eyes. Neither is it featured by the mere understanding of the intelligibility underlying the universe. Rather, this new world points to the radical transcendence over that which is given, in search of an *ultimate meaning*, the deepest truth, the core of wisdom. The most genuine sense of *philosophia* as "love of wisdom" teaches us that it does not consist of the unfolding of the mysteries of the world. Philosophy is *creative*, because the love of wisdom is the rubric of the highest possible reality to which the human being can aspire: its power to love, to commit himself to that which is different, to achieve detachment from himself in order to propitiate the flourishing (through the quest for understanding) of purity, the unconditioned, that which obeys nothing but the sweetness of love.

Love of wisdom moves the philosopher to create a world beyond the given world. Any consciousness is potentially a philosopher, not only those who claim for themselves the cultivation of this beautiful flower as their sole patrimony. Philosophy cannot be hypostasized in the professional activity of those who call themselves philosophers. Nothing can deprive it of its vitality: philosophy is life; it is the pleasure of thinking for its own sake, of exploring the meaning of reality through imagination. The intelligibility which philosophy seeks cannot be reduced to the realm of scientific inquiry. Philosophy does long for grasping the truth of the world, but its task does not end here: philosophy is aimed at *creating*, at offering a meaning through the world which philosophy itself patiently and passionately edifies, with greater mastery in the case of those authors who have shown a higher degree of sharpness and penetration.

However, and as a relevant difference with art, the free world that consciousness creates (in its wish for contemplating the meaning which the universe does not offer), the world meant to grant a word inside the vast and dark silence of the universe, is not deliberately detached from the sphere of intelligibility. Philosophy does not renounce reason. Philosophy does not surrender to pure arbitrariness. Philosophy is a mixture of art and science. It constitutes that inscrutable bridge which connects freedom and intelligibility, spontaneity and necessity. Through philosophy, consciousness is committed to the unconditioned, but this horizon is not the result of a desperate lack of satisfaction with the world: philosophy tries to understand the world in its truth. Thus, it wants a new world: it longs for creativity. The light of philosophy points to the illuminating power of love, beauty, and wisdom. Philosophy beautifully loves wisdom; it is committed to the fathomless beauty which emanates from understanding that the world in its sameness would never satiate the human longing for meaning. Consciousness realizes that it incarnates an unceasing capacity for questioning and challenging that which is given. Consciousness perceives of its vocation to *novum*, to expanding the frontiers of being, to the *growth* of humanity, to collaboration, to life in common. Philosophy is therefore love of mankind. He who venerates wisdom, he who entirely commits himself to the quest of a kind of wisdom which the world could never offer, is eagerly longing for the growth of humanity, for the life of humanity, for the display of its vital energies. The wish for creation manifests love of humanity.

If art can be compared to pure spontaneity, philosophy reflects that order of freedom which has understood the world in its truth, so that it looks for a meaning that the world does not yield. Nevertheless, this valiant wish for meaning, this "love of wisdom" (which is will to grow, to live, and to propagate such an overwhelming eagerness for life to the whole of humanity), is manifested in a reflexive way. The new world which philosophy seeks is not edified for its own sake. Rather, the goal is love, the peak is beauty, and the pinnacle is wisdom: the goal is not the challenge to the world but the unconditional commitment to a purity which shines as love, beauty, and wisdom; to a longing which philosophy envisions under the shape of *intelligible creation*. The creativity of philosophy is intertwined with the discoveries of science. Philosophy creates a new world without rejecting the fruits of the intellectual endeavor represented by modern science. Philosophy drinks in the same fountains from which the infinite longing for freedom flows, a longing that inspires artistic fervor, but it translates it into a language intelligible for all: into a discourse that may propitiate the growth of humanity. Philosophy seeks, just as science, to understand the world, but this longing leads to the creation of a new world in which meaning may flourish. Unlike art, philosophy creates its own world because it seeks to understand and it loves wisdom: philosophy creates, in order to understand the ultimate truth, the unconditioned, the inveterate power from which everything comes and to which everything leads.

The will to understand which ignites the flame of philosophy reflects such a profound love for wisdom that meaning has to be discovered *in a creative way*. Philosophy cannot limit its task to recognizing the absence of a meaning or the presence of a hypothetical sense in world and history. Rather, it delves into reality in such a deep way as to construct that meaning in the very act of creating, of expanding the energies of being, of broadening any given frontier, of opening itself to the possibility of *novum*. In the most beautiful act of abnegation, in the most sublime act of detachment, philosophy is committed to that which is impossible. Philosophy offers a meaning to humanity, a form of understanding which necessarily transcends the explanation provided by the natural sciences and approaches art inasmuch as creation. But this world is intelligible, it is the fruit of reflection, it is the result of the conscious realization of the insufficiency of the world and the need to challenge the cosmos.

Philosophy is open to creation without taking a radical, insurmountable distance from the world. It is true that art does not create against the world: it uses the world in order to edify its own aesthetic world. However, art reflects the solitude of consciousness, its sadness before the tormenting absence of meaning. This pain is venturous, because it lightens artistic creativity. This pain radiates passion and commitment; it is a form of fortunate suffering, for it has fostered the emergence of the greatest artistic works in history, of those works which can hardly cease to evoke thoughts and feelings. Nevertheless, the solitude with which philosophy must deal is no longer silent: it is a kind of solitude that has meditated upon its own state. Its commitment to creation is the fruit of its longing for understanding and discovering such a deep truth that only the creation of a *novum* might unfold it. The truth which philosophy seeks leads to dreaming of the growth of humanity through love, beauty, and wisdom.

Through philosophy, consciousness discovers that love, beauty, and wisdom are its innermost possibilities. It is consciousness that creates love, beauty, and wisdom. Art represents the attempt at edifying a world in which dreams, the recondite intuition that is cultivated in the intimacy of consciousness, the profoundest and most overwhelming longing, may find a dwelling, so that consciousness can listen, beyond the silence of this immense world, the word which it anxiously desires, a word that has to be its own creation. Through philosophy, consciousness realizes that this ideal, this *truth*, this *novum*, this *freedom* . . . must be *created*, and it must be the result of the activity of thought and sentiment, of understanding and will. Philosophy is art turned into thought: the art of thinking, the aesthetics of wisdom, the instauration of a space of true freedom, in which consciousness does not suffer the constraints of the urgency to explore the world in its sameness, of unveiling the structure and functioning of the universe, but it can courageously open itself to creating a meaning. Love, beauty, and wisdom, the golden fruits of free creation committed to the intuition of the unconditioned, pure, and inexhaustible; love, beauty, and wisdom, that which stands as end in itself, can never "appear." Philosophy comes to the awareness that the ideal cannot set its feet on the arid surface of the Earth. However, this both empirical and "metaphysical" evidence does not discourage consciousness from looking for the ideal, for that which is "impossible." Its commitment to creation is so intense and honest that not even the impossible can destroy the longing for novelty and purity. Behold the abnegation of consciousness, its detachment, its diaphanous generosity: to live for the impossible.

Love, beauty, and wisdom cannot "appear;" otherwise, they would lose their unconditional nature, their freedom, their unceasing creativity. They would become "exhausted," "closed" over their own objectification inside the rigid limits of a world that constantly returns to its sameness (we can appreciate at this point the resonances of the German theologian Dietrich Bonhoeffer's statement: "Einen Gott, den es gibt, gibt es nicht"[4]). But it is in the longing for love, beauty, and wisdom, in the presage that timid gleams of the unconditioned may blunt, where the fountain of creativity dwells.

To renounce the possibility that love, beauty, and wisdom may "appear" in their purity in the *hic et nunc* of world and history does not obey a strategy of "conscious seclusion," meant to flee from the evidence that the ideal can never be enthroned in the vulnerability of space and time. The wish for the unconditioned, accompanied by the awareness that it cannot be fully realized in history, is not the fruit of a perpetual "exoneration" of consciousness, which aims to identify that pure freedom in spite of understanding that everything in the world is governed by the inexorable concatenation of causes and effects. Consciousness does not take refuge in the placidity of the impossible ideal in order to gain perennial consolation against the vicissitudes of history. That which is hidden, the "*absconditus*"

---

4. "A God that 'exists' ['is given'] does not exist ['is not given']." Bonhoeffer, *Akt und Sein*, 94.

of love, beauty, and wisdom, the "impossibility" of creation, freedom, and the broadening of the frontiers of being, does not represent an empty song to fathomless abysses capable of captivating our poetic imagination. The awareness of this impossibility is a source of commitment, which contributes to changing history here and now. It leads to challenging the world and to propitiate the advent of a new spring. It implies to capture the moment of "inexhaustibility." It poses the need to preserve an unrestrained ontological space in which purity may truly shine. Consciousness anticipates this inscrutable enclave in the exercise of its most intimate power. Consciousness "appears without appearing" in the world, so that it reflects, with clarity and evocation, the rubric of the unconditioned: of that which, despite being, is not; of that which, in spite of its power, cannot be; of *novum*, true creation, *pure freedom*.

EXCURSUS: A SALVIFIC HISTORY FOR ALL

We have to find salvation in history, because thought lives in history. Thought, in fact, gives life to history. Conceiving of ourselves as historical beings is the inexorable moment in our quest for a path of salvation, in our search for the incarnation of love, beauty, and wisdom in the colorful home of space and time.

Marx offered a reflection on history whose trace can be felt in almost every single branch of the social sciences, and in whose legacy so many political movements have found their source of inspiration since the 19th century. There is therefore a legitimate question: what is the principal contribution of Marx to human thinking?

The topic is extremely complex on account of the multiple dimensions of Marx's work, and we could even say that it adopts different levels of meaning depending upon the realm in which his ideas are actually applied. However, I believe that there is a fundamental core in Marx's thought which synthesizes, better than any other one, the true scope of his thesis: the stress on the historicity of the spheres of human life. In this way, Marx dissolves the natural into the historical. The natural, eternal, and permanent falls, under the concomitant effects of the critique of the great German philosopher, into the kingdom of the historical, temporal, and variable reality. What seemed to be part of a set of invariable and universal laws is now regarded as the result of the dynamics of history. Nature transforms itself into history and therefore into the object of human action.[5]

If, according to Roland Barthes, a myth makes that which is historical become natural, and it attributes to a representation which is the result of time an eternal and immutable character, as if it belonged to the primeval and inexorable constitution of the world,[6] then we can say that Marx is the great "demystifier" of modernity. With his radical suspicion about anything that pretends to appear as a natural reality

---

5. On the central categories of Marx's social thought, cf. Unger, *Social Theory, Its Situation and Its Task*, 96–119.

6. This idea is key to Roland Barthes's *Mythologies* (1957), in which he applies this series of considerations to the realm of politics, as in the case of the bourgeois myths: "Le statut de la bourgeoisie est particulier, historique: l'homme qu'elle représente sera universel, éternel; (. . .) Enfin, l'idée première du monde perfectible, mobile, produira l'image renversée d'une humanité immuable, définie par une identité infiniment recommencée" (250–51). The bourgeoisie tries to make the historical seem natural: that which is changeable, immutable, and that which has been created by the human beings, an eternal law of the universe.

(by means of unveiling the process of its historical genesis), Marx has opened the highest liberating potential which humanity possesses: its own rationality, critically directed towards the examination of the circumstances in which we live.

The humanizing potential of historical reason, which does not limit itself to the analysis of things as they are manifested in the present reality but interprets them in a broader perspective (that of history), capable of relativizing present structures and inaugurating the hope in a different future, resembles the liberating power of the natural sciences. The natural sciences demythologize the world, because in their examination of physical phenomena they look for their deeper causes, with the intention of grasping the ultimate laws that rule upon them. The world is no longer the expression of unintelligible randomness, a mere present structure; rather, it is the result of millions of years of a vast cosmic and biological evolution under the irrevocable government of a series of laws. In a similar way, Marx demythologizes social reality by showing that it is the vivid fruit of history, not the product of an impersonal nature which escapes human action. Marx humanizes the present as he delivers it to the hands of humanity. The present is the outcome of the past, and it is destined to change.

Looking at things from a historical perspective is the only way to achieve the necessary critical distance from the present in order to understand why things are the way they are and if it is possible for them to be otherwise; moreover, it is the only way to understand if things must be otherwise. Judgments about "be" and "must be" are born in history, and they are orientated towards history. They do not stem from an impersonalized but a historicized nature. The historicity of the human world enlightens hope for humanity. It offers the confidence in the possibility of a different future: the contradictions of a present time are not final.

The essential difference between progressive and conservative approaches to the human world has been, is, and will always reside in the assimilation and the rejection of a historical perspective.[7] In conservatism, things are just as they have to be. Social and economic structures respond to natural, eternal laws, not to the contingency of history. The balances of power between human beings must be maintained since

---

7. Europe's long history of achievements and tragedies must help it contribute to the avant-garde of a humane project for the world, redeeming itself from its past mistakes by becoming "the Europe of ethics," a Europe which may be synonymous with pluralism, tolerance, and commitment.

they reflect the imperishable order of cosmos. Humanity has no real future but a past transformed into a necessary present.[8]

In a progressive conception, humanity is the owner of its own destiny. There is fatality, but it is negligible in comparison with the human capacity for modifying a contradictory present and creating a future which may bring hope for those who do not envision it. Things are the way they are not on account of universal laws but as the result of a historical process. Present relations of power have undergone different stages, adopting different forms; they have been often subverted, and they can still generate a new, even unpredictable, scenario. The challenge for progressivism is to become aware that the beauty and richness of history for the human spirit resides in its "openness": there must always be future, and no generation has the right to extinguish the flame of history by reaching its hypothetical final stage.

By accentuating the historicity of the human world Marx has liberated mankind from the chains of the present. Jürgen Habermas has also highlighted, in *The Theory of Communicative Action*, that Marx's great discovery is the historicity of social relations. The imprint of Hegel is clear, and it stands above all other possible traces that can be identified in Marx's work, but what Hegel contemplated as the history of the spirit looking for itself is for Marx the history of a torn humanity which longs for a final reconciliation, for a definitive kingdom. Both of them, however, think that *being* is *history*.

The attribution of the condition of "ontological space" *par excellence* to history in the understanding of the human being has allowed Marx to unfold the huge, and almost infinite, power of liberation of the collective action over time. It is true that the future does not always bring newness, but it is perennially open, and in this sense Wolfhart Pannenberg is right in claiming that the future is a power which liberates the present from the determinations of the *hic et nunc*.[9] The hope in change resides in the future, in its differentiation from a present in which truth does not exist, because humanity has not found itself yet.

The optimism inspired by our condition of historical beings faces a problem: history is also the narration of the unceasing will of power and domination. Truth cannot appear in a history in which

---

8. As Marx and Engels wrote in *The Communist Manifesto*, part 2: "In bourgeois society, the past dominates the present. In communist society the present dominates the past."

9. Cf. Pannenberg, *Theology and the Kingdom of God*.

reconciliation cannot be achieved, because the will of power prevails, and it separates human beings from themselves and nature. A history based exclusively upon the pursuit of power has not achieved reconciliation with itself. That which is true is definitive, immutable, and permanent: it is an asymptotic limit, but in history there is only contingence, whose highest expression is the will of power. We seek power because we are aware that we lack the light of an ultimate reality. We feel the need to dominate others and to subjugate nature because we have not yet found something capable of overcoming any wish and bringing the final peace.

We may be unable to find truth in history. There must always be a future, and truth cannot appear in its fullness. Eschatology is impossible, because history cannot become consummated if we still want to be human beings endowed with a future and a latent hope. A creative tension emerges, and no reconciliation is envisioned. However, it is legitimate to think that even in a perennially opened history we could still have a truly absolute scenario: the possibility of an infinite openness of the human mind, which would never exhaust the power of thought. We are servants of thought. Being always transcends itself in thought, it "ulteriorizes" itself, and its only limit is infinity. This may seem frustrating and tiring, but in each moment, subject, and history something "ultimate" has been achieved: we are edifying a path for thought, and we must not be discouraged by the fact that it may be potentially infinite, because we are part of it. The radical openness of history constitutes an exhortation for identifying that which, in spite of its "inexhaustibility," its "lack of resolution," could grant us even a fragile intuition of the purest, ultimate goal: love, beauty, and wisdom.

The principal obstacle against freedom of thought is the absolutization of the present, the objectification of the will of power in the structures of social relations in a given moment. This prevents the envisioning of the future. The loss of the sense of history is the greatest tragedy of humanity. Forgetting the past, and closing our minds to the power of the future by consecrating the present as a definitive reality, divides humanity. We become condemned to accepting that which is given, and our capacity for creation vanishes. Memory is the foundation of our hopeful looking at the future. We must remember that we, as humanity, are the children of history, after having overcome past stages and having suffered incommensurable horrors.

Solidarity beyond Itself: Creation

By preserving the sense of history we save ourselves as humanity. If we accept reification as an inexorable dynamic, then we become instruments of strategic actions which lack historical perspective and which do not aim to edify a history that may be meaningful (formal, intangible condition) for the whole of humanity (material, tangible condition). This is our great challenge: to build a history that may be meaningful for everyone and not only for few. Humanity cannot reify itself in ages, cultures, and powers: it needs to reach emancipation and become the age, the culture, and the power. The denial of this possibility eclipses any idea of justice.

Where is the utopia that may unite us, and which may be not only of mine but also yours, and his, and hers, and theirs? This is already a utopia: the union of human spirits, as if subjectivities might edify a realm of objectivity. I believe that such a utopia must embrace the quest for a meaningful history for everyone: the utopia of "conscience" in "consciences," of "universality" in "particularities." A meaningful history is the condition of possibility for everyone to find a sense in history without preventing others from doing so. It is therefore the utopia of toleration. As Habermas has suggested in several of his works, truth must be the universal reconciliation, the emancipation of mankind through the resurrection of nature. Reason, if it becomes an instrument for reconciliation and not for domination, transcends the stage of a mere means: it reaches the category of an end, since it is not possible to expect anything else beyond the reconciliation of all that seems divided and confronted.

The idea of reconciliation allows us to envision a way out of the labyrinth of the absence of meaning in human life. Solidarity, in the epistemological realm, is equivalent to an intersubjective, pluralistic rationality which assimilates everything that instrumental rationality dissociates: human beings, humanity, and nature. By founding identity not upon the isolated *ego* but on a form of intersubjectivity which is capable of thinking of the universal and realizing it as praxis in history, we can edify a free society. Against the myth of an already constituted subject it is necessary to remark that conscience as reflection demands a moment of "positing itself" and "returning to itself," both in nature and history. The subject is not constituted in advance: he needs to go out of himself in order to become more of "himself," and this is perhaps the greatest philosophical contribution of German idealism.

Part 2: *Fundamentum* in History

The recuperation of the "intersubjective subject" represents the rediscovery of solidarity as the epicenter of the discourse that proclaims the edification of a truly humane history. The defense of intersubjectivity is actually a political struggle: what should prevail, whether a history condemned to reproducing the present relations of power or a history opened to a different future, in which it may be possible to dream of a truly fraternal humanity? The canonization of the present is analogous to the consecration of instrumental rationality. In it, domination perpetuates itself and there is no possible reconciliation beside false consciousness. The hope for the future is therefore similar to the quest, although imperfect, for a reconciliation which may heal the wounds of an aggrieved humanity and an injured nature, and which may find an authentic and melodic harmony not in the mythological representation that seeks to discourage the ardor of honestly revolutionary spirits, by spreading the conviction that things cannot be otherwise, but by achieving a space in which domination may be substituted with understanding.

It is true that we cannot reach the security that, even if communicative action prevailed, real understanding would have been actually achieved. However, we can suppose that the conditions for reason to overcome itself (in order to become eventually transformed into action) and to question the present determinations (that darken reconciliation among human beings) might be set. The most surprising capacity of human reason resides in its inexhaustible disposition to transcending its present state.

Any given interpretation of world and history has been overcome by proposing, in a rational, argumentative way, an alternative view which also stemmed from the fountains of reason. Reason seems to gravitate around itself: scientific hypotheses, philosophical schools, religious worldviews which, behind their rich symbolism, try to express a certain rational conception: reason and more reason. There is room for the legitimate suspicion that it may all consist of a process which happens within the rigid limits of our own rational constitution, and which is self-referential to reason, instead of pointing to an external objectivity that might be identified with an effective understanding.

The latter problem is undoubtedly complex, and it brings about many serious questions on the viability of reason to organize the world and to edify a more just society. However, we cannot renounce reason, because there is no possible substitute. We must achieve a truly critical rationality through which to open reason itself, transforming it into an even greater power. This process of "healing" reason is not always inspired by reason itself: the non-rational (the beauty of intuition, imagination, and sentiment) often motivates a critique of reason, but this appreciation is always formulated in a rational way. We cannot escape reason. Nietzsche was right: we will believe in God as long as we believe in grammar. We will believe in reason as long as we believe in language, and we are linguistic beings. Our challenge lies in achieving a genuinely critical rationality which, aware of its limitations and its lack of *fundamentum* (since we can never be sure that the contents elucidated by reason actually correspond to an objective reality, external to ourselves), is constantly ready to think in a deeper way and to think of a vaster range of possibilities: infiniteness resides in the unceasing quest for a new future.

Versus the objection that any discourse about rationality and communication hides a cultural prejudice it is legitimate to establish a critical postulate: the belief that all cultures can open themselves, both internally and externally, in order to overcome their tensions and to grant a higher degree of freedom to their members. A position that takes refuge in the mere analysis of discourses as a strategy to avoid dealing with the most urgent problem, which is that of a humanity divided because domination prevails over understanding and solidarity, will necessarily be regressive, and it will justify the present order of things and its structures of power. Against such an attitude there is no better intellectual weapon than the emphasis on a historical perspective: cultures have changed over history, and they will do so in the future.

We need to discover signs of "transcendence" in the midst of history. That which recalls transcendence (the condition of possibility of any reflection that seeks to be universal) is the historicity of humanity. The normative consequence of this statement becomes clear: the right of humanity to possess a meaningful history is the fundamental truth of ethics. Humanity has a history if it can understand itself in history: the edification of a meaningful history for everyone is the great challenge of both thought and action, and it goes beyond any circumstance, any culture, any partiality, because in every time and space it must be possible to build a history endowed with meaning for the whole of humanity. The transcendental realm is therefore the utopian postulate of a society where, to follow Ernst Bloch in *The Principle of Hope*, *homo homini homo*, "man is a man for man." Behold how history becomes meaningful.

In our advanced industrial societies, whose system of production is capitalism, the search for a meaningful history becomes a crucial need. The transformation of capitalism into the expression of a universal law of nature has to be confronted by critical rationality, capable of showing that capitalism is the result of history, that it has vividly evolved over time and that it will inexorably change, and even disappear, so that its achievements must be judged on the basis of their potential to edify a meaningful history.

Capitalism accentuates the primacy of instrumental rationality in its aim to dominate human beings and nature. Capitalistic ethics does not foster the human quest for a meaningful history as the goal of collective actions. Capitalism only looks for power, power as bargaining. Solidarity is always extrinsic to capitalism, and it is imposed from outside. In capitalism, the historical dimension is annulled: immutable relations of production become perpetuated. Even if the whole of humanity eventually profited from its relations of production it would still be impossible to eradicate domination and to serve the ideal of solidarity. The structures of capitalism are too rigid as to embrace the human longing for a new future.

Capitalism consecrates efficiency as the highest norm of life. The goal of history is not meaning, the acquisition, by means of discovery or by means of construction, of something "pure," of love, beauty, and wisdom, but the production of goods and services which may satisfy the ever-increasing necessities of humanity. For capitalism, infiniteness resides in the unceasing potential of production of the market system, in the blind faith in the constant possibility of identifying new needs which may generate new economic dynamism, new entrepreneurial spirits, always within the frigid scheme of the relations of production.

In capitalism, infiniteness is not envisioned in the sincere quest for a meaningful history for all. This is why capitalism cannot properly recognize the victims, and it cannot appreciate the wound of humanity and the longing for reconciliation if it is not as a potential object for the market. If capitalism saves the victims (human beings and an exploited nature) it does so because it believes that it will be able to extend, even more broadly, the margins of its action. Capitalism embraces solidarity when it can benefit from it; it embraces solidarity if it is able to "capitalize" on the world and humanity.

Subordination of vital and social reality is intrinsic to capitalism: nature becomes subject to the human being, and some human beings to others. The spirit of democracy is alien to capitalism, and their eventual conjugation is not due to the nature of this economic system but to a process which is frequently strange to it.[10] The discriminating potential of capitalism is so dangerous that it may stifle the collective aspirations for a shared future. The achievements of capitalism seem overwhelming, and they are automatically used to neutralize any critique of the system. However, they are not the expression of the success of capitalism alone but (and principally) of the organized human labor within an institutional and juridical arrangement which, in fact, limits the scope of capitalism and even denaturalizes it. A purely capitalistic society has never existed.

Science is the human enterprise that looks for knowledge and the emancipation of reason from the atavism of ignorance. Science has been the principal driving force of capitalism, but science was born outside capitalism. Science precedes capitalism both historically and ontologically, just as philosophy and art. That capitalism has been promoted by the different spheres of the human knowledge and that, on its way, capitalism has also contributed to them, does not mean that we have to attribute all the colorful accomplishments of contemporary progress to capitalism

The transformation of industrial capitalism into financial capitalism has preserved the quintessence of the system, but it has highlighted its most perverse and discriminating aspects. Through the predominance of the financial world, the capitalistic imagination believes that it can conquer a world for itself, so that it can turn that which does not exist into existence, obtaining prosperity in the absence of labor and real production. Classical capitalism managed to generate wealth from the exploitation of labor force, but financial capitalism intends to create it by exploitation of the results of classical capitalism. It is, so to speak, a duplication of capitalism, a second order capitalism, which redoubles its dehumanizing, hierarchical potential.

The unsustainability of capitalism does not emerge from external factors but from internal elements that make it unsuitable as a universal

---

10. A completely democratic capitalism is a contradiction in terms. Capitalism is necessarily associated with the negation of fundamental aspects of democracy, for its decisions are based upon theoretically voluntary agreements between the individual parts, not on the general, Rousseaunian will (*volonté génerale*) of the political community.

system. Capitalism produces the illusion that its horizon of prosperity is universal: everyone will participate in it. Nevertheless, by analyzing its deepest structure we realize that such a universal goal is actually unattainable. In order for capitalism to subsist, a large part of humanity has to be deprived of the status of capitalist. Capitalism would fulfill its ideals and promises if everyone might become a capitalist and if everyone might display his creative energies, his entrepreneurial spirit, without being forced to sell himself to the highest bidder.

Capitalism is the negation of universality. In order to persist it needs to be partial, and if it becomes universal, it does so by betraying its deepest foundations. The improvement in the life of the middle classes in the Western world has been generally done at the expense of capitalism, through the approval of laws that guarantee labor rights, contradicting the spirit of *laissez faire* which is consubstantial to key doctrines of capitalism. The European welfare system has been capable, to a certain extent, of "taming" capitalism, while at the same time fostering its creative impetus. But the equilibrium is too fragile, especially in a globalized world in which no global government, no global political action, no global aspiration seems to exist. The success of the European model would mean the triumph of a humane form of capitalism. Its failure would destroy almost all hopes for finding harmony between individual freedom and collective goals.

In addition to its internal unsustainability (which might be interpreted as analytical or conceptual) capitalism faces three principal external limits:

1. An ecological limit: the Earth cannot be infinitely exploited, and human consumption cannot indefinitely increase. This dependency-effect responds to the fact that the Earth is not an unrestricted space. The urgent problem of climate change has underscored the existence of winners and losers in capitalistic growth.

2. An economic limit: capitalism seeks accumulation for its own sake. The goal is not production but the profit that may be obtained out of it. The excess of production is the consequence of an exclusive focus on earnings. The problem is therefore clear: the constant threat of overproduction bears the danger of a potential crisis, since the excess of production will not be distributed altruistically among those who are incapable of acquiring it by their own means (this is, according to the conditions imposed by the system of the free fixation of prices through supply and demand).

3. A human limit: capitalism necessarily generates deep social inequalities, and there is a natural aversion towards those disparities which exceed the reasonable limit that understanding, helped by historical experience and aware of the current state of civilization, is willing to admit.[11]

Against the perpetuation of a system which is alienating for so many members of the human family, and to whose essence instrumental domination over human beings and nature is linked, it is legitimate to oppose a critique whose deepest fountains lie in the assumption of a historical perspective. History will liberate us, and we can embrace hope for the possibility that one day we will regard ourselves as beings endowed with a meaning: the dream that all human beings will be treated as ends and not as means.

Critical reflection is essential for the recovery of social conscience, which, in capitalism, is necessarily subordinated to individual selfishness. Human beings, in capitalism, are violently separated from the dream of edifying a society in terms of fraternity and sorority. These ideals become juvenile whims which have no place in a mature mind. The spirit that seeks to build something new, capable of integrating all human beings instead of excluding them, fades before the primacy of an economically oriented pragmatism which actually hides a will of domination of some beings upon others. As Albert Einstein wrote, "this crippling of individuals I consider the worst evil of capitalism. Our whole educational system suffers from this evil. An exaggerated

11 If, let us say, a person could be twice, or even thrice as intelligent as another (something exceptional from the point of view of intelligence tests), and leaving behind the randomness of luck, it is difficult to understand why certain individuals can be hundreds or even thousands of times as prosperous as others. This excess of success cannot be achieved through their own means alone. It must be accomplished through the work of others and the conditions imposed by a system that allows for such a high degree of accumulation of wealth. The argument that holds that people who have gathered large fortunes have worked harder or have contributed more to society is not convincing at all. Even if the wealthy have worked harder or have contributed more to society, the question is, what is the limit? Can anyone, in normal conditions, work, let us say, a hundred times more or a hundred times more intensely than anyone else? The idea of responsibility (i.e., that those people earning more have greater responsibility and higher "marginal utility" for society) does not solve the problem because responsibility appears within a system that enables it to be distributed and valued in an unequal way. Upon this basis, democratically elected presidents should be the wealthiest people on earth. Responsibility has to be shared by all in solidarity. The "social utility" of someone's work is a social construction: society decides that which is more useful and that which should be valued more. In the same way, society, illuminated by a new spirit (that of solidarity), could decide to value all works in a more equitable way.

competitive attitude is inculcated into the student, who is trained to worship acquisitive success as a preparation for his future career."[12]

Capitalism inherits a history of tragedy, of oppression and triumph of the stronger over the weaker, but it does not seek to achieve a truly just society that may break from that chain of inhumanity. Capitalism is not capable of proposing a goal that may unite human beings beyond their individual profit. Capitalism denies the possibility of collective aspirations of humanity, and it therefore denies the very possibility of humanity, now reduced to a mere sum of individuals who can be profitable for each other. In capitalism, history crystallizes in an immutable order, and the river of time leads to a monotonous ocean, which is the infinite will of accumulation, instead of creating exuberant valleys that may foster the blossoming of the true forces of human nature, finding the infinite not in having but in being.

Any form of liberation bears the danger of promoting a new kind of slavery. In this sense, historical experience shows that we can never abdicate from critical rationality. The aim to defeat the numerous alienations that divide humanity (on the basis of gender, race, social class, religion) poses the risk of creating new types of servitude and reproducing the previous ones. Only critical rationality, which thinks from the perspective of history and which is constantly willing to look at the future, can become a truly humane and humanizing reason.

The ambiguity of history is distressing. On the one hand, it seems to be the result of an unending struggle for power between individuals and communities, indifferent to any possible meaning, acting in an anarchical way that exhibits no goal at all, but, on the other hand, there is an almost instinctive resistance to accepting this depiction. It is difficult to waive the possibility of seeing a will of meaning in the course of times, a higher conscience of the human capacity for creating, enjoying, and discovering. Maybe the true goal of history resides in serving as the abode of thought, so that we stand in history in order to extend the horizon of being through thinking. Thus, the lack of meaning in history becomes replaced by the edification of a space of signification through thought, capable of revealing the horizon of permanence. This is salvation. And this "kingdom of meaning" demands the pursuit of "purity," of inexhaustible realities which cannot be "possessed" but must be lived: love, beauty, and wisdom.

---

12. Einstein, "Why Socialism?"

EXCURSUS: FROM THE "THROWNNESS"[13] INTO THE WORLD TO THE KINGDOM OF ENDS

True: no one has asked me for permission to exist. I have come into this world without looking for it. My existence is due to the will of other people. This may seem sad, and it is so indeed. There are, in fact, many questions that one would like to pose, but is there anyone who has the answer to them? Is there anyone who knows, after all, why I am living? I feel myself thrown into a world which I have not created. I feel part of a world which has been given to me, but on which I have not had any responsibility at all.

Nobody has asked us, as humanity, if we wanted to live. We could ask our parents why they wanted us to come to this world. They could offer different reasons and, for sure, the most powerful one would be that of love. They loved us, and that is why we were born. We are children of love, and so are our parents, and their parents, and their parents' parents, as far as the dawn of humanity. But one is not always a son of love. We do not know what love is, and love often hides other realities. We do not know the reason why we are here. We have come, and that is all. It seems that an insurmountable barrier emerges, which prevents thought from giving any clear step forward. There is only darkness, as if we were in an infinite tunnel from which no light is envisioned beyond what we ourselves can light inside it.

No one called us asking if we wanted to exist: *ecce nos quia nemo vocabit nos*. Our existence is indebted to others, and since we have little power over its origin, we want at least to have power over its development and its outcome. We seek to be worthy of our existence, and we feel the duty to affirm ourselves as existing. We must do something

---

13. Heidegger's *Geworfenheit*: "This characteristic of Dasein's Being—this 'that it is'—is veiled in its 'whence' and 'whither,' yet disclosed in itself all the more unveiledly; we call it the '*thrownness*' of this entity into its 'there'; indeed, it is thrown in such a way that, as Being-in-the-world, it is the 'there.' The expression 'thrownness' is meant to suggest the *facticity of its being delivered over*" (*Being and Time*). According to J.-F. Suter, the idea of "thrownness" raises an important difference between the philosophies of Dilthey and Heidegger. For Heidegger, the human being has been thrown into the world and is abandoned to the power of destiny. Dilthey, however, believes in the human vocation to safeguard the cultural heritage of the past by inserting itself in a history that may transcend its particularity. Cf. Suter, *Philosophie et Histoire chez Wilhelm Dilthey*, 185–86. In any case, we should not forget that in his *Letter on Humanism*, Heidegger grants unquestionable relevance to the perspective of the "care of being" and man as the "shepherd of being" (ideas that might be interpreted as an expression of a "vocation" for humanity), even in spite of *Geworfenheit*.

that may justify our existence, as if we all had a vocation. It is difficult to speak in terms of vocation when we have suddenly appeared, without wishing to do so, but once we are in the world, once, by virtue of unknown ultimate causes, we are in the midst of the turbulent vortex of existence we have the duty to give reason for that existence. Knowledge, love, beauty, pleasure—they are all ways to affirm ourselves: even if no one asked us, we would have agreed to come into this world, and we would have given the unusual permission to exist.

Perhaps we will never be able to overcome the state of philosophical indigence generated by the vertigo of an existence in which we simultaneously face life and death, beauty and horror, knowledge and ignorance. Who is going to release us from this prison of ignorance and lack of understanding? The uncertainty concerning the meaning of our existence may be regarded in a negative way, as an expression of our fragility, of our contingency, and our lack of meaning. However, we can choose a positive interpretation: meaning is not closed, and we can build it. This is our divine possession: we are the agents of a history which is constantly opened to a new future. Why should we choose a negative hermeneutics of existence? We must learn to adopt a positive outlook to the world, because this is the only way to bring justice to the victims of history and to the collective aspirations of humanity.

Distress concerning the meaning of life cannot eclipse the necessity for a commitment to the history of mankind, to the edification of a more just, more humane world. We do not have the right to appropriate the profound anguish produced by the problem of the meaning of existence, because there are millions of human beings who everyday hover between life and death, and nonetheless look forward. While there is no social justice in this world, while the sentiment of solidarity is not capable of defeating the power of individual selfishness, and while it has not become true that, as medieval philosophers proclaimed, good may be *diffusivum sui*, each lamentation which paralyzes action will be a concession to the unfair and inhuman order that governs most of humanity.

One of the formulations of Immanuel Kant's categorical imperative is the following: "Act in such a way that you treat humanity, whether in your own person or in the person of any other, never merely as a means to an end, but always at the same time as an end."[14] The consideration of the human person as an end and never as a means to

---

14. Cf. Kant, *Groundwork of the Metaphysics of Morals*.

an end constitutes the greatest ideal of ethics. The history of human progress has consisted of the increasing capacity of society for providing more spaces of autonomy, knowledge, and creativity. With the development of both the sciences of nature and the sciences of the spirit, by means of extending individual and social rights, and through the great edifications of art and culture, the human being has been able to regard himself, with an ever growing conscience, as a true end.

However, progress exhibits a dimension of negativity which may become a source of fear: science and technique allow us to explore unknown, even unimaginable, scenarios, but they also enslave us with their destructive power; the rationalization of social organizations contributes to the possibility of a shared progress, so that we can propose common goals, but it may also stifle the creative energies of the individual, by submitting us to inexorable social dynamics, becoming means serving alien ends. Economic development does not always help people become an end, but it often transforms us into means in the midst of a process, that of economic growth, which is not necessarily beneficial or humanizing.

The ambivalence of history may never be solved at all, not even in the most idyllic future. The contradiction *par excellence* to any positive enthusiasm about the edification of a more humane history will always persist: death as radical non-utopia, death as the expression of the fact that the human being is condemned to be a means in the process that brings our species towards a destiny which is hardly intelligible for us. It is always possible to regard ourselves as a form of "creative negativity," since by virtue of our death we allow for the birth of new realities, and we help the world change in the path of evolution and history. However, that to which Max Horkheimer referred as the "longing for fulfilled justice," so that the executioner may not succeed over his victim and the injustices of history may not pass unpunished, still remains. This longing generates a nostalgia for something totally other to the world and history. There was nothing new in Horkheimer's wish, which is shared by many religious traditions, but as the historian Harry Austryn Wolfson wrote: "novelty in philosophy is often a matter of daring rather than of invention,"[15] and Horkheimer had the courage to formulate what many had felt before him.

Are we condemned to conceiving of ourselves as ends only as long as it constitutes a utopian, unreachable ideal of reason? Science,

---

15. Cf. Wolfson, *The Philosophy of Spinoza*, 2:331.

philosophy, art, and, in general, any human quest for something that overcomes the contingency of the present, are expressions of the will to achieve the condition of ends. The human struggles for a better world, for an ethical action, for an answer to the questions of science, for a space of beauty and compassion . . . , they all point to the longing for a meaning. The meaning is given by the end, not by the means. The means necessarily leads to the end as the category that explains the nature and significance of the means. If we look for a meaning of our existence and of human aspirations throughout history, we do so because we seek to be ends instead of means. And the end is permanence. The end remains even if the means is exhausted. To speak about the human being in terms of "ends" and not of "means" is equivalent to imagining the presence of a permanent reality in history, of a *Geist*, of a spirit which unites what is apparently divergent in a dimension of unifying totality. The infinite non-satisfaction of humanity shapes the "mediated meaning," this is, the meaning of each age, which always possesses an "antecedent" and a potential "consequent" over the course of times, but it does not create the final meaning of history. In every age we can find the opportunity for a new beginning which may correct the deviations of the former times in the path towards a more just world.

The truth is that we live between heavens that surpass us, a vast cosmic horizon of constellations and remote celestial bodies, in which our smallness is threatening, and an earth which we are learning to know and dominate, discovering the huge potential that resides inside us. Let us recall Kant's final words in his *Critique of Practical Reason*: "Two things fill the mind with ever-increasing wonder and awe, the more often and the more intensely the mind of thought is drawn to them: the starry heavens above me and the moral law within me." Every new answer has opened a new question, every achievement has inaugurated a new challenge, and every system of thought has generated new views of the world, but perplexity before the world, history, and human beings persists. The shining of the stars has made us create the natural sciences, and the flame of morality is the source of philosophy, ethics, social reflection, and art, as the mirror of our desires. The frontier between the transcendent, the starry sky that shines above us, and the immanent, the moral law which exists in our hearts, is the human hope for the universal kingdom of ends,[16] in which nature and freedom may converge.

---

16. The philosophy of Kant attributes absolute value to the individual existence

Solidarity beyond Itself: Creation

As history goes on, we become aware of its deep contradictions, but we still look up to the starry sky above us, and we still continue to listen to the moral law that dwells inside us; we still look for an answer to the urgent question about our position in the universe and the meaning of all things, and through dialogue, meditation, and the permanent intellectual and moral eagerness to know, we expand the frontiers of our humanity. The effort to bequeath something that may remain after our death, especially in the realms of knowledge and goodness, links us to the unconditioned, and it manifests the "ultimate" in ourselves: love, beauty, and wisdom.

We have compelling reasons to be optimistic because, in spite of the contradictions of history, we have pursued a scenario ruled by a state of greater knowledge and greater capacity for the good. This is actually the Kingdom of God imagined by several religions, the paradise of love, beauty, and wisdom, which is initiated in the *hic et nunc* of the world and history, and points to the realm of the unconditioned *fundamentum*, of the ultimate reason: the universal kingdom of ends, the highest of unrealized utopias, but the only one capable of satisfying our infinite wish for knowledge, justice, love, and beauty: the dream of the salvation of humanity through thought, action, and hope, a redemption that is unveiled in the edification of a history that may be meaningful for all.

In that kingdom, of which the music of Bach is only a glimpse of beauty and the formulae of Einstein a timid expression of its sophistication, the human being will be an end in itself, an unconditioned meaning in communion with other unconditioned and permanent meanings. The concept of the universal kingdom of ends should not be understood as a concession to religious faith, as a result of fear of death and distress before the possibility of the absence of meaning in history. It is, on the contrary, an idea that reason discovers through its own virtue, on the basis of its dignity and its infinite longing, which

---

of each human being. One of the possible formulations of the categorical imperative, which is the supreme and unconditional norm of practical reason, is that of being obliged to treat every person as an end, never as a means, in a universal kingdom of ends (the individual does not become subordinated to the goals of the spirit). This universal kingdom of ends demands that practical reason postulate an infinite space in which the balance of justice be equilibrated, so that happiness and the fulfilment of duty become ultimately reconciled, as it is expressed by Kant in his *Critique of Practical Reason*. On the idea of the immortality of the soul in Kant, cf. Gómez Caffarena, *El Teísmo Moral de Kant*, 120–38. For an examination of the moral philosophy of Kant from the analytic perspective, cf. Korsgaard, *Creating the Kingdom of Ends*.

demand an equally infinite answer. Here, the salvific power of thought appears in its most sumptuous manifestation. Only love, beauty, and wisdom could answer the depth, sincerity, and scope of our profoundest questions.

The kingdom of ends is already built in history when we edify a scenario in which to conceive of every human being as an end, never as a means for ends other than his personal realization and his own dignity. Meanwhile, in a world in which so many men and women are used as means for economic development and for the enrichment of others, in a society in which so many people lack what is necessary, having been deprived of access to the nobles fruits of knowledge and the high pinnacles of beauty created by their fellow human beings throughout the centuries, it will be impossible for mankind to reach what reason seems to impose to all of us: the condition of ends, the salvific horizon of thought and action. And only from the consideration of the human being as an end is it possible that peace among individuals, peoples, cultures, and religions may arise. Let us look for our true humanity through our quest for love, beauty, and wisdom: behold our salvation.

EXCURSUS: THE CONCEPT OF RELIGION AND THE SCOPE OF THEOLOGY

The idea of religion cannot be understood without taking into consideration its intimate association with the search for meaning. Consciousness enables humanity to create its own world, but mankind is constantly threatened by the evidence of a silent universe with which it cannot engage in a satisfactory dialogue. Religions try to provide the missing interlocutor: whether it be nature, or a personal and transcendent being, or the self-liberation from wishes, religiosity always refers to a sphere of meaning, to a realm of answers for human questions, in which communication can actually take place, even if through the mediation of different sets of rites and practices that establish the channels from which to access that semantic space.

What we have just said suggests that religion is not necessarily connected with the belief in God. The reason behind this presupposition is that the notion of God is problematic even within the different religious traditions. For example, the doctrine of a personal God seems to be absent from *Theravada* Buddhism,[17] and the very understanding of God as a personal being is irreparably mediated by the specific religious tradition, in such a way that the question about who God is does not yield to a simple, generalizing answer but it must inevitably confront the various expressions of religiosity that nowadays exist and have existed in the past.[18]

---

17. For an introduction to *Theravada* Buddhism, cf. Williams, *Buddhism: Critical Concepts in Religious Studies* vol. 2, *The Early Buddhist Schools and Doctrinal History*; *Theravada Doctrine*. On the philosophical dimensions of Buddhism, cf. Taliaferro et al., *A Companion to Philosophy of Religion*, 13–22. For the relationship between Buddhist and Hindu philosophies of religion in India, cf. Patil, *Against a Hindu God*.

18. In his book *The Meaning and End of Religion*, Wilfred Cantwell Smith questions the legitimacy of the concept of "religion," which he regards as a European construct. The category of "religion" would be the result of the apologetic efforts of European scholars and the affirmation of an identity of political nature. However, do these considerations allow for the invalidation of the use of the idea of "religion"? Isn't any scientific and academic category a construct, including those of "culture" and "identity"? Can scientific analysis renounce any form of generalization and abstraction so that it must surrender to the pretensions of uniqueness that each religious tradition claims for itself, with the well-known danger of sectarianism and lack of objectivity? In any case, it is true that the focus on "traditions" rather than hypothetical "essences" (of which an eminent example is Robinson and Koester, *Trajectories through Early Christianity*) helps to overcome the temptation of replacing the rich variety within the different religious traditions with a uniform conception that disregards their intrinsic plurality.

Part 2: *Fundamentum* in History

The philosophical reflection about religion has been a constant theme for the major thinkers of the West. The attempt at explaining the presence of religion in human life has not been a mere appendix to a certain philosophical discourse: it has normally conveyed the full power of that philosophical proposal, so that, in the analysis of religious experience, the range and scope of a certain philosophy can be fully assessed.

The outstanding variety of theories about the origin and nature of religion should not make us forget that, beyond the richness and plurality of views, it is possible to identify common aspects, a series of fundamental assumptions which facilitate a classification of these theses in accordance with the degree of "purity" that they attribute to the religious experience. By "purity" we mean, in a Kantian sense, the independence of the religious dimension from other experiences of human life (psychological, social, ethical, aesthetic. . .). The "purest" possible approach to the nature of religion would be that which regarded it as an absolutely irreducible experience in human being, which could not be justified in terms of other experiences, as if it were a subsidiary form to something else. Religion would therefore be something radically primary and unconditional, some sort of *causa sui* which would recall a fundamental experience in human life that cannot be assimilated into more basic experiences. If we admit this criterion, it is possible to distinguish the following principal theses about the core nature of the religious experience:

1. *A priori in descendo*: religion as perception of something that is ultimate. There is no projection of the self onto a different realm, for the "ultimate" is apprehended within the sphere of consciousness itself, generally on account of its insufficiency and finiteness.

    a) Unconditional priority of the religious experience. Absolute immediacy: religion as radical intuition of the totally other (Rudolf Otto).[19]

---

19. According to Rudolf Otto, religion has to do with the experience of the "numinous," and *das Numinose* cannot be reduced to anything else. *Das Numinose* expresses the intuition that there is something totally-other to the world which radically challenges cosmos. Therefore, it cannot be derived from the world, but it is radically prior to it. Cf. Otto, *The Idea of the Holy*; *Das Gefühl des Über-weltlichen (sensus numinis)*.

Solidarity beyond Itself: Creation

b) Relative priority of the religious experience. "Mediated" immediacy: religion as a sentimental intuition (Friedrich Schleiermacher).[20]

c) Absolute subordination of the religious experience to the real *a priori*, which is the spirit. "Mediated" mediation towards the final concept in the realm of the aprioristic knowledge of the different formations that consciousness generates in its path towards its absolute stage: religion as a supreme determination of the spirit, destined to be overcome by philosophy (Georg Hegel).[21]

2. *A posteriori in crescendo*: religion as projection of something that is prior to it.

---

20. For Schleiermacher, religion is an intuition (expressed through the feelings) of dependency upon an absolute reality that overcomes us. In his *On Religion: Speeches to Its Cultured Despisers* (1799), Schleiermacher indicates that religion cannot be explained as the product of fear or ignorance but as the intuition and sentiment of our radical need of something that has to stand beyond us. Thus, religion points to a direct relationship with the infinite. On the connection of intuition with religion in Schleiermacher in the context of German romanticism, cf. Brandt, *The Philosophy of Schleiermacher*, 95–144).

21. Both in Hegel's *Phenomenology of the Spirit* and *Encyclopaedia of the Philosophical Sciences in Basic Outline* religion appears as a supreme determination of the spirit, that is to say, as one of the highest formations of consciousness that can be achieved. However, there is a higher possible state of consciousness, offered by philosophy. Philosophy is the true supreme determination of the spirit when it returns to itself as absolute spirit, with the full knowledge of its freedom. The religious representation [*Vorstellung*] is to be overcome by the philosophical concept [*Begriff*], just as the religious representation overcomes the artistic intuition [*Anschauung*]. The emphasis on rationality makes Hegel distance himself from the philosophy of religion of Schleiermacher. For Hegel, religion is not a sentimental intuition but one of the three supreme determinations of the spirit. The spirit settles down in religion in its path towards its absolute self-understanding. As Hegel explains in the *Encyclopaedia*, in art there is an immediate unity of nature and spirit, whereas in (revealed) religion the absolute spirit manifests itself without any veil in order to be overcome by the self-conscious thinking that takes place in philosophy, in which unilateral, specific, and contingent representations do not prevail. Rather, we are before the supreme form, which is the very act of thinking. Situating religion in the realm of intuition and feeling darkens the possibility of grasping the dynamic of the spirit. The absolute does not belong to the sphere of sentiments: it is an object of thought. There is no universality in sentiment, which is intrinsically subjective, whereas reason looks for objectivity. This criticism can also be found in Hegel's *Lectures on the Philosophy of Religion*, 27–39 and his *Elements of the Philosophy of Right*, where he argues that the reduction of religion to the sphere of sentiments, to the realm of subjectivity, leaves the "ethical world [*sittliche Welt*]" in a state of "atheism," for religion would have nothing to say about the objectivity of moral life. On this point, cf. Pannenberg, "Die Bedeutung des Christentums in der Philosophie Hegels," in *Gottesgedanke und menschliche Freiheit*, 91.

Part 2: *Fundamentum* in History

2.1.: religion as projection of the *ego*.

a) Religion as immediate projection of our finite, conscious *ego* onto an infinite *alter* (Ludwig Feuerbach).[22]

b) Non-immediacy of the repressed unconscious, projected onto an *alter*: relative immediacy of the experience of oneself (mediated by the influence of the unconscious) and its projection as religion (Sigmund Freud).[23]

c) Mediation of the experience of oneself through the ethical action and its projection as religion (Immanuel Kant).[24]

2.2. Religion as projection of oneself through the mediation of nature, society, and history:

a) Religion as the result of the relationship between human beings and nature: "immediate" mediation of nature and its projection as religion through the experience of unknown powers as "*alter*" to *ego*: religion as the product of magic (Sir James Frazer);[25] religion as an expression of the distinction between the sacred and the profane (Mircea Eliade).[26]

---

22. In *The Essence of Christianity* (1841), Feuerbach expresses the thesis that the Christian idea of God constitutes an anthropomorphic projection. The human being conceives of a different entity, an *alter* that possesses our own attributes elevated to the highest possible exponent. A finite being imagines an infinite being: its impotency becomes omnipotence, its ignorance, omniscience, and its moral imperfection, supreme goodness. God is made in our image and likeness and the discourse of theology can be interpreted as anthropology.

23. Freud developed his treatment of religion in works like *Totem and Taboo* (1915), *The Future of an Illusion* (1927), and *Moses and Monotheism* (1938). Religion, according to Freud, is a form of neurosis, an illusion aimed at satisfying a wish deeply rooted in our psychic structures.

24. The subordination of religion to ethics in Kant is particularly patent in *Religion within the Limits of Reason Alone* (1793). In the *Critique of Pure Reason*, the existence of God and the immortality of the soul, fundamental doctrines of many religious traditions, are assimilated to postulates of practical reason. The understanding of religion as ethics in Kant is therefore clear: ideas such as God and the immortality of the soul can only be interpreted through the mediation of the ethical realm, that is, so to speak, "prior" to religion (which is the expression of the imperatives of practical reason viewed as divine mandates).

25. The principal work of Frazer is *The Golden Bough*. On Frazer and Edward Burnett Tylor (who was very influential on the first), cf. Pals, *Eight Theories of Religion*.

26. On the differentiation between the realms of the sacred and the profane as the fundamental feature of the religious experience, cf. Eliade, *The Sacred and the Profane*. Although the influence of Otto on Eliade is noticeable, as the Romanian thinker himself acknowledges, it needs to be noticed that in the case of Eliade the

b) Religion as the result of the relationship between individuals and the community: "immediate" mediation of society and its projection as religion (Émile Durkheim).²⁷

c) Religion as the result of the relationship between individuals, community, and history: "mediated" mediation of society through history and its projection as religion; religion as a transitory stage in human history (Comte)²⁸; "mediated" mediation of society through the experience of conflict and its projection as religion (Marx).²⁹

---

idea of "hierophanies" has a closer relationship with the role of nature in shaping the religious experience. In Otto, on the contrary, religion seems to be the primary intuition of something totally-other, which escapes the power of conceptualization and is absolutely non-reducible to any mediation: it is the immediate perception of radical "otherness." The category of "*das Heilige*" cannot be apprehended through concepts. Cf. Otto, *The Idea of the Holy*, 9.

27. The theories of Durkheim on religion are condensed in *The Elementary Forms of the Religious Life* (1912). According to him, religion has a social origin, characterized by its capacity for contributing to the strengthening of links among the individual members of the community. Religion is therefore some sort of divinization of society.

28. This is the approach that underlies Comte's famous law of the three stages of humanity: religious (divided into three sub-stages, too: animistic, polytheistic, monotheistic), metaphysical, and scientific. Religion is the form that governs the human conscience at a specific historical period. The very nature of human progress in history makes religion a transitory phenomenon, whose destiny is to be overcome first by metaphysics and finally by science as the definitive power to offer explanations about the world. On this famous law, cf. Bourdeau, *Les Trois États: Science, Théologie et Métaphysique chez Auguste Comte*.

29. According to Marx, "The struggle against religion is, therefore, indirectly the struggle against that world whose spiritual aroma is religion. Religious suffering is, at one and the same time, the expression of real suffering and a protest against real suffering. Religion is the sigh of the oppressed creature, the heart of a heartless world, and the soul of soulless conditions. It is the opium of the people. The abolition of religion as the illusory happiness of the people is the demand for their real happiness. To call on them to give up their illusions about their condition is to call on them to give up a condition that requires illusions. The criticism of religion is, therefore, in embryo, the criticism of that vale of tears of which religion is the halo" (*A Contribution to the Critique of Hegel's Philosophy of Right*. In *Collected Works*, vol. 3). Religion is therefore an expression of the real suffering of humanity, a translation of the deep conflicts that subsist within society projected onto a divine "hypostasis" (as Ernst Bloch remarked in *The Principle of Hope*), whose real content is that of protest against the situation of sorrow that afflicts humankind. Religion is neither an intuition nor a projection of the *ego* taken in isolation but a projection of the individual *ego* inserted into a social body which is, by its inner nature, contradictory. The conflictive character of society mediates the way in which religion emerges as a projection. The final reconciliation, the moment of definitive happiness which we are unable to construct on Earth, becomes imagined as *alter*, as other-worldly reality, as a different realm in which the synthesis

Religion constitutes an expression of our ineradicable orientation towards questioning. The different religious experiences account for the different ways of formulating and answering the fundamental question. The development of human consciousness is accompanied by an ever-increasing capacity for posing questions that always overcome any eventual response: the act of asking is constantly ahead of that of replying. The genuine religious spirit serves the imperious necessity for a radical questioning of the world, history, and mankind, but the spirit of questioning can be easily assassinated through the institutionalization of religion. It is precisely this tendency to "petrify" questions in a set of defined religious traditions that makes them extremely vulnerable, because the flame of questioning cannot be tamed. This intrinsic fragility of religions is also the strength of "religiosity": religions may die, but religiosity persists in various ways, as the prevalence of the question over any answer, of the spirit over the structures. There is a radical priority of questioning in the human life: questioning is both antecedent and consequent to any human enterprise. The inevitability of religion is also the irresistibility of philosophy: we will never cease to carry the torch of questioning.

What religions call God is the question of questions.[30] Religions cannot pretend to be the only way of expressing the question that defines the human being, as if they could exhaust all the channels that transport the longing for something capable of transcending the present frontiers of our thought. Kant's philosophical "agnosticism" regarding the existence of God has to be interpreted not as the faltering of reason but as the recognition that only the infiniteness of consciousness and the radical openness to being constitute the proper ontic moments for dealing with the most transcendental and ultimate question that intelligence can pose: the one referring to the absolute, to being in its purity, to the ultimate fountain of love, beauty, and wisdom. Our home has been built upon contingency and temporality, in whose realm we are compelled to perennially oscillate, following the pendulum of the dualities which characterize reality: finite/infinite, nature/freedom, etc. This is our prison, and we can never escape it unless we are released, saved by a thought which may bear an infinite power inside it, reaching

---

is possible.

30. There is therefore no reason to keep silent about God, as Heidegger recommended in *Identität und Differenz*, 51: we have to pose the question of the questions, even if the answer does not exist, because we will be enlarging the horizons of our thought and action and we will grow as humanity. Behold salvation.

the ultimate *fundamentum* of everything. Thinking about the *fundamentum* is the only path towards salvation.

It is impossible to cease to wonder at the amazing variety of religious beliefs that we find in the world. There are two principal and confronted views regarding religion and its future: on the one hand, the supposition that the religious phenomenon constitutes a transitory stage in the human spirit, being condemned to disappear, or that at least its relevance will radically decrease, and, on the other hand, the idea that the importance of religion will persist as long as humanity is alive.

We are unable to comprehend the meaning of our present, of our "here and now," as it represents a mystery.[31] "Know thyself": this is a vivid exhortation that many philosophies and religions have often repeated, but we know that such a task is impossible, since it overflows the limits of our cup. Our true vocation is to remain in suspense regarding the meaning of our lives, in a state of permanent "ontic vigil." Thus, we can respect the integrity of mystery, which takes its dwelling in thought, and thought finds a home in philosophy: *la philosophie est la demeure de la pensée*.

Faith will never grant full tranquility to our spirit, and it will never defeat the fear that invades us, inspired by this huge and enigmatic world that torments us. Religion builds no refuge, since it makes the act of questioning even harder, and it reveals the problem of existence with an even higher intensity. Had we stayed with science and reason alone, maybe we would have been able to understand something, but when humanity chose the path of religion, the impossibility to understand has become the defining feature of our existence. Joy and anguish may be overcome, however, in the act of looking forward with hope and looking backwards with condescendence, being aware that in the ineffability of the present a world which is always new emerges.[32] The

---

31. The human being, within the limits of the world, is in need of the discursive, logical clarity offered by the order of contingency, which is ruled by the principle of non-contradiction, but there is an inevitable aspiration to ascend into the superform and moreover, into the ultraform, in order to contemplate being as mystery, as dynamism, as trans-reason.

32. Whether the belief in God actually provides something real for the human being, instead of being a merely illusory conviction with no effective practical translation, is a question that can only be answered by means of appealing to the individual conscience (which is capable of *religatio* to being, of creating ontic spaces of immanence, transcendence, and tendency towards absoluteness, synergic realms in which any opposition is reconciled in the subject that knows, loves, and wishes). To choose is to extend the space of opposition, to realize that in the infiniteness of being there will

richness of faith can only be met by the autonomous exercise and the free deliberation of subjective conscience.[33]

---

always be room for the overcoming of any antinomy and the harmonic reconciliation of all with all. However, in the concrete existence, in its finiteness and limitation, the human being needs to make a decision, trying to broaden his horizon in such a way that the alternatives may actually approach, with the hope that any opposition will be finally overcome in the infinite spaces of being. Such a choice is, by its very nature, uncertain, but the leap to which Kierkegaard referred may bring us comfort, and it may provide us the security that we have, at least, undertaken the path of quest, the path of being. Any human certainty is at the same time an expression of uncertainty, and this is the perennial paradox of humanity, which also invades the religious feeling: mankind is forced to suspend its ontic place in order to jump, to throw itself into a vacuum which, *qua* vacuum, offers a mysterious horizon that also situates humanity in the path of being with a new and original sense, which only the individual, in his uniqueness, is entitled to grasp.

33. Kant's clairvoyance regarding the latter consideration appears with its full power in the following passage from the preface to the second edition of *Critique of Pure Reason*: "This important change in the field of the sciences, this loss of its fancied possessions, to which speculative reason must submit, does not prove in any way detrimental to the general interests of humanity. The advantages which the world has derived from the teachings of pure reason are not at all impaired. The loss falls, in its whole extent, on the monopoly of the schools, but does not in the slightest degree touch the interests of mankind. I appeal to the most obstinate dogmatist, whether the proof of the continued existence of the soul after death, derived from the simplicity of its substance; of the freedom of the will in opposition to the general mechanism of nature, drawn from the subtle but impotent distinction of subjective and objective practical necessity; or of the existence of God, deduced from the conception of an *ens realissimum*—the contingency of the changeable, and the necessity of a prime mover, has ever been able to pass beyond the limits of the schools, to penetrate the public mind, or to exercise the slightest influence on its convictions. It must be admitted that this has not been the case and that, owing to the unfitness of the common understanding for such subtle speculations, it can never be expected to take place. On the contrary, it is plain that the hope of a future life arises from the feeling, which exists in the breast of every man, that the temporal is inadequate to meet and satisfy the demands of his nature. In like manner, it cannot be doubted that the clear exhibition of duties in opposition to all the claims of inclination, gives rise to the consciousness of freedom, and that the glorious order, beauty, and providential care, everywhere displayed in nature, give rise to the belief in a wise and great Author of the Universe. Such is the genesis of these general convictions of mankind, so far as they depend on rational grounds; and this public property not only remains undisturbed, but is even raised to greater importance, by the doctrine that the schools have no right to arrogate to themselves a more profound insight into a matter of general human concernment than that to which the great mass of men, ever held by us in the highest estimation, can without difficulty attain, and that the schools should, therefore, confine themselves to the elaboration of these universally comprehensible and, from a moral point of view, amply satisfactory proofs. The change, therefore, affects only the arrogant pretensions of the schools, which would gladly retain, in their own exclusive possession, the key to the truths which they impart to the public" (B XXXII–XXXIV; cf. also B666 and

"Deep calls to deep" (*abyssus invocat abyssum*),³⁴ and whoever truly loves that which is deep does not seek to impose his own perception of it on others but only to make it loveable for all hearts: *cor ad cor loquitur* (John Henry Newman). Only the potential infiniteness which every person represents is able to understand the veritable scope of the profoundest intuitions of love, beauty, and wisdom.

To believe in God is equivalent to relying upon what being can offer: it implies opening oneself to being and to the wish for a final certainty, which becomes joyful uncertainty, happy mystery, and unrestricted extension of the horizon of each subject. It involves trusting the existence of a meaning for the vast and colorful display of being. If there is a God, such a deity can only be that which radiates the intuition of permanence and salvation: love, beauty, and wisdom.

The acceptance of a particular religious option should not exclude the possibility of considering other varieties of the religious experience and engaging into a critical examination of one's own choice,³⁵ even without abandoning it in its fundamentals.³⁶ Behold one of the greatest contributions of the discourse of modernity: the amplitude of subjectivity and its capacity for transcending any opposition by virtue of action. Reason cannot seek to standardize reality: it must discover the full scope of its dynamism, the beauty of imagination, phantasm, and the many

---

B668).

34. Ps 42:7 expresses this intuition in a truly profound way: "Deep calls to deep in the roar of your waterfalls; all your waves and breakers have swept over me."

35. As Professor Francis X. Clooney writes: "no theological topic, even the most seemingly concrete and tradition-specific, profits from being considered in isolation from comparable theological reflections in other traditions" (*Hindu God, Christian God. How Reason Helps Break Down the Boundaries between Religions*, 101). In this sense, the discipline of "comparative theology," for which Clooney is a strong advocator, may render a great service not only to particular religious traditions like Christianity and Hinduism but to philosophy of religion in general, as it can show that beyond any difference there is always room for some form of convergence, manifested in the capacity for recognizing common points of concern that encourage engagement in an honest communication between equals.

36. In this sense, it is interesting to recall Jan Assmann's remarks on the necessity to abolish that which he calls the "Mosaic distinction," the radical differentiation between the true and the false in religion. Cf. Assmann, *Moses the Egyptian*, 1–23 and 218. On the Mosaic distinction and the problem of intolerance, see also Assmann, *The Price of Monotheism*. However, it is sometimes hard to understand how a religious tradition could define its identity without appealing, in some way or another, to a distinction, to a "binomial." The flexibility of the terms of its identity, rather than the "lack" of identity, will perhaps be more practical for their self-awareness and their relationship to other religious and cultural traditions.

landscapes of human creativity. Mythology has historically constituted a genuine religious way to express what is ineffable, what escapes us and transcends us, but in all the concretions of the religious phenomenon (in both doctrines and rituals) the human conscience must always try to unveil their true meaning, their deepest value for our present time, looking to the past with understanding and to the future with hope. We cannot limit ourselves to accepting the representations provided by religious language: philosophy, as Hegel proclaimed,[37] has to reach the concept. Rational introspection needs to highlight the historical path leading to religious symbolism and its potential connections with the contemporary mind, achieving a way of understanding that may underscore identity and openness instead of disjunction, and which may accentuate the centrality of the human phenomenon, guided by the developments carried out by the sciences of nature and the sciences of the spirit.[38] Let religions help thought to discover trails of love, beauty, and wisdom, of the ultimate meaning of that which they call "salvation": this is the challenge of our time.

Conceiving of God as the question of questions, not as the answer for what we now ignore, is the only possible way to avoid all the fruitless conflicts between religion and science, between religions, and between religion and society. God cannot become the apodictic response to the arcane mysteries of science and philosophy but the catalyst for undertaking the noble path of searching. Can, in fact, a purely scientific explanation in terms of material, sociological, and cultural causes replace any form of theological, religious, and transcendental introspection? Science attempts to identify different types of causes behind all phenomena: material, social, economic, political, psychological—all of them susceptible to a rational treatment. However, the transfiniteness of being, its infinite transcendence, its inexhaustibility, they all mean that an element which is unsuitable for explanation will always persist. This limit is not a defeat of science and rationality: it is actually the expression of the infinite possibility of posing questions and extending the scientific enterprise. The fact that we wonder about the ultimate reason of all things in the world

---

37. Cf. Hegel's "preface" to his *Phenomenology of Spirit*: it is necessary to undertake the "effort of the concept [*Die Anstrengung des Begriffs*]."

38. Within many religious traditions, and in particular in the context of Christianity, it is necessary to pose the question that refers to the limit of interpretation: what is the theological limit? The theological limit resides in the scope that every age may be prepared to assume. Moreover, the limit lies in mystery, in its infiniteness, and the limit is in every individual conscience, since subjectivity alone can know the mystery.

and history lacks a scientific justification, and the highest mystery of science is science itself. There will always be room for whatever cannot be explained. Religion holds the advantage, because it points to the absolute horizon of questioning, which never fades.

Religions have participated in the creation of cultures, and nowadays they must also feel the responsibility to contribute to building a truly humane civilization, capable of assuming the infinite longing of humanity for self-transcendence. Culture is the ontic space in which mankind comes into dialogue with being and humanity discovers its singularity, its uniqueness, by contemplating being in its vivid display. Unlike religions, the works of writers and philosophers do not expect to impose anything upon the conscience of their fellow human beings: they just want to bequeath a word to mankind. Ideally, religions would share the same goal: to speak and listen, because we are striving for words, for a speech that should involve no power. Pure words, beyond any form of constraint: this is the utopia of thought. After all, philosophy is more idealistic than religion.

Part 2: *Fundamentum* in History

EXCURSUS: THE NAMES OF HUMANITY AND THE UTOPIA OF A REDEEMED PAST

The Judeo-Christian eschatological conception of history is based upon the idea that time has an end, in which both chronology and eternity will finally meet. The contradictions that are inherent to any given moment of the historical process will be ultimately resolved. However, the possibility of the existence of an end for history is difficult to appreciate. Even from a Judeo-Christian perspective it is not easy to explain why if God is the maker of the world, He has not fulfilled his plan yet: why does history have to wait for a consummation which is hard to envision?[39] The doctrine of the Kingdom of God can be interpreted, from a purely philosophical perspective, as the utopia of a definitive reconciliation of nature, humanity, and God. This ultimate harmony would encompass the past, present, and future. Of course, the principal problem of this doctrine has to do with the notion of *eskhaton*, that is to say, the idea of the full and definitive consummation which will reveal the meaning of everything that is.[40]

A theologian like Wolfhart Pannenberg, who is deeply committed to the eschatological conception of history, thinks that every individual experience has to be inserted into a totality of experiences. Individual experiences can be understood only in light of the broader context to which they belong and ultimately the totality of contexts, which is the

---

39. Pannenberg thinks that the divine plan on the world has not been fulfilled yet because God wants his creation to possess autonomy (cf. *Systematic Theology*, 2:175). However, it is legitimate to think that if God were omnipotent and omniscient, he could have found a way to reconcile autonomy and plenitude so that it were possible to enjoy freedom without suffering the contradictions of history. Of course, this question recalls the traditional problems of theodicy, which seem to find no satisfactory answer from a theistic perspective (cf. Mackie, "Evil and Omnipotence," 200–212). In any case, Pannenberg believes that the end of history has been anticipated in the life and destiny of Jesus Christ: resurrection is the fate of humanity, and the victims will be finally vindicated by God. This is certainly one of the most important dimensions of the Judeo-Christian doctrine of a general resurrection of the dead at the end of time, but it is hard to deny that it may simply represent the expression of the collective aspiration of humanity for life and justice, being more of a wish than a reality.

40. The idea of an eschatological consummation of history is rooted in the most genuine tradition of the biblical prophets, although it only became explicit with the advent of apocalypticism in the third and second centuries BC. A paradigm of the apocalyptic doctrine of a consummated history can be found in the book of Daniel (cf. Dan 2:44; 7:14). On apocalyptic eschatology, cf. Koziel, *Apokalyptische Eschatologie als Zentrum der Botschaft Jesus und der frühen Christen?*; Russell, *Divine Disclosure*. On the prophetic substrate of apocalyptic eschatology, cf. Hanson, *The Dawn of Apocalyptic*.

whole of reality. This idea is inspired by the philosophy of Dilthey[41] and moreover, by the Hegelian identification of truth and wholeness.[42]

According to Pannenberg, individual experiences can only be meaningful in the frame of the totality of experiences. However, should this statement be regarded as a postulate or a form of discursive argument? It seems to be a postulate in the Kantian sense: the idea of an end of history as the "transcendental condition" (condition of possibility) of the historical experience in general:[43] without a final point of history it is not possible to understand the historical experience of each individual. The "co-belonging" of the different individual experiences of history makes it necessary to project the historical discourse from the individual experience onto universal history. The acceptance of an end of history is the only way to admit that the true meaning of every individual experience will be finally revealed.

However, and as Kant noticed in his essay *Das Ende aller Dinge*, of 1794, the idea of an end of time goes beyond the power of the human imagination. The possibility of a consummation of history is nebulous, and it is equally obscure that such a culmination would be profitable and "salvific" for mankind. It could be an act of destruction, the annihilation of present reality.[44] Judeo-Christian theology believes, in any case, that such an act of consummation will mean the transition into eternity and the overcoming of temporality, but it also defends the idea that this transformation is not linear: between time and eternity the mediation of divine judgment stands. The dialectic between the temporal and the eternal does not become solved in a spontaneous

---

41. According to Dilthey, every spiritual unit is centred upon itself, since it possesses a "closed horizon," like that of a certain historical time (cf. *Der Aufbau der geschichtlichen Welt in den Geisteswissenschaften*, 188). However, the meaning of each action, thought, and common creation demands that each part be put in relationship with the historical whole in which it is integrated. The meaning of each action, thought, and common creation must be submitted to universal history. Ultimately, one should wait until the end of history has taken place in order to reach a "determination [*Bestimmung*]" of the meaning of the individual realities. In Dilthey's own words, "Erst im letzen Augenblick eines Lebens kann der Überschlag über seine Bedeutung gemacht werden . . . Man müsste das Ende des Lebenslaufes abwarten und könnte in der Todesstunde erst das Ganze überschauen, von dem aus die Beziehung seiner Teile feststellbar wäre" (ibid., 237, 233); "man müsste das Ende der Geschichte erst abwarten, um für die Bestimmung ihrer Bedeutung das vollständige Material zu besitzen" (ibid., 233). Cf. "Inwerden, Realität: Zeit" (ibid., 236–42).

42. Cf. Hegel's preface to his *Phenomenology of Spirit*.

43. Cf. Pannenberg, *Systematic Theology*, 3:591.

44. Pannenberg is aware of this theoretical difficulty. Cf. *Systematic Theology*, 3:521.

way: there is a judgment that will determine whether the irruption of eternity is going to be positive or negative. Nevertheless, this is a theological asseveration which is difficult to share on a purely rational basis.

The idea of an eternal life is tempting, but the difficulties which it poses cannot be disdained. Several religions, and especially Christianity, promise an unending existence together with God. Nonetheless, human imagination cannot conceive of life without temporality. Eternity resembles immutability and absence of activity rather than vital reality, on the one hand, and it does not necessarily imply positive connotations, on the other. If eternity were a mere revival of temporal existence, those who suffered injustice in life would enjoy no comfort at all. The abstraction of the essence of each individual being and its projection onto the realm of eternity does not solve the ethical problem of vindication. Some religions teach that there will be a final judgment that will bring the justice that has been absent in history, but this is too anthropomorphic a hypothesis to be rationally accepted. Such a doctrine will not be easily absolved from the accusation of refusing to confront the reality of suffering in history, whose solution is postponed to the future. Moreover, the focus on a final eschatology (as *endzeitliche Eschatologie*) disregards the possibility of a "supratemporal" (*überzeitliche*) or anticipated eschatology, in which the realm of eternity may be experienced in the present without the necessity to await the definitive future.[45] The future could be perennially opened while, at the same time, eschatology would be possible as the present realization of a meaning through the purest intuitions which we can find in human life: love, beauty, and wisdom.

The only way to preserve the centrality of the question is to leave history open: the beauty of an unsolved history. The meaning of history is the possibility of formulating the question of questions. This is, in fact, the most encompassing meaning: that which integrates both meaning and absence of meaning. Questioning does not impose a definitive, discernible significance and, nonetheless, it does not close the horizon of meaning. We cannot know whether history as such can illuminate the meaning of each individual experience. However, we do know that the possibility of questioning is always there.

It is true that many people have passed through life without enjoying any kind of recognition. Moreover, some of them can only be

---

45. On the distinction between *endzeitliche* and *überzeitliche Eschatologie*, cf. Hjelde, *Das Eschaton und die Eschata*, 432–33.

Solidarity beyond Itself: Creation

known on the basis of their suffering. Disgrace, not fortune, was their sole horizon. Their names will not be written in any golden book, in no collective memory, and perhaps not even in the remembrance of their relatives. The fact that many of our fellow human beings have only experienced misfortune has to inspire sadness and solidarity in every one of us, and it is the vivid manifestation of the inscrutable limitations and the vast fragility of our intellect. We feel the need to believe that life has a meaning and that our adventures have not been in vain. This is probably the only way to live: dreaming of a future in which these stories of tragedy, loneliness, and pain will not be repeated. In the act of making the world and history meaningful, humanity assumes the avant-garde of being. Meaning is, yes, a human creation, and it is the proof that we are now responsible for extending the horizons of being. Renouncing a meaning is undermining our humanity.

It is hard not to wish that all men and women who have lived on earth might be remembered, dwelling in the reverberating and colorful memory of the present and the future generations, so that no one felt orphaned in our only fatherland, which is humanity. However, we know well how difficult, how utopian, how far away this dream remains, but we also feel that we have to preserve this avid hope. We could reasonably accept an explanation of the world that excluded the possibility of a meaning, as if we were the products of the blind and deaf process that has led to the emergence of life and consciousness, but there is something inexplicable that encourages us to reject this view. The reason may be that we do not want to leave so many people who have suffered in this world without a final success, without any prospect of recognition. Maybe it is enough to think that we are all part of something that transcends us, be it the world or history. The sentiment of belonging to a reality which goes beyond our individuality is also suitable for those who had no fortune in life and whose names will not be written in the noblest books of history, because everyone has shaped space and time in a unique way, as if the world and history needed us as their integrating elements in their path towards an unknown destination. We are already necessary, for without us things would not have been the way they were.

Let us wish that we all could assume the weight of history, bringing justice to all those who did not enjoy it while they existed in this strange world. Why has humanity had so many faces? Why is it that we live and die? Until when is humanity going to adopt so many names, in so many prolix places and algid ages? How should we understand the violent reality that many people will be born in misfortune, without having chosen it, and that many will be condemned to being the last in a society in which only the first shine? Our world will not have achieved justice while it does not preserve the memory of all the names that humanity has had throughout its history. Only when we were prophetically aware of the necessity of remembering all those who came before us, and once we had acknowledged the vibrant responsibility of carrying the solicitous flame of collective reminiscence, we would have created a truly just world.

Let us therefore share the utopia of a full, concerted memory of humanity, the dream of the greatest possible concord, in which every single name shall be remembered, every single story shall find vindication, and nothing will have been in vain. It is the utopia of a history that may be meaningful for everyone, the dream of a *bibliotheca* which actually surpasses the infinite library of Jorge Luis Borges and the magnificence of the greatest temples of wisdom, because behind its august walls all the names and hopes of humanity are solicitously contained. Compassion will make us even forgive those who did not ennoble mankind, since mercy is also a synonym for pardon. This dream could be regarded as a passionate expression of profound madness,[46] but what is wrong with insanity if it is capable of inspiring creation and helps us to open the golden window to the inaugural scenario that we have not explored yet? Let us wish that we were all captives to a divine *delirium tremens* that moved us to envision this highest utopia, for, as Calderón de la Barca foresaw, living is dreaming and dreaming is living.[47] We must remember the past of furtive disgrace in order to invite ourselves into a future of

---

46. This expression of "madness" can be seen in Walter Benjamin's *Theses on the Philosophy of History*. Benjamin did not want to surrender to the idea that the past had been closed forever, without any possibility of radical transformation that might bring justice to the victims of history. Benjamin could not accept the immutability of past time: he was unable to admit that the past of sorrow had defeated humanity. He preferred the utopian wish for a messianic angel that could appear in history, bringing a message and a reality of hope. But the past, even a past of misfortune, can inspire compassion: it can light the torch of love, beauty, and wisdom. Behold its deepest meaning.

47. ¿Qué es la vida? Un frenesí.
¿Qué es la vida? Una ficción,
una sombra, una ilusión,
y el mayor bien es pequeño.
¡Que toda la vida es sueño,
y los sueños, sueños son!
From *La Vida es Sueño*.

utopian and invigorated happiness. This is the only way to inaugurate the Hegelian new spring of the spirit and to reach the noon-land in which the sunset has not started yet, creating a humanity in which no one will be a foreigner. Evoking a past of misfortune encourages us to take the path that will introduce us into the exotic scenario in which salvation dwells, in which love, beauty, and wisdom reign, so that we can say, together with Heine, "come with me, oh beautiful Sara, to another land; we want to leave misfortune behind us."[48]

---

48. Heine, *Der Rabbi von Bacherach* (1840): "Komm mit mir, schöne Sara, nach einem anderem Land, wir wollen das Unglück hinter uns lassen."

PART 3

Questioning as Salvation

7

Death as Challenge

DEATH IN HEIDEGGER AS THE RADICAL POSSIBILITY OF EXISTENCE

THE MOST ENDURING BOOK of Martin Heidegger (1889–1976), *Sein und Zeit* (1927), is aimed at working out "the question of the meaning of *Being*," examining "time as the possible horizon for any understanding whatsoever of Being."[1] The hermeneutical keys to understand the meaning of being will come from the union of being and time.

The clarification of the meaning of being is, however, eclipsed, as Heidegger remarks, by the historical development of Western philosophy, which has obscured question about being. In characterizing being as the most universal, as the indefinable, and as the self-evident, metaphysics has veiled both the answer and the question concerning the meaning of being. However, "every questioning is a seeking,"[2] and the question about the meaning of being appears as a task for whoever may formulate it, since "all ontology, no matter how rich and tightly knit a system of categories it has at its disposal, remains fundamentally blind and perverts its innermost

---

1. Heidegger, *Being and Time*. For the original German text, cf. *Sein und Zeit*.
2. Heidegger, *Being and Time*, 3.

intent if it has not previously clarified the meaning of being sufficiently and grasped this clarification as its fundamental task."[3]

The confusion between the entity and the being of the entity constitutes a serious obstacle for the proper formulation of the question, even more so if we realize that the one asking the question is actually an entity. In this way, posing the question about the meaning of being involves making an entity (the one that is questioning) become transparent in its being. The entity that wonders about the meaning of being is *Dasein*, and questioning is a possibility of *Dasein*, of the being-there which has been thrown into the world, but it is not just any kind of possibility, since "understanding the meaning of being is itself a determination of being of *Dasein*."[4]

The question about the meaning of being reflects the centrality of questioning for *Dasein*. The act of questioning is essential to all sciences, and "the real 'movement' of the sciences takes place in the revision of these basic concepts, a revision which is more or less radical and lucid with regard to itself. A science's level of development is determined by the extent to which it is capable of a crisis in its basic concepts,"[5] as it has happened in twentieth-century physics, with the introduction of quantum mechanics and the theory of relativity. According to Heidegger, "fundamental concepts are determinations in which the area of knowledge underlying all the thematic objects of a science attains an understanding that precedes and guides all positive investigation."[6] Fundamental concepts enable us to comprehend a science before achieving specific results. The particular aspect of the entity that is Dasein is that the act of understanding being (the task for which it poses the question about the meaning of being) cannot be separated from that of determining the being of *Dasein*. *Dasein* is not an ordinary entity that simply occurs among other entities. The burden of posing the question about being and searching the understanding of its meaning is carried by *Dasein*, in such a way that it is impossible to understand being without understanding *Dasein*.

However, "*Dasein* always understands itself in terms of its existence, in terms of its possibilities to be itself or not to be."[7] This ontic-ontological primacy of *Dasein* for the understanding of being in general and the mode of being of every entity in particular is assimilated by Heidegger to Aristo-

---

3. Ibid., 9.
4. Ibid., 10.
5. Ibid., 8.
6. Ibid.
7. Ibid., 10.

tle's statement that "the soul is, in some way, all things."[8] *Dasen* is an entity capable of considering any class of entities, and this is the reason why the mission of formulating the question about the meaning of being, and of looking for the understanding of being, falls upon *Dasein*.

To interrogate *Dasein* and to elucidate its existential analytic are necessary steps in order to adequately pose the question about being, because, as Heidegger remarks, the question about being cannot be artificially disconnected from the question about the being of *Dasein*. The goal of Heidegger's extensive study of the existential analytic of *Dasein* in *Being and Time* is to offer a hermeneutical foundation for the question about the meaning of being, which needs, first of all, to be asked about the form in which being determines itself in *Dasein*. The key for the understanding of being resides in the being of *Dasein*, and this assignment has to be carried out, according to Heidegger, within the horizon of time, for *Dasein* has temporality as its own being.

Contrary to Hegel, Heidegger thinks that the realm of universal history has no centrality for the understanding of the historical being. It is the "historicity [*Geschichtlichkeit*]" of *Dasein* that founds any possible universal history. Historicity is one of the possibilities of *Dasein*: the hermeneutical primacy belongs to the existential analytic of *Dasein*, not to universal history as the scenario in which *Dasein* is inserted. Knowledge about history [*Historie*] is only possible as a mode of being of *Dasein* in its being questioned. The historicity of *Dasein* founds the being of history, which seems to be a projection of individual existence rather than a substantive reality. According to Heidegger, the historicity of *Dasein* belongs to its fundamental ontological constitution, and it makes possible an ontic understanding (concerning entities) of universal history. The historicity of *Dasein* founds the possibility of historical understanding [*historisches Verstehen*]: the scientific interpretation of history is the result of the historicity of *Dasein*, not of the intelligibility of the historical process as such.

Dasein is an entity that constitutes itself as being-in-the-world [*in-der-Welt-sein*]: being-in-the-world is essential to any characterization of *Dasein*. As an entity that is in the world, *Dasein* shows a series of fundamental structures that, according to Heidegger, are centered upon the idea of "openness [*Erschlossenheit*]." The totality of this structure of *Dasein* appears as "care" [*Sorge*]: world, openness, and care are the three basic categories in the Heideggerian understanding of individual existence. *Dasein* is a temporal entity that is in the world, and as such, it

---

8. Cf. Aristotle, *De Anima* G8, 431b 21.

opens itself to other entities and takes care of itself. This "taking care of itself" has a primary moment: that of "anticipating itself" [*Sich-vorweg-sein*], what means that *Dasein* exists for its own sake and, while existing, it always behaves in relation to its being-able. There is a permanent state of incompleteness that belongs to the fundamental constitution of *Dasein*. This incompleteness means that *Dasein* is always a "being-able-to," and the notion of anticipation concerns the disposition by *Dasein* of its own possibilities of existence. Anticipation means that *Dasein* does not have an existence alien to its intrinsic possibilities of existing, but, rather, it exists in being turned to them.

Possibilities and existence cannot be separated in *Dasein*. Through anticipation, *Dasein* actualizes its possibilities of existence, taking the lead in its own life. Anticipation expresses the state of incompleteness, of being-able, that defines *Dasein*. It means that *Dasein* can never achieve its integrity while it is: it cannot reach its plenitude if it does not cease to be a "being-in-the-world," if it does not lose its determination as an entity in the world, open to other entities, and taking care of itself. Behold the tragedy of *Dasein*: its integrity demands its death, and *Dasein* has to lose the *da* of its *sein* in such a way that it is no longer an entity thrown into the world but a being which is not "there," because it has lost its "rootedness" in the world. Since the question about the meaning of being is linked to the meaning of *Dasein*, ceasing to be in the world is the only way for *Dasein* to reveal the meaning of its own being and, therefore, of being as such. As human beings, we experience the death of other people, not their "act of dying," which belongs to the most intimate dimension of every *Dasein*. We can witness death, not the very act of dying: we can never know the nature and meaning of death. In many actions, one *Dasein* can act in the place of another. This is not the case with death: my death is mine. The death of *Dasein* entirely belongs to it. No one else can assume it. While it is, *Dasein* is a "not-yet." However, the accomplishment of its end means that it no longer exists [*Nichtmehrdasein*], and reaching its end is an irreplaceable way of being: the act of dying is unique for every *Dasein*.

On the basis of the former remarks, how should we conceive of the death of *Dasein*? Is it the consummation of a process? Death cannot be imagined as the act of reaching an end [*Zu-Ende-sein*] but as the state of being turned to the end [*sein zum Ende*]. There is no life without death and the constant anticipation of death as the supreme possibility of *Dasein*. According to Heidegger, his analysis of death does not necessarily lead to a decision capable of elucidating whether there is an afterlife. Rather, it is intended at clarifying how death becomes present within each *Dasein*, as a reality that reveals the possibility of *Dasein* in its most radical form. Death reveals the true possibilities of *Dasein* and moreover, its most radical possibility: the possibility of the radical impossibility to exist [*Daseinsunmöglichkeit*]. Death is a task that *Dasein* has to assume. Otherwise, it will fall into inauthenticity. Death should not be the object of a mere empirical certainty (we are all going to die) for we need to be existentially convinced about death.

The importance of the notion of anticipation lies in its special conceptual condition: it is not simply one possibility among others of *Dasein* but it is the expression of the incompleteness of *Dasein*, of its not-yet, which should be regarded neither as an appended moment to be added, as one step more to be overcome, nor as something that has not become accessible yet but as a proper "not-yet" that *Dasein* needs to be at every time. As an entity thrown into the world, *Dasein* is a "not-yet," and the only way to cease to be a "not-yet" is to lose its character of *Dasein* with the advent of death. Anticipation allows *Dasein* to be turned to its end and become convinced about its inexorability. Anticipation is therefore a sign of authenticity. An authentic existential project is based upon the understanding of death: it is not based upon the attempt at escaping it. The fact of being turned to death does not mean, according to Heidegger, that *Dasein* has to commit suicide in order to exist in an authentic way but that it needs to understand the power of death, as a radical possibility, by anticipating itself to it. Anticipation is necessary for *Dasein* to understand that death is an ineluctable reality that expresses its fundamental ontological constitution as care. Death, for Heidegger, vindicates *Dasein* in its singularity, since it can only be assumed by every *Dasein*.

The proper meaning of "care" appears in temporality: temporality determines the being of *Dasein*. Because it is temporal, *Dasein* can achieve its integrity by anticipating itself to the end through resolution. However, this act of anticipating itself can only be based, as Heidegger highlights, upon the future: one can only anticipate what is to come. Future is, above all, the future of *Dasein*. Future is the realm of projection that reflects the possibilities of *Dasein*. Future enables *Dasein* to envision the meaning of its being as a temporal reality and to understand itself as care turned to its end, which is death. *Dasein* is the "in-between" that links birth and death: it is a finite project developed over time. Although *Dasein* has been thrown, it is capable of turning to its end, interlacing the origin (the fall, the act of having been thrown) and the end (death) through care, which allows it to anticipate itself. Temporality is the foundation of the historicity of *Dasein*.

By rooting history in the historicity of *Dasein*, Heidegger is actually assimilating it to worldliness. The historicity of *Dasein* is, essentially, historicity of the world. History, just as the world, responds to the condition of "having been thrown into the world" that defines *Dasein* as being-in-the-world. From this perspective, the question about the meaning of history loses its power, for history has been dissolved into historicity, and moreover, into the worldliness of *Dasein*. If history is not independent from the possibilities of *Dasein*, the question must be referred to the meaning of *Dasein*, not to the meaning of history. However, *Dasein* is an entity that has been thrown into the world, and it is turned to death: the meaning of *Dasein* is death as its radical possibility, because it is the only way for *Dasein* to achieve its integrity as a finite being.

THE CHALLENGE TO DEATH

The distressing presence of death in the horizon of the human existence has not necessarily inflicted upon humanity a sentiment of defeat. Rather, the vacuum and nothingness of the sudden cease of life, which we cannot escape, have actually stimulated our constant will to create a world and a history.

Humanity has not surrendered to death, nor has it wasted its energy in trying to cope with the fear that it generates. Rather, it has tried to transform its existence in the world into a creative scenario, into the life of the spirit, of the human action projected onto the infinite and unlimited: death has been the gate of the true being of mankind. In this sense, no one "dies," since death has opened mankind to being and to the horizon of its deepest quest. Death is the first fruit of ulteriority: *primitia ulterioritatis*.[9]

---

9. We do not know what will happen after death in its dimensional projection (in space and time), but we do know (in the most genuine sense of knowing: the knowing of mankind in its awareness of its vocation to being) that everything that happens cannot be alien to the horizon of being. Where does death come from? What establishes it as the frontier of the temporal human existence? Death is imposed by being; death is the border between concretion and radical openness; it is the very frontier between being perceived as mystery and being perceived as absoluteness, between mankind limited in its openness to the absolute and the overcoming of each limit in being as such, in the dynamic-absolute: death is the link between being and non-being, the fundamental identity, the gate to trans-being and to non-trans-non-being, the inaugural entrance to *categorumen*, to absoluteness ever transcended and transcendent, to the totality which overcomes and overcomes itself. Why to live and

Death as Challenge

The acceptance of death as the genuine horizon of every human being constitutes an abnegated capitulation to the world. Life consists of a constant struggle for the preservation of a realm of autonomy, in opposition to a material world that continuously threatens our independence. The vulnerability of life, its deepest tendency towards death, is perhaps its most important feature. However, consciousness cannot merely admit

---

why to die? Why death, after all? The power of the question is almost invincible, as it was in Unamuno's *Sentimiento trágico de la vida*, but it takes us to the horizon of existence and death, which is ulteriority. Is not, by any means, the absolute precisely the "trans," the "not-being-itself" and tending towards itself, the inscrutable power of that which separates and joins, of non-being and being, of the "beyond," of the possibility of constantly formulating questions that may constitute (in themselves) the absoluteness, as the perennial possibility of extending the space of what is unknown and becomes known in the act of questioning? However, if the absolute is also totality and plenitude, how and to what can it open itself? A similar aporia appears in our own individual life: if we are already, in a certain way, absoluteness and greatness, why should we live? What else can we do if we already exist, if we are already situated in the realm of being, so that, in the very act of existing, we have already achieved some sort of eternity, since we are already participating in something that cannot be annihilated (the truth about our having existed; a similar consideration can be found in the thought of Spinoza, as Gilles Deleuze has shown in a series of lectures: *Spinoza: immortalité et eternité*). However, we live in order to ask, and this is the beginning of our salvation. We live in order to open openness itself, and to discover that the absolute is being conceived as questionability, as tendency to the trans-absolute and to transcending trans-absoluteness. What is undetermined is not susceptible to proof (for a proof is a determination). Therefore, the non-existence of a limit in thought and progress is not susceptible to demonstration, if by it we understand the presence of a hypothetical-deductive argument, starting from clear, well-known premises and arriving at a universally valid conclusion with regard to its premises. Such a degree of clarity is alien to the power of questioning, which is above any further clarification. What we state, or moreover, presuppose (as an ontic postulate that gathers the conditions of possibility for mankind to apprehend the display of being) is that thinking is infinite and infinitesimal and reason, the human being, and reality project themselves onto ulteriority, onto the capacity for a "beyond," onto progress. Otherwise, we would be setting a limit without any legitimacy to do so. It is necessary to make a decision. Culture, thought, philosophy, and religion have tried to prepare us for it throughout the centuries, but it is the personal task of each individual. However, if a more convincing argument were needed (even though such a "demonstration" would always be limited, for conscience has the last word, and it is not always convinced by the evidence of the logical discourse but by the ineffable power of that which conscience itself wants to assume), Gödel's theorem might serve as an orientation, because it proves that no single axiomatic system can be both consistent and complete. No single axiomatic system can justify itself. It is necessary to bring about another system that may offer a justification, but this process goes on ad infinitum: we need this potential infiniteness in order to give meaning to the world and our mind. Plenitude can only be given in the fact of transcendence itself, which unifies any opposition in progress: in the entatic quest. Death needs to be arrogated by everyone.

the inexorable nature of death. Consciousness has to affirm itself through an attempt to challenge the irrevocable character of death. Consciousness represents a perpetual challenge to that which we have called the "sameness of the world," the fact that the vastness of phenomena which take place in the visible universe only reinforce the primacy of the inexorable laws of nature. No novelty, no purity, no real imagination, no authentic challenge to the cyclic reiteration of matter and its incessant transformation can happen within the world. The most severe expression of the sameness of the world is death. The struggle against death is the quest of freedom and purity: the search for something that may be unconditioned. The longing for permanence is the will of life, the endeavor to create. The edification of history is the result of this ambition to commit oneself to something that may transcend the "mediation" of the world.

Death is a phenomenon of life. Because death exists, renewal inside the sphere of nature is possible. Nevertheless, death emerges as an "insurmountable horizon" which plants the seed for its own challenge. Death is the condition of possibility of any *potential will* to challenge that which is given. Life involves the ineluctable orientation towards death. The awareness of this fact, the precise understanding that our destiny is death, reintegration into a silent nature, rubricates authenticity: the recognition that we are a "limit." In death we discover our "truth," our condition of natural beings that have received the "gift" of the highest existing complexity, but are nonetheless bound to the cycles of life and death. The finite character of our existence grants us the chance to expand the energies of life and to assume a vivid longing for life. Because existence is inextricably linked to time and space, because existence is finite, we learn to love life and its profoundest treasures: love, beauty, and wisdom. Because existence is finite, we truly become individual beings, whose vocation is no other than leaving their most genuine trace in the paths of life. Because existence is finite, time and space are meaningful for us, so that can we feel the exhortation to enlarge the frontiers of thought.

In an infinite existence, no commitment to broadening the scope of life and thought would be felt. Dissipation would prevail, a disdaining attitude towards time and space. Within infiniteness, everything is old, the vestige of a seed which has been already planted. In finiteness there is room for novelty, freshness, and youth. We can dream of infinity and we can seek an inexhaustible realm of purity, free from the concatenation of causes and effects (the concourse of wills of power and the inexorable cycles of nature) which darkens our finite existence.

Death as Challenge

A being whose destiny is death anxiously longs for permanence. The understanding of our finite nature opens the possibility for challenging death. We know that death cannot be defeated. We know that we must die. However, we feel the most powerful calling to challenge death through creation. By grasping our finite nature, we realize about the tyrannical character of the frontier that we face. We therefore feel committed to challenging such an indolent limit. There is no room for "more" within infiniteness, for every *plus* has been diluted into that which is unlimited. In a finite existence it is possible to long for "more."

The acceptance of the inexorability of death is captive to the solitude of consciousness. Self-satisfied consciousness will trumpet the merit of having understood its intrinsically mortal nature. Turned into "heroic consciousness," its courage will generate before death. However, heroic consciousness will not lose its passion for life, its commitment to the transformation of the world, and its consecration to humanity. Self-satisfied consciousness believes that the goal of life resides in achieving happiness and the mitigation of suffering. Pleasure (not a selfish pleasure which inspires indifference towards the world but a wise *hedone*, the awareness that the highest aspiration of the human life cannot be alien to obtaining the greatest degree of fruition and personal satisfaction) and the edification of a different future, emancipated from the chains of the present, will be regarded as the aims of existence. Apathetic consciousness will accept death as the inevitable destiny of life. However, it will show no commitment to creation. Apathetic consciousness will feel no fascination for life and history. It will experience no vocation for changing the world and leaving its most genuine trace. Its life will be enslaved by the rhapsody of phenomena that fall upon it. Apathetic consciousness will deprive itself of any attachment to life and any longing for creation. It will not seek to challenge death and finiteness. It will not look for *novum*.

Distressed consciousness will attack, with no piety, all those who want to challenge death. Absorbed by its own and tormented solitude, distressed consciousness seems to accept death guided by the spirit of humble resignation (although the truth is that it is possessed by a deep fear towards death and its dissolution into the vastness of the universe; distressed consciousness conceals this profound fear behind the mask of maturity and courage). Also, distressed consciousness looks with malice and rancor to all those who wish to "defeat" death (even if subjugated by a delusory longing) through creation. Distressed consciousness will proclaim that any project of "transcending" the *hic et nunc* of present existence is vain, the manifestation of candid naivety, the expression of self-incurred immaturity. The creative will, the wish for planting the seed of freshness, wonder, and ineffability, is the principal enemy of distressed consciousness. In suicidal consciousness, its courage will allow it to assume its mortal nature through the anticipation of death. Deprived of any attachment to life, suicidal consciousness will discover death as a radical possibility, as the eminent symbol of existential authenticity. Suicidal consciousness will answer that which Camus called "the only truly serious problem of philosophy."[10] The shadow of meaninglessness encourages suicidal consciousness to look for a "meaning": death, its dilution into the enormity of the world; its return to the arcane fountains of being, matter, and transformation. Suicidal consciousness will turn death into its "life." It will anticipate its ineluctable end by rejecting the horizon of possibilities that life can offer. It will renounce its power in space and time, the displaying of its vital energy, in order to submerge itself into being, the vastness of the world and the dissolution of any vestige of its individuality. Suicidal consciousness will not commit itself to creation, *novum*, the *orientation* of the multiple paths that life can take towards the growth of world and thought.

Consciousness that abandons the roughness of its solitude commits itself to the creative capacity of life: it shows a creative acceptance of death. Creative consciousness offers itself to a goal which transcends its narrow limits, thereby contemplating a vast ocean of possibilities, a task, a vocation: that of broadening the horizons of being and expanding the energies of life. It does not reject death, nor does it try to elude its presence. Creative consciousness accepts the reality of death. This is the reason why it seeks to challenge death. Creative consciousness does not hide itself from something that will eventually happen. Rather, it learns to look to death in a different way. It is no longer afraid by death or possessed by resignation: it is moved by the longing for tasting all the possibilities of life. Its desire is focused on creating. Because of having contemplated death as challenge instead of inexorability, creative consciousness takes advantage of all its possibilities in each moment of its existence. To challenge death is equal to delving into life. To drain the cup of life demands the longing for beauty, love, and wisdom. Pleasure is the rubric of life in its most genuine nature. The most iridescent manifestation of the gift of life shines in thought, for the act of thinking allows us to become aware of the possibilities of life.

10. Cf. the beginning of *Le Mythe de Sisyphe* by Albert Camus: "Il n'ya qu'un problème philosophique vraiment sérieux: c'est le suicide."

Death as Challenge

Thought is already a victory over the imminence of death. Through thinking, we open ourselves to the infinite space of being. Thinking is therefore the *fundamentum* of our salvation, greatness, and dignity.[11] We must challenge death through creativity, through our quest of a real *novum*; of purity, limpidness, and inexhaustibility: through our search for love, beauty, and wisdom. We challenge the finitude of life when we commit ourselves to goals that do not demand a further "reward": love, beauty, and wisdom. Even if constrained to finitude, even if condemned to perish with the destruction of our material world, by seeking them we have shown faith in the idea that life and creativity are worthy, because they allow us to contemplate signs of love, beauty, and wisdom: we have believed in an "ultimate end," in that which is worth being sought for its own sake, even if the shadow of annihilation darkens its future and inundates our souls with the waters of nostalgia and the tears of melancholy.

---

11. The greatness and dignity of the human being are beautifully expressed by Leibniz: "A single spirit is worth a whole world, because it not only expresses the whole world, but it also knows it and governs itself as does God. In this way we may say that though every substance expresses the whole universe, yet the other substances express the world rather than God, while spirits express God rather than the world. This nature of spirits, so noble that it enables them to approach divinity as much as is possible for created things, has as a result that God derives infinitely more glory from them than from the other beings, or rather the other beings furnish to spirits the material for glorifying him. This moral quality of God which constitutes him Lord and Monarch of spirits influences him so to speak personally and in a unique way" (*Discourse on Metaphysics*, 36). The relationship between totality and singularity, infiniteness and infinitesimalness, reaches one of its culminating points in the work of Leibniz, especially in his idea of "monads without windows," of an autonomous universe that contains in its own notion the totality of its possible determinations (*praedicatum inest subiecto*: an intellect knowing the subject in its "selfness" might deduce all the predicative determinations to follow, in Leibniz's view). Mankind therefore appears as *un petit dieu*. In order to be coherent with that which we have said about ulteriority and the transfinitization of being we must hold Leibniz's idea to be incomplete, because the deduction of any possible predicate from the analytic apprehension of the subject meets the following ineluctable difficulty: being is displayed in the ontic space, which transcends any previous ontic space; being "broadens itself," it "grows," it is subject of dynamism, and it creates new possibilities in the context of *categorumen*, which integrates both being and non-being (being goes beyond being, it *progresses*).

8

Wisdom, Love, and Beauty

WISDOM AS THE GOAL OF LIFE

SURROUNDED BY DATA, OVERWHELMED by information, we feel tempted to believe that by merely accumulating knowledge we have reached a deep understanding of reality. Moreover, we believe that we have conquered wisdom. However, information darkens the power of questioning and shadows the light of understanding, the freshness of a serene, profound, and courageous reflection that does not take refuge in the analysis of data but dares to think. Deep thinking is the prelude of wisdom, and it consists of a struggle against an uncontrolled curiosity which, blinded by details, does not delve into the core, as it becomes paralyzed by the large trees which hide the vastness and beauty of the forest.

The task of philosophy cannot consist of examining the data provided by other disciplines, in order to simply accumulate erudition concerning the history of the different schools and trends: philosophy is called to think, to formulate claims, to understand, to link; philosophy needs to be turned into a life; it has to "incarnate" itself in a vital project. The act of thinking is an exercise of freedom. To interrogate an object means to liberate oneself from the tyranny of specific representations in order to transcend reality through thinking: in Pliny the Younger's words, "*non multa, sed multum.*" Behold the most noticeable difference between the human mind and a computer: our intellect explores the semantic dimension of reality, whereas a computer remains in the sphere of syntax, "kidnapped" by ruled-based information processing. A computer is incapable of understanding, as John Searle remarked in his argument of the Chinese room.[1] Indeed, piling up information poses a very serious challenge for the task of philosophy. We nowadays enjoy access to information as no one could have ever imagined before. The greatest dream of Leibniz, who so eagerly searched for a *characteristic universalis* that might express all the ideas of human knowledge in a language intelligible for the whole of humankind, and the enlightened utopia of a universal dissemination of knowledge as the most eminent path to reach the unity of humanity, seem to have been materialized in the Internet.

However, this superabundance of information bears the danger of suffocating the fire of wisdom, the light of understanding. In order to think, we need to relativize, to "forget," to leave information aside and to concentrate on that which is fundamental.[2] We need to generalize, to abstract, and to relate: we must reach the substance beyond the "accidents" (through some sort of phenomenological *epojé*). The risk of underestimating the importance of details is much less compelling than the danger of renouncing thought and failing the quest of wisdom.

Knowledge, interpreted both as explanation (Dilthey's *erklären*) and understanding (Dilthey's *verstehen*),[3] demands the power of discriminating that which is fundamental from that which remains secondary. In knowledge, the factual multiplicity has to be related through its underlying unity. We must become fascinated by the vast reality which surrounds us, but we have to complement this moment of wonder with that of criticism, with that of thinking, with that of attempting to reach the nucleus of intelligibility of reality. Contemplation must be conjugated with an attitude that may allow us to "humanize" experience through its categorization into concepts. Science, philosophy, and theology can open the window to wisdom, but they can also conceal its vibrant light, if they lose themselves in an unredeemed search of information which is not tied to an equally enthusiastic quest of an "existential meaning" that can propitiate the ethical growth of humanity.

1 Cf. Searle, "Mind, Brain, Programs," 417–57.

2. As Jorge Luis Borges writes in his short story "Funes, the Memorious": "To think is to forget a difference, to generalize, to abstract. In the overly replete world of Funes there were nothing but details, almost contiguous details" (*Ficciones*, 90).

3. Cf. Dilthey, *Einleitung in die Geisteswissenschaften*.

Part 3: Questioning as Salvation

WISDOM AND SCIENCE

Few adventures have been as fruitful for the development of the human spirit as that of the natural sciences. Progress in the scientific view of the world has been outstanding since the time of Copernicus, Galileo, Kepler, and Newton. The basic features of the scientific method, as formulated in the sixteenth and seventeenth centuries, have remained unchanged: science is its method, and the scientific method which we nowadays use is basically the same as Galileo's and Newton's, who applied it to unfolding the structure and functioning of the physical world.

Physics has discovered the four fundamental forces and the prolix elenchus of elementary particles. It is currently in search of the unification of those basic interactions and a refinement of the so-called standard model. In the macroscopic realm, Einstein's findings have led us to a new understanding of the nature of space, time, and the force of gravity. It has also opened the way to the idea of "evolution of the universe," as shown in the pioneering works of Lemaître, Friedmann, and Gamow. The universe, just as life, has a history. The achievement for which physics is eagerly looking consists of the integration of its theory for the microcosm (epitomized in quantum mechanics) and its theory for the macrocosm into a unified theory of fundamental forces.

Regarding the life sciences, the consolidation of biology as a science in the nineteenth century (with Schwann and Schleiden's cell theory and Darwin's and Wallace's theory of evolution through natural selection), together with the revolution inaugurated by genetics since Mendel, has fostered the elucidation of the "key of life," the structure of DNA, the "secret" of the transmission of genetic information. We now possess a deep understanding of how living organisms function. This pinnacle in the scientific enterprise raises hope concerning the possibility of healing different pathologies. However, two deep "fundamental" mysteries remain: the first one refers to the origin of life (although the "RNA world" hypothesis seems to be a plausible explanation[4]) and the second one concerns the nature of consciousness. As Sir Francis Crick noticed, consciousness represents the major unsolved problem of biology.[5] However, as Professor Eric Kandel[6] has remarked, the synthesis of neurobiology, cognitive

---

4. Cf. Zimmer, "On the Origin of Life on Earth," 198–99.

5. "Consciousness is the major unsolved problem in biology" (prologue to Koch, *The Quest for Consciousness*).

6. Kandel won the Nobel Prize in Medicine or Physiology in 2000 for his contributions to the study of elementary forms of learning and behavior in invertebrates.

psychology, neurology, and psychiatry anticipates a very promising future for solving this deep question.[7]

The existence of scientific mysteries constitutes a vivid proof of vitality, freshness, and youth. The scientific enterprise still has a future, a purpose, a calling. The provisional nature of many scientific statements does not invalidate that which they affirm: it only darkens the pretension of having exhausted our understanding of the world. The theory of relativity does not refute classical mechanics but integrates it into a broader picture that is endowed with a higher power of explanation, just as it happens in the realm of quantum mechanics. Methodical science builds rather than destroys.

Science offers a most valuable knowledge of the world and our own nature, which philosophy, "love for wisdom," cannot underestimate. Technique may represent the happiest consequence of science, as it improves our material conditions of life (although it also shows a huge destructive potential), but the deepest fascination with science lies in its explanatory power. The fact that Einstein's genius was capable of predicting the deviation in the movement of Mercury's perihelion with respect to the calculations of classical mechanics is utterly amazing. By admiring this achievement we shall pay a tribute to the power of human intelligence and to the fruitful path inaugurated by the scientific method (and its fortunate conjunction of physics and mathematical formalism).

Science unveils the mystery of the world, but it does not solve "my mystery," "my problem," as Wittgenstein noticed. This *Unbefriedigtheit* generated by science, this lack of satisfaction for my deepest interests, lies in the fact that our problem is still "alive."[8] The most inscrutable mystery is: "why is there anything instead of nothing?," as both Leibniz and Heidegger remarked. Possibly, the deepest mystery is actually: "Why this unceasing formulation of questions? Why have we created philosophy and science? Why do we possess such an excess of energy?" Science does not solve the mystery of the meaning of my existence. Science does not teach me how I must live in the *hic et nunc* of history. No far-reaching ethics stems from science alone. Wisdom must therefore transcend the constellation of science, as it points to a profound reflection on how to dispose of scientific knowledge in order to grow as humans.

His book *In Search of Memory: The Emergence of a New Science of Mind* constitutes a wonderful introduction to the study of neuroscience.

7. See the final chapters of Kandel et al., *Principles of Neural Science*.
8. Cf. Wittgenstein, *Notebooks 1914–1916*.

Part 3: Questioning as Salvation

WISDOM AND PHILOSOPHY

If by "philosophy" we understand the way in which this discipline has been cultivated over the twentieth century, no conclusion can be drawn from the examination of trends such as analytic philosophy, phenomenology, existentialism, Marxism, hermeneutics, and postmodernism. Suspicion against the "great tales" of the past has grown stronger, and the perspective inaugurated by Marx, Nietzsche, and Freud through their "genetic, infrastructural" analysis of philosophical theses seems to be the prevailing framework in the Western world. Also, the failure of the so-called real socialism has almost entirely extinguished the flame of confidence in reason to orientate collective action towards building a new future. What is therefore left? Disenchantment, fragmentation, limit...

However, the variety of movements compels us to wonder about the real meaning of philosophy. We need to liberate ourselves from the tyranny of this rhapsody of trends and interpretations, which can conceal the task of our time and of every individual: to think of our own. Philosophical erudition is not philosophy. We must mediate on life with depth and courage. This is the task of philosophy. Philosophy must recover enthusiasm at thinking, audacity to revisit old themes and to offer new light on them. Philosophy cannot remain in a nostalgic return to great authors: philosophy has to think, *hic et nunc*, on how we must live as men and women of the twenty-first century. Thinking is the goal of any age and any human being. The great authors of the past will not cease to illuminate us, given the depth and sharpness of their penetration into the nature and scope of humanity, but we must deliver ourselves to thinking with enthusiasm and hope.

We must "reconquer" the genuine meaning of philosophy as "love of wisdom." Love of wisdom is itself a form of wisdom, for it entails a way of life that invites us to grow, to deliver ourselves to that which is noble and evoking. Love of wisdom shines in love of deep thought: philosophy must therefore dare to link the parts with their whole; to think about totality; to reflect on the past, the present, and the future. This inclination towards universality that underlies the philosophical endeavor calls for the commitment of extending philosophy to everyone: each individual must become a philosopher; each individual must be able to create his own space of freedom and solidarity in which to display human creativity. Love of wisdom requests us to turn knowledge into life.

WISDOM AND THEOLOGY

It is impossible to summarize the *status quaestionis* of theology. How should we account for the different theological schools within Protestantism (dialectical theology, existential theology, theologies of history, theology of hope, and so forth) and within Catholicism (*nouvelle théologie*, which anticipated the Second Vatican Council, liberation theology, personalism, and so forth), not to speak about Judaism (Buber, Rosenzweig, Levinas, and the like) and other religious creeds?

However, systematic theology represents only a fraction of the full set of theological disciplines. The development of biblical studies, through the application of the different hermeneutic tools to the Holy Scriptures of Judaism and Christianity, in addition to our increasing knowledge of the history of the various religious traditions, has caused a deep impact in systematic theology. We cannot understand Bultmann's existential theology without taking into consideration his work as a New Testament scholar. We cannot capture the essence of his New Testament research without fully grasping the scope of his theological orientation, mostly inspired by Heidegger's existential analytic. His theology and his biblical scholarship intertwine. Great theologies stem from a synergy of a deep and sharp reading of biblical texts and the assumption of a certain philosophical paradigm. The sentence "*nemo theologus nisi philosophus*" of Scholasticism has not lost its currency. Any influential theological movement is determined by a certain philosophical orientation in its approach to biblical sources.

However, accumulating theological knowledge is different from "cultivating theology." It is far more removed from holding the torch of wisdom. In Christianity, theology demands the continuous return to the same sources: the Bible, theological traditions, great spiritual writings, but this meditation needs to be focused on the present and the future. The question on how to conjugate the Bible and today's newspaper, which so deeply concerned Karl Barth, is still appealing, as it was in ancient times. Saint Augustine reflected upon his time, upon the twilight of an age, upon the fall of Rome, and so he came to meditate about the truly eternal city, about the divine kingdom of imperishable life, love, and beauty. Saint Thomas Aquinas discovered a *corpus philosophicum*, that of Aristotle, which was full of wisdom but had not been as influential for Christian theology as it had been for Jewish (e.g. Maimonides) and Muslim (e.g. Avicenna and Averroes) thought. He therefore sought to unfold its rational potential in order to express, even within its inexorable limits, the genuine Christian truth in which he firmly believed. Scheleiermacher built his theology in the climax of romanticism and idealism, when the spiritual energies had been shed on feeling instead of reason, and he conceived of religion as the sentimental intuition of our dependence upon that which is absolute.

Theology condenses the will to discover God, that which is unconditioned, absolute love, in the *hic et nunc* of history, of this vast palimpsest of wishes. Theology invites us to search for the meaning of life: it exhorts us to "live in a humane way." If theology wants to have something to say to mankind, it must delve into its own fountains, but it has to shine as universal wisdom: it needs to reveal something about how we should live today in order to grow as humanity.

WISDOM AS COMMITMENT

No one can possess wisdom: it is wisdom that possesses us. Wisdom is not an object of having but a recondite ideal that we never capture, for it recalls freedom in its highest degree. Wisdom cannot be exhausted through a definition. Wisdom, insofar as it is freedom, is never the patrimony of a culture or an individual. We are servants, not masters of wisdom. Wisdom belongs to the sphere of "being," not of "having," to bear in mind Erich Fromm's famous distinction. Wisdom is free because it can never be captured as something "at hand" (Heidegger's *zu Handen*). We do not dispose of wisdom in the same way as we can use a tool, a piece of information, or even a content of science. Wisdom must be "lived": wisdom is the *wise person*.

The wise person contemplates knowledge as a source of freedom. She is committed to turning knowledge into a way of uniting human beings, into a foundation of peace and creativity. The wise person does not recreate herself in that which she already knows: she delves into knowledge in order to turn it into a way of life. She becomes fascinated by knowledge, and she perceives of its "mysticism." She is delighted at each concept, and she entirely assumes the content of each idea with "*esprit de finesse*." This is the reason why she wants to diffuse the enthusiasm which she feels to all those around her. She conceives of the cultivation, propagation, and extension of knowledge as a preeminent form of a full life. The search for knowledge, which has now been transfigured into the wish for wisdom and the desire that knowledge may become life and inspiration for her existence, invites her to commit herself to the growth of mankind. She therefore works to improve the material conditions of life of humanity. She delivers herself to the service of justice and the mitigation of human suffering. She aspires to use her knowledge and her longing for wisdom to help humanity.

Her unceasing wish for wisdom inspires her to expand her mind and to tolerate other opinions; to look for truth without any prejudice; to listen, to learn, and to become submerged into history and the prodigious variety of cultural and philosophical traditions. She wants to extend the frontiers of life and the territories of thinking. This quest may turn into dissipation, but wisdom consists of the capacity for finding something that is permanent in the midst of that which is mutable: a "spirit," an ideal, a way of life. Wisdom resists the temptation of diluting thought into a gallery of data and dissonant opinions. That which is permanent is wisdom itself, for it never becomes "consumed" in a specific manifestation, in a particular philosophy, in a concrete work: it refers to that which is ultimate, to that which is unconditioned, to that which cannot be incarcerated into sensations and concepts. The same can be said about beauty: it never "appears"; it never becomes materialized in an object. It is by virtue of its endlessly evoking nature, of its unlimited capacity for being suggestive for our mind, that our minds admit so different aesthetic criteria. Wisdom cannot be expressed in a set of propositions: it is *lived*, it is "captured" as an inscrutable reality into which we can always delve.

Wisdom, as an end in itself, as a goal instead of an instrument to conquer anything else, plants the seed of love. The wish to become wise is the desire to commit oneself to something limpid, to something unconditioned, to something which does not serve a higher goal: it is the purity of service. The light of beauty also shines at this commitment: that which transcends our own narrowness and opens us to universality, to humanity, and truth is beautiful, for it is contemplated for its own sake. Wisdom as commitment and vocation is life, because it exhorts us to meditate upon the knowledge which we have acquired, in order to realize that its meaning "for me" lies in adopting a form of life: it points to ethics, to commitment to humanity, to fleeing my own selfness, to delving into myself so that I may learn that I urgently need to open my spirit to the world and mankind. Sapiential introspection leads to an intense desire for life, experience, and humanity. Moreover, it leads to longing for that which is unconditioned.

Part 3: Questioning as Salvation

WISDOM, BEAUTY, AND LOVE

Three ages condense, I think, the most "vivid experience" of wisdom, its "incarnation" into a time and a space: classical Athens, the Italian Renaissance, and German Romanticism. During the climax of Athens, when the Sun passionately shone upon the souls of Socrates, Plato, Pericles, and Aristotle, wisdom was regarded as an end in itself. Philosophy was the instrument for achieving self-knowledge (*gnothi seauton*) in order to grow as *polis*, as a community in which to display everyone's vital energies. Wisdom was focused on the conception of a political existence, of a project that might unite human beings (we know that in a very limited way) through the cultivation of the same goods: the spirit, truth, righteousness. For Plato, it is not possible to philosophize without loving wisdom: the highest form of wisdom consists of a sincere commitment to wisdom as a way of life, as participation in that which is eternal. As we read in *Symposium*, in words that Socrates attributes to Diotima of Mantineia: "For wisdom is surely among the most beautiful of things, but Eros is love of the beautiful, so Eros is necessarily a philosopher, a lover of wisdom, and, being a philosopher, intermediate between wisdom and ignorance."[9]

In Aristotle, the superiority of contemplative over active life should not be interpreted as a withdrawal from the ethical and political task. Rather, it rubricates the conviction that the goal of life in common resides in committing oneself to a pure end (contemplation is equivalent to offering ourselves to that which fascinates us), to an end in itself, to a good which does not require further justification: to true wisdom, to free happiness.[10] As we read in *Nicomachean Ethics*: "The activity of a god, superior as it is in its blessedness, will be one of reflection; and so too the human activity that has the greatest affinity to this one will be most productive of happiness . . . Happiness too extends as far as reflection does, and to those who have more of reflection more of happiness belongs too, not incidentally, but in virtue of the reflection; for this is in itself to be honoured. So then happiness will be a kind of reflection."

In the Renaissance, wisdom was "tasted" as beauty. To incarnate the most sublime beauty, as Michelangelo and Leonardo da Vinci eagerly sought (in spite of their awareness of the impossibility of emulating the omnipotence of God to obtain perfection, the divine power to create *ex nihilo*), meant to discover in the highest art the truth of life, the most

---

9. Plato, *The Symposim*, 147.
10. *Nicomachean Ethics*, book 10, chap. 8 (Rowe translation).

intense life: wisdom. If genuine wisdom exhorts us to orientate all means, and specially knowledge, to contribute to our growth as humanity, to a fuller and deeper life, the Renaissance identified this desire for life with the contemplation of beauty and artistic creation. The goal of life converged with the instauration of beauty, with creativity, with the sweet exercise of freedom focused on art. The ornamentation of Renaissance cities with the most outstanding works of art allowed for the sharing of beauty, for the translation of beauty into a form of life in common. The dignity of life shone in the splendor of aesthetic beauty. The act of "tasting" the same cup of beauty, art, and commitment to creation was an exhortation to live in a humane way and to consecrate oneself to the utopia that the divine kingdom might descend to Earth in the form of art.

Romanticism understood love as the goal of mankind. Religion, for young Hegel, is love.[11] The great idealist thinkers attribute to love the primeval unity that founds and unifies everything. Love is the truth of life for romanticism, and wisdom can be tasted as love. It is true that Hegel finishes his *Phänomenologie des Geistes* with a chapter on absolute knowledge, but in order to properly understand this Hegelian concept (which recalls Aristotle's *noesis noeseos*) it is necessary to realize that absolute knowledge is a form of *amor sui* of the spirit for itself. The spirit has alienated itself from its own initial selfness, from its initial indeterminacy, because it freely looks for itself: it wants to know itself, to "possess" itself, and to love itself. Its love is unquestionably selfish, as it can be noticed in the threatening severity of the central thesis of Hegel's philosophy of history, according to which suffering is inexorable so that the spirit may reach the full knowledge of itself. However, the spirit has also suffered: it has succumbed to "infinite pain," to its "speculative Good Friday," on behalf of love. In Schelling, God creates the world moved by love. God allows that his own *alter Deus* may rebel against him and "fall" into the world. God contracts himself, just as in the Jewish mystical tradition of *tzim-tzum* (as exposed by Isaac Luria in the sixteenth century, whose trace can be found in Jacob Böhme, one of the precursors of German idealism as early as the seventeenth century). God cedes his "vital space" because of pure love, pure abnegation, and in doing so He propitiates the birth of the "age of the world" (*Weltalter*).[12]

---

11. Cf. Hegel, "Tübinger Fragment," in Nohl, *Hegels theologische Jugendschriften*; cf. Paredes, "G. W. F. Hegel: el 'Fragmento de Tubinga,'" 139–76. On the philosophy of young Hegel, cf. Legros, *Le Jeune Hegel et la Naissance de la Pensée Romantique*.

12. Cf. Schelling, *Werke* 4:331.

Part 3: Questioning as Salvation

Idealism is the philosophy of love, of fathomless and unconditional purity. Idealism "tastes" infiniteness and freedom in that which is finite and determined. Romanticism is the aesthetic translation of idealism: it is Goethe who, in the eternal city of Rome, does not ask for the science of antiquity or the revival of past glories but for "Amor's temple":[13]

> Speak, ye stones, I entreat! Oh, speak, ye palaces lofty!
> Utter a word, O ye streets! Wilt thou not, Genius, awake?
> All that thy sacred walls, eternal Rome, hold within them
> Teemeth with life; but to *me,* all is still silent and dead.
> Oh, who will whisper unto me,—when shall I see at the casement
> That one beauteous form, which, while it scorcheth, revives?
> Can I as yet not discern the road on which I forever
> To her and from her shall go, heeding not time as it flies?
> Still do I mark the churches, palaces, ruins and columns,
> As a wise traveller should, would he his journey improve.
> Soon all this will be past; and then will there be but *one* temple,
> Amor's temple alone, where the Initiate may go.
> Thou art indeed a world, O Rome; and yet, were Love absent,
> Then would the world be no world, then would e'en Rome be no Rome.

Romanticism itself knew, however, that its twilight meant the sunset of a golden age. The spirit that vivified Athens, the Italian Renaissance and romanticism, the "faith" in an end in itself which were capable of orienting individual and collective life, would never return. It is in fact difficult to think of an age as full of splendor and creative fecundity as the ones mentioned above. Goals such as wisdom, beauty, and love cannot be contemplated with so much purity any longer. The suspicion that they represent mere delusions, consoling fantasies, "metaphysical impossibilities" darkened in a net of concatenated interests which fills everything, compels us to believe that there is only will of power. Nothing limpid can be seen, nothing authentic remains; no goal stands beyond a powerful life which affirms itself. The irreversible process of rationalization and disenchantment of the world, which "demythologizes" all spheres of existence, seems to subsume ourselves into the coldness of objectivity, of an intellect which cannot aspire to transcend that which is given (the *positum*) except through art and imagination.

Max Weber recalls the nostalgia for the twilight of romanticism in his famous study on the influence of the Protestant *ethos* upon the genesis

---

13. Goethe, *Roman Elegies*, elegy I.

Wisdom, Love, and Beauty

of capitalism (Calvinism is responsible, in his view, for the consolidation of the rationalizing tendency in Western culture"):[14]

> The idea that modern labor has an ascetic character is of course not new. Limitation to specialized work, with a renunciation of the Faustian universality of man which it involves, is a condition of any valuable work in the modern world; hence deeds and renunciation inevitably condition each other today. This fundamentally ascetic trait of middle-class life, if it attempts to be a way of life at all, and not simply the absence of any, was what Goethe wanted to teach, at the height of his wisdom, in the Wanderjahren, and in the end which he gave to the life of his Faust. For him the realization meant a renunciation, a departure from an age of full and beautiful humanity [vollen und schönen Menschentums], which can no more be repeated in the course of our cultural development than can the flower of the Athenian culture of antiquity. The Puritan wanted to work in a calling; we are forced to do so. For when asceticism was carried out of monastic cells into everyday life, and began to dominate worldly morality, it did its part in building the tremendous cosmos of the modern economic order. This order is now bound to the technical and economic conditions of machine production which today determine the lives of all the individuals who are born into this mechanism, not only those directly concerned with economic acquisition, with irresistible force. Perhaps it will so determine them until the last ton of fossilized coal is burnt.

The impossibility to revive the "idealism" of times past would be ratified by the scientific view of the world, which may seem desolating: it reveals that we are a lately product of a certain evolutionary path, and that we live in a recondite region of a vast universe which is almost fourteen billion years old. In this huge cosmos, the most threatening silence prevails: "le silence éternel de ces espaces infinis m'effraie,"[15] as Pascal wrote in the beginning of a scientific revolution which deprived us of any hope of enjoying a "central position" in the universe (and, to recall Sigmund Freud, this revolution wounded our narcissistic self-pride). The conclusions of science, if analyzed without poetic or theological willingness, seem frightening. Bertrand Russell summarizes them in the following way:[16]

---

14. Weber, *The Protestant Ethic and the Spirit of Capitalism*, 181.
15. Pascal, *Pensées*, 1669.
16. Russell, "A Free Man's Worship," 67.

Part 3: Questioning as Salvation

> That man is the product of causes that had no prevision of the end that they were achieving; that his origin, his growth, his hopes and his fears, his loves and his beliefs, are but the outcome of accidental collocations of atoms; that no fire, no heroism, no intensity of thought and feeling, can preserve individual life beyond the grave, that all the labours of the ages, all the devotion, all the inspiration, all the noonday brightness of human genius, are destined to extinction in the vast death of the solar system, and that the whole temple of Man's achievement must inevitably be buried beneath the debris of the universe in ruins—all these things, if not quite beyond dispute, are yet so nearly certain that no philosophy which rejects them can hope to stand."

However, science also shows that we possess the highest degree of complexity within nature. Our brain, with almost a hundred billion neurons and a hundred trillion synapses, endowed with the capacity for thinking, creating, imagining, building its own world, and discovering the permanent truths of logic and mathematics, occupies some sort of "central position." As Pascal proclaimed: "l'homme n'est qu'un roseau, le plus faible de la nature; mais c'estun Roseau pensant."[17] The problem of human loneliness in the midst of our huge universe can be solved by thinking about cosmos, by giving a meaning to it, by looking for the *fundamentum*, by making of the universe an *ego*.

Science does not only infuse sadness on account of our smallness in the midst of these vast sideral spaces: it also exhorts us to become fascinated by the extraordinary complexity of the universe and the harmony of its laws (which so deeply amazed Einstein). It also invites us to show gratitude for the gift of life. Whoever dares to understand the universe can perceive its *creating power*, the force from which everything emanates and to which everything points. He can feel the commitment to exercise his own power, his own spirit of creation, his *freedom*.

The rejection of death does not emerge from fear alone. It does not refer only to the frightening presence of death and the fugacity of joy. It is not only the result of an « inauthentic existence » in Heideggerian terms, which pretends to conceal our finiteness. The rejection of death also recalls the conviction that the human effort to create, to bring beauty to the world, to discover, to think, and to love *deserves* reward. Without this conscience of merit it is not possible to understand the spirit of religions. The human struggle to transmit love, beauty, and wisdom cannot be in vain. Many will think that enjoying a finite existence is enough.

---

17. Pascal, *Pensées*, 1670.

The prize will be present happiness, the reward of having created beauty and having discovered new truths, of having loved and having dreamt of new worlds, but many people will still feel that humanity has been called to higher destinies.

In any case, the contemplation of the glories of the past must not inspire melancholy, as if it had been better not to have participated in the advancement of science and technology in order to remain alien to the process of rationalization, which deprives us of "tasting" something permanent and transcendent to world and history. Let us not proclaim, just as Mephistopheles:[18]

> Ich bin der Geist, der stets verneint!
> Und das mit Recht; denn alles, was entsteht,
> Ist wert, daß es zugrunde geht;
> Drum besser wär's, daß nichts entstünde.

Even if life is necessarily followed by death, and everyone is "sein zum Todde," we have the power to create, to build our own world, to serve love, wisdom, and beauty. To look at the serene magnificence of the Caryatids, at the captivating intensity of Sistine Chapel and to listen at the unredeemed sentiment exhaled by the verses of Goethe should not inspire nostalgia but desire of life, longing for a future. History must move forward. History must still offer the chance to search for knowledge and to long for wisdom. The future generations must have something to say : they must be able to live their own existence and to fully dispose of their own capabilities.

We must lead the future and we must learn to contemplate the past with depth, sharpness, and gratitude. It is our responsibility to devoutly preserve the legacy which we have received. Dilthey conceived of this "care" for the past as the key of the human vocation.[19] In our time, a preeminent task for great religions resides in linking us to a past which is essential for many of them. The evocation of the past will help us to take care of the historical legacy that binds us as humanity. Great religions must also contribute to the creation of a space in which to meditate upon our ultimate concerns and "taste" something pure, something limpid behind this net of interests and wills of power which darkens the perception of wisdom, love, and beauty.

---

18. Goethe, *Faust*, "ersterTeil," "Studierzimmer."
19. Suter, *Philosophie et Histoire chez Wilhelm Dilthey*, 85–186.

WISDOM AND THE UNCONDITIONED

Wisdom, beauty, and love converge with the unconditioned: they are ends in themselves, a triumvirate of purity and commitment. They invite us to look for them with enthusiasm and fascination. They exhort us to consecrate our lives to their quest. The unconditioned can never be exhausted. It can never become objectified in a specific structure. It is utterly free.

Wisdom is not given: it is conquered. It is the result of a process of personal growth, because wisdom does not exist "in abstract" but in those who seek it with prudence and commitment. The gate into wisdom is fascination. The superabundance of information and knowledge in our world darkens the possibility of enthusiasm and wonder. We do not appreciate the value of that which is known, of the huge effort made by our ancestors to discover what now belongs to universal culture. If wisdom is life; if to be wise means to translate knowledge into life, growth, service, and ethical improvement, wisdom must also inspire fascination for the richness of knowledge and the complexity of the universe, for the diversity of arts and the variety of cultures. The great British neurophysiologist Sir Charles Sherrington, winner of the Nobel Prize in Medicine or Physiology in 1932, referred to the necessity of "wonder" in his Gifford lectures: "The wonder is still there. It rests on different way. Nature is not made less wonderful because her rule of working begins to be intelligible. If it be a question of wonder, rather the more wonderful."[20] The moment of perplexity must be complemented with that of criticism, but its primordial goal resides in evoking our full commitment to admiration and to consecrating our lives to love, wisdom, and beauty.

Wisdom demands the awareness of the provisional nature of any acquired knowledge. Scientific propositions, as Sir Karl Popper remarked, are inherently provisional. A single experiment contrary to a hypothesis forces us to correct its presuppositions. This conscience of the limited scope of our knowledge admonishes us to "taste finiteness" and to long for more knowledge, for more questioning, for more life.

Science cannot exhaust the truth about the world, because any new form of knowledge raises a flamboyant constellation of new questions. A "pending rest" will always remain: the question concerning the ultimate origin, the meaning of everything. The act of appealing to the incapacity of science to answer this question does not stem from a strategy of building a "philosophical fortress" against the advancement of science and its gradual

---

20. Sherrington, *Man on His Nature*, chapter 4.

"invasion" of spaces traditionally reserved to the humanities. Rather, it obeys the evidence that we can always pose a further question. Our capacity for questioning is virtually unlimited. This "lack of limitation" is the truth of knowledge: nothing can exhaust it. No scientific theory could ever become a "final theory," not only because of Gödel's theorem but on account of this fundamental "inexhaustibility" of the human intellect. The quest of a deeper *fundamentum* is always possible. However, philosophy cannot compete against the natural sciences in the search for the elucidation of the structure and functioning of the natural world. Philosophy must aspire to creation, to love for wisdom. Philosophy is not called to interpret scientific data. It should not become some sort of *ancilla scientiae* it has to promote the broadest possible space of reflection, in which knowledge may be oriented towards unfolding and creating the future.

Through philosophy, humanity exercises its own freedom, because it looks for wisdom as an end in itself, as an unconditioned goal. Philosophy learns from science, history, sociology, psychology, etc., but it dares to think about the meaning of that which surrounds us. At this point, philosophy approaches art, as it recalls a free and humanizing creation.

True wisdom exhorts us to humility, for it stems from the awareness that knowledge cannot be exhausted. We can always learn more and understand in a deeper way. Any given knowledge is but a drop in a vast sea of possibilities. Any human achievement trembles before the magnificence of nature, which has created such a variety of beings and has ultimately led to the birth of consciousness.

Finiteness, compared to infiniteness, seems to us emptiness, nothingness. It is useless to long for understanding, to wish to discover truth, and to aspire to creating beauty, for we shall always realize that any achievement will be incommensurable with the potential infiniteness of knowledge. In a virtually infinite path, the vigor of any step succumbs before the perception of impotence. Nevertheless, the key to wisdom resides in understanding that the very fact of its search is the highest form of wisdom: it is already "infiniteness," it is already "meaning," it is already "commitment." In delivering ourselves to love, beauty, and wisdom, to pure goals which never become exhausted in any given reality and which no one can possess, we reach the unconditioned, and we find a meaning for a life which is worth being lived.

Epilogue
Only a God Can Still Save Us

ONLY A GOD CAN still save us [*Nur noch ein Gott kann uns retten*]. The sole possibility that is left for us is to prepare a sort of readiness, through thinking and poeticizing, for the appearance of the god or for the absence of the god in the time of foundering [*Untergang*]," as Heidegger said,[1] but such a god is elusive. The god of religions is too far away from humanity. We would love a god, but we would need a deity who spoke to us today, here and now, and who had not limited itself to revealing its will to the prophets of ancient times, to the peoples of a world which we no longer understand, of an inveterate age which is now absent.[2]

We often feel tempted to wish that someone were listening to us in these huge cosmic spaces, in which reticent silence seems to be the only ruler; a powerful, painful, and frightening muteness that reminds us of our fugacity and littleness. We seldom wish that there were an *alter ego* for this humanity in quest of answers to its questions. However, this evanescent God may not be so remote, after all, because in philosophy we can find a language that meets our profoundest expectations. Its effort to create constitutes the unparalleled epitome of that which humanity deserves: a thought that may give life. Through thinking, humanity enters into the future, and it discovers itself capable of inaugurating worlds and opening horizons that have not been unveiled. Through thinking, mankind learns

---

1. Cf. Heidegger, "Interview with *Der Spiegel*" (1966).
2. This sentiment was brilliantly expressed by Antonio Machado in a series of poetic compositions sent to Miguel de Unamuno in 1913: "Señor, me cansa la vida / tengo la garganta ronca / de gritar sobre los mares, / la voz de la mar me asorda. / Señor, me cansa la vida / y el universo me ahoga. / Señor, me dejaste solo, / solo, con el mar a solas. / O tú y yo jugando estamos / al escondite, Señor, / o la voz con que te llamo / es tu voz. / Por todas partes te busco / sin encontrarte jamás, / y en todas partes te encuentro / sólo por irte a buscar."

that it has received a power, which goes beyond any worldly power. Philosophy, the act of thinking to light a flame that may guide our existence, is the "divine" in humanity.

How could we intend to encounter salvation outside humanity? Who would understand our words, if not mankind? Nature is supremely eloquent, but its language is not appealing for us. No true wisdom, no free beauty, no real love emanates from the colorful territories of nature. Humanity alone, only the language that expresses our longing for creating a humane future, can be meaningful. The only god that can still save us must speak a human language, and it must be capable of listening to our shout and pronouncing a word of salvation. And the god that can still save us builds a dwelling in thought. Only in the context of an emancipated individual and an emancipated society could the longing for the absolute be authentic, as it would not be the result of any previous condition: it would not be the product of fear but the fruit of a pure, irreducible will. Only in that scenario god would be truly existent, the god who is being itself that speaks to us through thought. Thought is called to redeem human power by transforming it into a non-power, into a non-void, into a veritable free energy, which is not determined by the imperious desire to dominate but has become a means for dialogue and voluntary exchange between equals.

We deserve a god. Even if god did not exist, humanity would still be meritorious of divine reality. Our struggle, suffering, and the frequent absence of words to calm our anguish cannot be in vain. The divine salvation announced by different religions is anticipated in the *hic et nunc* of history when we philosophize, when we turn world and humanity into the object of our thought, and when we discover the infinite in the finite. To anticipate is to make the future present by taking possession of the meaning of time, so that we may not fall captives to the tyranny of randomness. To anticipate is therefore to defeat the arbitrariness of an ever open future, in which human aspirations and conquests become diluted into an infinite ocean. To anticipate is, after all, to humanize time, and to seek the infinite in the finite, the pure and ultimate in the inexorable fragility of space and time: a goal in the midst of blind, silent, and perishable phenomena. Thought and poetry, truth and beauty, anticipate the salvation for which we are longing, because they allow the future to dwell in the present. They build an abode for that which is unknown, and in bringing it they open a new path for that which is known. That which is unknown challenges that which is known, but salvation means that both the unknown and the known will be finally able to find a utopian harmony, a peace that

Epilogue: Only a God Can Still Save Us

overflows the power of human imagination, but which is "sensed" in philosophy, mysticism, and art.

The salvation anticipated in philosophy, as the quintessential expression of human thinking (and of our attempt to create a world which may justify our longing for an inexhaustible scenario), reflects that which is "final." This definitive intuition remains beyond diversity and links the diverse *qua* diverse, although it stays apart from that diversity; it is the eternal "beyond," the perennial ulteriority of all things, that which gives sense to difference itself. The spirit is being in its act of self-transcendence: it is the thought that overcomes itself. To save is, then, to bring a spirit that may illuminate that which is diverse and can constitute a world meaningful for all. To save is to disseminate the exultant joy of meaning. To save is to proclaim that nothing has been in vain. Both philosophy and art dignify the life of humanity, for the fact of belonging to the same race that has enabled Plato to write his *Dialogues* and Beethoven to compose his symphonies makes life worth having been lived. Moreover, it calls us to dream (even if we know that it is ultimately impossible) of healing any vestige of suffering, so that the sour constellation of tragedies that darkens our history may be replaced by the radiant stars of love, beauty, and wisdom.

There can be no pre-established meaning for history: history must be free to receive its sense from the thought and the actions of humanity; otherwise it would not be a humane history. There is no liberty in a history whose meaning has been written in advance. History cannot be the mechanical fulfillment of an essence, in which there is no end, but merely a beginning that contains any potential finality. We can always envision the prospect of a humane history: it exists in our minds, our imagination, and our conscience that there is always a future at our disposal. Let us dare to think of the novelty of being; let us have the courage to conceive of the possibility of an extension of being beyond its current boundaries; and let us dare to consider that the meaning of history is history itself. Through the thought and action of humanity in time any form of meaning emerges. This is a pre-eminent way to bring justice to the victims of the past, for history is not closed: we can construct it and therefore reinterpret it from a different perspective. History can only be meaningful for us if it is actually the product of mankind. And in the very action of shaping history, humanity is broadening the horizon of being: we are the avant-garde of being.

Critical reason, instrumental reason, utopian reason: we need salvific reason, which may go beyond reason itself, an "ulteriorized" reason, capable of being nurtured by all forms of rationality and fearless to offer a scope of permanence and universality which, why not, may compete with that of religions. Moreover, it has to serve as a reason that aspires to anticipate salvation for us, as the meaning in the midst of contingency. We should therefore speak in terms of the "salvific interest" of reason, which is that of liberating us to a kingdom of ends: the goal of supra-humanizing us. We often wish that the divine salvation promulgated by some religions actually came, but we must be convinced that we can foresee such a redemptive ideal in philosophy, through thinking of the world, humanity, and history in such a way that everyone may find a meaning of his own.

Only a God who could help us to grow as humanity would be worthy of our faith. Any deity whose sole commitment consisted of tormenting our flagellated conscience with the remembrance of the gravity of our mistakes, vices, and perversions; any supernatural being from whose voice only the wind of recriminations and martyrizing words emanated towards our spirit; a divinity that only radiated the dark ray of fear, the constant threat of an implacable punishment, of the submission of our deepest desires to the cold-hearted action of a severe father who does not tolerate the freedom of his children, their right to emancipation; such a creator of the universe and sovereign of life would not deserve our confidence, our adherence. Faith must be the source of courage, will, and love; an exhortation to knowing and exploring new paths in the adventure of life. Faith cannot torture us with panic and the sour prophecies of terrible flames that shall consume our souls as the penalty for our wickedness. Goodness and iniquity share the vastness of our souls, but we shall not conquer the pinnacle of love if those divine heights which have fascinated us, and from which the fountain of our consolation has flown throughout the centuries, distress us with the overwhelming and frightening agony of condemnation. We do not want tears and revenge to fall from heavens: we seek the waters of hope. We need compassion and understanding, not rigor and cruelty. If we believe, our faith must correspond to an intense longing for life, discovery, maturity, and freshness. If we believe, our faith must be free: the fruit of tenderness and gift, not the product of fear and inclemency. We shall only edify a future of wisdom, beauty, and love if our will is entirely committed to something worthy of humanity, to a power that may encourage us to grow, to improve ourselves, to expand the energies of life and the horizons of thought.

Appendices

The aim of the following appendices is to develop, in a more detailed and technical way, several basic elements of the thought of different philosophers whose ideas have been influential in shaping some of the theses of the present book.

Appendices

Appendix A
Hegel: History, Theodicy, Art, and Redemption

HISTORY AS THEODICY

THE SYSTEMATIC EXPOSITION OF the philosophy of history of Hegel can be found in his *Lectures on the Philosophy of World History* [*Vorlesungen über die Philosophie der Weltgeschichte*], a recompilation of a series of courses dictated at the University of Berlin in 1822, 1828, and 1830. The first edition of these lectures was done by Eduard Gans in 1837, a few years after the death of Hegel in 1831, and it was based on the notes of Hegel himself and his students. In this work, Hegel explains what Karl Löwith has called an "eschatological construction [*endgeschichtliche Konstruktion*]," which manifests a clear orientation towards an end that may be determined by thought.[1]

Hegel wants to think of history in such a way that it may not appear as a meaningless process but as a reality that manifests rationality. Philosophy discovers that what, *prima facie*, lacks the guidance of reason, actually responds to the display of the spirit, the substantive reason, so that history is directed by the thoughts which philosophy elucidates: philosophy is capable of constructing, *a priori*, a history. The philosophy of history is not deduced from the observation of history itself but from the very act of thinking. There is no material antecedent to thought: philosophy precedes history itself. We should not forget that the whole philosophical project of Hegel (and especially his *Phenomenology of the Spirit*) can be regarded as an ambitious attempt at showing that what is real is rational and that

---

1. Cf. Löwith, *Von Hegel zu Nietzsche*, 44–48.

Appendix A

the rational necessarily becomes real.² Nature is the determination of the idea and history is not a rhapsody of events but a continuous display of rationality. The idea cannot be subordinated to the factual reality of history, as if philosophy (the activity itself of the concept) were forced to obey the demands of the empirical realm, but the concept is independent and acts by itself in history. Hegel is perfectly aware that this thesis will raise the fierce opposition of historians, but he still believes that the task of philosophy has to be carried out. The thought that philosophy offers is simple: reason guides the world, and therefore, universal history proceeds in a rational way.³ The Schylla and the Charybdis of the philosophy of history are, to some extent, these two opposite views: a radical historical rationalism, inspired in absolute idealism, which deduces, *a priori*, history from the dynamic of the idea, on the one hand, and, on the other, the rejection of this perspective by conceiving of history as an autonomous reality that is ruled by blind forces.

In any case, is the Hegelian teaching that reason guides the world a presupposition, an act of faith in the rationality of the historical process, or rather, is it susceptible to proof? Are we before some sort of Kantian

---

2. As Herbert Marcuse writes about the *Phenomenology of the Spirit* of Hegel: "When, at the end of the Age of Reason, with Hegel, Western thought makes its last and greatest attempt to demonstrate the validity of its categories and the principles which govern this world, it concludes again with the *nous theos*. Again, fulfilment is relegated to the absolute idea and to absolute knowledge. Again, the movement of the circle ends the painful process of destructive and productive transcendence. Now the circle comprises the whole: all alienation is justified and at the same time cancelled in the universal ring of reason which is the world. But now philosophy comprehends the concrete historical ground on which the edifice of reason is erected. The *Phenomenology of the Spirit* unfolds the structure of reason as the structure of domination—and as the overcoming of domination. Reason develops through the developing self-consciousness of man who conquers the natural and historical world and makes it the material of his self-realization . . . The *Phenomenology of the Spirit* would not be the self-interpretation of Western civilization if it were nothing more than the development of the logic of domination. The *Phenomenology of the Spirit* leads to the overcoming of that form of freedom which derives from the antagonistic relation to the other. And the true mode of freedom is, not the incessant activity of conquest, but its coming to rest in the transparent knowledge and gratification of being . . . The *Phenomenology of the Spirit* throughout preserves the tension between the ontological and the historical content: the manifestations of the spirit *are* the main stages of Western civilization, but these historical manifestations remain affected with negativity; the spirit comes to itself only in and as absolute knowledge . . . Being is no longer the painful transcendence toward the future but the peaceful recapture of the past . . . Freedom implies reconciliation—redemption of the past" (*Eros and Civilization*, 113, 116, 117,118).

3. Cf. Hegel, *Lectures on the Philosophy of World History*, 27–43.

postulate, just as the existence of God and the immortality of the soul? According to Hegel, it is an imperative of philosophy itself in its search of truth, and history demonstrates *a posteriori* what philosophy deduces *a priori*. Hegel's philosophy of history is dependent on his system as a whole, and history does not enjoy any privilege for the philosophical reflection: it is another form that reason takes to express itself, and the interest in history lies in the fact that it is ruled by reason. The *a priori* condition of reason over the factual character of history may be seen as an arbitrary postulate, but it is a firm certainty for the philosophy of Hegel, according to which reason is infinite substance, infinite potency, infinite matter, and infinite form. If reason is a reality absolutely autonomous and self-sufficient, history is going to be considered as a product of reason, as the result of its activity. Reason would not be absolute if history were alien to its power. The philosophical density of these ideas summarizes Hegel's philosophy of universal history, which, like nature, can only be governed by reason. Reason is the substance *par excellence*, the absolute might that rules nature and history and excludes any form of contingency by subsuming it into the realm of necessity.

In his prologue to the second edition of the *Encyclopaedia*, of 1827, Hegel says that the intention of his work, both past and present, is the scientific knowledge of truth. The object of philosophy is not the partial reflection about reality but the consideration of the absolute and moreover, the absolute reflection about the absolute, which displays itself in nature and history. Hegel's philosophy looks for the absolute in the midst of contingency and the infinite in the finite. He wants to find a universal "end" in history, and such an ultimate goal is the highest interest of reason. Reason cannot be interested in any particular, finite end. Reason flows throughout history and acquires different determinations in the form of the spirits of the peoples. It seems patent that the admission of the rationality of history constitutes the cornerstone of Hegel's philosophy, and whoever is not

Appendix A

ready to accept it must wait to see the results which, for Hegel, show, beyond any doubt, that universal history has followed a rational path, as the necessary direction taken by the universal spirit, which is the substance of history. As Hegel himself notices, his ideas will be criticized as aprioristic, but he believes that historians are not alien to apriorism because they inevitably bear previous categories in their approaches to the study of historical reality.[4] Hegel has his own prejudice: the rational outlook on the world. Reason alone is capable of elucidating the ultimate meaning of history. It is clear, in any case, that by "reason" Hegel understands the pure use of rationality as it occurs in philosophical thinking.

Hegel wants to discover the universal in the midst of the particular: universal history beyond particular histories, which are not true history, because they are unable to fully reflect reason. However, universality becomes infinitely concrete in each event and particular spirit, as if they were "infinitesimals" of rationality in history. In the different episodes of history, universality appears as concrete, not abstract. The fundamental categories that history offers to thought (which manifest its nature, its submission to a prior rational order which is displayed in it) are the following:

a. Variation: the change of individuals, peoples, and states. Historical transformations may generate nostalgia, since reason had become accustomed to admiring goodness, beauty, and magnificence in certain civilizations. However, there can be no peace in history but only the unceasing mutation of individuals, peoples, and states. New life emerges from death. The spirit, in a dialectical perspective, negates itself in order to acquire a new determination, and this process of negation is necessary: the phoenix has to die in order to arise from

---

4. In light of the work of Gadamer, it is inevitable to see in this Hegelian remark a precedent of the principle of hermeneutic circularity. On this principle, cf. Gadamer, *Truth and Method*, part 2, chapter 4. Gadamer's idea of the anticipation of meaning as the condition of possibility of the elaboration of hermeneutics as the science of understanding (whose goal is not to eliminate prejudices, for this is impossible, but to contribute to their elucidation) has generated much criticism. According to Derrida, the centrality that Gadamer bequeaths to understanding hides a will of power, whose objective is to see oneself reflected on the other. In order to preserve *alteritas* (on which Levinas so much insisted: cf. *Totalité et Infini. Essai sur l'Extériorité*, 28) it is necessary to renounce the "good will of understanding." Cf. Derrida, "Bonnes volontés de puissance (Une réponse à Hans-Georg Gadamer," 343). Gadamer, on the contrary, thinks that an absolutized concept of *alteritas* cannot be held, because, even though it is true that there is no understanding without rupture with the other, dialogue is still possible as the initial point of any relationship with others and moreover, as the precondition of any form of human solidarity. Cf. Gadamer, "Et pourtant, puissance de la bonne volonté " (Une réplique à Jacques Derrida, 346).

its own ashes. For Hegel, negativity is history, and it is actually the driving force of historical change. The implacable dynamic of death and life exhibits necessity, its subordination to the realm of reason.

b. Rejuvenation: the spirit creates new activity, a new material of work, and the past is never repeated, for the spirit is constantly taking new forms. The goal of the activity of the spirit is not individuals, peoples, or states: the spirit acts for its own sake, which is its final reconciliation with itself.

c. Ultimate end: if individuals, peoples, and states are not the goal of the activity of the spirit, why does it express itself in history? What is it looking for? There must be an ultimate goal that cannot be alien to the spirit itself. Reason is the absolute power that freely determines itself, so supreme freedom must be the ultimate end of the spirit. Individuals, peoples, and states serve reason and its freedom. [/LL]

Reason rules the world and, in an absolute sense, reason is divine. This divine reason is the providence to which religions refer, and it governs history following a plan. However, are we capable of knowing such a plan? In light of Hegel's philosophical program the answer seems to be obvious: we can understand it because thought can elevate itself over the particular determinations, discovering the universal spirit in nature and history. The Christian idea of Providence has to be assimilated to the philosophical concept of rationality as the guiding principle of history. The religious representation must become the content of philosophy in order to be overcome by purely rational reflection. Philosophy, for Hegel, sees divine wisdom in the rationality underlying both nature and history. Religion has to cede its place to philosophy. If in medieval Scholasticism philosophy had been *ancilla theologiae*, Hegel regards theology (the rational systematization of the content of the revealed religion) as *ancilla philosophiae*, as the antecedent and necessary determination to be overcome in the final determination of the spirit. It is not reason that makes room for faith but faith that makes room for reason. The conviction of faith (that there is providence) is rationally developed by philosophy. Theodicy cannot be abstract, as in Leibniz,[5] but it must reconcile the thinking spirit with its negation in the particular events of history: philosophy of history is actually the true theodicy.[6]

---

5. For an introduction to the role of theodicy in the thought of Leibniz, cf. Rateau, *La Question du Mal chez Leibniz*; Rateau, *L'Idée de Théodicée de Leibniz à Kant*.

6. Cf. Löwith, *Von Hegel zu Nietzsche*, 60.

Appendix A

ART AS REDEMPTION

Hegel had an enduring passion for the arts. We know that he travelled to the Netherlands in 1822, to Vienna in 1824 and to Paris in 1827. It seems that listening to Johann Sebastian Bach's *The Passion according to St. Matthew*, as performed by Mendelssohn after decades of oblivion of the work of the great composer from Eisenach, left a perdurable trace in our philosopher.[7] His *Aesthetics: Lectures on Fine Art* [*Vorlesungen über die Ästhetik*], compiled and edited by Heinrich Gustav Hotho in 1835 taking as reference the courses offered by Hegel himself, show the intellectual depth of his analysis of the nature of art and his exceptional knowledge of its history. They irradiate vivid and inspiring enthusiasm for the arts.

The aesthetic philosophy of Hegel examines art not as an isolated manifestation of human creativity but as a culminating moment in the evolution of the spirit. The triad *pulchrum, bonum, verum* of Scholastic thought turns into art, religion, and philosophy as the supreme determinations of the spirit. In art, the spirit initiates its final reunion with itself as absolute spirit, whose pinnacle is philosophy, in which the absolute spirit becomes *noeses noeseos*, "the thought that thinks about itself," a concept that had been formulated by Aristotle in book XII of his *Metaphysics*. The essence of art is beauty, of religion, goodness, and of philosophy, truth. The spirit, after the traumatic process of self-alienation that makes it go through natural objectivity and history, is able to return to itself as absolute spirit, which assumes and overcomes subjectivity and objectivity, infinity and finiteness, in the true infinite.

Hegel integrates his conception of art into a historical perspective. He is not aiming at offering universal canons of beauty and harmony but at understanding why the history of art has experienced certain stages throughout its evolution. The insertion of art into the dynamic of the spirit is therefore the intention of Hegel's aesthetics. He wants to combine the metaphysical universality of the idea of beauty in itself and the genuine particularity of the specific artistic works which express the idea of beauty in their own way. Artistic beauty belongs to the deepest aspirations of the spirit and it therefore necessarily surpasses natural beauty. The goal of art is not the faithful imitation of nature but the expression of our concept of beauty, which is not taken from our observation of the world but from our introspection into our own being. The beauty of the arts is the result of the activity of the human mind. It is not spontaneous but deliberately pursued

---

7. Cf. Paolucci, *Hegel: On the Arts*, x.

beauty. As a consequence of this approach, the philosopher is interested as an absolute necessity of the human being, for "man's need for art, no less than his need for religion and philosophy, is rooted in his capacity to mirror himself in thought."[8] The dynamic of the spirit inexorably leads to art. For Hegel, mankind cannot live without art, just as it cannot live without religion or philosophy. The reason is simple but inevitably threatening: humanity does not exist for its own sake but on behalf of the spirit.

The human being is a thinking consciousness. This means that he has abandoned the realm of immediacy in order to become a being for itself. In thinking, man achieves some sort of reduplication, and this ability to mediate with respect to his own being is the root of his spiritual freedom. In art, mankind is reflecting the highest idea of the spirit as an objective intuition of a concept which can only be reached in philosophy: art is the intuition of the absolute truth, its immediate apprehension through sensitive forms, and "the sensuous shapes and sounds of art present themselves to us not to arouse or satisfy desire but to excite a response and echo in all the depths of consciousness of the mind."[9] Art is the material expression of a question addressed to the human soul. In it, the spiritual acquires a sensuous shape: art stems from the spiritual world, fusing both sensibility and understanding as an undivided unity, and "this is what constitutes genuinely artistic productive imagination, or fantasy."[10] The creative mind of the artist is capable of giving material expression to the profoundest and most universal interests of humanity.

If art were a mere imitation of nature, it would not constitute a new world. The copy of the existing reality is superfluous. The most genuine human activity is not imitation but creation: mankind gives life through art. The natural world cannot become the rule of art but its servant. The greatness and power of art are visible in its capacity for expressing the contradiction between matter and idea. Art mirrors a reality that is not peaceful but dialectical. Beauty cannot emerge from the harmonious peace among the opposites but from a sincere struggle, looking for an overcoming synthesis that can create a new world within human subjectivity and history. The awareness of contradiction opens the gate for the contemplation of beauty, goodness, and truth, and "when the cultural experience of an entire age sinks into this contradiction, it becomes philosophy's task to show that neither side possesses truth in itself, that each is one-sided

---

8. Ibid., 3.
9. Ibid., 4.
10. Ibid.

Appendix A

and self-dissolving, that the truth lies in the conciliation and mediation of the two, and that such mediation or reconciliation is in reality accomplished and is always self-accomplishing."[11] The philosopher must become the herald of the necessity of a new world, and art is its beginning, for it reconciles the sensuous and the spiritual in the truth that it expresses.

The reconciliation of spirit and matter in art had been highlighted by Kant in his *Critique of Judgment* [*Kritik der Urteil*]. The problem, according to Hegel, is that the distinguished son of Königsberg refers to a purely subjective reconciliation. For both Kant and Hegel, in knowing, the human being unifies perception and sensation, an internal and an external world, into a concept. However, Hegel thinks that Kant has not grasped the full nature of the real reconciliation, which does not simply consist of achieving a concept but it demands the manifestation of the truth of art in itself as a supreme determination of the spirit.[12] We need to recognize that art responds to the universal movement of the spirit: it is the absolute spirit that recognizes itself through the human mind in the work of art. Art is not a mere product of the human mind but it reflects how the spirit conceives of itself in an absolute way. It therefore transcends the scope of human interests, because it points to the ultimate goal of the spirit. The immediate apprehension of the absolute in art paves the way for its mediated grasping, through the religious symbolic representations, in order to finally become a philosophical concept, a universal content that is independent from sensibility and representation and achieves definitive freedom. The greatness of the work of art, as an open question addressed to the human soul, implies that it does not surrender to the particularity imposed by sensibility. A work of art can always inspire the human spirit beyond the constraining limits of its material form: its determinate material character can convey an indeterminate range of sense. Appearance becomes defeated by the act of grasping a deeper meaning. Behold the triumph of the absolute, for art embodies the reconciliation of the particularity of the sensuous expression and the universality of the world of meaning.

Artistic beauty demands a specific harmonization of form and content: "in ideal artistic beauty, perfection of form derives ultimately from perfection of content."[13] Ideal beauty underlines the correspondence between the true idea and the true form, and artistic beauty is actually the

---

11. Ibid.
12. Cf. ibid., 6.
13. Ibid., 9.

totality of specific stages required to be experienced in order to achieve a final reconciliation between the idea and its artistic representation. Art has evolved, just as the spirit, and in its earliest manifestations it did not express the definitive reconciliation of matter and idea. History has been necessary as the scenario of an arduous struggle that can be summarized in three major moments: symbolic, classical, and romantic art.[14] Symbolic art looks for the perfect unity of form and content, which is found in classical art and transcended in romantic art. In symbolic art, the idea has not found its true form yet. It acquires natural forms that it does not alter. The universal meaning is expressed through natural figures, but the idea cannot be satisfied with them alone: it needs more. The natural forms are unable to convey the full meaning that the idea wants to reveal. In classical art, the form reaches such a degree of correspondence with the content that true beauty and true art are accomplished. In it, the power of the idea is so overwhelming that it determines the form of the work of art. The spirit becomes the content of the artistic work. In Greek culture, quintessential, paradigmatic instantiation of classical art, the idea that the spirits seeks to materialize is so high that only the human body is capable of giving it a form. Nevertheless, the classical ideal of beauty was exhausted. Its depletion was, however, substituted with the romantic form of art, and "to express its new and higher spiritual content, romantic art abandons the self-limiting perfection of the classical ideal of artistic beauty."[15] If the concept of perfection in the classical world was bounded to the perception of limit and proportion, modernity understands it in terms of infiniteness and transcendence of any limitation.

In symbolic art, matter determines form; in classical art, form shapes matter; in romantic art, true matter and true form are discovered to inhabit the interiority of the human person. Romantic art, inspired by Christianity, is the self-transcendence of art itself. Art is no longer enslaved to a form. In romanticism, there is a perception of the infinite subjectivity of God as the true content of the work of art. The romantic God is visible in his invisibility. Romanticism gives artistic expression to the idea of divine redemption, which "consists in God's reconciliation with the world and thereby with himself, through man."[16] The phenomenological depiction of the stages of the spirit is actually the philosophical expression of the Christian faith in redemption. In classical art, there was no possibility of

14. On the three forms of art in Hegel, cf. Löwith, *Von Hegel zu Nietzsche*, 49–50.
15. Ibid., 36.
16. Ibid., 39.

introducing the negativity of the world, the infinite pain. This kind of art was alien to history and was constrained to universal forms: art was self-enclosed, and it was not open to the dialectical process that defines reality. Romantic art, on the contrary, overcomes all opposition through love. Love becomes the content and the form of romantic art: it does not only externalize the idea in matter, but it also internalizes it. The idea returns to the world of interiority after having transcended the opposition between the external and the internal, and it is therefore suitable to express the truth of the spirit. Love is self-forgetfulness, in such a way that the true possession of oneself is achieved. God has to be love.

These three universal forms of art (symbolic, classical, and romantic) are still mere abstractions until they are not incorporated into real works of architecture, sculpture, painting, music, and poetry. The most spiritual way of artistic representation in romanticism is poetry, not music. Not even Beethoven's sonatas are able to reach our intimacy as deeply as Goethe's and Schiller's verses. Poetry is the truly universal art, as it assumes all the other modes of representation. Poetry integrates both the visual and the musical arts. Its means is imagination. The task of the philosopher who thinks about art cannot be the mere criticism of the specific works but the search of the fundamental concept of beauty through its different historical stages. Philosophy has to realize that art is a supreme determination of the spirit.

Appendix B
Dilthey and the Legitimacy of the "Sciences of the Spirit"

AN ESSENTIAL ELEMENT IN the philosophy of Wilhelm Dilthey (1833–1911) is the differentiation of the method of the sciences of nature [*Naturwissenschaften*] from that of the sciences of the spirit [*Geisteswissenschaften*], which to a large extent defines his entire intellectual trajectory.[1]

According to Dilthey, there is a different "constitution [*Aufbau*]" for the sciences of nature and the sciences of the spirit.[2] Every operation of the sciences of the spirit is associated with the identification of a sense and a meaning [*Sinn und Bedeutung*], which appear in the working of the spirit. There is an immanent dimension in the sciences of the spirit: to understand [*verstehen*] a meaning referred to the subject. Contrary to what happens in the natural world, in the realm of the spirit the context [*Zusammenhang*] is "lived [*erlebt*]" and understood, whereas the context of nature remains abstract for us. In spirit and history the context is alive.[3]

The approach of Dilthey to history emerges as an application of the methodology of the sciences of the spirit to the study of the objectivation of the human life in the course of times.[4] Individuals, communities, and

1. Cf. Dilthey, *Einleitung in die Geisteswissenschaften*.
2. Cf. Dilthey, *Der Aufbau der geschichtlichen Welt in den Geisteswissenschaften*, 140.
3. Cf. ibid. 142.
4. According to José Ortega y Gasset, "junto a la *Crítica de la Razón Pura*, esto es, física, Dilthey se propone una crítica a la razón histórica. Lo mismo que Kant se preguntó: ¿cómo es posible la ciencia natural?, Dilthey se preguntará: ¿cómo es posible la historia y las ciencias del estado, de la sociedad, de la religión y del arte? Su tema es, pues, epistemológico, de crítica del conocimiento, y en este punto Dilthey no es más que un hombre de su tiempo" ("Guillermo Dilthey y la Idea de la Vida" (*Obras*

Appendix B

the works that reflect life and spirit constitute "the external kingdom of the spirit [*das äussere Reich des Geistes*]."[5] They all represent something "common [*Gemeinsames*]" that makes them intelligible for the subject, because the spirit only understands that which it has actually brought into effect.[6] Dilthey acknowledges the influence of Hegel and his notion of "objective spirit," but he interprets it in a different way. For Hegel, the objective spirit is a level in the development of the spirit on its way towards the absolute spirit (its highest stage, consisting of the knowledge of the spirit about itself), but Dilthey thinks that the presuppositions of Hegel's idea cannot be maintained any longer: it is not possible to start with the general rational will, for it is necessary to begin from the reality of life.[7]

The philosophical consideration of history cannot be based upon a metaphysical construction but on the analysis of "what is given [*das Gegebene*]," by considering the reality of the objective spirit in its historical substrate. The object of study has to be how the spirit becomes individualized in history and how the individual turns into the representative of

---

Completas, 6:186). Ortega embraces an idea of rationality which, trying to overcome the limits imposed by positivism, may open itself to life and history: "para mí es razón, en el verdadero y riguroso sentido, toda acción intelectual que nos pone en contacto con la realidad, por medio de la cual topamos con lo trascendente . . . Hasta ahora, la historia era lo contrario a la razón. En Grecia, los términos razón e historia eran contrapuestos. Y es que hasta ahora, en efecto, apenas se ha ocupado nadie de buscar en la historia su sustancia racional . . . Mi propósito es estrictamente inverso. Se trata de encontrar en la historia misma su original y autóctona razón. Por eso ha de entenderse en todo su vigor la expresión 'razón histórica' . . . La razón histórica . . . no acepta nada como mero hecho, sino que fluidifica todo hecho en el fieri de lo que proviene: ve como se hace el hecho" (*Historia como Sistema y del Imperio Romano*, 73, 78–79).

5. Cf. Dilthey, *Der Aufbau der geschichtlichen Welt in den Geisteswissenschaften*, 178, and, in general, the section on "Die Objektivation des Lebens" (177–85).

6. In Dilthey's words, "nur was der Geist geschaffen hat, versteht es" (ibid., 180), and this principle is narrowly connected with Giambattista Vico's *verum esse ipsum factum*, which underlies his original approach to the realm of human society based upon the consideration that "questo mondo civile egli certamente è stato fatto dagli uomini, onde se ne possono, perché se ne debbono, ritruovare i principi dentro le modificazioni della nostra medesima mente umana" (*Principi di Scienza Nuova*, book I, section 3).

7. Dilthey, *Der Aufbau der geschichtlichen Welt in den Geisteswissenschaften*, 183. In the section "Der objektive Geist und das elementare Verstehen" (256–58), Dilthey says that by "objective spirit" he refers to "die mannigfachen Formen, in denen die zwischen den Individuen bestehende Gemeinsamkeit sich in der Sinneswelt objektiviert hat" (256). In the section "Die Menschheit und die Universalgeschichte" (335–42), Dilthey insists on his idea that Hegel's principal mistake is the attempt to construct the levels of the spirit in an immanent way instead of considering them from the "working together [*aus dem Zusammenwirken*]" with the historical situation [*Lage*].

Dilthey and the Legitimacy of the "Sciences of the Spirit"

history in the community that nurtures him. The individual is capable of understanding history because he is a historical being himself. There is a mutual implication that makes the objectivity of history become a subjective experience of meaning. The importance of the individual as agent of history, and as the carrier of a spirit which does not flow independently, introduces a key qualification to the philosophy of Hegel. Dithery cannot be accused of underestimating the role of the individual as a mere moment in the path of the spirit looking for itself.[8]

If Hegel situates himself directly in the realm of the spirit in order to examine how it becomes objectivized in nature (and this is the reason why, according to him, the question concerning the legitimacy of the sciences of the spirit poses no problem at all), Dilthey is aware of the fact that a method is needed to highlight the viability of a universal knowledge of the historical world.[9] The integration of singularity and totality is a fundamental step for this task: understanding the singular is only possible through the presence of the general knowledge that appears in it,[10] because the comprehension of the part demands its insertion into the whole. In every individual fact of the sciences of the spirit it is necessary to see the historical totality of the community. There is therefore a reciprocal dependency between the general and the singular realities. The world of the spirit appears as a "context of working [*Wirkungszusammenhang*],"[11] which is the object of the sciences of the spirit. The *Wirkungszusammenhang* of the sciences of the spirit is different from the *Kausalzusammenhang* that prevails in the realm of nature, because the former (that could be translated "connection of working," or simply "interdependence") generates values [*Werte*] and performs ends [*Zwecke*]. This is what Dilthey calls the "teleological-immanent character of the spiritual *Wirkungszusammenhänge*."[12]

---

8. Dilthey thinks that the problem of the "intellectualization" of history by means of concepts (undertaken, in his view, by Hegel) consists of the impossibility of such an enterprise to take individuals into serious consideration. Individuals appear as separated entities. According to Dilthey, individuals cannot be understood conceptually, because this type of comprehension will be necessarily based upon their "equality [*Gleichkeit*]," not on their uniqueness. Cf. ibid., 320.

9. Cf. ibid., 185.

10. Ibid.

11. Cf. "Die geistige Welt als Wirkungszusammenhang" (ibid., 185–96).

12. According to Dilthey, values are the "material [*das Material*]" of the historical world. Hegel spoke in terms of "materialization" of the spirit in history through state, *Rechtsstaat*, religion, spheres of the life of a people, and constitution in his *Vorlesungen über die Philosophie der Weltgeschichte*, although Dilthey has a different concept of objective spirit.

Appendix B

The spirit establishes worlds, and this task is performed by individuals, communities, and cultural systems.[13]

Dilthey regards the idea of *Wirkungszusammenhang* as the "fundamental concept" [*Grundbegriff*] of the sciences of the spirit, which "grasp" [*erfassen*] the spiritual world under the form of "*Wirkungszusammenhänge*."[14] In nature, on the contrary, no internal context is given:[15] there is no unity of life, no principle of action, but, in the "living experience [*Erlebnis*]" with which the sciences of the spirit deal, we are contexts for ourselves. All life appears and works together in every operation of the spirit, not as a totality composed of differentiated parts but as a unitary whole. We are therefore homogeneous systems, and the individual intervenes as a vital unity in *Wirkungszusammenhang*, in whose externalization the individual acts as a whole.[16]

The understanding of history demands the application of the systematic sciences of the spirit. However, the spiritual world appears as a creation of the subject, while history intends to reach an objective knowledge. How is it possible to define a science of history if such identification exists between the subject and the object? Dilthey believes that a critique of historical reason is needed in order to underscore the legitimacy of the knowledge about the spiritual reality in its historical dimension.[17] In any case, the key idea needed to achieve this goal is the awareness that the causality that is present in the realm of the sciences of the spirit is not analogous to that of the sciences of nature.[18] The mission of the sciences of the spirit is not to unveil a causal relationship but to understand the proper meaning[19] which links the parts to the whole. It consists of

---

13. On these elements, cf. "Die Geschichte und ihr Verständnis vermittels der systematischen Geisteswissenschaften" (Dilthey, *Der Aufbau der geschichtlichen Welt in den Geisteswissenschaften*, 196–230).

14. Cf. ibid., 191.

15. Ibid. 195.

16. Ibid. It is interesting to notice that Dilthey's idea keeps some connection with Aristotle's substantial form, which, in opposition to a mechanistic view, acts as the principle of operations that grants unity to the working of the living being, in particular to that of the rational agent. On Aristotle's substantial form, cf. *Metahysics* Z, 4ff.

17. Cf. "Die Aufgabe einer Kritik der historischen Vernunft," in Dilthey, *Der Aufbau der geschichtlichen Welt in den Geisteswissenschaften*, 235.

18. Ibid., 243.

19 According to Dilthey, "Jedes Leben hat einen eigenen Sinn. Er liegt in einem Bedeutungszusammenhang, in welchem jede erinnerbare Gegenwart einen Eigenwert besitz, doch zugleich im Zusammenhang der Erinnerung eine Beziehung zu einem Sinn des Ganzen hat. Dieser Sinn des individuellen Daseins, ist ganz singular, dem

discovering a "spirit," seen as *Zusammenhang*, as context. The fact that a historical subject is undertaking the scientific examination of history is not, in the philosophy of Dilthey, an obstacle but a condition of possibility of the science of history: in order for it to exist, the subject must be a historical being, so that whoever is exploring history may be, at the same time, the one bringing history into realization.[20]

Historical life is a part of life in its most radical sense, and life is a "basic fact [*Grundtatsache*]," a point of departure irreducible for philosophy. Life becomes historical when its *Wirkungszusammenhang* is perceived in time. As a consequence, the possibility of historical knowledge resides in the "reconstruction [*Nachbildung*]," in the sphere of memory, of the course of time. However, it is not the individual that is reproduced but the context itself, for in their approach to history the sciences of the spirit study the set of externalizations of life within the connections they generate. In this way, the first condition to build the historical world is the "purification [*Reinigung*]" of memories through criticism, and philology becomes the fundamental science of history, because traditions have been primarily expressed through languages.[21]

In the study of history, as in that of life, the whole has to be constructed from the parts, and the meaning of each part lies in the whole. However, the sciences of the spirit cannot ignore historical individuality. In the sciences of nature it is possible to subsume the individual into a "prototype," but in the sciences of the spirit the individual is irreducible, although it can only be understood in the context of history.[22]

Erkennen unauflösbar, und er repräsentiert doch im seiner Art, wie eine Monade von Leibniz, das geschichtliche Universum" (ibid., 246).

20. Cf. ibid., 347.

21. Cf. ibid., 324.

22. Cf. "Das Grundverhältnis: Die Struktur der historischen Gebilde" (ibid., 314–25). This perspective is also present in Wolfhart Pannenberg's *Anthropologie in theologischer Perspektive*.

Appendix C
Religion as Illusion in Sigmund Freud

THE FATHER OF PSYCHOANALYSIS applied his influential theories to the study of a phenomenon present in the practical totality of human cultures: religion. Freud's examination of religion in general and Judeo-Christianity in particular is in continuity with the great nineteenth century anthropological critiques of religion (Feuerbach, Marx, Nietzsche), although it is aimed at identifying the root of the problem, the true genesis of the idea of God: how and why it emerges and to what kind of reality the religious phenomenon is actually pointing.

Feuerbach's theory of religion had circumscribed the domain of theology to anthropology: the true essence of the divine is not to be found in the world or history but inside the human mind. For both Feuerbach and Freud, the critique of religion has a humanistic goal: that of liberating the energy absorbed by religion in order to direct it to the real, earthly benefit of humankind. The innovative nature of the Freudian scrutiny of religion, at least in comparison to Feuerbach's, lies in his use of the methodology and conceptual tools of psychoanalysis, which allow him to "situate" the origin of the projection unveiled by the author of *The Essence of Christianity* in the deep structures of the human *psyche*. Freud devoted three important works to religion: *Totem and Taboo* (1915),[1] *The Future of an*

---

1. Freud's essay *Totem and Taboo* tries to explain the origin of the prohibition of incest and the obligation to exogamy, which he justifies as a process of internalization of the Oedipus complex through the way of the *super-ego*, leading to the assimilation of the paternal values: "anyone approaching the problem of taboo from the angle of psychoanalysis, that is to say, of the investigation of the unconscious portion of the individual mind, will recognize, after a moment's reflection, that these phenomena are far from unfamiliar to him ... The most striking point of agreement between the obsessional prohibitions of neurotics and taboos is that these prohibitions are equally lacking in motive and equally puzzling in their origin. Having made their appearance at some unspecified moment, they are forcibly maintained by an irresistible fear. No

Illusion (1927), and *Moses and Monotheism* (1938).² The second title offers a valuable, condensed synthesis of his views on religion.

In *The Future of an Illusion*, Freud tries to provide a functional depiction of religion and its role in human culture or civilization (between

---

external threat of punishment is required, for there is an internal certainty, a moral conviction, that any violation will lead to intolerable disaster" (*Totem and Taboo*, 26–27). The taboo of incest generates an emotional ambivalence of neurotic nature: "taboos, we must suppose, are prohibitions of primeval antiquity which were at some time externally imposed upon a generation of primitive men ... These prohibitions must have concerned activities towards which there was a strong inclination ... Possibly, however, in later generations they may have become 'organized' as an inherited psychical endowment ... They must therefore have an ambivalent attitude towards their taboos. In their unconscious there is nothing they would like more than to violate them, but they are afraid to do so; they are afraid precisely because they would like to, and the fear is stronger than the desire. The desire is unconscious, however, in every individual member of the tribe just as it is in neurotics" (ibid., 31). Taboos are based upon the prohibition of something towards which there is an intense predisposition. Thus, Freud argues that an intrinsic, even though unconsciously repressed inclination towards incest exists in the human mind, as if it were some sort of *fomes peccati*: it is inevitable for us, but we are compelled to control it, in the dialectic that any law shows between its fulfilment and the incorrigible temptation to violate it, which was so brilliantly analyzed by St. Paul in the seventh chapter of his *Letter to the Romans* (echoed by Lacan, *The Ethics of Psychoanalysis*, 83). In the Freudian perspective, this emotional ambivalence shapes our moral conscience. Freud finds the ultimate origin of the religious projection of a paternal God in "the elimination of the primal father by the company of his sons," which "must inevitably have left ineradicable traces in the history of humanity" (Freud, *Totem and Taboo*, 155). It is clear, in any case, that the story of a primitive horde that kills the father because of his monopoly of females (subsequently creating a complex of guilt) cannot be taken as a historical fact, of which there is no proof, but as a metaphor, as a literary fiction with a didactic goal (it is a "scientific myth"; cf. Gómez, *Freud, Crítico de la Ilustración*, 59). The most relevant conclusion of Freud's study of totemism and taboo is therefore the dependency that he establishes between the image of God that the human beings form and the paternal figure. This aspect constitutes a "concretion" of the anthropological projection that Feuerbach had interpreted as the essence of religion, which Freud situates in the "sublimation of the father."

2. In *Moses and Monotheism*, Freud tries to apply his method of "psychohistory" to the study of the figure of Moses, an Egyptian who would have been killed by his own followers. The rebels, regretting their action, internalized a guilt that was to persist in Judaism. Although the utility of psychoanalysis for history, at least as employed by Freud and authors like Erikson (cf. *Young Man Luther*) has been generally contested (cf. Stannard, *Shrinking History*), it has enjoyed some important defences, notably that of Gay, *Freud for Historians*. In any case, it seems clear that the application of psychoanalytic apriorisms to the study of history can hardly produce good fruits for our understanding of historical phenomena. Perhaps, it will be useful for the examination of specific topics (e.g. the psychology of certain historical characters) but not for the elucidation of historical processes, a task for which the range of "prejudices" needs to be minimized, and it must be constantly submitted to contrast with "factual" evidence.

which he deliberately refuses to distinguish), which are integrated, in his view, by "all those respects in which human life has raised itself above its animal status and differs from the life of beasts."[3] Freud thinks that culture has undertaken two fundamental directions: one makes reference to the attempt at dominating nature through science and technique, while the second points to the creation of organizations that regulate human life. The first tendency seems to manifest an increasing degree of accumulated progression. The second, however, exhibits no clear, continued improvement at all. In any case, it seems patent that any form of culture needs to be based upon "coercion and renunciation of instinct."[4] Otherwise, it would be impossible to edify a society, which ineluctably demands some sort of individual sacrifice. Nevertheless, the foundations of culture are constantly being threatened, because its existence is subsidiary to the "inexistence" (through repression) of our natural inclinations. The cost is colossal: behold the "original sin" of human culture. The three principal wishes that, according to Freud, must be suppressed by culture if it wants to subsist are incest, cannibalism, and homicide.[5]

Culture gravitates towards a relentless battle against the destructive instincts that emerge from human nature and which produce multiple manifestations. As Freud writes in *Civilization and Its Discontents*, "the meaning of the evolution of civilization is no longer obscure to us. It must present the struggle between Eros and Death, between the instinct of life and the instinct of destruction, as it works itself out in the human species. This struggle is what all life essentially consists of, and the evolution of civilization may therefore be simply described as the struggle for life of the human species."[6] However, the evolution of culture is characterized by a gradual transformation of external into internal coercion, in such a way that "aggressiveness is introjected, internalized. There it is taken over by a portion of the ego, which sets itself over against the rest of the ego as super-ego, and which now, in the form of 'conscience,' is ready to put into action against the ego the same harsh aggressiveness that the ego would

---

3. Freud, *The Future of an Illusion*, 5–6.

4. Cf. ibid., 7.

5. For a detailed analysis of incest, cannibalism, and homicide and their role, as repressed instincts, in the formation of culture, cf. Freud, *Civilization and Its Discontents*, whose capital idea is that "civilization is built upon a renunciation of instinct ... This 'cultural frustration' dominates the large field of social relationships between human beings. As we already know, it is the cause of the hostility against which all civilizations have to struggle" (97).

6. Ibid., 122.

have liked to satisfy upon other, extraneous individuals. The tension between the harsh super-ego and the ego that is subjected to it, is called by us the sense of guilt, it expresses itself as a need for punishment."[7] The super-ego is therefore the internalization of the parental figures, and it becomes a structural level of the human *psyche*, which imposes the internalization of the cultural values that have been transmitted from one generation to another as a means of safeguarding culture itself, even though in this process it creates different pathologies within the individual. Moreover, the internalization of the laws demanded by culture for its own preservation against the instinctive dangers of the human being becomes interpreted as a universal and natural truth. What is the result of the pragmatic interest of culture is regarded as a natural law.

It is clear, in any case, that such a great individual sacrifice only makes sense if the profit is high enough. The benefit, which is culture itself, is worth the effort. The ideals of culture reward the onerous sacrifice of instincts. The sense of belonging to a great project (that of civilization) brings protection and self-realization, and it affects everyone, regardless of his or her social condition. The Freudian analysis of culture is, so to speak, prior to any social critique, for it departs from the structure of the human *psyche*. The great creations of culture, just as art, can compensate the renunciation of individual instinctive wishes. What for Hegel were the supreme determinations of the spirit (art, religion, and philosophy) Freud viewed as the principal retributions that culture offers individuals. They may grant satisfaction: confronted by factuality and fatality, in art we can vivify our deepest ideals, in religion we try to defeat our fears before the hostility of nature and our finiteness and contingency, and in philosophy we aim to achieve universal truths that may help us to overcome our state of ignorance. Civilization, in summary, grants us the possibility, both individually and as mankind, to bear a life in all respects hard. In culture, men and women have found the most efficient tool of survival. Cooperation allows for endurance and it is, after all, the most successful evolutionary strategy.

The genesis of religious representations is precisely associated with this need for consolation before the overwhelming power of nature. The relief that they offer is extremely fructiferous for culture, because it

---

7. Ibid., 123. As Freud explains further, "the analogy between the process of civilization and the path of individual development may be extended to an important respect. It can be asserted that the community, too, evolves a super-ego under whose influence cultural development proceeds" (141).

contributes to the dissipation of eventual hostilities. The peace and comfort inaugurated by religious representations serves the goal of the self-perpetuation of culture. Religion immunizes the individual against the fear of nature, death, and fate, and "thus a store of ideas is created, born from man's need to make his helplessness tolerable and built up from the material of memories of the helplessness of his own childhood and the childhood of the human race."[8] The imaginary world of religions is a refuge against the crude reality of a speechless, merciless universe.

According to Freud, the first step of the process that leads to religion is the humanization of nature. The human being represents the physical world in his image and likeness. Animism, which Freud analyses both in *Totem and Taboo* and *The Future of an Illusion*, constitutes the quintessential example of this tendency to conceive of the universe as inhabited by spirits and powers whose nature is similar to that of human beings, so that mankind finds some sort of *alter ego* in the invisible forces that govern the cosmos. This situation, however, "has an infantile prototype, of which it is in fact only the continuation. For once before one has found oneself in a similar state of helplessness: as a small child, in relation to one's parents."[9] Again, this is the key innovation of Freud with respect to the earlier anthropological critiques of religion: the identification of the *locus* of the illusion, which Freud associates with infantile traumas that leave a perennial trace in the human *psyche*. The attribution of a personal character to the powers of nature is a mechanism analogous to that of a child, who assumes the image of the father in his conception of the world. Animistic religions, for Freud, fulfill a threefold function: they dissipate our natural fears, offer peace before the horizon of a cruel, hostile destiny, and compensate the pains and deprivations which civilization, even in its most primitive stages, necessarily imposes.

The next step in this dynamic is defined by the advancement of humanity in its knowledge of nature. The deities can no longer be identified with the powers of nature, since mankind is on the path to understanding the impersonal laws that rule upon it, and they must be elevated to a superior realm. The gods are not the powers of nature but the authors of those powers. In *Totem and Taboo*, following a similar logic of Comte's law of the three stages, Freud develops the idea that the human conception of the world has experienced three principal paradigms: animistic, religious, and scientific. "Religious" actually means the evolution that generates the

8. Freud, *The Future of an Illusion*, 18.
9. Ibid., 17.

gradual abandonment of the animistic beliefs, motivated by the acquisition of a deeper knowledge of nature and its laws. Nevertheless, the persistence of our sense of helplessness and solitude in this vast universe obliges us to displace the realm of the divine from the physical world to an invisible, inscrutable, and purely spiritual sphere. The divine makes no sense if constrained to nature: the divine cannot be inside nature but it has to belong to the realm of the ultimate causes of everything that exists. The reality of the divine loses its association with nature and it becomes concentrated on ethics. The divine is not an anthropomorphic representation of nature any more but an anthropomorphic projection onto a transcendent being that is over nature, whose importance is particularly visible in morality: ethical norms are interpreted as divine mandates, and they are conceived of as universal laws. They come from a supreme being who is beyond both nature and society and has power over the two of them. Believers will be therefore convinced that their lives serve a higher goal and that everything is ruled by a sublime intelligence that looks after the world.

The Freudian examination of religion thinks that it is capable of deducing, in an almost aprioristic way, the possible contents of every religion, precisely because it has been able to find the essence of religion in the ambivalence, of neurotic nature, that the human being manifests concerning himself, the physical universe, and society. This makes humankind appeal to a hypothetical supreme entity that brings comfort, peace, and meaning against an inhospitable reality. These "materials" of religiosity appear, of course, in monotheism, which "concentrates" the belief in spiritual forces on a single being that "absorbs" all the power. Religion, just as the idea of God, is nothing, for Freud, but the search of relief. It is an illusion produced by the human *psyche*. Freud does not seek to ridicule religion, for he is aware that it is the only available way to answer the question about the ultimate purpose of life. Science cannot offer a response to this challenge, but it can help us to recognize the true origin of religion in our intrinsic necessity (which resembles a narcissistic, anthropocentric orientation) to focalize the projection of our anguish on a supreme being who guarantees sense and stability on the basis of a paternal figure.

It is hard to deny that the great monotheistic religions (Judaism, Christianity, and Islam) project an anthropomorphic representation on a divine being which possesses our attributes in their most eminent degree. However, the Holy Scriptures of these religions warn not only against the idolatrous association of God with material powers (at least in their later stages, when the distance from a more animistic, naturalistic conception is clearer), but they also proclaim that God is *absconditus*. The *Vere Tu es Deus Absconditus* of Deutero-Isaiah (45:15) synthesizes the perception that God cannot be constrained to the realm of nature and our representations of it. Rather, God is beyond the world and the human mind. God is "hidden" and, as Dietrich Bonhoeffer stated, "Einen Gott, den es gibt, gibt es nicht":[10] a God that "exists" cannot exist, meaning that a "visible" God in our finite world would no longer be the supreme God. This thesis will be, in any case, accused of exonerating God from any interaction with the real world in order to conceal the lack of evidence of his existence, but religions have no other alternative: they must necessarily conceive of God as an entity which belongs to a sphere different from our world, otherwise it would not be God. The most outstanding theological systematizations of the monotheistic religions have realized that any anthropomorphic image of God is always relative and provisional, so that the realm of the divine has to be found in something that transcends the world and remains unknown: the "totally-other."

The process of gradual concentration of what used to be interpreted in terms of the deific powers of nature on a more spiritualized, intellectualized idea of the divine constitutes, according to Freud, the basis of monotheistic religions. The advantages of this dynamic are patent: by focusing all the attributes and qualities for which the human being is anxiously looking on a single entity, the fears derived from the tragic confrontation with the natural and the social realities, which bear *in nuce* the possibility of neurotic experiences, seem to vanish before the consciousness that there is a supreme and omnipotent being that rules everything. All our now wishes have a single target, a single object of desire, so that their "psychological intensity" is, so to speak, stronger, and "now that God was a single person, man's relations to him could recover the intimacy and intensity of the child's relation to his father,"[11] a statement which summarizes the understanding of religion as a form of collective neurosis based upon the Oedipus complex that Freud has exposed in *Totem and Taboo*.

For Freud, Christianity incorporates, more than any other religion, the necessity of conceiving of God as a kindhearted father that protects us and bequeaths upon us innumerable goods and favors. Christianity is, in a sense, the epitome of the common source of all religious sentiments of mankind, and it carries the shared and captivating secret that has made

---

10. Cf. Bonhoeffer, *Akt und Sein*, 94; cf. M. Fraijó, *Das Sprechen von Gott bei W. Pannenberg*, 127.

11. Freud, *The Future of an Illusion*, 19.

religions capable of exerting such an enduring social and psychological influence on human history: the need to defend ourselves against the overwhelming power of nature and to correct the imperfections of civilization. Nature treats us just as any other biological entity, in a hostile despotism that challenges our tendency to think that we have a special role in the universe. Christianity, through the idea of a God that governs the world in wisdom and providence, offers a solution to this problem, as it does to the challenge of the ethical life and the inherent dangers to the antagonistic relationship of individuals. Injustice will be repaired, and the imperfections of the earthly city will be replaced by the glories of the heavenly kingdom towards which we are walking *in statu viae*. Behold the social function of religion in its most evident expression. Christianity, just as Judaism, Islam, and any other similar monotheistic creed, will try to vindicate its legitimacy by appealing to the concept of revelation, claiming that what it teaches is the result of neither the exercise of reason nor historical experience but divine communication. However, this pretension is part of the religious system itself, and it is therefore not susceptible to criticism from the outside, what makes the intellectual enterprise impossible.

We don't ourselves acquire religious ideas and representations. Rather we inherit them from the past. They are "teachings and assertions about facts and conditions of external (or internal) reality which tell one something one has not discovered for oneself and which lay claim to one's belief. Since they give us information about what is most important and interesting to us in life, they are particularly highly prized."[12] The individual adheres to a series of conceptions received from his or her ancestors. A question could be posed concerning the origin of those representations in the case of the founders of the great religions, but the theoretical perspective inaugurated by Freud would compel us to look for precedents of those religious beliefs and to explain the emergence of the new creeds in terms of a dynamic evolution of some basic elements, instead of referring to some sort of *ex novo* invention, even less to a revelation.

For Freud, there are two alternatives for the survival of the religious creeds: the attitude, exemplified in Tertullian's *Credo quia absurdum* in his *De Carne Christi*, a proclamation of radical fideism in his controversy against Docetism, and the attempt "made by the philosophy of 'as if.'"[13] The problem of the first option is that it "is only of interest as a self-confession. As an authoritative statement it has no binding force. Am I obliged to

12. Ibid., 25.
13. Ibid., 28.

Appendix C

believe every absurdity? And if not, why this one in particular? There is no appeal to a court above that of reason."[14] The difficulties involved by the second position, which tries to convince that religious doctrines, on account of their importance in the maintenance of human society, must be preserved, is that "a man whose thinking is not influenced by the artifices of philosophy will never be able to accept it; in such a man's view, the admission that something is absurd or contrary to reason leaves no more to be said."[15] However, and since the power of the rationalistic critique is so overwhelming, how should we explain the fact that religions still persist? According to Freud, the answer is clear: religious ideas are illusions which are firmly rooted in our *psyche*, and they express the oldest and strongest aspirations of humanity, our most vivid desire to overcome our state of impotency before the cosmos and society. Religion has "performed great services for human civilization. It has contributed much towards the taming of asocial instincts—but not enough. If it had succeeded in making the majority of mankind happy, in comforting them, in reconciling them to life and making them into vehicles of civilization, no one would dream of attempting to alter the existing conditions."[16]

Religion is therefore an illusion that stems from the omnipotence of the unfulfilled wish within the human mind. This is the best summary of Freud's approach to the topic. This psychological characterization possesses key social implications. Religion can offer no knowledge about external reality: science is the only path towards our understanding of the world, and "the scientific spirit brings about a particular attitude towards worldly matters, before religious matters it pauses for a little, hesitates, and finally there too crosses the threshold. In this process there is no stopping; the greater the number of men to whom the treasures of knowledge become accessible, the more widespread is the falling away from religious belief."[17] Cultural precepts should be founded upon reason, not on religious beliefs. Is this not an expression of passionate confidence in the ideals of the Enlightenment? Is Freud an *Aufklärer*? It is well known that psychoanalysis constitutes a form of criticism of the rationalistic conception of the human being as self-consciousness, and it is therefore suspicious of any attempt at overcoming our natural impulses by the exercise of our higher mental faculties. The unconscious cannot be discarded, and the power of reason falls

14. Ibid.
15. Ibid., 29.
16. Ibid., 37.
17. Ibid., 38.

before the evidence of the prevalence of our repressed natural instincts: "man's intellect is powerless in comparison with his instinctual life,"[18] but there is something special about the intellect: its voice is soft, "but it does not rest till it has gained a hearing . . . The primacy of the intellect lies, it is true, in a distant, distant future, but probably not in an infinitely distant one."[19]

The contradiction between the confidence in human rationality and the awareness of the legitimacy of a critique of its foundations is not easy to overcome. The "unreasonableness" of reason is there, but Freud does not renounce a social project that keeps a close connection with the enlightened dream of a society guided by reason. In any case, the kind of rationality to which Freud refers does not exclude taking into account the unconscious and instinctive dimension of the human being, and psychoanalysis finds its *raison d'être* in offering a "rational" awareness of the importance of the repressed contents of our *psyche* in our lives, both individual and collective.

The disappearance of religion will not mean, according to Freud, the achievement of a full liberation of humanity. We will still feel fear and anguish and seek consolation. However, it is better to know the truth about religion than to conceal it in a self-guilty state of ignorance, for "our science is no illusion. But an illusion it would be to suppose that what science cannot give us we can get elsewhere."[20] Undoubtedly, Freud would share the entire content of the final paragraph of Bertrand Russell's *Why I Am Not a Christian*: "We want to stand upon our own feet and look fair and square at the world—its good facts, its bad facts, its beauties, and its ugliness; see the world as it is and be not afraid of it. Conquer the world by intelligence and not merely by being slavishly subdued by the terror that comes from it . . . We ought to stand up and look the world frankly in the face. We ought to make the best we can of the world, and if it is not so good as we wish, after all it will still be better than what these others have made of it in all these ages. A good world needs knowledge, kindliness, and courage; it does not need a regretful hankering after the past or a fettering of the free intelligence by the words uttered long ago by ignorant men. It needs a fearless outlook and a free intelligence. It needs hope for the future, not looking back all the time toward a past that is dead, which we trust will be far surpassed by the future that our intelligence can create."

18. Ibid., 53.
19. Ibid.
20. Ibid., 56.

Appendix C

The God of great religions can only stand before human reason if it is contemplated as "*Deus Absconditus*," as the question of all questions, as the ineffable synthesis of immanence and transcendence, as the highest expression of the purest intuition: wisdom, beauty, and love. Fragile but enlightening gleams from the divine realm will therefore shine in the pinnacles of wisdom, beauty, and love conquered by humanity; distressing signs of its remoteness will emanate from the vast tragedies of history and the painful darkening of beauty, wisdom, and love; vivid encouragement to crown the peaks of love, beauty, and wisdom will be irradiated from both the conscience of its presence and the awareness of its absence.

Appendix D
The Conception of God as Das Ganz-Andere *in Rudolf Otto*

THE IDEA OF GOD as the "wholly-Other" [*Das Ganz-Andere*] plays a fundamental role in the thought of Rudolf Otto (1869–1937). The aim of this paper is to examine the nature and scope of this conception of God in the work of the renowned German theologian and philosopher of religion.

Otto's influence in the fields of comparative religions, philosophy of religion, and systematic theology has been acknowledged by authors of such influence as Paul Tillich (1886–1965),[1] Mircea Eliade (1907–1986),[2] and Gustav Mensching (1901–1978).[3] One of his most powerful ideas, actually the basis underlying both his notion of "the numinous" and his understanding of religion as a whole, is his conception of God as "*das Ganz-Andere*." A solid formulation of this understanding of divine reality can be found in Otto's most celebrated book, *The Idea of the Holy* [*Das Heilige*], first published in 1917, which "recognizing the profound impact of the non-rational for metaphysics, makes a serious attempt to analyze all the more exactly feeling which remains where the concept fails."[4]

Thinking of God in analogy with the human reality easily falls captive to the critique of Ludwig Feuerbach (1804–1872) in *The Essence of Christianity* (1841), who regards the Christian idea of God as an anthropomorphic projection of our own nature. As a possible alternative,

---

1. Cf. Tillich, *Dynamics of Faith*, 13.

2. Cf. Eliade, *Sacred and the Profane*, 10, although Eliade intends to present "the phenomenon of the sacred in all its complexity, and not only in so far as it is *irrational.*"

3. Cf. Mensching, "Rudolf Otto und die Religionsgeschichte," in Benz, *Rudolf Otto's Bedeutung für die Religionswissenschaft und die Theologie heute.*

4. Otto, *Idea of the Holy*. For the German text, cf. *Das Heilige*.

Appendix D

the so-called *via eminentiae*[5] tries to safeguard divine transcendence by overcoming any possible analogical relationship: it intends to preserve God as a *Deus absconditus*. According to Otto, however, the danger of this theological path is that of reducing the being of God to mere concepts [*Begriffe*], which "can be grasped by the intellect" and "can be analyzed by thought; they even admit definition."[6]

Conceptualization implies rationalization, and whatever is rational is susceptible to some kind of knowledge, even if it is through faith and its articulation into doctrines. We conceptualize because we want to know, and this need for expressing our ideas in terms of rational concepts makes us prisoners of language. As Otto remarks, "all language, in so far as it consists of words, purports to convey ideas or concepts—that is what language means—and the more clearly and unequivocally it does so, the better the language. And hence expositions of religious truth in language inevitably tend to stress the 'rational' attributes of God."[7]

Religions have created a challenge of their own to the temptation of becoming rationalized: mysticism.[8] In mysticism there is a deep awareness of ineffability, although this does not mean "that absolutely nothing can be asserted of the object of the religious consciousness; otherwise, mysticism could exist only in unbroken silence, whereas what has generally been characteristic of mystics is their copious eloquence."[9]

Mysticism accentuates negation, but in doing so it maintains the affirmation as well: mysticism negates in order to affirm the absolute transcendence of God and its irreducibility to any given category. "In mysticism," writes Otto, "we have in the 'beyond' (*epekeina*) again the strongest stressing and over-stressing of those non-rational elements which are already inherent in all religion. Mysticism continues to its extreme point this contrasting of the numinous object (the *numen*), as the 'wholly other,' with ordinary experience. Not content with contrasting it with all that is of nature or this world, mysticism concludes by contrasting it with Being itself and all that is [*dem 'Sein' und dem 'Seienden' selber*], and finally actually calls it 'that which is nothing [*'das Nichts' selbst*].' By this 'nothing' is meant not only that of which nothing can be predicted, but that which is

---

5. On the importance of analogy in Christian theology, cf. Mondin, *Principle of Analogy in Protestant and Catholic Theology*.

6. Otto, *Idea of the Holy*, 1.

7. Ibid., 2.

8. For an introduction to mysticism, cf. Woods, *Understanding Mysticism*; Katz, *Mysticism and Religious Traditions*.

9. Otto, *Idea of the Holy*, 2.

The Conception of God as Das Ganz-Andere in Rudolf Otto

absolutely and intrinsically other than and opposite of everything that is and can be thought [das schlechthin und wesentlich Andere und Gegensätzliche zu allem was ist und gedacht werden kann]."[10]

According to Otto, the nature of religion cannot be grasped through the opposition of rationality with irrationality. Even the doctrine of miracles is already "rational." Neither rationality nor irrationality can account for what religion actually is, and religious experience cannot be reconstructed from a basis or structure: it is unique, and it does not yield to any categorization, even in terms of irrationality. Otto seems to be seeking a deeper category, some sort of Hegelian "true infinite."[11] For him, religion has a specific *fundamentum*, and it constitutes a category of its own: *das heilige*, "the holy." The holy goes beyond the opposition of rationality and irrationality. "The holy" escapes conceptualization, and it therefore flees from the rational: it "remains inexpressible—an *arreton* or *ineffabile*—in the sense that it completely eludes apprehension in terms of concepts."[12]

Heilige is not derived from ethics, although it can be related to it.[13] Religious concepts such as *qadosh, hagios, sanctus,* and *sacer* respond to

---

10. Ibid., 29. In *West-Östliche Mystik* (*Mysticism East and West*), Otto states that the mystical escapes any possible definition: "in the language of secular speech we should have to say: 'knowledge of the (mystical) unity of the universe and my own unity with it is knowledge *a priori*.' The senses provide the raw materials for this. But what this 'is,' what it 'is' in truth, wherein lies its depth meaning and essence, the senses do not reveal. This is also discovered immediately by the soul 'through itself,' and that means that the soul find it 'indwelling' in itself [*sie zugleich selbst der Erkenntnisgrund ist, sofern sie nämlich selbst ist, was sie erkennt*]" (ibid., 281). However, Otto warns against the temptation of regarding mysticism as "one and ever the same" throughout all religions. On the contrary, he thinks "that in mysticism there are indeed strong primal impulses working in the human soul which as such are completely unaffected by differences of climate, of geographical position or of race," but "there are within mysticism many varieties of expression which are just as great as the variations in any other sphere of spiritual life . . . We affirm that these variations as such are not determined by race, or geographical situations, by they may appear side by side" (ibid., 14).

11. On the importance of Hegel's idea of "the true infinite [*das wahre Unendlichkeit*]," as it is expressed in works such as *Phenomenology of the Spirit*, cf. Pannenberg, *Metaphysik und Gottesgedanke*, 94ff.

12. Otto, *Idea of the Holy*, 5.

13. Concerning Otto's approach to ethics, cf. Otto, *Verantwortliche Lebensgestaltung*; cf. Otto, *Aufsätze zur Ethik*. According to Otto, a fundamental problem of ethics is the determination of the relationship between the "autonomy of values [*Wertautonomie*]" and the "will of God [*Gotteswille*]" (ibid., 215), what Nicolai Hartmann calls the "Antinomie zwischen Ethik und Religion" (Otto, *Ethik*). However, and against the temptation of paying much attention to ethics in the philosophical and theological discourse, Otto remarks that "der Wille ist nicht der ganze Mensch, und die Ethik, ja auch die Moral hat nicht nur vom Menschen als Willenswesen zu redden" (Otto,

a certain "ethical schematization [*ethische Schematisierung*] of what was a unique original feeling response."[14] In order to distinguish "the holy" from its potential ethical surplus, Otto introduces the category of "*das Numinose*," "the numinous." Otto is asking us to recall the moment which comes before any form of "moralization": the *numen*, for "this mental state is perfectly *sui generis* and irreducible to any other, and therefore, like every absolutely primary and elementary datum [*Grund-datum*], while it admits of being discussed, it cannot be strictly defined."[15] In religious experience, we stand before the "non-thematic intuition" (to use Karl Rahner's expression)[16] that something inexplicable exists and always transcends us, as it cannot be exhausted by any human desire.

In *Kantisch-Fries'sche Religionsphilosophie*, a book published before *Das Heilige*, Otto had spoken in terms of *Ahnung*, a category inspired by the work of Jacob Friedrich Fries (1773–1843), which could be understood as man's deepest need and longing. However, "it is not a scientific principle to be used for explanation; it is an 'aesthetic' principle which serves for the religious interpretation of historical development," consisting of some sort of "divination of the government of the world in history [*Ahnung der Weltregierung in der Geschichte*]."[17]

It is interesting to notice that in *Das Heilige* the category of *Ahnung* seems to have ceded its power to that of "*numen*," in which the fundamental dimensions of the former have been condensed. Nevertheless, in both works there is a clear statement of the centrality of *Erlebnis*, which cannot be reduced to a concept, as it is rather an experiential "ideogram [*Ideogramm*]," because "the focal point, the starting point for all science of religion, and especially for the Christian branch of that science, is religious experience [*religiöse Erlebnis*], a thing that is not interpreted by mythology

---

Aufsätze zur Ethik, 214).

14. Otto, *Idea of the Holy*, 6.

15. Ibid., 7.

16. For an exposition of Rahner's concept of the "non-thematic," cf. *Grundkurs des Glaubens*.

17. Otto, *Philosophy of Religion based on Kant and Fries*, 144. For the original German text, cf. *Kantisch-Fries'sche Religionsphilosophie und ihre Anwendung an die Theologie*. In close connection with philosophy of religion is Otto's distinction between theology and history of religions: "Theology is not a history of religion . . . It is not a collection of propositions developed by methods of profane science, but of formulations of religious faith, even when these are critical judgements of one's own, or of an alien, religion. Its fundamental category is that of 'revelation' [*Offenbarung*], in India as well as among us" (Otto, *India's Religion of Grace and Christianity*, 61). For the original German text, cf. *Die Gnadenreligion Indiens und das Christentum*.

The Conception of God as Das Ganz-Andere in Rudolf Otto

or archaeology, that in default of immediate personal knowledge must be understood from the life of those who are religious in the narrower and more forcible sense."[18] This religious experience "is the obscure knowledge [*dunkle Erkennen*] of the Eternal in general and the eternal determination of Existence, which comes to life in Feeling [*das im Gefühl lebendig werdende*]."[19]

For Otto, the experience of the numinous cannot be reduced to a "feeling of dependence [*Gefühl der Abhängigkeit*]," as in the philosophy of Friedrich Schleiermacher (1768–1834),[20] because this kind of sentiment is not exclusive to the religious experience. Schleiermacher's notion of dependence is primarily concerned with human self-consciousness, but Otto refers to something that is external to us: the numinous, which we experience as *numen praesens*, being "thus felt as objective and outside the self."[21]

To take the uniqueness of religion seriously implies granting it an *a priori* status within the human mind, and even though Schleiermacher considers the state of dependence to be "absolute," in contrast with any sort of relative dependence, Otto goes even further: he does not want analogy, for the numinous not only overflows any kind of analogy but also negates it. The numinous, which is the core of any religious experience, "cannot be expressed by means of anything else."[22] It defines itself, as if it were some sort of *causa sui*. It finds its reason to exist in itself. The numinous is neither result of social structures nor a psychological experience of fear and incompleteness: it constitutes a realm of its own. As Otto writes, the

---

18. Otto, *Philosophy of Religion based on Kant and Fries*, 227.

19. Ibid., 229. As Octavio Paz writes, "La concepción de Otto recuerda la sentencia de Novalis: Cuando el corazón se siente a sí mismo y, desasido de todo objeto particular y real, deviene su propio objeto ideal, entonces nace la religión." La experiencia de lo sagrado no es tanto la revelación de un objeto exterior a nosotros—dios, demonio, presencia ajena—como un abrir nuestro corazón o nuestras entrañas para que brote ese "Otro" escondido. La revelación, en el sentido de un don o gracia que viene del exterior, se transforma en un abrirse del hombre a sí mismo. Lo menos que se puede decir de esta idea es que la noción de trascendencia—fundamento de la religión—sufre un grave quebranto. El hombre no está "suspendido de la mano de Dios," sino que Dios yace oculto en el corazón del hombre. El objeto numinoso es siempre interior y se da como la otra cara, la positiva, del vacío con que se inicia toda experiencia mística. ¿Cómo conciliar este emerger de Dios en el hombre con la idea de una Presencia absolutamente extraña a nosotros? ¿Cómo aceptar que vemos a Dios gracias a una disposición divinizante sin al mismo tiempo minar su existencia misma, haciéndola depender de la subjetividad humana?" (*El Arco y la Lira*, 140–141).

20. Cf. Schleiermacher, *On Religion*.

21. Otto, *Idea of the Holy*, 11.

22. Ibid., 9.

numinous affects the senses, but "it does not arise out of them, but only by their means [*es entspringt nicht aus ihnen sondern nur durch ihnen*]."[23] In his work *Das Gefühl des Über-weltlichen (sensus numinis)*, Otto says that "*sensus numinis*" is the "historical origin of religion [*geschichtlicher Ursprung der Religion*]."[24] The "numinous" is therefore the "*Grund-Datum*" of religious experience. According to him, Nicolaus Ludwig Zinzendorf (1700–1760), a key exponent of German pietism, had already discovered this category in the eighteenth century.[25]

The human mind must be prepared to accept fundamental, non-reducible concepts, and it is hard to imagine how sciences such as physics could possibly exist without the ultimate categories of matter, energy, space, and time. Nevertheless, the *Grund-Datum*, which Otto mentions, could be skeptically regarded as an expression of a core *Grund-Datum* that is shared by all the dimensions of human life, instead of being exclusively constrained to the sphere of religiosity. Otto admits that it actually addresses a fundamental feeling, which is the "creature-feeling [*Kreaturgefühl*]," "the emotion of a creature, submerged and overwhelmed by its own nothingness in contrast to that which is supreme above all creatures."[26] In any case, this is not an attempt to offer a conceptual explanation of what, by its own nature, cannot be explained.[27] Just as art, and even as philoso-

---

23. Ibid., 113.

24. Otto, *Das Gefühl des Über-weltlichen (sensus numinis)*, 11.

25. The experience of the numinous is a feeling [*Gefühl*]: "es ist nicht eine blosse subjektive Befindlichkeit sondern hat einen dunklen Vorstellungsgehalt, den es nicht fantasiemässig aus natürlichen Gegebenheiten konstruiert sondern der ihm als allem natürlichen Gegebenen völlig fremder, ganz-anderer Gestalt zunächst ohne allen Namen und Begriff 'kommt' und der sich spatter in 'Ideogrammen' und auch in immer klaren Begriffen wie übernatürlichen, überweltlichen, jenseitig verdeutlichen muss. Es ist als solches 'unmittert' von der spezifisch numinosen Emotionen, die wir beschrieben haben" (ibid., 2).

26. Otto, *Idea of the Holy*, 10.

27. The numinous, according to Otto, is non-rational, in the sense that it challenges rationality. In his study of the theology of Sankara and Meister Eckhart (seeing in both authors a "common theistic foundation [*Gemeinsamertheistischer Unterbau*]"), Otto realizes that the two mystics arrive at something "completely non-rational, or as we should say, a 'numinous' value. From this viewpoint it becomes clear that for Eckhart as for Sankara the whole scheme of speculation about Being is in itself only a preliminary task, undertaken in the service of another and higher idea. In the light of this, Being itself takes on a new aspect. It is removed from the rational sphere to which it unquestionably belonged at first, and becomes simply an ideogram of the "wholly Other," of the *anyad*, the *alienum*, the *dissimile* . . . In the writings of both Masters it is clear that the idea of pure Being (in spite of their own assertions) is nevertheless merely the utmost which concept or 'ratio' can offer in the approach to the highest of

The Conception of God as Das Ganz-Andere in Rudolf Otto

phy, religion (to mention the three supreme determinations of the spirit in Hegel[28]) cannot be "expressed" conceptually. Human beings feel ineluctably overwhelmed by it and they can only make reference to something which evades any cognitive dimension (Saint John of the Cross's "un no sé qué que quedan balbuciendo"[29]). Art, religion, and philosophy appeal to the individual himself, and in these realities it is possible to perceive the presence of something that cannot be controlled at all by ourselves: beauty, the numinous, and the idea which, once it has been formulated, reaches some sort of eternity, escaping our power.

Mystery only becomes accessible as *Erlebnis*, as a "living experience,"[30] and this is narrowly connected with the philosophy of Wilhelm Dilthey (1833–1911): meaning is "lived [*erlebt*]," and it cannot be reduced to an explanation in terms of causes and effects, for it constitutes a subjective core, an inexhaustible limit.[31] Just as Dilthey, Otto believes that the domain of the spirit goes beyond the limits of the natural sciences, since "nature can only be explained by an investigation into the ultimate fundamental forces of nature and their laws: it is meaningless to propose to go further and explain these laws themselves, for in terms of what are they to be explained?," whereas in the realm of the spirit "the corresponding principle from which an explanation is derived is just the spirit itself," and "this has to be presupposed: it cannot itself be explained [den man voraussetzen muss, den man seller aber night erklären ken]."[32]

---

all things. But it still falls short of the summit itself, and finally reveals itself as only a rational 'schema' (model) of something which is fundamentally transcendent—something numinous. '*Sa atma. Tat tvan asi.*' '*Brahmasmi*': that is palpably something more and something 'wholly other' than the rational expression: 'I have become pure Being. I am Being itself . . . Every concept fails utterly here . . . He [Eckhart] is then no longer in the sphere of Being: he is purely and absolutely in the sphere of 'wonder [*Wunder*]' (as he himself calls it), in the region of a purely numinous and non-rational valuation [*im Bereiche rein numinous-irrationaler Setzung und Wertung*]" (*Mysticism East and West*, 41–45).

28. Cf. Hegel, *Encyclopaedia of the Philosophical Sciences in Basic Outline*, part 3.

29. Y todos cantos vagan,
 de ti me van mil gracias refiriendo.
 Y todos más me llagan,
 y déjame muriendo
 un no sé qué que quedan balbuciendo."
  From *Cántico Espiritual*, 5.31–35.

30. Cf. Otto, *Idea of the Holy*, 33.

31. Cf. Dilthey, *Der Aufbau der geschichtlichen Welt in den Geisteswissenschaften*, 142.

32. Otto, *Idea of the Holy*, 114. Otto's idea of the infeasability of the scientific

Appendix D

The numinous, according to Otto, exhibits a series of moments. The first one is what he names *mysterium tremendum*. *Tremendum* means "awful." It is "das Moment des Schauervollen," and it "is something more than 'natural,' ordinary fear: it implies that the mysterious is already beginning to loom before the mind, to touch the feelings. It implies the first application of a category of valuation which has no place in the everyday natural world of ordinary experience, and is only possible to a being in whom has been awakened a mental predisposition, unique in kind and different in a definite way from any 'natural' faculty."[33] Otto associates this emotion with the "daemonic dread" of ancient religions, and it very much responds to Isaiah's *sanctus, sanctus, sanctus* (Isaiah 6:3): "the 'shudder' has here lost its crazy and bewildering note, but not the ineffable something that holds the mind. It has become a mystical awe, and sets free as its accompaniment, reflected in self-consciousness, that 'creature-feeling' that has already been described as the feeling of personal nothingness and submergence before the awe-inspiring object directly experienced."[34]

The numinous is therefore intrinsically contradictory, for "the daemonic-divine object may appear to the mind an object of horror and

---

conception of the world for a proper understanding of religion is detailed in his book *Naturalistische und religiöse Weltansicht*, published in 1904, in which he explains that "if religion is to live, it must be able to demonstrate—and it can be demonstrated—that its convictions in regard to the world and human existence are not contradicted from any other quarter, that they are possible and may be believed to be true" (*Naturalism and Religion*, 6). Religion, according to Otto, does not emerge, as in natural theology, from the evidence that finite realities can offer of an infinite reality. On the contrary, its sources "lie deep in the human spirit, and have had a long history . . . In fact, religion and religious interpretations are nothing if not 'enthusiasms,' that 's to say, expressions of the art of sustaining a permanent exaltation of the spirit" (ibid., 8–13). Against the pretensions of religion, rationalism points out that "instead of the naïve, poetical, and half mystical conceptions of nature we must have a really scientific one, so that, so to speak, the supernatural may be eliminated from nature, and the apparently irrational rationalised; that is, so that its phenomena may be traced back to simple, unequivocal, and easily understood processes, the actual why and how of all things perceived, and thus, it may be, understood; so that, in short, everything may be seen to come about 'by natural means'" (ibid., 23). However, Otto believes that the religious conception of the world is legitimate. In order to justify this assumption, it is necessary to defend the autonomy of the realm of the spirit from the sphere of nature: "religion cannot represent, or conceive, or possess its own highest good and supreme idea, except by thinking in terms of the highest analogies of what it knows in itself as spiritual being and reality . . . If spirit is not real and above all other realities; if it is derivable, subordinate and dependent, it is impossible to think of anything whatever to which the name of "God" can be given" (ibid., 282).

33. Otto, *Idea of the Holy*, 15.
34. Ibid., 17.

dread, but at the same time it is no less something that allows with a potent charm."[35] This is what Otto calls the "Kontrast-Harmonie" and the "Doppel-Charakter" of the numinous, and it is impossible for the intellect to choose one of both extremes (awfulness and wonderfulness). Any attempt of providing a rational articulation of the numinous reaches contradiction, because the synthetic moment itself, the act of grasping the full scope of the ineffable, exceeds the power of reason. As Otto writes: "above and beyond our rational being lies hidden the ultimate and highest part of our nature, which can find no satisfaction in the mere allaying of the needs of the sensuous, psychical, or intellectual impulses and cravings. The mystics called it the basis or ground of the soul [*Seelengrund*]."[36]

The biblical God, just as the deities of other religions, manifests "wrath": it is the so-called *ira deorum*, the Pauline *orgue theou*,[37] which challenges any rational, theological approach, as it may seem capricious, at least if one does not realize that it is not rational but it is a power, the '*tremendum*' of mystery. Wrath is actually an ideogram, not a concept.[38] It is something that challenges any analogical conception of the divine.

The experience of *mysterium* as *tremendum* is immediately followed, according to Otto, by its perception as *majestas*, as "overpoweringness" [*das Übermächtige*],[39] as "absolute unapproachability" [*schlechthinnige Unnahbarkeit*]. This *tremendous majesties* "forms the numinous raw material for the feeling of religious humility."[40] If Schleiermacher thought that the feeling of dependence makes us realize our "relatedness" [*Geschaffenheit*], Otto gives a step forward: it is not simply that we regard

---

35. Ibid., 31.
36. Ibid., 36.
37. For an important instantiation of the idea of the wrath of God, see Rom 1:18.
38. In *West-Östliche Mystik*, Otto uses again the category of "ideogram," in contrast with that of "concept": "we have no longer any concept, only the ideogram as a vessel of pure, inexplicable, numinous feeling" (*Mysticism East and West*, 268). However, and as González de Mendoza explains, for Otto the "non-rational" is expressed in rational moments, "die sind nicht keine Ideogramme, sondern eigentliche Begriffe, die sie mit den numinosen Gefühlen und deren Ideogrammen verbinden, um mit ihnen die komplexe Kategorie des Heiligen zu bilden" (González de Mendoza, *Stimmung und Transzendenz*, 271).
39. Otto insists on this idea in his work *Gottheit und Gottheiten der Arier*: "Das Moment des 'Ganz andern'; das allem Vertrauen und Hiesigen zunächst qualitative entgegengesetzt, sodann ihm durch Machtgemalt überlegen ist ... es ist ein 'anderes' und ein übermächtiges" (ibid., 6), whose power "aller bekannten natürlichen Macht entgegengesetzt ist" (ibid., 7).
40. Otto, *Idea of the Holy*, 20.

ourselves as created beings but that we perceive our "creaturehood" [*Geschöpflichkeit*], the consciousness of impotency and nullity, the awareness that we are nothing. It does not manifest our condition of created beings but our state of impotency.

In mysticism, this is experienced as self-depreciation: the *ego* is denied in order to affirm the supremacy of a power which is alien to me, which is *other* than me: *ich nights, du alles*, "I am naught, thou art all." There is actually no binomial dependence, because linearity has been broken. There is no possible continuity, no Hegelian synthesis as the result of *Aufhebung*, but only negation as the means to enter the world of supreme affirmation. However, there is no place for a new negation, for "*negatio negations*":[41] we have to remain in negation itself, returning to something which recalls the beginning of Hegel's *The Science of Logic*: pure being is pure nothingness.[42] There is no aspiration to build a synthesis, and we must yield to the complete abandonment of any affirmation, of any *positivitas* (as the world is).

The third moment of the numinous is that of *energy*, of vitality, of what makes the God of Abraham so different from the God of philosophers and sages: "der lebendige Gott." Many philosophers would consider this view as anthropomorphic, because the *Deus absconditus* appears, as Otto remarks, as a deeply passionate being. This is certainly an analogy, but it is intended to express the power of negation as a "refusal" of the world. Such a depiction of God involves the affirmation of power and life over the world, as in Luther's idea of *omnipotentia Dei* in *De Servo Arbitrio*, in contrast with the serenity of the God of geometers. Here there is a God that challenges the world, instead of founding its intelligibility. It would be a mistake, however, as Otto reminds us, to try to conceptualize it.[43] No architectonics of science can emerge from this radical intuition.

What is therefore the "wholly-Other"? What role does the idea of "*das 'Ganz Andere'*" play in the context of the experience of the numinous? The "wholly-Other" is, for Otto, the object of the numinous consciousness. The mysterious is the "wholly-Other": *anyad, thareton, alienum*, "that which is quite beyond the sphere of the usual, the intelligible, and the

---

41. Nevertheless, Otto, in his study of Sankara and Eckhart, thinks that *via negationis* actually consists of *negatio negationis*, because "it is intended as the very highest positive. And so the *via negationis*' emerges not as contrary to the *via eminentiae*, not even as a merely parallel mode of expression, but really as a continuation of the *via eminentiae* itself" (*Mysticism East and West*, 128).

42. Cf. Hegel, *Science of Logic*, 1:67.

43. Cf. Otto, *Idea of the Holy*, 23.

familiar."⁴⁴ It is "das Fremde und Befremdende," and it generates *stupor*, "an astonishment that strikes us dumb."⁴⁵ We feel proximity and distance towards it, and we can echo Saint Augustine's words: "Quis comprehendet? quis enarrabit? quid est illud quod interlucet mihi et percutit cor meum sine laesione? et inhorresco et inardesco: inhorresco, in quantum dissimilis ei sum, inardesco, in quantum similis ei sum."⁴⁶

As Otto explains, the "wholly-Other" poses at least three principal implications:

1. It does not yield to concepts or predicates that could be abstracted from something.
2. It does not yield to concepts or predicates that could be named in some way.
3. Its being does yield to any concept or predicate at all.⁴⁷

God as the "wholly-Other," which is the result of *via negationis*, means, in the philosophy of Otto, that "God is not merely the ground and superlative of all that can be thought; He is in himself a subject on His own account and in Himself" [*Gott ist, in sich selbst, noch eine Sache für sich*].⁴⁸ God must be affirmed *de iure*, not simply as the culmination of the world. In order to affirm what is in itself it is necessary to negate the world and to look for a subjective core that may be different from that of the world. Then, God is not the elevation of the world and humanity but their negation, their challenge: religion cannot be introduced, as Kant sought, within the limits of reason alone⁴⁹, because it denies the very essence of

---

44. Ibid., 26.
45. Ibid.
46. St. Augustine, *Confessiones* 11.9.11.
47 Cf. Otto, *Das Gefühl der Über-weltlichen (sensus numinis)*, 219. The statements we have just considered imply that it is not possible to conceive of God in terms of the categories of cause and effect and of substance and accident, because the relationship of God to the world is "ganz anders," "entirely other" (ibid., 220). See also Otto, *Aufsätze das Numinose Betreffend*, 24. Otto thinks that the doctrine of *simplicitas Dei* is influenced by the perception of God as the "wholly-Other": "Gott ist 'einfach' schlechthin, weil er es das 'Ganz Andere' ist schlechthin" (ibid., 24).
48. Otto, *Idea of the Holy*, 36.
49. Cf. Kant, *Religion within the Limits of Reason Alone*.

reason.⁵⁰ If, as Levinas said, "mourir pour l'infini, voilá la métaphysique,"⁵¹ religion can be described as the act of "dying" for the sake of non-reason, by accepting a world which runs parallel to reason. If, to follow Spinoza, "omnis determinatio est negatio,"⁵² the negation of any determination of the world is actually the affirmation of the numinous: to negate the world is to affirm all that is indeterminate. To negate in order to affirm, just as to die in order to live.

The numinous refers to the absolute, but our reason is not capable of understanding the absolute, which "is within the reach of our conceiving [*Begriffsvermörgen*], but it is beyond the grasp of our comprehension [*Fassungskraft*]."⁵³ However, the category of "the absolute" should not be simply identified, according to Otto, with that of the "wholly-Other." They inevitably converge, but there is an important difference: the absolute cannot be understood, although we can conceive of it, whereas the "wholly-Other," by its own nature, challenges any possible conception: it is the utterly mysterious. The absolute is, then, "that which surpasses the limits of our understanding [*Fassungskraft*], not through its actual qualitative character, for that it is familiar to us, but through its formal character. The mysterious, on the other hand, is that which lies altogether outside what can be thought, and is, alike in form, quality, and essence, the utterly 'wholly other' [*das 'Ganz Andere'*]."⁵⁴

---

50. According to Otto, the perception of something that radically challenges our rational capacity can be extrapolated to the realm of music: "musical feeling is rather (like numinous feeling) something 'wholly other,' which, while it affords analogies and here and there will run parallel to the ordinary emotions of life, cannot be made to coincide with them by a detailed point-to-point correspondence." (*The Idea of the Holy*, 49). The "wholly-Other" does not yield, in fact, to any kind of analogy ("*Das 'Ganz Andere' des Numinosen widerstrebt in der Tat jeder Analogie, jede Vergleichbarkeit und damit jeder begrifflichen Determination*," in *Das Gefühl des Über-weltlichen*, 266).

51. Levinas, *Totalité et Infini; Essai sur l'Exteriorité*, 6.

52. Cf. Spinoza, "Epistle 59," in *Complete Works*. In any case, Otto thinks that Spinoza did not go as far as he should have in order to liberate God from all our categories, not only from those of space and time, an enterprise for which the characterization of God as "wholly-Other" is aimed: "Solche hohen Dinge aber mit 'Pantheismus' verwechseln kann man nur, wenn man jeder Begriff von Sachen verloren hat—übrigens auch Spinoza lehrt nicht Pantheismus, sondern Theopantismus. Und das ist von Pantheismus das diametrale Gegenteil" (ibid., 28). Thus, Spinoza still applies categories of the understanding such as substance and cause to that which is "wholly-Other" and therefore escapes any categorization. On Spinoza and "*Theopantismus*," cf. Otto's translation of *Visnu-Narayana*, Buch 2, Einleitung, 85.

53. Otto, *Idea of the Holy*, 141.

54. Ibid.

The Conception of God as Das Ganz-Andere in Rudolf Otto

Both the absolute and the mysterious stand outside our realm of understanding, although on account of different reasons: the absolute, on the basis of impotence, and the mysterious, on the basis of impossibility, for "the absolute exceeds our power to comprehend; the mysterious wholly eludes it" [*Das Absolute ist unerfasslich, das Mysteriöse unfasslich*].[55] The "wholly-Other" is rationalized as the "absolute"[56] in what Otto calls the "schematization [*Schematisierung*] of the numinous moment of the wonderful through the moment of the absolute."[57]

Otto regards mankind as *capax religionis* because, in his view, humanity possesses an *a priori* which comes before any historical explanation. He does not justify how this *a priori* could possibly emerge, as he restricts his work to showing that in the constitution of the human being there is a religious *a priori*: the "holy," which points to a *mysterium tremendum et fascinans*. This *a priori* represents an *Anlage*, a "predisposition,"[58] being "a faculty of receptivity" [*Vermögen der Empfänglichkeit*], a "principle of judgment and acknowledgement" [*Prinzp der Beuerteilung*].[59] As Otto explains in *Kantisch-Fries'sche Religionsphilosophie*, what is *a priori* is different from the innate. *A priori* is whatever we are all capable of having, whereas "innate" is whatever we actually have ("specific cognitions").[60]

The use of the category of *a priori* by Otto immediately recalls Immanuel Kant, but Otto warns against the relegation of *a priori* to the realm of *Idealität*, as if it lacked validity outside our representations: "Kant infers that, since this knowledge is altogether *a priori*, it can only hold good for the subjective world of our conceptions, not for an objective world of Being-in-itself, independent of ourselves. From the *a priori* nature of categories he concludes that they are ideal."[61] Otto vindicates the philosophy of Jakob Friedrich Fries as an alternative position to the Kantian conception of the *a priori*, and, just as him, our theologian argues that Kant presupposes that the fact that an object affects us is the criterion of objective validity [*objektive Gültigkeit*], but such "affection" is already a

---

55. Ibid.
56. Cf. Otto, *Visnu-Narayana*, 127.
57. Otto, *Aufsätze das Numinose Betreffend*, 33.
58. Cf. Otto, *Idea of the Holy*, 177.
59. Ibid.
60. Cf. Otto, *Philosophy of Religion based on Kant and Fries*, 42.
61. Ibid., 52.

Appendix D

form of causality, and "at this point Kant is forced to attribute reality to the category of causality [*Kausalität*] which he precisely declares to be ideal."[62]

The originality of Rudolf Otto's approach to the understanding of the nature of religion is visible not only in the importance that he attributes to the "numinous," as an experience which is independent from other realms of individual and the social life, but also in the philosophical implications derived from his depiction of God as "the wholly-Other" and in the consequences that this has for the conception of the scope and the limitations of human rationality.

His understanding of God as a reality that radically challenges any rational category poses a legitimate question: can we accept that which, by its deepest nature, rebels against all concepts? Doesn't progress consist, to a certain extent, of the gradual acquisition of concepts that liberate us from the tyranny of specific representations?

These questions point to the human aspect of thinking of God as "wholly-Other" to the world. The "social" implications of the idea of the "wholly-Other" have not remained unnoticed to Otto who, in his *Reich Gottes und Menschensohn: Ein religionsgeschichtlicher Versuch*, relates "das Ganz Andere" with the kingdom of God, for "the term 'kingdom' and 'coming of the kingdom' imply the idea of an absolute domain of salvation [*Heilsgutes*], indefinable and undefined as are all domains of salvation . . . Because the connotation of the wholly other and the supramundane belongs to the moral kingdom, the modernistic idea of a crisis—Jesus knew nothing of crisis—does not belong to it, but rather the idea of a supernatural breaking off the entire world process."[63] In the teaching of Jesus, the kingdom "was the inbreaking power of God into salvation" [*hereinbrechende rettende Gottesmacht*].[64]

According to Otto, Jesus did not bring a new theology, and his doctrine "could not be characterized as a new 'knowledge of God,' or as a profound all-embracing theology, or a new theoretic conception of the relation of the Godhead to the world, or of the infinite ground of things to its phenomena and its effects, or of the eternal to the temporal, or of the present to that which lies beyond . . . He did not bring a new theology, but a new piety; not a new theoretic conception of eternity, but a new practical conduct and disposition toward it."[65]

62. Ibid.
63. Otto, *Kingdom of God and the Son of Man*, 56.
64. Ibid., 375.
65. Otto, *Life and Ministry of Jesus*, 59. For the original German text, cf. *Leben und*

The Conception of God as Das Ganz-Andere in Rudolf Otto

Although in a rather speculative form, we can realize that the idea of God as "wholly-Other" to the world does not involve the denial of the very reality of the world and of the profoundest aspirations of humanity in history. On the contrary, one of the considerations that legitimately follow from Otto's philosophy is the need for a deeper knowledge of humanity.

The "wholly-Other" is the unconditioned: no power of the world can rule over it, and it therefore stands in permanent contradiction to the world and its finiteness. The "other" is revelation, as Levinas foresaw[66], not simply discovery. If there is an "other," then someone can reveal something to me, and there is room for gratitude, surprise, and novelty in this world. On account of this, the "wholly-Other," even while escaping my power, humanizes me to the highest degree, for in negating me it is encouraging me to know myself, and in negating me it is revealing something about my own finiteness.

God is totally alien to me if I am "wholly-I," "ein Ganz-Ich," and here we have the principle of humanization and freedom: I can only adequately perceive the "wholly-Other" if I feel that I am "wholly-I," with full disposition of my own capacities. This is actually the ideal which guides any attempt to emancipate humanity, and it shows interesting resonances with Max Horkheimer's longing for the "*Ganz Andere*."[67] Mysticism cannot deny the utopia of an emancipated humanity, because *Deus absconditus* has *homo absconditus* as its mirror, and the infinite distance that separates us from the "wholly-Other" is also the infinite distance that separates us from ourselves: we have to be ourselves so that God may be the "wholly-Other."

Wirken Jesu.

66. Cf. Levinas, *Totalité et Infini*.
67. Cf. Horkheimer, *Die Sehnsucht nach dem ganz Anderem*.

Appendix E
God, the Future, and the Fundamentum *of History in Wolfhart Pannenberg*[1]

GOD AND THE RATIONAL CRITIQUE OF RELIGION

THE HISTORY OF WESTERN philosophy seems to point to the inevitability of atheism, to the inexorable advent of a godless *Zeitgeist*, capable of assuming the best of the theistic proposal, while at the same time depriving it of its "continent," of its expression in terms of a divinized entity that is transcendent to mankind: the human being is the true infinite, as Feuerbach envisioned in *The Essence of Christianity* (1841), and what used to be predicated of God has to be attributed to humanity as a whole (to its generic essence) in its openness towards a future which it is able to master.[2]

---

1. A version of this article has appeared in *The Heythrop Journal* (2012).

2. As Ernst Bloch remarked, Christianity itself leads to atheism, which keeps the deepest content of this religion without the "hypostasis" of God, liberating its utopian message from religious heteronomy. According to his famous aphorism "Nur ein Atheist kann ein guter Christ sein, gewiss aber auch: nur ein Christ kann ein guter Atheist sein" (cf. Bloch, *Atheismus im Christentum*, 87-98). On the influence of Bloch on the theologian Jürgen Moltmann and his proposal of a "theology of hope," cf. Moltmann, *Theology of Hope*; Marsch, *Diskussion über die "Theologie der Hoffnung,"* 11; Mardones, *Teología e Ideología*; Fraijó, *Jesús y los Marginados*, 201-15. The idea that modern European atheism is actually a "Christian" atheism is also present in Karl Löwith. According to this author, modern atheism is a "monotheistic" atheism, founded upon the radical separation of creator and creation. In a post-Christian world we have creation without creator. Behold the paradox of modern history: it has a Christian "origin [*Herkunft*]" but an anti-Christian "result [*Ergebnis*]." Cf. Löwith, *Weltgeschichte und Heilsgeschehen*, 184.

God, the Future, and the Fundamentum *of History in Wolfhart Pannenberg*

The criticism of Christianity by Feuerbach has found a courageous response in the work of the German theologian Wolfhart Pannenberg (1928-).[3] Pannenberg has tried to show, on the one hand, that the idea of God may not have been the result of an anthropomorphic projection (as a contestation of the genetic critique of religion) and, on the other, that it is possible to conceive of God in such a way that it does not become one entity in coexistence with others. In order to achieve this goal, Pannenberg uses the category of "futurity." According to him, theology and metaphysics are largely responsible for the emergence of the genetic criticism of religion, because both of them, at least in their classical expressions, have considered God as one substance among others [*als seines vorhandenen Seienden*], despite being endowed with eminent characteristics (infiniteness, omniscience, omnipotence). God has become "finalized." This reflection seems rather similar to Heidegger's denunciation of the oblivion of being in Western philosophy, replaced by the focus on "entity": God, instead of being treated as "the being," has been considered the most perfect entity. In addition to this, Pannenberg thinks that idealism has also contributed to the genetic criticism of religion, because it has underlined the primacy of self-consciousness as the foundation and truth of any form of awareness of an object, planting the seed so that any possible idea of the absolute should be regarded as a projection of self-consciousness.[4]

Nevertheless, the criticism of the idea of God cannot be artificially separated from the broader process defined by the suspicion about religion and the reaction against the *guerres de religion* that devastated Europe in the sixteenth and seventeenth centuries. The crisis of religion is not therefore solely the result of an intellectual dynamic, but also of the historical and social changes that put under scrutiny those political structures with which the Christian religion had been traditionally associated.[5] That religion was discredited made it necessary to find a new formulation for the bases of the unity of society and state, which now was going to be discovered in human nature. Religion was to become relegated to the

---

3. Cf. Pannenberg, "Das Heilige in der modernen Kultur," in *Beiträge zur systematischen Theologie*, 1:12.

4. Cf. Pannenberg, "Bewusstsein und Subjektivität," in *Metaphysik und Gottesgedanke*, 35. As Pannenberg writes: "Die Verbindung von Wissen und Selbsbewusstsein ist allerdings nicht immer schon für den Begriff des Wissens grundlegend gewesen. In den Anfängen griechischen Denkens war das Wissen ein Schauen des in sich selbst Ruhenden" (Ibid., 41).

5. Cf. Pannenberg, "Das Heilige in der modernen Kultur," in *Beiträge zur systematischen Theologie*, 1:12.

private sphere of the individual and, in contrast to most ancient cultures, in modernity, religion is no longer a fundamental reality. The human being can actually live without religion,[6] even if it is at the expense of what Peter Berger has called "the loss of meaning [*Sincere*]."[7]

A provisional answer to the challenge of Feuerbach's critique can consist of defending the idea that his judgment only affects the alienating representations or images of God, not its very notion. Theologians like Paul Tillich have tried to maintain some sort of conceptual core that goes beyond its historical representations. Tillich identifies this "core" with the foundation and the power of everything that exists.[8] However, and as Pannenberg points out, it is superfluous still to preserve the idea of God as the power of being, because this "potency" could be attributed to nature as totality instead of a reality that is hypothetically transcendent to the cosmos. God as the "power of being," in a romantic song to the fathomless abyss of all that exists, is subject to the same criticism that atheism launches against the representations of God as a personal being. The anthropological critique of theology is so compelling that there seems to be little room for the idea of God.

According to Pannenberg, the solution lies in the Bible, although not in a non-critical return to the sacred books of Judaism and Christianity as a sclerotic deposit of supernatural, revealed truths in a sentimental search of security and protection against the merciless attacks of modern rationality. Rather, what is needed is to interpret the Bible in light of the present reality. Pannenberg believes that the idea of God that is expressed by the Bible is inextricably linked to the Kingdom: God is the God of the Kingdom, a God of the future who leads history towards its eschatological consummation.

God is, for Pannenberg, the future to which all reality is opened. God does not become exhausted by the present, because the experience of God in history is never final: the definitive idea of God will only arrive once history has been consummated, once history has reached its true end. The atheistic critique of religion is therefore offering a priceless service: that of

---

6. Cf. ibid., 15.

7. Cf. Pannenberg, "Gottesbenbildichkeit und Bildung des Menschen," in *Grundfragen systematischer Theologie*, 2:209; "Eschatologie und Sinnerfahrung," in *Grundfragen systematischer Theologie*, 2:67. See also Pannenberg, *Die Erfahrung der Abwesenheit Gottes in der modernen Kultur*. On Peter Berger's views on "secularization" and "desecularization," cf. Berger, *Desecularization of the World*.

8. On God as the "power of being," cf. Tillich, *Systematic Theology*, 1:235–40.

obliging theology to clarify its idea of God.[9] The traditional proofs of the existence of God do not demonstrate the reality of God but the finiteness of the world and the human being.[10] From the structure of human subjectivity it is not possible to reach God but only to realize the problematic character [*Fraglichkeit*] of the human being as an open question.[11] Here, Pannenberg agrees with Hegel, for whom the proofs of the existence of God constitute a formal expression of the religious elevation [*Erhebung*] of the human being from finiteness to infiniteness.[12]

The association of God with the future in Pannenberg is connected with his attempt at elaborating an ontology of history that takes futurity as its basis. According to him, the problem of Bloch, who has also highlighted the centrality of the future, is that his *futurum* lacks an ontological autonomy: it is a psychological future founded upon the human wish. It is not a real *novum*. In Pannenberg, the future is self-subsistent, and it possesses an ontological consistency that enables it to become the hermeneutical clue to the world, history, and humanity. God *will be*: we cannot say, for the moment, that God is, since we would be representing the divinity as an existent entity in the present. The future is a power over the present, which keeps the present permanently open and undetermined. The future prevents the present from becoming enclosed by itself, from becoming "finitized." God is, for Pannenberg, "the power of the future," and because the future offers freedom, God can be regarded as the "origin [*Ursprung*] of freedom."[13] There has always been a future, and in this sense God is eternal, because the future has always existed. The opposition between time and eternity is overcome by the *eskhaton*, by the ultimate future, which is not to be replaced by a further future. Rather, it is a self-present, eternal, and free future.

The importance of eschatology resides in the possibility that it offers to "postpone" meaning about the individual and the collective life to the

---

9. Cf. Pannenberg, "Reden von Gott angesichts atheistischer Kritik," in *Gottesgedanke und menschliche Freiheit*, 41.

10. Cf. ibid., 46. Cf. Pannenberg, *Systematic Theology*, 1:63–118.

11. Cf. Pannenberg, "Anthropologie und Gottesfrage," in *Gottesgedanke und menschliche Freiheit*, 27. On the analysis of this position, cf. Koch, *Der Gott der Geschichte*, 180–210.

12. Cf. Hegel, *Vorlesungen über die Beweise vom Dasein Gottes*; cf. Fraijó, *Das Sprechen von Gott bei W. Pannenberg*, 120–32.

13. Cf. Pannenberg, "Reden von Gott angesichts atheistischer Kritik," in *Gottesgedanke und menschliche Freiheit*, 42. On God as future, cf. also Schillebeeckx, *Gott, die Zukunft des Menschen*, 87.

Appendix E

end of all of human history, as opposed to the existentialist perspective, in which, according to Pannenberg, any form of meaning is restricted to the realm of the individual experience of history as historicity [*Geschichtlichkeit*].[14] The object of religion is, for Pannenberg, the "totality of meaning of life [*Sinntotalität des Lebens*]." This idea seems to be closely related to Schleiermacher's depiction of religion as the sentiment of dependence upon an infinite, absolute reality, based on the acceptance that every individual being is part of larger whole, while, at the same time, such a whole, which is infinite, is present in every individual being. However, Pannenberg thinks that this totality cannot be understood as the totality of cosmic meaning but as the "unity of a divine reality [*Einheit einer göttlichen Wirklichkeit*]." The originality of Schleiermacher lies in his interpretation of religion through the lens of the experience of meaning, although Pannenberg believes that this hermeneutical approach is too individualistic, and it does not take into account the relevance of the historical process as such.[15] Pannenberg considers that Schleiermacher's analysis needs to be complemented by the examination of the historical nature of the human experience of meaning, as highlighted by Dilthey, in such a way that what is anticipated in every experience is the total meaning of reality, whose definitive form will only be decided in the ultimate future.[16]

Theology, for Pannenberg, has to leave behind hypnotic fascination with primeval time, with the protological moment of creation, in order courageously to open itself to the eschatological future.[17] The fear of this new paradigm might be justified, since the past is susceptible to control, whereas

---

14. Cf. Pannenberg, "Eschatologie und Sinnerfahrung," in *Grundfragen systematischer Theologie*, 2:74.

15. In any case, it needs to be noticed that the historical and collective dimensions of religious experience in general and the Christian idea of salvation in particular are not entirely absent from the thought of Schleiermacher, according to whom the Church is "Gesamtleben der Erlösung," and the "state of plenitude [*Vollendungszustand*] of the individual must take place together with the state of plenitude of *Gesamtleben*" (Weeber, *Schleiermachers Eschatologie*, 99). On the ecclesiology of Schleiermacher, cf. his *Der christliche Glaube*, 2:215–73, 274–40 (for the relationship between the church and the world), and 408–40 (for the relationship between ecclesiology and eschatology).

16. Cf. Pannenberg, "Eschatologie und Sinnerfahrung," in *Grundfragen systematischer Theologie*, 2:76–79. Pannenberg analyzes the philosophical and theological thought of Schleiermacher in *Schleiermachers Schwierigkeiten mit dem Schopfungsgedanken*, and in *Problemgeschichte der neueren evangelischen Theologie in Deutschland*.

17. A similar consideration on the liberating power of the historical perspective can be found in Dilthey, for whom "Die Geschichte macht uns frei, indem sie über Bedingtheit des aus unieren Lebensverlauf entstandenen Bedeutungsgeschichtspunktes erhebt" (*Der Aufbau der geschichtlichen Welt in den Geisteswissenschaften*, 311).

the future belongs to the sphere of all that remains unknown and is unpredictable. Religious discourse would lose its "doctrinal" force. Nevertheless, Pannenberg thinks that the future to which Christianity refers is luminous, for it has been anticipated as a present reality in the Incarnation of Christ. Hope, not angst, is to prevail. It is the world, not the future illuminated by Christian hope, that is obscure.[18] The future makes the human being free from the social structures that mankind has generated. The future allows for a rupture with the present and the inauguration of a new scenario.

However, and as an objection to the unquestionably suggestive approach of Pannenberg, it is hard to deny that his interpretation of God as "futurity" could be regarded as a strategy of self-immunization which tries to save, *in extremis*, the idea of God by alienating it from history as a not-yet that is nonetheless present in terms of the future of each time, something that inevitably flees from any possible thematization. This proposition resembles an attempt at finding some sort of permanent refuge for the idea of God, capable of exonerating it from any "relationship" to the present, by situating it in a future which, by its own nature, is ineluctably elusive for human thought. Is theology so intensely besieged by rational criticism that it is compelled to displace God to the future? Pannenberg is aware of this difficulty and he knows that his whole project could eventually fall into the same degree of uncertainty as classical theologies. The connection of God with the future makes it problematic to speak of the deity in terms of a personal being (what would be the role of prayer, for example?[19]). But, on the contrary, to retain a representation of God as a personal being is equally susceptible to criticism, as Feuerbach clearly showed.

Pannenberg thinks that it is still possible to attribute a personal nature to God, even if it is understood as identical with the power of the future. Conceiving of God as a personal being is justified, because our author considers that the idea of "personality" is not the result of a projection from the human realm to the numinous sphere. Rather, the procedure occurred inversely: human beings acquired conscience of their personality through assimilation of the divine as rooted in religious experience, so that the profane self-understanding of mankind is a "late product [*Spätprodukt*]" of the history of humanity. According to Pannenberg, human beings are religious by nature. This topic has been treated *in extenso* by the German theologian in his most recent writings, such as *Systematic*

---

18. Cf. Pannenberg, "Das Nahen des Lichts und die Finsternis der Welt" (*Beiträge zur systematischen Theologie*, 2:287).

19. Pannenberg deals with the topic of Christian spirituality in his *Christliche Spiritualität*.

Appendix E

Theology[20] and the second volume of *Beiträge zur systematischen Theologie*. Pannenberg is critical of authors who, like Émile Durkheim, defend the thesis that religion is a transitory phenomenon in human evolution, which will be finally overcome by the power of society.[21] He is also reluctant to believe that religion is the expression of a fundamental structure whose "language" would be totally secular. Religion is not an epiphany of human nature, and we are not secular beings on whom the religious element is eventually added on the basis of psychological or social circumstances. Rather, we are naturally religious. Pannenberg supports his considerations on the data provided by paleontology, ethnology, and history of culture, disciplines which would show, in his opinion, that humanity has been religious since the beginning of its rationality.[22] In any case, the constitutive priority of religion in human nature does not prove the existence of God, although Pannenberg thinks that it helps us realize, against the views of Feuerbach, that we are not secular beings who project their essence on a divine *alter ego* that possesses all the perfections that we lack.[23]

For Pannenberg, there are at least two possible interpretative hypotheses about the kind of reality that establishes the religious nature of man: it might be an inevitable illusion or the seal of its divine "source [*Herkunft*]." The latter is the Christian explanation: we have the idea of God because we

---

20. Cf. Pannenberg, *Systematic Theology*, 1:136-51.See also Pannenberg, *Sind wir von Natur aus religiös?*

21. According to Pannenberg, "der Mensch ist vom Natur aus religiös" ("Religion und menschliche Natur," in *Beiträge zur systematischen Theologie*, 2:270). For Durkheim, the "pan-sacredness" of primitive societies is substituted by society itself in the enlightened world, in such a way that religion is no longer necessary (cf. Pannenberg, "Das Heilige in der modernen Kultur," in *Beiträge zur systematischen Theologie*, 1:19). On the modern understanding of religion, cf. Pannenberg, "Macht der Mensch die Religion, oder macht die Religion den Menschen. Ein Rückblick auf die Diskussion des religionstheoretischen Arbeitskreises," in *Beiträge zur systematischen Theologie*, vol. II, 254-259.

22. Cf. Pannenberg, "Religion und menschliche Natur," In *Beiträge zur systematischen Theologie*, 2:261; "Das Heilige in der modernen Kultur," In *Beiträge zur systematischen Theologie*, 1:18.

23. Cf. Pannenberg, "Religion und menschliche Natur," In *Beiträge zur systematischen Theologie*, 2:270. Religion is therefore a fundamental projection, which cannot be derived from the alienation of the human conscience. This thesis is already present in his writings of the 1970s, such as *Gottesgedanke und menschliche Freiheit*, in which we read that "the history of human personality appears as a function of the history of religion (cf. Pannenberg, "Reden von Gott angesichts atheistischer Kritik," in *Gottesgedanke und menschliche Freiheit*, 46).

are creatures of God. Otherwise, his revelation would be an entirely "alien message [*fremde Botschaft*]" for us.[24]

Religion does not only refer to the separation between the sacred and the secular,[25] according to Pannenberg, but also to the *fundamentum* [*Grund*] of this world, to its "setting [*Ordnung*]" in the divine reality and its "reconciliation [*Versöhnung*]" with God: religion therefore points to the past, the present, and the future of the world in relation to God.[26] In any case, the religious element becomes expressed in different religions. As a Christian theologian, Pannenberg does not deny the fact that Christianity is one religion among others. Unlike Karl Barth in his dialectical theology and his radical contrasting of religion and revelation,[27] Pannenberg thinks that Christianity is indeed a religion, because it speaks about God, and the discourse about the divine constitutes the content of the religious conscience.[28] Also, Christianity admits the provisional character [*Vorläufigkeit*] of its

24. Cf. ibid. Pannenberg thinks that the explanation of religion in terms of a projection does not solve the problem of the origin of the idea of infinite in the human mind (Pannenberg, "Das Heilige in der modernen Kultur," in *Beiträge zur systematischen Theologie*, 1:19). As Descartes noticed in *Metaphysical Meditations*, third meditation, the concept of the finite logically presupposes that of infiniteness, but how is it possible that a finite being may conceive of something infinite? This difficulty makes Pannenberg reaffirm that religion must be a constitutive element of the human nature (cf. Pannenberg, "Das Heilige in der modernen Kultur," in *Beiträge zur systematischen Theologie*, 1:20). However, this proposal cannot ignore the fact that if this were true, it would be extremely complicated to justify the increasing presence of atheism in modern culture. Also, there is an important difference between regarding men as religious beings and deducing, based on this, their character of "creatures." Many religions do not, in fact, share the Judeo-Christian idea of creation.

25. Pannenberg believes that the distinction between the sacred and the profane is unable to explain why the religious conscience reaches such a duality. According to him, the binomial "sacred/profane" has to do with the "temporality of the religious experience [*Temporalität der religiösen Erfahrung*]." In the case of ancient Israel, it is closely associated to worship, which brings it back to some sort of mythical *Urzeit*, actualizing the "primordial mythical action of the deity [*das mythisch-urzeitliche Handeln der Gottheit*]." However, with the advent of prophetism the holiness of God transcends the realm of worship to be oriented to an eschatological future in which time and eternity will finally converge. Cf. Pannenberg, "Zeit und Ewigkeit in der religiösen Erfahrung Israels und des Christentums," in *Grundfragen systematischer Theologie*, 2:188–206.

26. Cf. ibid., 22.

27. The radical opposition between religion and revelation in Barth can be found in *Church Dogmatics* I.2. For a comparison of Barth's position with the discussions within Hindu theological traditions (such as *Mimamsa, Vaisnava Vedanta*, and *Saiva Vedanta*), cf. Clooney, *Hindu God, Christian God*, 129–62.

28. Cf. Pannenberg, "Das Christentum: Eine Religion unter anderen?," in *Beiträge zur systematischen Theologie*, 1:173.

knowledge about the eschatological revelation of God in Jesus Christ until the end of time has taken place.

However, Pannenberg believes that Christianity, even as a religion among others, has the obligation to proclaim the universal truth of the God revealed in Jesus Christ. In any case, Christianity possesses no privileged status over other religions or philosophies. Supernatural, divine revelation cannot be opposed to any "human religion": against dialectical theology, Pannenberg inserts Christianity within the horizon of the religions of the world and he also renounces offering a series of *a priori* conditions which, in a transcendental way, would enable the human subject to receive an eventual divine revelation, without paying attention to the phenomenological and historical constitution of different religions.[29] As I. Berten has noticed, Christianity, for Pannenberg, has to be comprehended in relation to the other religions of the world, the key problem being whether or not the God proclaimed by Christianity is capable of answering the question represented by what it is to be human.[30]

A THEOLOGICAL FUNDAMENTUM OF HISTORY?

In works such as "Heilsgeschehen und Geschichte" (1959) and *Offenbarung als Geschichte* (1961), Pannenberg insists on the substantial nature of history, which cannot be reduced, in his view, to a mere addition of individual historical experiences: *Geschichte* necessarily prevails over *Geschichtlichkeit*. This consideration marks a clear distance from the more existential perspective found in authors such as Heidegger and Bultmann.[31] This approach has two clear consequences: history can be properly regarded only as universal history (here, Pannenberg is very close to Hegel) and history cannot be secularized in the long term. The acceptance of a transcendental *fundamentum* of history is, for Pannenberg, the only possible way to defend the unity of the historical process.[32] The lens of a unitary history is, moreover, imperative if one wants to pose the question concerning the meaning of particular events.

---

29. Concerning the relationship of Christianity to the other religions of the world in Pannenberg, cf. *Systematic Theology*, 1:129–36, and his articles "Religion und Religionen," in *Beiträge zur systematischen Theologie*, 1:145–54; "Die Religionen als Thema der Theologie," in *Beiträge zur systematischen Theologie*, 1:160–72.

30. Cf. Berten, *Histoire, Révélation et Foi*, 14.

31. Cf. Fraijó, *El Sentido de la Historia*, 133.

32. Here, Pannenberg's position is close to the perspectiva of R. Wittram. Cf. Wittram, *Das Interesse an der Geschichte*, 135.

Pannenberg's rejection of any attempt at offering a purely secular understanding of history puts him in opposition to Hans Blumenberg.[33] If Romano Guardini had characterized modernity as the result of a process of secularization of Christianity[34] and Friedrich Gogarten had interpreted secularization as the effect of the Christian faith itself,[35] because the biblical conception of God deprived the world of its sacredness (an idea which seems to be closely related to Weber's "disenchantment of the world"), Blumenberg wants to break with the stigma of "illegitimacy" that has been thrown upon modernity through the category of "secularization." He prefers to speak in terms of "self-affirmation of reason [*Selbstbehaptung der Vernunft*]": modernity would be a "counter-proposal [*Gegenposition*]" to the theological absolutism of Christianity.[36]

According to Blumenberg, the notion of progress became an alternative to the failure of classical theodicy. Responsibility, in the discourse of modernity, is entirely human, with no attempt to explain how divine omnipotence and divine "omnibenevolence" may coexist. Pannenberg, on the contrary, believes that theodicy never acquired such a central role in Christianity as Blumenberg thinks, because theology has never exonerated God from the persistence of evil in the world. Rather, this religion hopes for a final "reconciliation [*Versöhnung*]" that will bring justice.[37] For Pannenberg, the Christian reflection on human freedom to choose between good and evil contributed to the emancipation of reason. Modernity, rather than reacting to the Christian idea of divine grace, rebelled against the positive, institutional structures of the ecclesiastical system, which had been denounced in the later Middle Ages by Meister Eckhart, Tauler, Bradwarine, and others, a criticism that became prominent and crucial with the advent of the Reformation.[38]

Pannenberg finds some positive aspects in the idea of secularization, especially those concerning human emancipation from tradition and

---

33. Cf. Pannenberg, "Die Christliche Legitimität der Neuzeit," in *Gottesgedanke und menschliche Freiheit*, 114–28.

34. Cf. Guardini, *Das Ende der Neuzeit*.

35. Cf. Gogarten, *Verhängnis und Hoffnung der Neuzeit*. On secularization, cf. Cox, *The Secular City*; Lübbe, *Säkularisierung*. For an examination of the so-called "theologies of secularization," cf. Camps, *Los Teólogos de la Muerte de Dios*; Dubach, *Glauben in säkularer Gesellschaft*.

36. Cf. Pannenberg, "Die Christliche Legitimität der Neuzeit," in *Gottesgedanke und menschliche Freiheit*, 116.

37. Cf. ibid., 119.

38. Cf. ibid., 125.

Appendix E

authority, but he thinks that if history is totally secularized it loses its *fundamentum*. However, he also wants to preserve the contingency of history, instead of submitting it to the fulfillment of a pre-established plan. He believes that there is *novum* in time and an ineluctable openness to the future. In any case, the future to which Pannenberg refers is an eschatological, consummated one, but if there is a *telos* that governs the historical process, where is contingency? The allusion to the category of anticipation of the eschatological future as a strategy to safeguard the openness of history in the present, while at the same time defending the fact that it is not left to randomness, does not solve the question at all, because history is still under the guidance of a higher rationality and is not actually susceptible to a real *novum*.

The latter problem is hardly answerable by philosophy. Pannenberg depends upon authors like Hegel and Dilthey, but he is, first of all, a Christian theologian, and he affirms that God is the *fundamentum* that grants unity and meaning to history. The philosophy of history of Pannenberg is therefore compelled to move into theological considerations. In this enterprise he finds an important ally: Karl Löwith, who in *Meaning in History* [*Weltgeschichte und Heilsgeschehen*], of 1949,[39] endorses the thesis that the modern philosophy of history is intrinsically bound to a series of "theological presuppositions [*theologische Voraussetzung*],"[40] which he discovers in authors like Voltaire (who wanted to study history not as a theologian looking for the imprints of divine providence but "comme historien et philosophe"),[41] Burckhardt, Marx,[42] and Hegel.[43] The Enlightenment kept the interpreta-

---

39. Cf. Pannenberg, "Christliche Anthropologie und Personalität," in *Beiträge zur systematischen Theologie*, 2:150–51.

40. Cf. Löwith, *Weltgeschichte und Heilsgeschehen*, 11–12.

41. Voltaire develops this perspective in his *Essai sur les Mœurs et l'Esprit des Nations et sur les Principaux Faits de l'Histoire depuis Charlemagnes jusqu'à Louis XIII*. According to Löwith, Vico and Voltaire "emanzipierten die irdische Geschichte von der himmlischen" (ibid., 175). In Vico, just as in Voltaire, the history of religion becomes subordinated to the history of civilization.

42. The presence of Judeo-Christian theology in Marx is clear for Löwith: "Der ganze Geschichtsprozess, wie er im 'Kommunistischen Manifest' dargestellt wird, spiegelt das allgemeine Schema der jüdischen-christlichen Interpretation der Geschichte als eines providentiellen Heilsgeschehens auf ein sinnvolles Endziel hin" (ibid., 48). In Marx, there is a struggle between Christ (the proletarians) and the anti-Christ (the bourgeoisie), and the proletarians possess, like Christ, a universal mission that has messianic connotations. Marx envisions a "kingdom of freedom" at the end of history, which is "ein Reich Gottes, ohne Gott—das Endziel des historischen Messianismus von Marx" (ibid., 46), so that, according to Löwith, "der historische Materialismus ist Heilsgeschichte in der Sprache der Nationalökonomie" (ibid., 48).

43. Löwith thinks that Hegel transforms the Christian theology of history into a

tion of history as a process oriented towards an end and, even though the subject of history was no longer divine will but human nature, *Les Lumières* inherited the outlook of providentialism, of patent Judeo-Christian roots, for they still conceived of the past as "preparation [*Vorbereitung*]" and the future as "fulfillment [*Erfüllung*]." This has been a common intellectual dynamic, at least until the emergence of a postmodern conscience that denies the existence of a final stage of history.[44] Modernity, according to Löwith, turns the category of salvation into an "impersonal teleology [*unpersönliche Teleologie*]" through the idea of progressive development,[45] in which each present period fulfils the previous historical preparation.

Pannenberg agrees with Löwith in pointing out that the importance of historical conscience in the West is largely indebted to the religious experience of Israel,[46] although the German theologian believes that Judeo-Christianity does not propose a *historia salutis* running parallel to secular history: the history of salvation is not a "supra-history" but, on account of its inherent aspiration to universality, is aimed at encompassing all possible events. An exclusively anthropocentric hermeneutics of history leads to its dissolution in individual history, since the only protagonist is the individual, with the result of "diminishing," and even destroying, historical consciousness.[47] In any case, and as a form of criticism of Pannenberg's remarks, it is extremely complicated to justify the idea that modernity has stunted historical conscience. The philosophies of Hegel and Marx are a good proof of the firm commitment of modernity to highlighting the inexorable centrality of history in all spheres of human life. It is clear, in any case, that the concerns of Pannenberg are basically related to the existentialist reduction of history into historicity that, in his opinion, is a manifestation of a common phenomenon: the progressive emancipation of human reason from God.

Pannenberg assumes Dilthey's idea of the priority of the whole over the part (which recalls Hegel, too), and he thinks that only the horizon of universal history enables the valuation of the meaning of each individual event. The isolation of different happenings responds to the need for a delimitation of the object of study of history, not to the truth of the intrinsic

---

speculative system (cf. ibid., 176). For a comparative study of the philosophies of history of Hegel and Marx, cf. Cohen, *Karl Marx's Theory of History*, 1–27.

44. On postmodernity, cf. Lyotard, *La Condition Postmoderne*.
45. Cf. Löwith, *Weltgeschichte und Heilsgeschehen*, 170.
46. Cf. Pannenberg, "Der Gott der Geschichte 2:118.
47. Cf. ibid.

Appendix E

interconnection of all its episodes. The theory of historical knowledge proposed by the English philosopher Robin George Collingwood (1889–1943) offers, according to Pannenberg, a solid basis to articulate these considerations on the unity of history.[48] Against historical positivism and its extrapolation of the hypothetical and deductive method of the natural sciences to the realm of historiography, Collingwood rejected the notion that the historian is exclusively centered upon individual events. The historian does not study isolated facts but connections. However, the emphasis on links might compromise a defense of the contingency of particular events. This is the reason why Pannenberg thinks that the interpretation of history as unity has to meet a series of conditions that may harmonize this position with the respect for the peculiarity of historical facts.

The former task is not easy, but Pannenberg is capable of indicating at least three models which, for sure, cannot be reconciled with the attempt at safeguarding the contingency and openness of history: historical evolutionism (history as the necessary display of an original core), the thesis that there are "structural typologies" (focused on cultures and historical cycles), and the idea of an "axial time," as proposed by Karl Jaspers, in which the fundamental categories of both Eastern and Western thought emerged.[49] Pannenberg thinks that Jaspers's position is a secularization of the Christian doctrine that the Incarnation constitutes the "focal point" of history, although he believes that a historical period (as the "axial time") cannot anticipate the eschatological end of history, because, unlike the figure of Jesus of Nazareth, it lacks internal unity.[50] Nevertheless, it is difficult to explain why the singular historical fact is the only legitimate aspect for anticipating the meaning of the totality of history. The demarcation of both the margins and the scope of a fact and an individual figure is not clear at all, especially from a perspective, like that of Pannenberg, which stresses, following Collingwood, the idea that history is a fabric of connections of facts. Moreover, from the approach of the theology of religious pluralism, it is even more complicated to argue that Christ must be the only definitive anticipation of a hypothetical *eskhaton* of history.

Pannenberg is convinced that those explanations that leave God aside are incapable of justifying the unity of history, but there is a legitimate question: does the historian need to commit himself to a theistic depiction? Isn't this attitude dangerous for the sake of scientific objectivity?

48. Cf. Collingwood, *The Idea of History*, of 1946.
49. Cf. Jaspers, *Vom Ursprung und Ziel der Geschichte*, of 1949.
50. This idea is detailed in "Heilsgeschehen und Geschichte."

Pannenberg does not pretend to subordinate scientific research to the acceptance of God as the foundation of history but, in practice if not in intent, the historian seems to have no other alternative than surrendering to divine reality: either he or she rejects the unity of history (refusing to acknowledge the deep connection between all events) or assimilates it without providing a sufficient rational basis for it. Pannenberg's theses may be more compelling for theologians than for historians. In any case, he agrees with Löwith in remarking that the question concerning the meaning of history is theologically grounded.[51] For Pannenberg, it is necessary to grant history a divine *fundamentum* and, in spite of the great challenge posed by the presence of evil and suffering in the world, he still believes that the reference to God allows for the envisioning of meaning for the course of times, since the idea of God represents the answer to the problem of the "sense [*Sinn*]" of reality as a whole.[52] Only God can grant history unity and meaning.[53] This is a courageous thesis which appears both in his early (like "Heilsgeschehen und Geschichte") and more recent writings (such as *Beiträge zur systematischen Theologie*). The central role that Pannenberg attributes to God in the elucidation of the nature of history, constitutes a valuable link between philosophy and theology of history, both of which converge, according to him, in the necessity of recognizing God as the *fundamentum* of history.

---

51. This thesis is also present in the analysis of the philosophy of history of the Frankfurt school elaborated by Theunissen (history as the process of emancipation of humanity; cf. *Der Andere*). Cf. Pannenberg, "Der Gott der Geschichte," in *Grundfragen systematischer Theologie*, 2:112.

52. Cf. Pannenberg, "Sinnerfahrung, Religion und Gottesgedanke," in *Beiträge zur systematischen Theologie*, 1:112.

53. On the importance of God as *fundamentum* of the unity of reality (as the encompassing process that integrates both nature and history), cf. Buller, *Unity of Nature and History in Pannenberg's Theology*, 63-79.

Appendix F
The Rose and Its Reason[1]

Die Rose ist ohne warum, sie blühet, weil sie blühet ... ("The rose does not have a reason, it blooms because it blooms ...")

—Angelus Silesius (1624–1677)

The mystics will never cease to puzzle us. One merely needs to venture into the texts of Saint Teresa and of San Juan de la Cruz, to introduce oneself within the metaphysical speculations of Meister Eckhart, to enfold oneself in the fascinating territory of Islamic Sufism, to plunge into the teachings of Sankara, or submerge oneself in the spiritual intensity radiating from the Rhenish mystics of the Low Middle Ages to be convinced of this. Yes, mysticism is a boundless source of surprise, a mystery incarnate in the form of letters, phrases, and discussions, which attempt to transmit a unique testimony that, by its nature, approaches the ineffable.

The capacity of mysticism to engender wonder in the minds of contemporary men and women, who are accustomed to pursuing strict processes of rationalization in all spheres of life—whereby the occult is relegated to a realm of mere fantasy or artistic creation—is indeed extraordinary. We are fully aware of our difficulty to consider the works of great mystic writers as anything more than exalted expressions of a strong psychological experience, as well as of the impassable barrier that science interposes between them and us. Yet, conversely, we also wish that there

---

1. A version of this article has appeared in *Apeira* 1 (2012) 83–87. This text has been generously translated from its original Spanish version ("La rosa y el porqué") by Mr. Étien Santiago.

truly existed a space for the indescribable, such that not everything be reducible to the often tyrannical dominion of intelligence. We would like to feel and learn only by feeling, for it is still true, as Pascal said, that the heart possesses reasons that reason cannot know. Thus a strange relationship exists between mysticism and our epoch: a nexus of love and hate, a vibrant enthusiasm for that which is inexpressible as well as for its intemperate opposite, before the vertigo produced by the sole idea that there might be an immeasurable abyss that human knowledge would never be able to exhaust.

The quote above by Silesius is indefinable. The rose lacks a reason why; it limits itself only to blooming, and it blooms because it blooms. Its own and exquisite explanation resides within itself, and it is useless to look for any justification transcending the basic fact that the rose blooms. Here the Leibnizian principle of sufficient reason, with its *nihil est sine ratione*,[2] finds itself vanquished. We are thus conquered by the captivating sameness of the rose, by the unbeatable power of the factual, which becomes elusive to us, and we rest in the melodious calm of harmony engendered by the absence of problematicity, by the annulment of all unknowns, which are transformed into something incongruous or even absurd. In such a setting, there is no room to investigate the reason for the rose. And, as a consequence, there is no room to investigate the reason for the world, which does exist, ever since it has been the world, and only the world that it is. From here stems the blatant tragedy of the philosopher, who cannot live without formulating questions, but whose curiosity inevitably leads down a path with no end—an unnecessary conundrum for his or her own head. How easy it would be to simply cower before the beauty of the rose, without saying a word, releasing ourselves to the peace generated by pure facts, without any mediation of understanding, abandoned to ourselves while letting other things interpellate us. Rather than depending on our lexicons and signs of interrogation, things in themselves would become the lively translation of our profuse vocabulary, and humanity could satisfy itself merely by directing its gaze at that which surrounds it, but at the same time would also cease its vehement endeavor to raise doubts about nature.

Yes, the rose blossoms, and let us not try to fathom why it does so, says the mystic. Let us deliver ourselves instead to the contemplation of blossoming itself; let us show confidence in the seductive magic of a reality that elucidates itself alone, and which does not require any human being to

---

2. "Nothing is without a reason."

Appendix F

stand in for the voice of those infinite spaces submerged in eternal silence. It is the mind that is empty, argues the mystic, whereas reality is blissfully replete of fruitful energy. The stark contrast Goethe noted between, on the one hand, the green and golden tree of life and, on the other hand, the grayness of theory also applies to this unyielding truth. Despite the numerous and divine inquires we initiate, on the behalf of all the things that we, like supplicants, painfully desire to know, the enigma of factuality stubbornly persists before us, as does the enigma regarding the degree of objectivity of one experience over another, of our own existence as beings upon this intractable earth.

Mystical "*Gelassenheit*"[3] is what he have here: an enraptured distraction, peaceful and almost hermit-like, renounces itself before what is, lies down amongst the green pastures and refuses to think, but only to feel—to feel life, to feel death, but not to investigate anything, because doing so would mean torment—while curtailing the anxiety of existence, sinking deep into despair when confronted with the thundering orphanhood of answers. We intend to know, but we are not sure if we are ready to undergo the ordeal that this entails. And yet, nonetheless, we do not abandon this sovereign task.

No, I cannot believe in the *Gelassenheit*, or accept that the rose stands without a reason, imposing itself upon me as if it were an unassailable wall. The rose is not a god to me, but only a miniscule part of this marvelous scenario in which I live, and which has entitled me to examine it. By doing so I also come to know myself, and I perceive that I am the one who creates the universe. The rose will continue to be an open question, and humanity cannot rest, because the grueling fatigue that results from its interrogation is a luminous sign of resplendent life, and we aspire to live as something more, more than the rose, which does not know why it blooms, when we intend to audaciously scrutinize the reasons why we live.

It is not that the rose is devoid of a reason, but rather that she eloquently defers the question of the 'why.' She is herself; she is the notable triviality that derives from the fundamental sameness of all being with itself, from the principle of identity. But she is not isolated, for she is not the only element in the vast cosmos. If the universe only were a rose, and no more, she would be her own question as well as her own answer. Yet within the colossal realm in which exists a humanity that survives by relentlessly enunciating that which remains unknown, and which advances along the path of time by constantly precipitating new topics, the rose cannot

3. "Serenity."

constitute an absolute, unqualified reality that escapes all interrogative faculties. Rather, the rose is a particular demonstration of the question defining the celestial firmament: "why do you exist, universe; and why you, instead of another?" And yes, I venture to suggest, due to this question I find myself commanded to investigate why the rose blossoms and to explore, with the minute tools that the venerable sciences offer us, the complex mechanisms underlying this biological process. Moreover, I search for the origin of all roses and all plants, of all living things, of the Earth, and, eventually, of our galaxy, in order to—oh, what a sublime abstraction!—climb all the way back to the obscure beginnings of the cosmos. Thus I link a hypothetically trivial act of philosophizing about a rose that blooms to a lucubration on the world as a cohesive whole, to why there is something rather than nothing, connecting everything to everything else. And here is the grandeur of the human mind, which, in the felicitous words of Aristotle, "is in a certain sense all things." By concatenation, one moves from the insignificant to the grandiose, for which nothing, neither human nor non-human, is alien.

Rose of mine, eternal mystery that you are, as you hold within yourself a unique witness to the universal arcane, continue blossoming; intoxicate us with the bountiful beauty of your petals. Yet do not oblige us to content ourselves with observing you as prisoners of overwhelming abnegation. Do not be so ruthless and ungrateful as to douse the untamed flame of the question that burns so ardently in us, which, if it were not to spill out into this vast world, would end up consuming us, devouring our fragile being.

No rose without an apparent reason could extinguish the legendary cry of a humanity that rebels against the contemptuous obscurity springing from the clamorous lack of answers. We want to know because we yearn to live; we exist to know, and, furthermore, to ask. No rose, regardless of how beautiful it might be, and no matter how closely it might embody the aesthetic ideal of philosophers and poets, should dare to annihilate this impulse born in us, and which will never languish. Unamuno was right when he wrote in *Del Sentimiento Trágico de la Vida en los Hombres y en los Pueblos* that "the visible universe, which is the son of the instinct of conservation, seems narrow, like a cage that is too small for me, and against whose bars my spirit presses in its agitation; there is not enough air to breathe. More, more, and always more, I want to be myself without ceasing to be so, and also to be others, to introduce myself in the totality of visible and invisible things, to extend myself into the boundlessness of

Appendix F

space and prolong myself into the endlessness of time. To not be everything, and forever, is like to not exist at all, or at least to be fully myself and to be so forever and ever. And to be all of myself is also to be all the others. Either everything or nothing!"

Bibliography

Adorno, Th. *Prismen: Kulturkritik und Gesellschaft*. Gesammelte Schriften 10. Frankfurt: Suhrkamp, 1997.
Aristotle, *Metaphysics*. Books 1–9. Translated by H. Tredennick. Loeb Classical Library. Cambridge: Harvard University Press, 1979.
Aristotle, *Nicomachean Ethics*. Translation (with historical introduction) by Christopher Rowe. Philosophical introduction and commentary by Sarah Broadie. Oxford: Oxford University Press, 2002.
Assmann, J. *Das kulturelle Gedächtnis: Schrift, Erinnerung und politische Identität in frühen Hochkulturen*. C. H. Beck Kulturwissenschaft. Munich: Beck, 1992.
———. *Moses the Egyptian: The Memory of Egypt in Western Monotheism*. Cambridge: Harvard University Press, 1997.
———. *The Price of Monotheism*. Translated by R. Savage. Stanford: Stanford University Press, 2010.
Augustine, Saint. *De Civitate Dei*, books 8–11. Bilingual edition. Translated by D. S. Wiesen. Loeb Classical Library. Cambridge: Harvard University Press, 1968.
Ayala, F., and Th. Dobzhansky, editors. *Studies in the Philosophy of Biology: Reduction and Related Problems*. Berkeley: University of California Press, 1974.
Barth, K. *Church Dogmatics*. Vol. 1.2, *The Doctrine of the Word of God*. Translated by G. T. Thomson and H. Knight. Edinburgh: T. & T. Clark, 1956.
Barthes, R. *Mythologies*. Translated by A. Lavers. New York: Hill & Wang, 1972.
Benjamin, W. "Theses on the Philosophy of History." In *Illuminations*, 253–64. Translated by H. Zohn. New York: Schocken, 1969.
Bensaïd, D. "L'Humanité au-delà du Capital." *Actuel Marx* 1 (2002) 139–46.
Benz, E., editor. *Rudolf Ottos Bedeutung für die Religionswissenschaft und die Theologie Heute: Zur Hundertjahrfeier seines Geburtstags*. Zeitschrift für Religions und Geistesgeschichte 14. Leiden: Brill, 1971.
Berdyaev, N. *The Meaning of History*. With a new introduction by M. Nemcova. New Brunswick, NJ: Transaction, 2006.
Berger, P., editor. *The Desecularization of the World: Resurgent Religion and World Politics*. Grand Rapids: Eerdmans, 1999.
Berten, I. *Histoire, Révélation et Foi: Dialogue avec Wolfhart Pannenberg*. Brussels: CEP, 1969.
Bloch, E. *Atheismus im Christentum: zur Religion des Exodus und des Reichs*. Gesamtausgabe 14. Frankfurt: Suhrkamp, 1968.
———. *The Principle of Hope*. Translated by N. Plaice et al. 3 vols. Oxford: Blackwell, 1986.

Bibliography

Blumenberg, H. *The Legitimacy of the Modern Age.* Translated by R. M. Wallace. Studies in Contemporary German Social Thought. Cambridge: MIT Press, 1983.

Bonhoeffer, D. *Akt und Sein. Transzendentalphilosophie und Ontologie in der systematischen Theologie.* Theologische Bücherei; Neudrucke und Berichte aus dem 20. Systematiche Theologie 5. Jahrhundert Munich: Kaiser, 1956.

Borges, J. L. *Ficciones.* Edited and with an introduction by Anthony Kerrigan. New York : Grove Weidenfeld, 1963.

Bourdeau, M. *Les Trois États: Science, Théologie et Métaphysique chez Auguste Comte.* Philosophie & théologie. Paris: Cerf, 2006.

Brandt, R. B. *The Philosophy of Schleiermacher: The Development of His Theory of Scientific and Religious Knowledge.* New York: Harper & Brothers, 1941.

Brentano, F. *Von der mannigfachen Bedeutung des Seienden nach Aristoteles.* Freiburg: Herder, 1862. Reprinted, Hildesheim: Olms, 1960.

Buller, C. A. *The Unity of Nature and History in Pannenberg's Theology.* Lanham MD: Rowman & Littlefield, 1996.

Bultmann, R. *The New Testament and Mythology and Other Basic Writings.* Selected, edited, and translated by S. M. Ogden. Philadelphia: Fortress, 1984.

Calderón de la Barca, P. *La Vida Es Sueño.* Edited by F. Antonucci. Barcelona: Crítica, 2008.

Camps, V. *Los Teólogos de la Muerte de Dios.* Barcelona: Nova Terra, 1968.

Camus, A. *Le Mythe de Sisyphe.* Paris: Gallimard, 1942.

Caputo, J. D. *The Mystical Element in Heidegger's Thought.* New York: Fordham University Press, 1986.

Carr, D. M. *The Formation of the Hebrew Bible: A New Reconstruction.* New York: Oxford University Press, 2011.

Certeau, M. de. *La Fable Mystique : XVIe–XVIIe Siècle.* Bibliothe[set grave]que des histoires. Paris : Gallimard, 1982.

Clooney, F. X. *Hindu God, Christian God: How Reason Helps Break Down the Boundaries between Religions.* Oxford: Oxford University Press, 2001.

Cohen, G. A. *Karl Marx's Theory of History: A Defence.* Princeton Paperbacks. Princeton: Princeton University Press, 2000.

Collingwood, R. G. *The Idea of History.* Oxford: Clarendon, 1946.

Collins, J.J. *Jewish Wisdom in the Hellenistic Age.* The Old Testament Library. Louisville: Westminster John Knox, 1997.

Collins, J. J., and G. E. Sterling, editors. *Hellenism in the Land of Israel.* Christianity and Judaism in Antinquity Series 13. Notre Dame: University of Notre Dame, 2001.

Cox, H. G. *The Secular City: Secularization and Urbanization in Theological Perspective.* New York: Macmillan, 1965.

Cullmann, O. *Christ and Time: The Primitive Christian Conception of Time and History.* Translated by F. V. Filson. Philadelphia: Westminster, 1950.

Deleuze, G. *Spinoza : "Immortalité et Éternité."* Lecture delivered on March 17th 1981. Online: http://www.webdeleuze.com/php/texte.php?cle=43&groupe=Spinoza&langue=1

Dennett, D. *Consciousness Explained.* Boston: Little, Brown, 1991.

Derrida, J. "Bonnes volontés de puissance (Une réponse à Hans-Georg Gadamer)." In *Revue Internationale de Philosophie* n. 151 (1984) 341–43.

Dilthey, W. *Der Aufbau der geschichtlichen Welt in den Geisteswissenschaften* Gesammelte Schriften 7. Frankfurt: Suhrkamp, 1970.

Bibliography

———. *Einleitung in die Geisteswissenschaften: Versuch einer Grundlegung für das Studium der Gesellschaft und der Geschichte.* Gesammelte Schriften 1. Stuttgart: Teubner, 1959.

Dubach, A. *Glauben in säkularer Gesellschaft: Zum Thema Glaube und Säkularisierung in der neueren Theologie, besonders bei Friedrich Gogarten.* Europäische Hochschulschriften 23. Theologie 17. Bern: Lang, 1973.

Durkheim, É. *The Elementary Forms of the Religious Life.* Translated by J. W. Swain. London: Allen & Unwin, 1976.

Einstein, A. "Why Socialism?" *Monthly Review* 1 (May 1949) n.p.

Eliade, E. *The Myth of the Eternal Return: Cosmos and History.* Translated by W. R. Trask, with a new introduction by J. Z. Smith. Princeton: Princeton University Press, 2005.

———. *The Sacred and the Profane: The Nature of Religion.* Translated by W. R. Trask. New York: Harcourt Brace, 1959.

Eliot, T. S. *Choruses from the Rock.* In *Collected Poems 1909–1935.* New York: Harcourt, Brace, 1936.

Erikson, E. *Young Man Luther: A Study in Psychoanalysis and History.* New York: Norton, 1958.

Evans, C. A., and E. Tov, editors. *Exploring the Origins of the Bible: Canon Formation in Historical, Literary, and Theological Perspective.* Acadia Studies in Bible and Theology. Grand Rapids: Baker Academic, 2008.

Feuerbach, F. *The Essence of Christianity.* Translated by G. Eliot. 1854. Reprinted, Mineola, NY: Dover, 2008.

Foucault, M. *Philosophie. Anthologie.* Paris: Gallimard, 2004.

Fraijó, M. *Das Sprechen von Gott bei W. Pannenberg.* Tübingen: Fotodrück Präzis Barbara v. Spangenberg, 1976.

———. *El Sentido de la Historia: Introducción al Pensamiento de W. Pannenberg.* Madrid: Cristiandad, 1986.

———. *Jesús y los Marginados: Utopía y Esperanza Cristiana.* Madrid: Cristiandad, 1985.

Frazer, J. G. *The Golden Bough: A Study in Comparative Religion.* Canongate Classicsl 114. Edinburgh: Canongate, 2004.

Freeman, K. *Ancilla to the Pre-Socratic Philosophers: A Complete Translation of the Fragments in Diels Fragmente der Vorsokratiker.* Oxford: Blackwell, 1956.

Freud, S. *Civilization and Its Discontents.* Standard Edition of the Complete Psychological Works of Sigmund Freud 21. Translated by J. Strachey, in collaboration with A. Freud. London: Hogarth, 1961.

———. *The Future of an Illusion.* Standard Edition of the Complete Psychological Works of Sigmund Freud 21. Translated by J. Strachey, in collaboration with A. Freud. London: Hogarth, 1961.

———. *Introductory Lectures on Psychoanalysis.* Translated and edited by J. Strachey; with a biographical introduction by P. Gay. New York: Norton, 1989.

———. *Moses and Monotheism.* Standard Edition of the Complete Psychological Works of Sigmund Freud 23. Translated by J. Strachey, in collaboration with A. Freud. London: The Hogarth Press, 1961.

———. *Totem and Taboo.* Standard Edition of the Complete Psychological Works of Sigmund Freud 13. Translated by J. Strachey, in collaboration with A. Freud. London: Hogarth, 1961.

Bibliography

Gadamer, H. G. "Et pourtant, puissance de la bonne volonté (Une réplique à Jacques Derrida." *Revue Internationale de Philosophie* n. 151 (1984) 341–43.

———. *Truth and Method*. 2nd rev. ed. Translation revised by J. Weinsheimer and D. G. Marshall. New York: Continuum, 1993.

Gay, P. *Freud for Historians*. New York: Oxford University Press, 1985.

Geertz, C. *Local Knowledge: Further Essays in Interpretative Anthropology*. New York: Basic Books, 2000.

Goethe, J. W. von. *Roman Elegies*. In *Goethe's Works*. Vol. 1, *Poems*. Edited by Hjalmar Hjorth Boyesen. 5 vols. Philadelphia: Barrie, 1885. Online: http://oll.libertyfund.org/?option=com_staticxt&staticfile=show.php%3Ftitle=2110&chapter=162946&layout=html&Itemid=27/.

Gogarten, F. *Verhängnis und Hoffnung der Neuzeit: die Säkularisierung als theologisches Problem*. Stuttgart: Friedrich Vorwek, 1953.

Gómez, C. J. *El Teísmo Moral de Kant*. Madrid: Cristiandad, 1983.

Gómez, C. *Freud, Crítico de la Ilustración*. Madrid: Crítica, 1998.

González de Mendoza, R. *Stimmung und Transzendenz: Die Antizipation der existenzialanalytischen Stimmungsproblematik bei Ignatius von Loyola*. Berlin: Duncker & Humblot, 1970.

Green, R. M. "Ernst Bloch's Revision of Atheism." *Journal of Religion* 49 (1969) 128–35.

Greimas, A. J. *On Meaning: Selected Writings in Semiotic Theory*. Translated by P. J. Perron and F. H. Collins. Open Linguistics Series. London: Pinter, 1987.

———. *Structural Semantics: An Attempt at a Method*. Translated by D. McDowell et al. Lincoln: University of Nebraska Press, 1983.

Guardini, R. *Das Ende der Neuzeit: Ein Versuch zur Orientierung*. 2nd ed. Basel: Hess, 1950.

Habermas, J. *Technik und Wissenschaft als "Ideologie."* Frankfurt: Suhrkamp, 1969.

———. *The Theory of Communicative Action*. 2 vols. Translated by Th. McCarthy. Cambridge: Polity, 1986–1989.

Hanson, P. D. *The Dawn of Apocalyptic: The Historical and Sociological Roots of Jewish Eschatology*. Philadelphia: Fortress, 1975.

Hartmann, N. *Ethik*. Berlin: de Gruyter, 1926.

———. *Zur Grundlegung der Ontologie*. Berlin: de Gruyter, 1965

Hegel, G. W. F. *Aesthetics: Lectures on Fine Art*. 2 vols. Translated by T. M. Knox. Oxford: Clarendon, 1975.

———. *Elements of the Philosophy of Right*. Edited by A. W. Wood. Translated by H. B. Nisbet. Cambridge Texts in the History of Political Thought. Cambridge: Cambridge University Press, 1991.

———. *Encyclopaedia of the Philosophical Sciences in Basic Outline*. Translated and edited by K. Brinkmann and D. O. Dhalstrom. Cambridge Hegel Translations. Cambridge: Cambridge University Press, 2010.

———. *Lectures on the Philosophy of Religion*. Translated by R. F. Brown et al. Berkeley: University of California Press, 1988.

———. *Lectures on the Philosophy of World History*. Translated by H. B. Nisbet. Cambridge Studies in the History and Theory of Politics. Cambridge: Cambridge University Press, 1975.

———. *Phenomenology of Spirit*. Translated by A. V. Miller with analysis of the text and foreword by J. N. Findlay. Oxford: Oxford University Press, 1977.

———. *The Science of Logic*. Translated and edited by G. di Giovanni. Cambridge Hegel Translations. Cambridge: Cambridge University Press, 2010.
———. *Vorlesungen über die Beweise vom Dasein Gottes*. Philosophische Bibliothek 64. Hamburg: Meiner, 1966.
Heidegger, M. *Being and Time*. Translated by J. M. Macquarrie and E. Robinson. Oxford: Blackwell, 1973.
———. *Holzwege*. Frankfurt: Klostermann, 1950.
———. *Identität und Differenz*. Pfullingen: Neske, 1957.
———. "Interview with *Der Spiegel*." In *The Heidegger Reader*, edited by G. Figal, 313–33. Translated by J. Veith. Studies in Continental Thought. Bloomington: Indiana University Press, 2009.
———. *Introduction to Metaphysics*. Translated by G. Fried and R. Polt. New Haven: Yale University Press, 2000.
———. *Letter on Humanism*. In *Basic Writings*, edited by D. F. Krell, 213–66. New York: Harper & Row, 1977.
———. *Der Satz von Grund*. Pfullingen: Neske, 1965.
———. *Vorträge und Aufsätze*. Pfullingen: Neske, 1978.
Heine, H. *Der Rabbi von Bacherach: Ein Fragment*. Frankfurt: Insel, 1985.
Hengel, M. *Judentum und Hellenismus: Studien zu ihrer Begegnung unter besonderer Berücksichtigung Palästinas bis zur Mitte des 2. Jh. v. Ch.* Wissenschaftliche Unterschungen zum Neuen Testament 10. Tübingen: Mohr, 1969.
Hjelde, S. *Das Eschaton und die Eschata: Eine Studie über Sprachgebrauch und Spracherwirrung in protestantischer Theologie von der Orthodoxie bis zur Gegenwart*. Beiträge zur evangelischen Theologie 102. Munich: Kaiser, 1987.
Horkheimer, M. *Anhelo de Justicia. Teoría Crítica y Religión*. Edited by J. J. Sánchez. Madrid: Trotta, 2000.
Hume, D. *A Treatise of Human Nature*. London, 1739.
Hyppolite, J. *Genèse et Structure de la Phénoménologie de l'Esprit de Hegel*. Philosophie de l'esprit. Paris : Aubier, 1946.
Jaspers, K. *Vom Ursprung und Ziel der Geschichte*. Zurich: Artemis, 1949.
John of the Cross, Saint. *Cántico Espiritual y Poesía Completa*. Edited by P. Elia and M. J. Mancho, with a preliminary study by D. Ynduráin. Barcelona: Crítica, 2002.
Kandel, E. *In Search of Memory: The Emergence of a New Science of Mind*. London: Norton, 2006.
Kandel, E. R. et al., editors. *Principles of Neural Science*. New York: McGraw-Hill Health Professionals Division, 2000.
Kant, I. *Critique of Judgement*. Translated by J. C. Meredith. Revised, edited, and introduced by N. Walker. Oxford World's Classics. Oxford: Oxford University Press, 2007.
———. *Critique of Practical Reason*. Translated by W. S. Pluhar. Indianapolis: Hackett, 2002.
———. *Critique of Pure Reason*. Translated, edited, with an introduction by M. Weigelt. Penguin Classics. London: Penguin, 2007.
———. *Groundwork of the Metaphysics of Morals*. Translated and analysed by H. J. Paton. New York: Harper Perennial Modern Thought, 2009.
———. *Kants Schrift: Das Ende aller Dinge*. Edited by H. A. Salmony. Zurich: EVZ, 1962.

Bibliography

Katz, S. T., editor. *Mysticism and Religious Traditions*. New York: Oxford University Press, 1983.
Kaufman, G. *In Face of Mystery: A Constructive Theology*. Cambridge: Harvard University Press, 1993.
Kirschner, M. W., and J. C. Gerhart. *The Plausibility of Life: Resolving Darwin's Dilemma*. New Haven: Yale University Press, 2005.
Koch, Ch. *The Quest for Consciousness. A Neurobiological Approach*. Denver: Roberts, 2004.
Koch, K. *Der Gott der Geschichte: Theologie der Geschichte bei Wolfhart Pannenberg als Paradigma einer philosophischen Theologie in ökumenischer Perspektive*. Tübinger Theologische Studien 32. Mainz: Grünewald, 1988.
Korsgaard, Ch. M. *Creating the Kingdom of Ends*. Cambridge: Cambridge University Press, 1996.
Koziel, B. Z. *Apokalyptische Eschatologie als Zentrum der Botschaft Jesus und der frühen Christen? Ein Diskurs zwischen Exegese, Kulturphilosophie und systematischer Theologie über die bleibende Bedeutung einer neuzeitlichen Denklinie*. Bamberger theologische Studien 33. Frankfurt: Lang, 2007.
Kuhn, Th. *The Structure of Scientific Revolutions*. Chicago: University of Chicago Press, 1970.
Lacan, J. *The Ethics of Psychoanalysis, 1959–1960*. Translated by D. Porter. New York: Norton, 1997.
Legros, R. *Le Jeune Hegel et la Naissance de la Pensée Romantique*. Ousia 4. Brussels: Ousia, 1981.
Leibniz, G. W. *Discourse on Metaphysics and Other Essays*. Edited and Translated by D. Garber and R. Ariew. Indianapolis: Hackett, 1991.
Levinas, É. *Totalité et Infini. Essai sur l'Exteriorité*. Phaenomenologica: collection publiée sous le patronage des Centes d'archives-Husserl 8. The Hague: Nijhoff, 1961.
Löwith, K. *Meaning in History: The Theological Implications of the Philosophy of History*. Chicago: University of Chicago Press, 1949.
———. *Von Hegel zu Nietzsche: Der revolutionäre Bruch im Denken des neuzehnten Jahrhunderts*. Hamburg: Meiner, 1978.
———. *Weltgeschichte und Heilsgeschehen: Die theologischen Voraussetzungen der Geschichtsphilosophie*. 2nd ed. Urban-bücher 2. Stuttgart: Kohlhammer, 1953.
Lübbe, H. *Säkularisierung: Geschichte eines ideenpolitischen Begriffs*. Freiburg: Alber, 1965.
Luc, L.-P. "Le statut philosophique du 'Tübinger Fragment.'" *Hegel Studien* 16 (1981) 69–98.
Lucas, J. "Minds, Machines and Gödel." *Philosophy* 36 (1961) 112–27.
Lyotard, J.-F. *La Condition Postmoderne: Rapport sur le Savoir*. Collection «Critique.» Paris: Minuit, 1979.
Mackie, J. "Evil and Omnipotence." *Mind* 254 (1955) 200–212.
Marcel, G. *The Mystery of Being*. Translated by G. S. Fraser. South Bend, IN: St. Augustine's, 2001.
Marcuse, H. *Eros and Civilization: A Philosophical Inquiry into Freud*. Humanitas: Beacon Studies in the Humanities. Boston: Beacon, 1955.

Mardones, J. M. *Teología e Ideología. Confrontación de la Teología Política de la Esperanza de J. Moltmann con la Teoría Crítica de la Escuela de Frankfurt*. Bilbao: Mensajero, 1979.
Marsch, W.-D. *Diskussion über die "Theologie der Hoffnung."* Munich: Kaiser, 1967.
Marx, K. *A Contribution to the Critique of Hegel's Philosophy of Right*. Collected Works 3. New York: International Publishers, 1976.
―――. *Critique of the Gotha Program*. Library of Marxist-Leninist Classics. Moscow: Foreign Languages, 1954.
Marx, K., and F. Engels. *The Holy Family, or, Critique of Critical Critique*. Moscow: Foreign Languages, 1956.
―――. *The Communist Manifesto*. Edited with an introduction and notes by D. McLellan. Oxford World Classics. Oxford: Oxford University Press, 2008.
Mayr, E. *The Growth of Biological Thought*. Cambridge: Harvard University Press, 1982.
Mill, J. S. *On Liberty*. Edited by A. S. Kahan. Bedford Series in History and Culture. Boston: Bedford/St. Martins, 2008.
Moltmann, J. *A Theology of Hope: On the Grounds and Implications of Christian Eschatology*. Translated by J. W. Leitch. San Francisco: HarperSanFrancisco, 1991.
Monod, J. *Chance and Necessity: An Essay on the Natural Philosophy of Modern Biology*. Translated by A. Wainhouse. New York: Knopf, 1971.
Nagel, Th. "What Is It Like to Be a Bat?" *Philosophical Review* 83 (1974) 435–50.
Neruda, P. "Pablo Neruda: Nobel Lecture." Website: Nobelprize.org. Online: http://www.nobelprize.org/nobel_prizes/literature/laureates/1971/neruda-lecture.html.
―――. "Towards the Splendid City." In *Nobel Lectures: Literature 1968–1980*, edited by T. Frängsmyr and S. Allén, n.p. Singapore: World Scientific, 1993.
Newton, I. *Mathematical Principles of Natural Philosophy*. Translated by R. Thorp. London: Dawsons, 1969.
Nietzsche, F. *Thus Spoke Zarathustra: A Book for All and None*. Edited by A. del Caro, R. B. Pippin. Translated by A. del Caro. Cambridge Texts in the History of Philosophy. Cambridge: Cambridge University Press, 2006.
―――. *Twilight of the Idols, or How to Philosophize with a Hammer*. Translated with an introduction and notes by D. Large. Oxford World's Classics. Oxford: Oxford University Press, 2008.
Ortega y Gasset, J. "Guillermo Dilthey y la Idea de la Vida." In *Obras Completas* 6:165–213. Madrid: Revista de Occidente, 1964.
―――. *Historia como Sistema y del Imperio Romano*. Madrid: Revista de Occidente, 1942.
Otto, R. *Aufsätze zur Ethik*. Edited by J. S. Boozer. Munich: Beck, 1981.
―――. *Das Gefühl des Über-weltlichen (sensus numinis)*. Munich: Beck, 1932.
―――. *Gottheit und Gottheiten der Arier*. Aus der Welt der Religion . . . Religionswissenschaft 20. Giessen: Töpelmann, 1932.
―――. *The Idea of the Holy*. Translated by J. W. Harvey. Oxford: Oxford University Press, 1958. *Das Heilige: Über das Irrationale in der Idee des Göttlichen und sein Verhältnis zum Rationalen*. Beck'sche Reihe 328. Munich: Beck, 2004.
―――. *India's Religion of Grace and Christianity*. Translated by F. H. Foster. London: Student Christian Movement Press, 1930. *Die Gnadenreligion Indiens und das Christentum. Vergleich und Unterscheidung*. Munich: Beck, 1930.

Bibliography

———. *The Kingdom of God and the Son of Man.* Translated by F. V. Filson and B. L. Woolf. Boston: Starr King, 1957. (Orig. pub.: *Reich Gottes und Menschensohn: Ein religions-geschichtlicher Versuch.* Munich: Beck, 1934).

———. *Leben und Wirken Jesu: nach historisch-kritischer Auffassung.* Göttingen: Göttingen: Vandenhoeck & Ruprecht, 1902.

———. *The Life and Ministry of Jesus: According to the Historical and Critical Method.* Translated by H. J. Whitby. Chicago: Open Court, 1908.

———. *Mysticism East and West: A Comparative Analysis of the Nature of Mysticism.* Translated by B. L. Bracey and R. C. Payne. New York: Macmillan, 1972. *West-Östliche Mystik: Vergleich und Unterscheidung zur Wesensdeutung.* Bücherei der christlichen Welt. Gotha: Klotz, 1926.

———. *Naturalism and Religion.* Translated by J. A. Thomson an M. R. Thomson. London: Williams and Norgate, 1907. *Naturalistische und religiöse Weltansicht.* Lebensfragen : Schriften und Reden 2. Tübingen: Mohr/Siebeck, 1904.

———. *The Philosophy of Religion based on Kant and Fries.* Translated by E.B. Dicker. London: Williams Norgate, 1931. *Kantisch-Fries'sche Religionsphilosophie. Religionsphilosophie und ihre Anwendung auf die Theologie: zur Einleitung in die Glaubenslehre für Studenten der Theologie.* Tübingen: Mohr, 1909.

———. *Verantwortliche Lebensgestaltung: Gespräche mit Rudolf Otto über Frage der Ethik.* Edited by K. Küssner. Stuttgart: Kohlhammer, 1943.

———. *Visnu-Narayana.* Religiöse stimmen der völker. . .[1] Die Religion des alten Indien. Jena: Diederichs, 1917.

Pals, D. L. *Eight Theories of Religion.* 2nd ed. New York: Oxford University Press, 2006.

Panikkar, R. *Invitació a la Saviesa.* Barcelona: Proa, 1997.

Pannenberg, W. *Anthropologie in theologischer Perspektive.* Göttingen: Vandenhoeck & Ruprecht, 1983.

———. *Beiträge zur systematischen Theologie.* 3 vols. Göttingen: Vandenhoeck & Ruprecht, 1999.

———. *Christliche Spiritualität: theologische Aspekte.* Kleine Vandenhoeck-Reihe 1519. Göttingen: Vandenhoeck & Ruprecht, 1986.

———, editor. *Die Erfahrung der Abwesenheit Gottes in der modernen Kultur.* Göttingen: Vandenhoeck & Ruprecht, 1984.

———. "Heilsgeschehen und Geschichte." *Kerygma und Dogma* 5 (1959) 218–37. 259–88.

———. *Gottesgedanke und menschliche Freiheit.* Göttingen: Vandenhoeck & Ruprecht, 1972.

———. *Grundfragen systematischer Theologie. Gesammelte Aufsätze 2.* Göttingen: Vandenhoeck & Ruprecht, 1980.

———. *Metaphysik und Gottesgedanke.* Kleine Vandenhoeck-Reihe 1532. Göttingen: Vandenhoeck und Ruprecht, 1988.

———. *Problemgeschichte der neueren evangelischen Theologie in Deutschland: von Schleiermacher bis zu Barth und Tillich.* Uni-Taschenbücher 1979. Göttingen: Vandenhoeck und Ruprecht, 1997.

———, editor. *Sind wir von Natur aus religiös?* Schriften der Katholischen Akademie in Bayern 120. Düsseldorf: Patmos, 1986.

———. *Schleiermachers Schwierigkeiten mit dem Schopfungsgedanken.* Sitzungsberichte /Bayerische Akademie der Wissenschaften, Philosophisch-Historische Kl.3.; Jahrg. 1996, 3. Munich: Bayerischen Akademie der Wissenschaften, 1996.

———. *Systematic Theology*. 3 vols. Translated by G. W. Bromiley. Grand Rapids: Eerdmans, 1991–1998.

———. *Theology and the Kingdom of God*. Philadelphia: Westminster, 1969.

Paredes, M. C. "G. W. F. Hegel: el 'Fragmento de Tubinga.'" *Revista de Filosofía* 11 (1994) 139–76.

Paolucci, H. *Hegel: On the Arts; Selections from G. W. F. Hegel's "Aesthetics or Philosophy of Fine Arts," abridged and Translated with an Introduction by H. Paolucci*. Smyrna, DE: Griffon House, 2001.

Pascal, P. *Pensées*. Paris: Classiques Garniers, 2010.

Patil, P. *Against a Hindu God: Buddhist Philosophy of Religion in India*. New York: Columbia University Press, 2009.

Paz, O. *El Arco y la Lira*. Mexico: Fondo de Cultura Económica, 1986.

Plato. *The Symposium*. Translated with an analysis by R. E. Allen. The Dialogues of Plato 2. New Haven: Yale University Press, 1991.

Popper, K. R. *Objective Knowledge: An Evolutionary Approach*. Oxford: Clarendon, 1972.

Pushkin, A. *The Complete Works of Alexander Pushkin*. 15 vols. Downham Market, England: Milner, 1999–2003.

Rahner, K. *Schriften zur Theologie*. Vol. 6. Einsiedeln: Benziger, 1960.

Rateau, P., editor. *L'Idée de Théodicée de Leibniz à Kant: Héritage, Transformations, Critiques*. Studia Leibnitiana Sonderheft 36. Stuttgart: Steiner, 2009.

———. *La Question du Mal chez Leibniz: Fondements et Élaboration de la Théodicée*. Paris: Champion, 2008.

Rilke, R. M. *Sämtliche Werke*. 6 vols. Frankfurt: Insel, 1955–1966.

Robinson, J. M., and H. Koester. *Trajectories through Early Christianity*. Philadelphia: Fortress, 1971.

Rosenberg, A., and R. Arp, editors. *Philosophy of Biology: An Anthology*. Blackwell Philosophy Anthologies 32. Chichester: Wiley-Blackwell, 2010.

Russell, B. *Why I Am Not a Christian, and Other Essays on Religion and Related Subjects*. With a new preface by S. Blackburn. Routledge Classics. London: Routledge, 2004.

———. "A Free Man's Worship." In *The Basic Writings of Bertrand Russell*, edited by L. E. Dennon and R.E. Egner, 38–44. London: Allen & Unwin, 1961.

Russell, D. S. *Divine Disclosure: An Introduction to Jewish Apocalyptic*. London: SCM, 1992.

Sartre, J.-P. *Being and Nothingness: An Essay on Phenomenological Ontology*. Translated by H. E. Barnes. London: Routledge, 2003.

———. *Critique of Dialectical Reason: Theory of Practical Ensembles*. Translated by A. Sheridan-Smith. Edited by J. Rée. London: NLB, 1976.

Scheler, M. *Die Stellung des Menschen im Kosmos*. Berna: Francke, 1978.

Schelling, F. W. J. *Werke*. 10 vols. in 11 bks. Historisch-kritische Ausgabe. Reihe 1. Stuttgart: Frommann-Holzboog, 1976.

Schillebeeckx, E. *Gott, die Zukunft des Menschen*. Mainz: Grünewald, 1969.

Schleiermacher, F. *Der christliche Glaube: nach den Grundsätzen der evangelischen Kirche im Zusammenhange dargestellt*. De Gruyter Texte. Berlin: de Gruyter, 2008.

———. *On Religion: Speeches to Its Cultured Despisers*. Translated and edited by R. Crouter. Cambridge Texts in the History of Philosophy. 2nd ed. Cambridge: Cambridge University Press, 1996.

Bibliography

Schluchter, W. *Die Entzauberung der Welt: sechs Studien zu Max Weber.* Tübingen: Mohr/Siebeck, 2009.

Schopenhauer, A. *The World as Will and Representation.* Translated by E. F. J. Payne. New York: Dover, 1969.

Searle, J. "Mind, Brain, Programs." *Behavioral and Brain Sciences* 3/3 (1980) 417–57.

Sen, A. "Rational Fools: A Critique of the Behavioural Foundations of Economic Theory." *Philosophy and Public Affairs* 6/4 (1977), 317–44.

Sen, A. "Equality of What?" In *The Tanner Lectures on Human Values*, edited by S. M. McMurrin, 195–220. Salt Lake City: University of Utah Press, 1980.

———. *The Idea of Justice.* Cambridge: Belknap, 2009.

Sherrington, C. S. *Man on His Nature.* Cambridge: Cambridge University Press, 1940.

Silesius, A. *Cherubinischer Wandersmann, Oder, Geistreiche Sinn und Schlussreime.* Edited by L. Gnädinger. Manesse Bibliothek der Weltliteratur. Zurich: Manesse, 1986.

Smith, W. K. *The Meaning and End of Religion: A New Approach to the Religious Tradition of Mankind.* New York: Macmillan, 1963.

Spinoza, B. de. *Complete Works.* With translations by S. Shirley. Edited, with introduction and notes, by M. L. Morgan. Indianapolis: Hackett, 2002.

Stannard, D. *Shrinking History: on Freud and the Failure of Psychohistory.* New York: Oxford University Press, 1980.

Stauffer, R. C., editor. *Charles Darwin's Natural Selection: Being the Second Part of His Big Species Book Written from 1856 to 1858.* London: Cambridge University Press, 1975.

Suter, J.-F. *Philosophie et Histoire chez Wilhelm Dilthey: Essai sur le Problème de l'Historicisme.* Studia philosophica; Jahrbuch der Schweizerischen Philosphischen Gesellschaft. Supplementum 8. Basel: Recht & Gesellschaft, 1960.

Taliaferro, Ch et al., editors. *A Companion to Philosophy of Religion.* 2nd ed. Blackwell Companions to Philosophy 9. Chichester: Wiley-Blackwell, 2010.

Taylor, Ch. *Hegel.* Cambridge: Cambridge University Press, 1977.

Teilhard de Chardin, P. *The Phenomenon of Man.* With an introduction by J. Huxley. Translated by B. Wall. New York: Harper & Row, 1975.

Tertullian. *De Carne Christi liber: Tertullian's Treatise on the Incarnation.* Edited with an Introduction, Translation, and Commentary. London: SPCK, 1956.

Theunissen, M. *Der Andere: Studien zur Sozialontologie der Gegenwart.* 2nd ed. Berlin: de Gruyter, 1965.

Thoreau, H. D. *Walden, Civil Disobedience, and Other Writings: Authoritative Texts, Journal Reviews and Posthumous Assessments, Criticism.* Edited by W. Rossi. Norton Critical Edition. New York: Norton, 2008.

Tillich, P. *Systematic Theology.* 3 vols. Chicago: University of Chicago Press, 1951–1963.

———. *Systematic Theology.* 3 vols. in 1. Chicago: Chicago University Press, 1967.

Tucker, R. C., editor. *The Marx-Engels Reader.* New York: Norton, 1972.

Uexküll, J. von. *Umwelt und Innenwelt der Tiere.* Berlin: Springer, 1909.

Unamuno, M. de. *Obras Completas.* Biblioteca Castro. Madrid: Fundación Juan Antonio de Castro, 1994.

———. *Del Sentimiento Trágico de la Vida.* Prologue by F. Savater. Madrid: Alianza, 1986.

Unger, R. M. *Social Theory, Its Situation and Its Task: A Critical Introduction to Politics, a Work in Constructive Social Theory.* London: Verso, 2004.

Bibliography

Vico, G. B. *Principi di Scienza Nuova, d'Intorno alla comune Natura delle Nazioni*. Naples: Stamperia Muziana, 1744.
Voltaire, *Essai sur les Mœurs et l'Esprit des Nations et sur les Principaux Faits de l'Histoire depuis Charlemagnes jusqu'à Louis XIII*. Paris: Garnier, 1963.
Wallace, A. R. *Natural Selection and Tropical Nature*. London: Macmillan, 1870.
Weber, M. *Gesammelte Aufsätze zur Religionssoziologie*. 3 vols. Tübingen: Mohr/ Siebeck, 1920.
———. *The Protestant Ethic and the Spirit of Capitalism*. Translated by S. Kalberg. New York: Scribner, 1958.
Weeber, M. *Schleiermachers Eschatologie*. Beiträge zur evangelischen Theologie 118. Gütersloh : Kaiser, 2000.
Wigner, E. "The Unreasonable Effectiveness of Mathematics in the Natural Sciences." *Communications in Pure and Applied Mathematics* 13/1 (February 1960) 1–14.
Williams, P., editor. *Buddhism: Critical Concepts in Religious Studies*. Vol. 2, *The Early Buddhist Schools and Doctrinal History; Theravada Doctrine*. Critical Concepts in Religious Studies. London: Routledge, 2005.
Wittgenstein, L. "Lectures on Religious Beliefs." In *Lectures & Conversations on Aesthetics, Psychology and Religious Belief* as compiled from notes taken by Y. Smythies, R. Rhees, and J. Taylor and edited by C. Barrett, 53–72. Oxford: Blackwell, 1966.
———. *Notebooks 1914–1916*. Edited by G. H. von Wright and G. E. M. Anscombe; with an English translation by G. E. M. Anscombe. Chicago: University of Chicago Press, 1979.
———. *Philosophical Investigations*. Translated by G. E. M. Anscombe et al. Rev. 4th ed. Chichester: Wiley-Blackwell, 2009.
———. *Wittgenstein's Tractatus*. Translated by D. Kolak. Mountain View, CA: Mayfield, 1998.
Wittram, R. *Das Interesse an der Geschichte; zwölf Vorlesungen über Fragen des zeitgenössischen Geschichtsverständnisses*. 3rd ed. Kleine Vanderhoek-Reihe 59, 60, 61. Göttingen: Vandenhoeck & Ruprecht, 1968.
Wolfson, H. A. *The Philosophy of Spinoza*. New York: Meridian, 1958.
Woods, R., editor. *Understanding Mysticism*. New York: Image, 1980.
Zimmer, C. "On the Origin of Life on Earth." *Science* 5911 (2009) 198–99.

www.ingramcontent.com/pod-product-compliance
Lightning Source LLC
Chambersburg PA
CBHW070237230426
43664CB00014B/2331